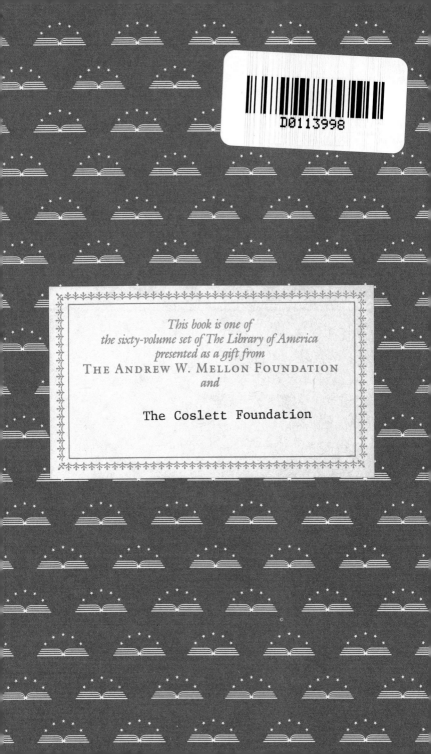

RALPH WALDO EMERSON

RALPH WALDO EMERSON

COLLECTED POEMS
AND TRANSLATIONS

THE LIBRARY OF AMERICA

Some of the material in this volume is reprinted by
permission of the holders of copyright and publication rights.
Acknowledgments will be found in the Note on the Texts.

The paper used in this publication meets the
minimum requirements of the American National Standard for
Information Sciences—Permanence of Paper for Printed
Library Materials, ANSI z39.48—1984.

Distributed to the trade in the United States
by Penguin Books USA Inc
and in Canada by Penguin Books Canada Ltd.

Library of Congress Catalog Number: 93–40245
For cataloging information, see end of Index.
ISBN 0–940450–28–3

First Printing
The Library of America—70

HAROLD BLOOM AND PAUL KANE
SELECTED THE CONTENTS AND WROTE THE NOTES
FOR THIS VOLUME

*The publishers express their appreciation
to the Houghton Library at Harvard University for the use
of Ralph Waldo Emerson materials.*

Contents

Each section has its own table of contents.

POEMS

(1847)

Contents

The Sphinx

The Sphinx is drowsy,
　Her wings are furled;
Her ear is heavy,
　She broods on the world.
"Who'll tell me my secret,
　The ages have kept?—
I awaited the seer,
　While they slumbered and slept;—

"The fate of the man-child;
　The meaning of man;
Known fruit of the unknown;
　Dædalian plan;
Out of sleeping a waking,
　Out of waking a sleep;
Life death overtaking;
　Deep underneath deep?

"Erect as a sunbeam,
　Upspringeth the palm;
The elephant browses,
　Undaunted and calm;
In beautiful motion
　The thrush plies his wings;
Kind leaves of his covert,
　Your silence he sings.

"The waves, unashamed,
　In difference sweet,
Play glad with the breezes,
　Old playfellows meet;

The journeying atoms,
　　Primordial wholes,
Firmly draw, firmly drive,
　　By their animate poles.

"Sea, earth, air, sound, silence,
　　Plant, quadruped, bird,
By one music enchanted,
　　One deity stirred,—
Each the other adorning,
　　Accompany still;
Night veileth the morning,
　　The vapor the hill.

"The babe by its mother
　　Lies bathed in joy;
Glide its hours uncounted,—
　　The sun is its toy;
Shines the peace of all being,
　　Without cloud, in its eyes;
And the sum of the world
　　In soft miniature lies.

"But man crouches and blushes,
　　Absconds and conceals;
He creepeth and peepeth,
　　He palters and steals;
Infirm, melancholy,
　　Jealous glancing around,
An oaf, an accomplice,
　　He poisons the ground.

"Outspoke the great mother,
　　Beholding his fear;—
At the sound of her accents
　　Cold shuddered the sphere:—
'Who has drugged my boy's cup?
　　Who has mixed my boy's bread?
Who, with sadness and madness,
　　Has turned the man-child's head?' "

I heard a poet answer,
   Aloud and cheerfully,
"Say on, sweet Sphinx! thy dirges
   Are pleasant songs to me.
Deep love lieth under
   These pictures of time;
They fade in the light of
   Their meaning sublime.

"The fiend that man harries
   Is love of the Best;
Yawns the pit of the Dragon,
   Lit by rays from the Blest.
The Lethe of nature
   Can't trance him again,
Whose soul sees the perfect,
   Which his eyes seek in vain.

"Profounder, profounder,
   Man's spirit must dive;
To his aye-rolling orbit
   No goal will arrive;
The heavens that now draw him
   With sweetness untold,
Once found,—for new heavens
   He spurneth the old.

"Pride ruined the angels,
   Their shame them restores;
And the joy that is sweetest
   Lurks in stings of remorse.
Have I a lover
   Who is noble and free?—
I would he were nobler
   Than to love me.

"Eterne alternation
   Now follows, now flies;
And under pain, pleasure,—
   Under pleasure, pain lies.

Love works at the centre,
　Heart-heaving alway;
Forth speed the strong pulses
　To the borders of day.

"Dull Sphinx, Jove keep thy five wits!
　Thy sight is growing blear;
Rue, myrrh, and cummin for the Sphinx—
　Her muddy eyes to clear!"—
The old Sphinx bit her thick lip,—
　Said, "Who taught thee me to name?
I am thy spirit, yoke-fellow,
　Of thine eye I am eyebeam.

"Thou art the unanswered question;
　Couldst see thy proper eye,
Alway it asketh, asketh;
　And each answer is a lie.
So take thy quest through nature,
　It through thousand natures ply;
Ask on, thou clothed eternity;
　Time is the false reply."

Uprose the merry Sphinx,
　And crouched no more in stone;
She melted into purple cloud,
　She silvered in the moon;
She spired into a yellow flame;
　She flowered in blossoms red;
She flowed into a foaming wave;
　She stood Monadnoc's head.

Thorough a thousand voices
　Spoke the universal dame:
"Who telleth one of my meanings,
　Is master of all I am."

Each and All

Little thinks, in the field, yon red-cloaked clown,
Of thee from the hill-top looking down;
The heifer that lows in the upland farm,
Far-heard, lows not thine ear to charm;
The sexton, tolling his bell at noon,
Deems not that great Napoleon
Stops his horse, and lists with delight,
Whilst his files sweep round yon Alpine height;
Nor knowest thou what argument
Thy life to thy neighbor's creed has lent.
All are needed by each one;
Nothing is fair or good alone.
I thought the sparrow's note from heaven,
Singing at dawn on the alder bough;
I brought him home, in his nest, at even;
He sings the song, but it pleases not now,
For I did not bring home the river and sky; —
He sang to my ear, — they sang to my eye.
The delicate shells lay on the shore;
The bubbles of the latest wave
Fresh pearls to their enamel gave;
And the bellowing of the savage sea
Greeted their safe escape to me.
I wiped away the weeds and foam,
I fetched my sea-born treasures home;
But the poor, unsightly, noisome things
Had left their beauty on the shore,
With the sun, and the sand, and the wild uproar.
The lover watched his graceful maid,
As 'mid the virgin train she strayed,
Nor knew her beauty's best attire
Was woven still by the snow-white choir.
At last she came to his hermitage,
Like the bird from the woodlands to the cage; —
The gay enchantment was undone,
A gentle wife, but fairy none.
Then I said, 'I covet truth;

Beauty is unripe childhood's cheat;
I leave it behind with the games of youth.'—
As I spoke, beneath my feet
The ground-pine curled its pretty wreath,
Running over the club-moss burrs;
I inhaled the violet's breath;
Around me stood the oaks and firs;
Pine-cones and acorns lay on the ground,
Over me soared the eternal sky,
Full of light and of deity;
Again I saw, again I heard,
The rolling river, the morning bird;—
Beauty through my senses stole;
I yielded myself to the perfect whole.

The Problem

I like a church; I like a cowl;
I love a prophet of the soul;
And on my heart monastic aisles
Fall like sweet strains, or pensive smiles;
Yet not for all his faith can see
Would I that cowled churchman be.

Why should the vest on him allure,
Which I could not on me endure?

Not from a vain or shallow thought
His awful Jove young Phidias brought;
Never from lips of cunning fell
The thrilling Delphic oracle;
Out from the heart of nature rolled
The burdens of the Bible old;
The litanies of nations came,
Like the volcano's tongue of flame,
Up from the burning core below,—
The canticles of love and woe;
The hand that rounded Peter's dome,

And groined the aisles of Christian Rome,
Wrought in a sad sincerity;
Himself from God he could not free;
He builded better than he knew;—
The conscious stone to beauty grew.

Know'st thou what wove yon woodbird's nest
Of leaves, and feathers from her breast?
Or how the fish outbuilt her shell,
Painting with morn each annual cell?
Or how the sacred pine-tree adds
To her old leaves new myriads?
Such and so grew these holy piles,
Whilst love and terror laid the tiles.
Earth proudly wears the Parthenon,
As the best gem upon her zone;
And Morning opes with haste her lids,
To gaze upon the Pyramids;
O'er England's abbeys bends the sky,
As on its friends, with kindred eye;
For, out of Thought's interior sphere,
These wonders rose to upper air;
And Nature gladly gave them place,
Adopted them into her race,
And granted them an equal date
With Andes and with Ararat.

These temples grew as grows the grass;
Art might obey, but not surpass.
The passive Master lent his hand
To the vast soul that o'er him planned;
And the same power that reared the shrine,
Bestrode the tribes that knelt within.
Ever the fiery Pentecost
Girds with one flame the countless host,
Trances the heart through chanting choirs,
And through the priest the mind inspires.
The word unto the prophet spoken
Was writ on tables yet unbroken;

The word by seers or sibyls told,
In groves of oak, or fanes of gold,
Still floats upon the morning wind,
Still whispers to the willing mind.
One accent of the Holy Ghost
The heedless world hath never lost.
I know what say the fathers wise,—
The Book itself before me lies,
Old *Chrysostom*, best Augustine,
And he who blent both in his line,
The younger *Golden Lips* or mines,
Taylor, the Shakspeare of divines.
His words are music in my ear,
I see his cowled portrait dear;
And yet, for all his faith could see,
I would not the good bishop be.

To Rhea

Thee, dear friend, a brother soothes,
Not with flatteries, but truths,
Which tarnish not, but purify
To light which dims the morning's eye.
I have come from the spring-woods,
From the fragrant solitudes;—
Listen what the poplar-tree
And murmuring waters counselled me.

If with love thy heart has burned;
If thy love is unreturned;
Hide thy grief within thy breast,
Though it tear thee unexpressed;
For when love has once departed
From the eyes of the false-hearted,
And one by one has torn off quite
The bandages of purple light;
Though thou wert the loveliest
Form the soul had ever dressed,

Thou shalt seem, in each reply,
A vixen to his altered eye;
Thy softest pleadings seem too bold,
Thy praying lute will seem to scold;
Though thou kept the straightest road,
Yet thou errest far and broad.

But thou shalt do as do the gods
In their cloudless periods;
For of this lore be thou sure, —
Though thou forget, the gods, secure,
Forget never their command,
But make the statute of this land.
As they lead, so follow all,
Ever have done, ever shall.
Warning to the blind and deaf,
'Tis written on the iron leaf,
Who drinks of Cupid's nectar cup
Loveth downward, and not up;
Therefore, who loves, of gods or men,
Shall not by the same be loved again;
His sweetheart's idolatry
Falls, in turn, a new degree.
When a god is once beguiled
By beauty of a mortal child,
And by her radiant youth delighted,
He is not fooled, but warily knoweth
His love shall never be requited.
And thus the wise Immortal doeth. —
'Tis his study and delight
To bless that creature day and night;
From all evils to defend her;
In her lap to pour all splendor;
To ransack earth for riches rare,
And fetch her stars to deck her hair:
He mixes music with her thoughts,
And saddens her with heavenly doubts:
All grace, all good his great heart knows,
Profuse in love, the king bestows:
Saying, 'Hearken! Earth, Sea, Air!

This monument of my despair
Build I to the All-Good, All-Fair.
Not for a private good,
But I, from my beatitude,
Albeit scorned as none was scorned,
Adorn her as was none adorned.
I make this maiden an ensample
To Nature, through her kingdoms ample,
Whereby to model newer races,
Statelier forms, and fairer faces;
To carry man to new degrees
Of power, and of comeliness.
These presents be the hostages
Which I pawn for my release.
See to thyself, O Universe!
Thou art better, and not worse.'—
And the god, having given all,
Is freed forever from his thrall.

The Visit

Askest, 'How long thou shalt stay,'
Devastator of the day?
Know, each substance, and relation,
Thorough nature's operation,
Hath its unit, bound, and metre;
And every new compound
Is some product and repeater,—
Product of the early found.
But the unit of the visit,
The encounter of the wise,—
Say, what other metre is it
Than the meeting of the eyes?
Nature poureth into nature
Through the channels of that feature.
Riding on the ray of sight,
More fleet than waves or whirlwinds go,
Or for service, or delight,

Hearts to hearts their meaning show,
Sum their long experience,
And import intelligence.
Single look has drained the breast;
Single moment years confessed.
The duration of a glance
Is the term of convenance,
And, though thy rede be church or state,
Frugal multiples of that.
Speeding Saturn cannot halt;
Linger,—thou shalt rue the fault;
If Love his moment overstay,
Hatred's swift repulsions play.

Uriel

It fell in the ancient periods,
    Which the brooding soul surveys,
Or ever the wild Time coined itself
    Into calendar months and days.

This was the lapse of Uriel,
Which in Paradise befell.
Once, among the Pleiads walking,
SAID overheard the young gods talking;
And the treason, too long pent,
To his ears was evident.
The young deities discussed
Laws of form, and metre just,
Orb, quintessence, and sunbeams,
What subsisteth, and what seems.
One, with low tones that decide,
And doubt and reverend use defied,
With a look that solved the sphere,
And stirred the devils everywhere,
Gave his sentiment divine
Against the being of a line.
'Line in nature is not found;

Unit and universe are round;
In vain produced, all rays return;
Evil will bless, and ice will burn.'
As Uriel spoke with piercing eye,
A shudder ran around the sky;
The stern old war-gods shook their heads;
The seraphs frowned from myrtle-beds;
Seemed to the holy festival
The rash word boded ill to all;
The balance-beam of Fate was bent;
The bounds of good and ill were rent;
Strong Hades could not keep his own,
But all slid to confusion.

A sad self-knowledge, withering, fell
On the beauty of Uriel;
In heaven once eminent, the god
Withdrew, that hour, into his cloud;
Whether doomed to long gyration
In the sea of generation,
Or by knowledge grown too bright
To hit the nerve of feebler sight.
Straightway, a forgetting wind
Stole over the celestial kind,
And their lips the secret kept,
If in ashes the fire-seed slept.
But now and then, truth-speaking things
Shamed the angels' veiling wings;
And, shrilling from the solar course,
Or from fruit of chemic force,
Procession of a soul in matter,
Or the speeding change of water,
Or out of the good of evil born,
Came Uriel's voice of cherub scorn,
And a blush tinged the upper sky,
And the gods shook, they knew not why.

The World-Soul

Thanks to the morning light,
   Thanks to the foaming sea,
To the uplands of New Hampshire,
   To the green-haired forest free;
Thanks to each man of courage,
   To the maids of holy mind;
To the boy with his games undaunted,
   Who never looks behind.

Cities of proud hotels,
   Houses of rich and great,
Vice nestles in your chambers,
   Beneath your roofs of slate.
It cannot conquer folly,
   Time-and-space-conquering steam;
And the light-outspeeding telegraph
   Bears nothing on its beam.

The politics are base;
   The letters do not cheer;
And 'tis far in the deeps of history,
   The voice that speaketh clear.
Trade and the streets ensnare us,
   Our bodies are weak and worn;
We plot and corrupt each other,
   And we despoil the unborn.

Yet there in the parlor sits
   Some figure of noble guise, —
Our angel, in a stranger's form,
   Or woman's pleading eyes;
Or only a flashing sunbeam
   In at the window-pane;
Or Music pours on mortals
   Its beautiful disdain.

The inevitable morning
   Finds them who in cellars be;
And be sure the all-loving Nature
   Will smile in a factory.
Yon ridge of purple landscape,
   Yon sky between the walls,
Hold all the hidden wonders,
   In scanty intervals.

Alas! the Sprite that haunts us
   Deceives our rash desire;
It whispers of the glorious gods,
   And leaves us in the mire.
We cannot learn the cipher
   That's writ upon our cell;
Stars help us by a mystery
   Which we could never spell.

If but one hero knew it,
   The world would blush in flame;
The sage, till he hit the secret,
   Would hang his head for shame.
But our brothers have not read it,
   Not one has found the key;
And henceforth we are comforted,—
   We are but such as they.

Still, still the secret presses,
   The nearing clouds draw down;
The crimson morning flames into
   The fopperies of the town.
Within, without the idle earth,
   Stars weave eternal rings;
The sun himself shines heartily,
   And shares the joy he brings.

And what if Trade sow cities
   Like shells along the shore,
And thatch with towns the prairie broad,
   With railways ironed o'er?—

They are but sailing foam-bells
   Along Thought's causing stream,
And take their shape and sun-color
   From him that sends the dream.

For Destiny does not like
   To yield to men the helm;
And shoots his thought, by hidden nerves,
   Throughout the solid realm.
The patient Dæmon sits,
   With roses and a shroud;
He has his way, and deals his gifts,—
   But ours is not allowed.

He is no churl nor trifler,
   And his viceroy is none,—
Love-without-weakness,—
   Of Genius sire and son.
And his will is not thwarted;
   The seeds of land and sea
Are the atoms of his body bright,
   And his behest obey.

He serveth the servant,
   The brave he loves amain;
He kills the cripple and the sick,
   And straight begins again.
For gods delight in gods,
   And thrust the weak aside;
To him who scorns their charities,
   Their arms fly open wide.

When the old world is sterile,
   And the ages are effete,
He will from wrecks and sediment
   The fairer world complete.
He forbids to despair;
   His cheeks mantle with mirth;
And the unimagined good of men
   Is yeaning at the birth.

Spring still makes spring in the mind,
  When sixty years are told;
Love wakes anew this throbbing heart,
  And we are never old.
Over the winter glaciers,
  I see the summer glow,
And, through the wild-piled snowdrift,
  The warm rosebuds below.

Alphonso of Castile

I, Alphonso, live and learn,
Seeing Nature go astern.
Things deteriorate in kind;
Lemons run to leaves and rind;
Meagre crop of figs and limes;
Shorter days and harder times.
Flowering April cools and dies
In the insufficient skies.
Imps, at high midsummer, blot
Half the sun's disk with a spot:
'Twill not now avail to tan
Orange cheek or skin of man.
Roses bleach, the goats are dry,
Lisbon quakes, the people cry.
Yon pale, scrawny fisher fools,
Gaunt as bitterns in the pools,
Are no brothers of my blood;—
They discredit Adamhood.
Eyes of gods! ye must have seen,
O'er your ramparts as ye lean,
The general debility;
Of genius the sterility;
Mighty projects countermanded;
Rash ambition, brokenhanded;
Puny man and scentless rose
Tormenting Pan to double the dose.
Rebuild or ruin: either fill

Of vital force the wasted rill,
Or tumble all again in heap
To weltering chaos and to sleep.

Say, Seigniors, are the old Niles dry,
Which fed the veins of earth and sky,
That mortals miss the loyal heats,
Which drove them erst to social feats;
Now, to a savage selfness grown,
Think nature barely serves for one;
With science poorly mask their hurt,
And vex the gods with question pert,
Immensely curious whether you
Still are rulers, or mildew?

Masters, I am in pain with you;
Masters, I'll be plain with you;
In my palace of Castile,
I, a king, for kings can feel.
There my thoughts the matter roll,
And solve and oft resolve the whole.
And, for I'm styled Alphonse the Wise,
Ye shall not fail for sound advice.
Before ye want a drop of rain,
Hear the sentiment of Spain.

You have tried famine: no more try it;
Ply us now with a full diet;
Teach your pupils now with plenty;
For one sun supply us twenty.
I have thought it thoroughly over,—
State of hermit, state of lover;
We must have society,
We cannot spare variety.
Hear you, then, celestial fellows!
Fits not to be overzealous;
Steads not to work on the clean jump,
Nor wine nor brains perpetual pump.
Men and gods are too extense;
Could you slacken and condense?

Your rank overgrowths reduce
Till your kinds abound with juice?
Earth, crowded, cries, 'Too many men!'
My counsel is, kill nine in ten,
And bestow the shares of all
On the remnant decimal.
Add their nine lives to this cat;
Stuff their nine brains in his hat;
Make his frame and forces square
With the labors he must dare;
Thatch his flesh, and even his years
With the marble which he rears.
There, growing slowly old at ease,
No faster than his planted trees,
He may, by warrant of his age,
In schemes of broader scope engage.
So shall ye have a man of the sphere,
Fit to grace the solar year.

Mithridates

I cannot spare water or wine,
  Tobacco-leaf, or poppy, or rose;
From the earth-poles to the line,
  All between that works or grows,
Every thing is kin of mine.

Give me agates for my meat;
Give me cantharids to eat;
From air and ocean bring me foods,
From all zones and altitudes; —

From all natures, sharp and slimy,
  Salt and basalt, wild and tame:
Tree and lichen, ape, sea-lion,
  Bird, and reptile, be my game.

Ivy for my fillet band;
Blinding dog-wood in my hand;

Hemlock for my sherbet cull me,
And the prussic juice to lull me;
Swing me in the upas boughs,
Vampyre-fanned, when I carouse.

Too long shut in strait and few,
Thinly dieted on dew,
I will use the world, and sift it,
To a thousand humors shift it,
As you spin a cherry.
O doleful ghosts, and goblins merry!
O all you virtues, methods, mights,
Means, appliances, delights,
Reputed wrongs and braggart rights,
Smug routine, and things allowed,
Minorities, things under cloud!
Hither! take me, use me, fill me,
Vein and artery, though ye kill me!
God! I will not be an owl,
But sun me in the Capitol.

To J. W.

Set not thy foot on graves:
Hear what wine and roses say:
The mountain chase, the summer waves,
The crowded town, thy feet may well delay.

Set not thy foot on graves;
Nor seek to unwind the shroud
Which charitable Time
And Nature have allowed
To wrap the errors of a sage sublime.

Set not thy foot on graves:
Care not to strip the dead
Of his sad ornament,
His myrrh, and wine, and rings,

His sheet of lead,
And trophies buried:
Go, get them where he earned them when alive;
As resolutely dig or dive.

Life is too short to waste
In critic peep or cynic bark,
Quarrel or reprimand:
'Twill soon be dark;
Up, heed thine own aim, and
God speed the mark!

Fate

That you are fair or wise is vain,
Or strong, or rich, or generous;
You must have also the untaught strain
That sheds beauty on the rose.
There is a melody born of melody,
Which melts the world into a sea:
Toil could never compass it;
Art its height could never hit;
It came never out of wit;
But a music music-born
Well may Jove and Juno scorn.
Thy beauty, if it lack the fire
Which drives me mad with sweet desire,
What boots it? what the soldier's mail,
Unless he conquer and prevail?
What all the goods thy pride which lift,
If thou pine for another's gift?
Alas! that one is born in blight,
Victim of perpetual slight:
When thou lookest on his face,
Thy heart saith, 'Brother, go thy ways!
None shall ask thee what thou doest,
Or care a rush for what thou knowest,

Or listen when thou repliest,
Or remember where thou liest,
Or how thy supper is sodden;'
And another is born
To make the sun forgotten.
Surely he carries a talisman
Under his tongue;
Broad are his shoulders and strong;
And his eye is scornful,
Threatening, and young.
I hold it of little matter
Whether your jewel be of pure water,
A rose diamond or a white,
But whether it dazzle me with light.
I care not how you are dressed,
In the coarsest or in the best;
Nor whether your name is base or brave;
Nor for the fashion of your behavior;
But whether you charm me,
Bid my bread feed and my fire warm me,
And dress up Nature in your favor.
One thing is forever good;
That one thing is Success,—
Dear to the Eumenides,
And to all the heavenly brood.
Who bides at home, nor looks abroad,
Carries the eagles, and masters the sword.

Guy

Mortal mixed of middle clay,
Attempered to the night and day,
Interchangeable with things,
Needs no amulets nor rings.
Guy possessed the talisman
That all things from him began;
And as, of old, Polycrates

Chained the sunshine and the breeze,
So did Guy betimes discover
Fortune was his guard and lover;
In strange junctures, felt, with awe,
His own symmetry with law;
So that no mixture could withstand
The virtue of his lucky hand.
He gold or jewel could not lose,
Nor not receive his ample dues.
In the street, if he turned round,
His eye the eye 'twas seeking found.
It seemed his Genius discreet
Worked on the Maker's own receipt,
And made each tide and element
Stewards of stipend and of rent;
So that the common waters fell
As costly wine into his well.
He had so sped his wise affairs
That he caught Nature in his snares:
Early or late, the falling rain
Arrived in time to swell his grain;
Stream could not so perversely wind
But corn of Guy's was there to grind;
The siroc found it on its way,
To speed his sails, to dry his hay;
And the world's sun seemed to rise,
To drudge all day for Guy the wise.
In his rich nurseries, timely skill
Strong crab with nobler blood did fill;
The zephyr in his garden rolled
From plum-trees vegetable gold;
And all the hours of the year
With their own harvest honored were.
There was no frost but welcome came,
Nor freshet, nor midsummer flame.
Belonged to wind and world the toil
And venture, and to Guy the oil.

Tact

What boots it, thy virtue,
  What profit thy parts,
While one thing thou lackest,—
  The art of all arts?

The only credentials,
  Passport to success;
Opens castle and parlor,—
  Address, man, Address.

The maiden in danger
  Was saved by the swain;
His stout arm restored her
  To Broadway again.

The maid would reward him,—
  Gay company come;
They laugh, she laughs with them;
  He is moonstruck and dumb.

This clinches the bargain;
  Sails out of the bay;
Gets the vote in the senate,
  Spite of Webster and Clay;

Has for genius no mercy,
  For speeches no heed;
It lurks in the eyebeam,
  It leaps to its deed.

Church, market, and tavern,
  Bed and board, it will sway.
It has no to-morrow;
  It ends with to-day.

Hamatreya

Minott, Lee, Willard, Hosmer, Meriam, Flint
Possessed the land which rendered to their toil
Hay, corn, roots, hemp, flax, apples, wool, and wood.
Each of these landlords walked amidst his farm,
Saying, ' 'Tis mine, my children's, and my name's:
How sweet the west wind sounds in my own trees!
How graceful climb those shadows on my hill!
I fancy these pure waters and the flags
Know me, as does my dog: we sympathize;
And, I affirm, my actions smack of the soil.'
Where are these men? Asleep beneath their grounds;
And strangers, fond as they, their furrows plough.
Earth laughs in flowers, to see her boastful boys
Earth-proud, proud of the earth which is not theirs;
Who steer the plough, but cannot steer their feet
Clear of the grave.
They added ridge to valley, brook to pond,
And sighed for all that bounded their domain.
'This suits me for a pasture; that's my park;
We must have clay, lime, gravel, granite-ledge,
And misty lowland, where to go for peat.
The land is well,—lies fairly to the south.
'Tis good, when you have crossed the sea and back,
To find the sitfast acres where you left them.'
Ah! the hot owner sees not Death, who adds
Him to his land, a lump of mould the more.
Hear what the Earth says:—

EARTH-SONG.

　　　'Mine and yours;
　　　Mine, not yours.
　　　Earth endures;
　　　Stars abide—
　　　Shine down in the old sea;
　　　Old are the shores;

But where are old men?
I who have seen much,
Such have I never seen.

'The lawyer's deed
Ran sure,
In tail,
To them, and to their heirs
Who shall succeed,
Without fail,
Forevermore.

'Here is the land,
Shaggy with wood,
With its old valley,
Mound, and flood.
But the heritors?
Fled like the flood's foam,—
The lawyer, and the laws,
And the kingdom,
Clean swept herefrom.

'They called me theirs,
Who so controlled me;
Yet every one
Wished to stay, and is gone.
How am I theirs,
If they cannot hold me,
But I hold them?'

When I heard the Earth-song,
I was no longer brave;
My avarice cooled
Like lust in the chill of the grave.

Good-Bye

Good-bye, proud world! I'm going home:
Thou art not my friend, and I'm not thine.
Long through thy weary crowds I roam;
A river-ark on the ocean brine,
Long I've been tossed like the driven foam;
But now, proud world! I'm going home.

Good-bye to Flattery's fawning face;
To Grandeur with his wise grimace;
To upstart Wealth's averted eye;
To supple Office, low and high;
To crowded halls, to court and street;
To frozen hearts and hasting feet;
To those who go, and those who come;
Good-bye, proud world! I'm going home.

I am going to my own hearth-stone,
Bosomed in yon green hills alone,—
A secret nook in a pleasant land,
Whose groves the frolic fairies planned;
Where arches green, the livelong day,
Echo the blackbird's roundelay,
And vulgar feet have never trod
A spot that is sacred to thought and God.

O, when I am safe in my sylvan home,
I tread on the pride of Greece and Rome;
And when I am stretched beneath the pines,
Where the evening star so holy shines,
I laugh at the lore and the pride of man,
At the sophist schools, and the learned clan;
For what are they all, in their high conceit,
When man in the bush with God may meet?

The Rhodora:

On Being Asked, Whence Is the Flower?

In May, when sea-winds pierced our solitudes,
I found the fresh Rhodora in the woods,
Spreading its leafless blooms in a damp nook,
To please the desert and the sluggish brook.
The purple petals, fallen in the pool,
Made the black water with their beauty gay;
Here might the red-bird come his plumes to cool,
And court the flower that cheapens his array.
Rhodora! if the sages ask thee why
This charm is wasted on the earth and sky,
Tell them, dear, that if eyes were made for seeing,
Then Beauty is its own excuse for being:
Why thou wert there, O rival of the rose!
I never thought to ask, I never knew;
But, in my simple ignorance, suppose
The self-same Power that brought me there brought you.

The Humble-Bee

Burly, dozing, humble-bee,
Where thou art is clime for me.
Let them sail for Porto Rique,
Far-off heats through seas to seek;
I will follow thee alone,
Thou animated torrid-zone!
Zigzag steerer, desert cheerer,
Let me chase thy waving lines;
Keep me nearer, me thy hearer,
Singing over shrubs and vines.

Insect lover of the sun,
Joy of thy dominion!
Sailor of the atmosphere;
Swimmer through the waves of air;

Voyager of light and noon;
Epicurean of June;
Wait, I prithee, till I come
Within earshot of thy hum,—
All without is martyrdom.

When the south wind, in May days,
With a net of shining haze
Silvers the horizon wall,
And, with softness touching all,
Tints the human countenance
With a color of romance,
And, infusing subtle heats,
Turns the sod to violets,
Thou, in sunny solitudes,
Rover of the underwoods,
The green silence dost displace
With thy mellow, breezy bass.

Hot midsummer's petted crone,
Sweet to me thy drowsy tone
Tells of countless sunny hours,
Long days, and solid banks of flowers;
Of gulfs of sweetness without bound
In Indian wildernesses found;
Of Syrian peace, immortal leisure,
Firmest cheer, and bird-like pleasure.

Aught unsavory or unclean
Hath my insect never seen;
But violets and bilberry bells,
Maple-sap, and daffodels,
Grass with green flag half-mast high,
Succory to match the sky,
Columbine with horn of honey,
Scented fern, and agrimony,
Clover, catchfly, adder's tongue,
And brier roses, dwelt among;
All beside was unknown waste,
All was picture as he passed.

Wiser far than human seer,
Yellow-breeched philosopher!
Seeing only what is fair,
Sipping only what is sweet,
Thou dost mock at fate and care,
Leave the chaff, and take the wheat.
When the fierce north-western blast
Cools sea and land so far and fast,
Thou already slumberest deep;
Woe and want thou canst outsleep;
Want and woe, which torture us,
Thy sleep makes ridiculous.

Berrying

'May be true what I had heard, —
Earth's a howling wilderness,
Truculent with fraud and force,'
Said I, strolling through the pastures,
And along the river-side.
Caught among the blackberry vines,
Feeding on the Ethiops sweet,
Pleasant fancies overtook me.
I said, 'What influence me preferred,
Elect, to dreams thus beautiful?'
The vines replied, 'And didst thou deem
No wisdom to our berries went?'

The Snow-Storm

Announced by all the trumpets of the sky,
Arrives the snow, and, driving o'er the fields,
Seems nowhere to alight: the whited air
Hides hills and woods, the river, and the heaven,
And veils the farm-house at the garden's end.
The sled and traveller stopped, the courier's feet
Delayed, all friends shut out, the housemates sit
Around the radiant fireplace, enclosed
In a tumultuous privacy of storm.

Come see the north wind's masonry.
Out of an unseen quarry evermore
Furnished with tile, the fierce artificer
Curves his white bastions with projected roof
Round every windward stake, or tree, or door.
Speeding, the myriad-handed, his wild work
So fanciful, so savage, nought cares he
For number or proportion. Mockingly,
On coop or kennel he hangs Parian wreaths;
A swan-like form invests the hidden thorn;
Fills up the farmer's lane from wall to wall,
Maugre the farmer's sighs; and, at the gate,
A tapering turret overtops the work.
And when his hours are numbered, and the world
Is all his own, retiring, as he were not,
Leaves, when the sun appears, astonished Art
To mimic in slow structures, stone by stone,
Built in an age, the mad wind's night-work,
The frolic architecture of the snow.

Woodnotes I

I.

For this present, hard
Is the fortune of the bard,
    Born out of time;
All his accomplishment,
From Nature's utmost treasure spent,
    Booteth not him.
When the pine tosses its cones
To the song of its waterfall tones,
He speeds to the woodland walks,
To birds and trees he talks:
Cæsar of his leafy Rome,
There the poet is at home.
He goes to the river-side,—
Not hook nor line hath he;
He stands in the meadows wide,—
Nor gun nor scythe to see;
With none has he to do,
And none seek him,
Nor men below,
Nor spirits dim.
Sure some god his eye enchants:
What he knows nobody wants.
In the wood he travels glad,
Without better fortune had,
Melancholy without bad.
Planter of celestial plants,
What he knows nobody wants;
What he knows he hides, not vaunts.
Knowledge this man prizes best
Seems fantastic to the rest:
Pondering shadows, colors, clouds,
Grass-buds, and caterpillar-shrouds,
Boughs on which the wild bees settle,

Tints that spot the violets' petal,
Why Nature loves the number five,
And why the star-form she repeats:
Lover of all things alive,
Wonderer at all he meets,
Wonderer chiefly at himself,—
Who can tell him what he is?
Or how meet in human elf
Coming and past eternities?

2.

And such I knew, a forest seer,
A minstrel of the natural year,
Foreteller of the vernal ides,
Wise harbinger of spheres and tides,
A lover true, who knew by heart
Each joy the mountain dales impart;
It seemed that Nature could not raise
A plant in any secret place,
In quaking bog, on snowy hill,
Beneath the grass that shades the rill,
Under the snow, between the rocks,
In damp fields known to bird and fox,
But he would come in the very hour
It opened in its virgin bower,
As if a sunbeam showed the place,
And tell its long-descended race.
It seemed as if the breezes brought him;
It seemed as if the sparrows taught him;
As if by secret sight he knew
Where, in far fields, the orchis grew.
Many haps fall in the field
Seldom seen by wishful eyes,
But all her shows did Nature yield,
To please and win this pilgrim wise.
He saw the partridge drum in the woods;
He heard the woodcock's evening hymn;
He found the tawny thrush's broods;

And the shy hawk did wait for him;
What others did at distance hear,
And guessed within the thicket's gloom,
Was showed to this philosopher,
And at his bidding seemed to come.

3.

In unploughed Maine he sought the lumberers' gang,
Where from a hundred lakes young rivers sprang;
He trode the unplanted forest floor, whereon
The all-seeing sun for ages hath not shone;
Where feeds the moose, and walks the surly bear,
And up the tall mast runs the woodpecker.
He saw beneath dim aisles, in odorous beds,
The slight Linnæa hang its twin-born heads,
And blessed the monument of the man of flowers,
Which breathes his sweet fame through the northern bowers.
He heard, when in the grove, at intervals,
With sudden roar the aged pine-tree falls,—
One crash, the death-hymn of the perfect tree,
Declares the close of its green century.
Low lies the plant to whose creation went
Sweet influence from every element;
Whose living towers the years conspired to build,
Whose giddy top the morning loved to gild.
Through these green tents, by eldest Nature dressed,
He roamed, content alike with man and beast.
Where darkness found him he lay glad at night;
There the red morning touched him with its light.
Three moons his great heart him a hermit made,
So long he roved at will the boundless shade.
The timid it concerns to ask their way,
And fear what foe in caves and swamps can stray,
To make no step until the event is known,
And ills to come as evils past bemoan.
Not so the wise; no coward watch he keeps
To spy what danger on his pathway creeps;

Go where he will, the wise man is at home,
His hearth the earth,—his hall the azure dome;
Where his clear spirit leads him, there's his road,
By God's own light illumined and foreshowed.

4.

'Twas one of the charmed days,
When the genius of God doth flow,
The wind may alter twenty ways,
A tempest cannot blow;
It may blow north, it still is warm;
Or south, it still is clear;
Or east, it smells like a clover-farm;
Or west, no thunder fear.
The musing peasant lowly great
Beside the forest water sate;
The rope-like pine roots crosswise grown
Composed the network of his throne;
The wide lake, edged with sand and grass,
Was burnished to a floor of glass,
Painted with shadows green and proud
Of the tree and of the cloud.
He was the heart of all the scene;
On him the sun looked more serene;
To hill and cloud his face was known,—
It seemed the likeness of their own;
They knew by secret sympathy
The public child of earth and sky.
'You ask,' he said, 'what guide
Me through trackless thickets led,
Through thick-stemmed woodlands rough and wide?
I found the water's bed.
The watercourses were my guide;
I travelled grateful by their side,
Or through their channel dry;
They led me through the thicket damp,
Through brake and fern, the beavers' camp,
Through beds of granite cut my road,

And their resistless friendship showed;
The falling waters led me,
The foodful waters fed me,
And brought me to the lowest land,
Unerring to the ocean sand.
The moss upon the forest bark
Was polestar when the night was dark;
The purple berries in the wood
Supplied me necessary food;
For Nature ever faithful is
To such as trust her faithfulness.
When the forest shall mislead me,
When the night and morning lie,
When sea and land refuse to feed me,
'Twill be time enough to die;
Then will yet my mother yield
A pillow in her greenest field,
Nor the June flowers scorn to cover
The clay of their departed lover.

Woodnotes II

As sunbeams stream through liberal space,
And nothing jostle or displace,
So waved the pine-tree through my thought,
And fanned the dreams it never brought.

'Whether is better the gift or the donor?
Come to me,'
Quoth the pine-tree,
'I am the giver of honor.
My garden is the cloven rock,
And my manure the snow;
And drifting sand-heaps feed my stock,
In summer's scorching glow.
Ancient or curious,
Who knoweth aught of us?

Old as Jove,
Old as Love,
Who of me
Tells the pedigree?
Only the mountains old,
Only the waters cold,
Only moon and star
My coevals are.
Ere the first fowl sung
My relenting boughs among;
Ere Adam wived,
Ere Adam lived,
Ere the duck dived,
Ere the bees hived,
Ere the lion roared,
Ere the eagle soared,
Light and heat, land and sea,
Spake unto the oldest tree.
Glad in the sweet and secret aid
Which matter unto matter paid,
The water flowed, the breezes fanned,
The tree confined the roving sand,
The sunbeam gave me to the sight,
The tree adorned the formless light,
And once again
O'er the grave of men
We shall talk to each other again
Of the old age behind,
Of the time out of mind,
Which shall come again.

'Whether is better the gift or the donor?
Come to me,'
Quoth the pine-tree,
'I am the giver of honor.
He is great who can live by me.
The rough and bearded forester
Is better than the lord;
God fills the scrip and canister,
Sin piles the loaded board.

The lord is the peasant that was,
The peasant the lord that shall be;
The lord is hay, the peasant grass,
One dry, and one the living tree.
Genius with my boughs shall flourish,
Want and cold our roots shall nourish.
Who liveth by the ragged pine
Foundeth a heroic line;
Who liveth in the palace hall
Waneth fast and spendeth all.
He goes to my savage haunts,
With his chariot and his care;
My twilight realm he disenchants,
And finds his prison there.

'What prizes the town and the tower?
Only what the pine-tree yields;
Sinew that subdued the fields;
The wild-eyed boy, who in the woods
Chants his hymn to hills and floods,
Whom the city's poisoning spleen
Made not pale, or fat, or lean;
Whom the rain and the wind purgeth,
Whom the dawn and the day-star urgeth,
In whose cheek the rose-leaf blusheth,
In whose feet the lion rusheth,
Iron arms, and iron mould,
That know not fear, fatigue, or cold.
I give my rafters to his boat,
My billets to his boiler's throat;
And I will swim the ancient sea,
To float my child to victory,
And grant to dwellers with the pine
Dominion o'er the palm and vine.
Westward I ope the forest gates,
The train along the railroad skates;
It leaves the land behind like ages past,
The foreland flows to it in river fast;
Missouri I have made a mart,
I teach Iowa Saxon art.

Who leaves the pine-tree, leaves his friend,
Unnerves his strength, invites his end.
Cut a bough from my parent stem,
And dip it in thy porcelain vase;
A little while each russet gem
Will swell and rise with wonted grace;
But when it seeks enlarged supplies,
The orphan of the forest dies.
Whoso walketh in solitude,
And inhabiteth the wood,
Choosing light, wave, rock, and bird,
Before the money-loving herd,
Into that forester shall pass,
From these companions, power and grace.
Clean shall he be, without, within,
From the old adhering sin.
Love shall he, but not adulate
The all-fair, the all-embracing Fate;
All ill dissolving in the light
Of his triumphant piercing sight.
Not vain, sour, nor frivolous;
Not mad, athirst, nor garrulous;
Grave, chaste, contented, though retired,
And of all other men desired.
On him the light of star and moon
Shall fall with purer radiance down;
All constellations of the sky
Shed their virtue through his eye.
Him Nature giveth for defence
His formidable innocence;
The mounting sap, the shells, the sea,
All spheres, all stones, his helpers be;
He shall never be old;
Nor his fate shall be foretold;
He shall see the speeding year,
Without wailing, without fear;
He shall be happy in his love,
Like to like shall joyful prove;
He shall be happy whilst he woos,
Muse-born, a daughter of the Muse.

But if with gold she bind her hair,
And deck her breast with diamond,
Take off thine eyes, thy heart forbear,
Though thou lie alone on the ground.
The robe of silk in which she shines,
It was woven of many sins;
And the shreds
Which she sheds
In the wearing of the same,
Shall be grief on grief,
And shame on shame.

'Heed the old oracles,
Ponder my spells;
Song wakes in my pinnacles
When the wind swells.
Soundeth the prophetic wind,
The shadows shake on the rock behind,
And the countless leaves of the pine are strings
Tuned to the lay the wood-god sings.
    Hearken! Hearken!
If thou wouldst know the mystic song
Chanted when the sphere was young.
Aloft, abroad, the pæan swells;
O wise man! hear'st thou half it tells?
O wise man! hear'st thou the least part?
'Tis the chronicle of art.
To the open ear it sings
The early genesis of things,
Of tendency through endless ages,
Of star-dust, and star-pilgrimages,
Of rounded worlds, of space and time,
Of the old flood's subsiding slime,
Of chemic matter, force, and form,
Of poles and powers, cold, wet, and warm:
The rushing metamorphosis,
Dissolving all that fixture is,
Melts things that be to things that seem,
And solid nature to a dream.
O, listen to the undersong—

The ever old, the ever young;
And, far within those cadent pauses,
The chorus of the ancient Causes!
Delights the dreadful Destiny
To fling his voice into the tree,
And shock thy weak ear with a note
Breathed from the everlasting throat.
In music he repeats the pang
Whence the fair flock of Nature sprang.
O mortal! thy ears are stones;
These echoes are laden with tones
Which only the pure can hear;
Thou canst not catch what they recite
Of Fate and Will, of Want and Right,
Of man to come, of human life,
Of Death, and Fortune, Growth, and Strife.'

Once again the pine-tree sung:—
'Speak not thy speech my boughs among;
Put off thy years, wash in the breeze;
My hours are peaceful centuries.
Talk no more with feeble tongue;
No more the fool of space and time,
Come weave with mine a nobler rhyme.
Only thy Americans
Can read thy line, can meet thy glance,
But the runes that I rehearse
Understands the universe;
The least breath my boughs which tossed
Brings again the Pentecost,
To every soul it soundeth clear
In a voice of solemn cheer,—
"Am I not thine? Are not these thine?"
And they reply, "Forever mine!"
My branches speak Italian,
English, German, Basque, Castilian,
Mountain speech to Highlanders,
Ocean tongues to islanders,
To Fin, and Lap, and swart Malay,
To each his bosom secret say.

Come learn with me the fatal song
Which knits the world in music strong,
Whereto every bosom dances,
Kindled with courageous fancies.
Come lift thine eyes to lofty rhymes,
Of things with things, of times with times,
Primal chimes of sun and shade,
Of sound and echo, man and maid,
The land reflected in the flood,
Body with shadow still pursued.
For Nature beats in perfect tune,
And rounds with rhyme her every rune,
Whether she work in land or sea,
Or hide underground her alchemy.
Thou canst not wave thy staff in air,
Or dip thy paddle in the lake,
But it carves the bow of beauty there,
And the ripples in rhymes the oar forsake.
The wood is wiser far than thou;
The wood and wave each other know.
Not unrelated, unaffied,
But to each thought and thing allied,
Is perfect Nature's every part,
Rooted in the mighty Heart.
But thou, poor child! unbound, unrhymed,
Whence camest thou, misplaced, mistimed?
Whence, O, thou orphan and defrauded?
Is thy land peeled, thy realm marauded?
Who thee divorced, deceived, and left?
Thee of thy faith who hath bereft,
And torn the ensigns from thy brow,
And sunk the immortal eye so low?
Thy cheek too white, thy form too slender,
Thy gait too slow, thy habits tender
For royal man; — they thee confess
An exile from the wilderness, —
The hills where health with health agrees,
And the wise soul expels disease.
Hark! in thy ear I will tell the sign
By which thy hurt thou may'st divine.

When thou shalt climb the mountain cliff,
Or see the wide shore from thy skiff,
To thee the horizon shall express
Only emptiness and emptiness;
There is no man of Nature's worth
In the circle of the earth;
And to thine eye the vast skies fall,
Dire and satirical,
On clucking hens, and prating fools,
On thieves, on drudges, and on dolls.
And thou shalt say to the Most High,
"Godhead! all this astronomy,
And fate, and practice, and invention,
Strong art, and beautiful pretension,
This radiant pomp of sun and star,
Throes that were, and worlds that are,
Behold! were in vain and in vain;—
It cannot be,—I will look again;
Surely now will the curtain rise,
And earth's fit tenant me surprise;—
But the curtain doth *not* rise,
And Nature has miscarried wholly
Into failure, into folly."

'Alas! thine is the bankruptcy,
Blessed Nature so to see.
Come, lay thee in my soothing shade,
And heal the hurts which sin has made.
I will teach the bright parable
Older than time,
Things undeclarable,
Visions sublime.
I see thee in the crowd alone;
I will be thy companion.
Let thy friends be as the dead in doom,
And build to them a final tomb;
Let the starred shade that nightly falls
Still celebrate their funerals,
And the bell of beetle and of bee
Knell their melodious memory.

Behind thee leave thy merchandise,
Thy churches, and thy charities;
And leave thy peacock wit behind;
Enough for thee the primal mind
That flows in streams, that breathes in wind.
Leave all thy pedant lore apart;
God hid the whole world in thy heart.
Love shuns the sage, the child it crowns,
And gives them all who all renounce.
The rain comes when the wind calls;
The river knows the way to the sea;
Without a pilot it runs and falls,
Blessing all lands with its charity;
The sea tosses and foams to find
Its way up to the cloud and wind;
The shadow sits close to the flying ball;
The date fails not on the palm-tree tall;
And thou,—go burn thy wormy pages,—
Shalt outsee seers, and outwit sages.
Oft didst thou thread the woods in vain
To find what bird had piped the strain;—
Seek not, and the little eremite
Flies gayly forth and sings in sight.

'Hearken once more!
I will tell thee the mundane lore.
Older am I than thy numbers wot;
Change I may, but I pass not.
Hitherto all things fast abide,
And anchored in the tempest ride.
Trenchant time behoves to hurry
All to yean and all to bury:
All the forms are fugitive,
But the substances survive.
Ever fresh the broad creation,
A divine improvisation,
From the heart of God proceeds,
A single will, a million deeds.
Once slept the world an egg of stone,
And pulse, and sound, and light was none;

And God said, "Throb!" and there was motion,
And the vast mass became vast ocean.
Onward and on, the eternal Pan,
Who layeth the world's incessant plan,
Halteth never in one shape,
But forever doth escape,
Like wave or flame, into new forms
Of gem, and air, of plants, and worms.
I, that to-day am a pine,
Yesterday was a bundle of grass.
He is free and libertine,
Pouring of his power the wine
To every age, to every race;
Unto every race and age
He emptieth the beverage;
Unto each, and unto all,
Maker and original.
The world is the ring of his spells,
And the play of his miracles.
As he giveth to all to drink,
Thus or thus they are and think.
He giveth little or giveth much,
To make them several or such.
With one drop sheds form and feature;
With the second a special nature;
The third adds heat's indulgent spark;
The fourth gives light which eats the dark;
In the fifth drop himself he flings,
And conscious Law is King of kings.
Pleaseth him, the Eternal Child,
To play his sweet will, glad and wild;
As the bee through the garden ranges,
From world to world the godhead changes;
As the sheep go feeding in the waste,
From form to form he maketh haste;
This vault which glows immense with light
Is the inn where he lodges for a night.
What recks such Traveller if the bowers
Which bloom and fade like meadow flowers

A bunch of fragrant lilies be,
Or the stars of eternity?
Alike to him the better, the worse,—
The glowing angel, the outcast corse.
Thou metest him by centuries,
And lo! he passes like the breeze;
Thou seek'st in globe and galaxy,
He hides in pure transparency;
Thou askest in fountains and in fires,
He is the essence that inquires.
He is the axis of the star;
He is the sparkle of the spar;
He is the heart of every creature;
He is the meaning of each feature;
And his mind is the sky,
Than all it holds more deep, more high.'

Monadnoc

Thousand minstrels woke within me,
  'Our music's in the hills;'—
Gayest pictures rose to win me,
  Leopard-colored rills.
'Up!—If thou knew'st who calls
To twilight parks of beech and pine,
High over the river intervals,
Above the ploughman's highest line,
Over the owner's farthest walls!
Up! where the airy citadel
O'erlooks the surging landscape's swell!
Let not unto the stones the Day
Her lily and rose, her sea and land display.
Read the celestial sign!
Lo! the south answers to the north;
Bookworm, break this sloth urbane;
A greater spirit bids thee forth
Than the gray dreams which thee detain.

Mark how the climbing Oreads
Beckon thee to their arcades!
Youth, for a moment free as they,
Teach thy feet to feel the ground,
Ere yet arrives the wintry day
When Time thy feet has bound.
Accept the bounty of thy birth,
Taste the lordship of the earth.'

   I heard, and I obeyed,—
Assured that he who made the claim,
Well known, but loving not a name,
   Was not to be gainsaid.

Ere yet the summoning voice was still,
I turned to Cheshire's haughty hill.
From the fixed cone the cloud-rack flowed,
Like ample banner flung abroad
To all the dwellers in the plains
Round about, a hundred miles,
With invitation to the sea, and to the bordering isles.

In his own loom's garment dressed,
By his own bounty blessed,
Fast abides this constant giver,
Pouring many a cheerful river;
To far eyes, an aerial isle
Unploughed, which finer spirits pile,
Which morn and crimson evening paint
For bard, for lover, and for saint;
The country's core,
Inspirer, prophet evermore;
Pillar which God aloft had set
So that men might it not forget;
It should be their life's ornament,
And mix itself with each event;
Their calendar and dial,
Barometer and chemic phial,
Garden of berries, perch of birds,

Pasture of pool-haunting herds,
Graced by each change of sum untold,
Earth-baking heat, stone-cleaving cold.

The Titan heeds his own affairs,
Wide rents and high alliance shares;
Mysteries of color daily laid
By the great sun in light and shade;
And sweet varieties of chance
And the mystic seasons' dance;
And thief-like step of liberal hours
Thawing snow-drift into flowers.
O, wondrous craft of plant and stone
By eldest science done and shown!

'Happy,' I said, 'whose home is here!
Fair fortunes to the mountaineer!
Boon Nature to his poorest shed
Has royal pleasure-grounds outspread.'
Intent, I searched the region round,
And in low hut my monarch found
He was no eagle, and no earl;—
Alas! my foundling was a churl,
With heart of cat and eyes of bug,
Dull victim of his pipe and mug.
Wo is me for my hope's downfall!
Lord! is yon squalid peasant all
That this proud nursery could breed
For God's vicegerency and stead?
Time out of mind, this forge of ores;
Quarry of spars in mountain pores;
Old cradle, hunting-ground, and bier
Of wolf and otter, bear and deer;
Well-built abode of many a race;
Tower of observance searching space;
Factory of river and of rain;
Link in the alps' globe-girding chain;
By million changes skilled to tell
What in the Eternal standeth well,
And what obedient Nature can;—

Is this colossal talisman
Kindly to creature, blood, and kind,
And speechless to the master's mind?
I thought to find the patriots
In whom the stock of freedom roots:
To myself I oft recount
The tale of many a famous mount,—
Wales, Scotland, Uri, Hungary's dells;
Roys, and Scanderbegs, and Tells.
Here Nature shall condense her powers,
Her music, and her meteors,
And lifting man to the blue deep
Where stars their perfect courses keep,
Like wise preceptor, lure his eye
To sound the science of the sky,
And carry learning to its height
Of untried power and sane delight:
The Indian cheer, the frosty skies,
Rear purer wits, inventive eyes,—
Eyes that frame cities where none be,
And hands that stablish what these see;
And by the moral of his place
Hint summits of heroic grace;
Man in these crags a fastness find
To fight pollution of the mind;
In the wide thaw and ooze of wrong,
Adhere like this foundation strong,
The insanity of towns to stem
With simpleness for stratagem.
But if the brave old mould is broke,
And end in churls the mountain folk,
In tavern cheer and tavern joke,
Sink, O mountain, in the swamp!
Hide in thy skies, O sovereign lamp!
Perish like leaves, the highland breed!
No sire survive, no son succeed!

Soft! let not the offended muse
Toil's hard hap with scorn accuse.
Many hamlets sought I then,

Many farms of mountain men;
Found I not a minstrel seed,
But men of bone, and good at need.
Rallying round a parish steeple
Nestle warm the highland people,
Coarse and boisterous, yet mild,
Strong as giant, slow as child,
Smoking in a squalid room
Where yet the westland breezes come.
Close hid in those rough guises lurk
Western magians,—here they work.
Sweat and season are their arts,
Their talismans are ploughs and carts;
And well the youngest can command
Honey from the frozen land;
With sweet hay the wild swamp adorn,
Change the running sand to corn;
For wolves and foxes, lowing herds,
And for cold mosses, cream and curds;
Weave wood to canisters and mats;
Drain sweet maple juice in vats.
No bird is safe that cuts the air
From their rifle or their snare;
No fish, in river or in lake,
But their long hands it thence will take;
And the country's iron face,
Like wax, their fashioning skill betrays,
To fill the hollows, sink the hills,
Bridge gulfs, drain swamps, build dams and mills,
And fit the bleak and howling place
For gardens of a finer race.
The World-soul knows his own affair,
Forelooking, when he would prepare
For the next ages, men of mould
Well embodied, well ensouled,
He cools the present's fiery glow,
Sets the life-pulse strong but slow:
Bitter winds and fasts austere
His quarantines and grottos, where
He slowly cures decrepit flesh,

And brings it infantile and fresh.
These exercises are the toys
And games with which he breathes his boys:
They bide their time, and well can prove,
If need were, their line from Jove;
Of the same stuff, and so allayed,
As that whereof the sun is made,
And of that fibre, quick and strong,
Whose throbs are love, whose thrills are song.

Now in sordid weeds they sleep,
Their secret now in dulness keep;
Yet, will you learn our ancient speech,
These the masters who can teach.
Fourscore or a hundred words
All their vocal muse affords;
These they turn in other fashion
Than the writer or the parson.
I can spare the college bell,
And the learned lecture, well;
Spare the clergy and libraries,
Institutes and dictionaries,
For that hardy English root
Thrives here, unvalued, underfoot.
Rude poets of the tavern hearth,
Squandering your unquoted mirth,
Which keeps the ground, and never soars,
While Jake retorts, and Reuben roars;
Tough and screaming, as birch-bark,
Goes like bullet to its mark;
While the solid curse and jeer
Never balk the waiting ear.
To student ears keen relished jokes
On truck, and stock, and farming folks, —
Nought the mountain yields thereof,
But savage health and sinews tough.

On the summit as I stood,
O'er the wide floor of plain and flood
Seemed to me, the towering hill

Was not altogether still,
But a quiet sense conveyed;
If I err not, thus it said: —

'Many feet in summer seek,
Betimes, my far-appearing peak;
In the dreaded winter time,
None save dappling shadows climb,
Under clouds, my lonely head,
Old as the sun, old almost as the shade.
And comest thou
To see strange forests and new snow,
And tread uplifted land?
And leavest thou thy lowland race,
Here amid clouds to stand?
And wouldst be my companion,
Where I gaze,
And shall gaze,
When forests fall, and man is gone,
Over tribes and over times,
At the burning Lyre,
Nearing me,
With its stars of northern fire,
In many a thousand years?

'Ah! welcome, if thou bring
My secret in thy brain;
To mountain-top may Muse's wing
With good allowance strain.
Gentle pilgrim, if thou know
The gamut old of Pan,
And how the hills began,
The frank blessings of the hill
Fall on thee, as fall they will.
'Tis the law of bush and stone,
Each can only take his own.

'Let him heed who can and will;
Enchantment fixed me here
To stand the hurts of time, until

In mightier chant I disappear.
   'If thou trowest
How the chemic eddies play,
Pole to pole, and what they say;
And that these gray crags
Not on crags are hung,
But beads are of a rosary
On prayer and music strung;
And, credulous, through the granite seeming,
Seest the smile of Reason beaming; —
Can thy style-discerning eye
The hidden-working Builder spy,
Who builds, yet makes no chips, no din,
With hammer soft as snowflake's flight; —
Knowest thou this?
O pilgrim, wandering not amiss!
Already my rocks lie light,
And soon my cone will spin.

'For the world was built in order,
And the atoms march in tune;
Rhyme the pipe, and Time the warder,
Cannot forget the sun, the moon.
Orb and atom forth they prance,
When they hear from far the rune;
None so backward in the troop,
When the music and the dance
Reach his place and circumstance,
But knows the sun-creating sound,
And, though a pyramid, will bound.

'Monadnoc is a mountain strong,
Tall and good my kind among;
But well I know, no mountain can
Measure with a perfect man.
For it is on temples writ,
Adamant is soft to wit:
And when the greater comes again
With my secret in his brain,

I shall pass, as glides my shadow
Daily over hill and meadow.

'Through all time,
I heard the approaching feet
Along the flinty pathway beat
Of him that cometh, and shall come;
Of him who shall as lightly bear
My daily load of woods and streams,
As now the round sky-cleaving boat
Which never strains its rocky beams;
Whose timbers, as they silent float,
Alps and Caucasus uprear,
And the long Alleghanies here,
And all town-sprinkled lands that be,
Sailing through stars with all their history.

'Every morn I lift my head,
Gaze o'er New England underspread,
South from Saint Lawrence to the Sound,
From Katskill east to the sea-bound.
Anchored fast for many an age,
I await the bard and sage,
Who, in large thoughts, like fair pearl-seed,
Shall string Monadnoc like a bead.
Comes that cheerful troubadour,
This mound shall throb his face before,
As when, with inward fires and pain,
It rose a bubble from the plain.
When he cometh, I shall shed,
From this wellspring in my head,
Fountain drop of spicier worth
Than all vintage of the earth.
There's fruit upon my barren soil
Costlier far than wine or oil.
There's a berry blue and gold,—
Autumn-ripe, its juices hold
Sparta's stoutness, Bethlehem's heart,
Asia's rancor, Athens' art,

Slowsure Britain's secular might,
And the German's inward sight.
I will give my son to eat
Best of Pan's immortal meat,
Bread to eat, and juice to drink;
So the thoughts that he shall think
Shall not be forms of stars, but stars,
Nor pictures pale, but Jove and Mars.
He comes, but not of that race bred
Who daily climb my specular head.
Oft as morning wreathes my scarf,
Fled the last plumule of the Dark,
Pants up hither the spruce clerk
From South Cove and City Wharf.
I take him up my rugged sides,
Half-repentant, scant of breath,—
Bead-eyes my granite chaos show,
And my midsummer snow;
Open the daunting map beneath,—
All his county, sea and land,
Dwarfed to measure of his hand;
His day's ride is a furlong space,
His city tops a glimmering haze.
I plant his eyes on the sky-hoop bounding:
"See there the grim gray rounding
Of the bullet of the earth
Whereon ye sail,
Tumbling steep
In the uncontinented deep."
He looks on that, and he turns pale.
'Tis even so; this treacherous kite,
Farm-furrowed, town-incrusted sphere,
Thoughtless of its anxious freight,
Plunges eyeless on forever;
And he, poor parasite,
Cooped in a ship he cannot steer,—
Who is the captain he knows not,
Port or pilot trows not,—
Risk or ruin he must share.
I scowl on him with my cloud,

With my north wind chill his blood;
I lame him, clattering down the rocks;
And to live he is in fear.
Then, at last, I let him down
Once more into his dapper town,
To chatter, frightened, to his clan,
And forget me if he can.'

As in the old poetic fame
The gods are blind and lame,
And the simular despite
Betrays the more abounding might,
So call not waste that barren cone
Above the floral zone,
Where forests starve:
It is pure use; —
What sheaves like those which here we glean and bind
Of a celestial Ceres and the Muse?

Ages are thy days,
Thou grand expresser of the present tense,
And type of permanence!
Firm ensign of the fatal Being,
Amid these coward shapes of joy and grief,
That will not bide the seeing!

Hither we bring
Our insect miseries to the rocks;
And the whole flight, with pestering wing,
Vanish, and end their murmuring, —
Vanish beside these dedicated blocks,
Which who can tell what mason laid?
Spoils of a front none need restore,
Replacing frieze and architrave; —
Yet flowers each stone rosette and metope brave;
Still is the haughty pile erect
Of the old building Intellect.

Complement of human kind,
Having us at vantage still,

Our sumptuous indigence,
O barren mound, thy plenties fill!
We fool and prate;
Thou art silent and sedate.
To myriad kinds and times one sense
The constant mountain doth dispense;
Shedding on all its snows and leaves,
One joy it joys, one grief it grieves.
Thou seest, O watchman tall,
Our towns and races grow and fall,
And imagest the stable good
For which we all our lifetime grope,
In shifting form the formless mind,
And though the substance us elude,
We in thee the shadow find.
Thou, in our astronomy
An opaker star,
Seen haply from afar,
Above the horizon's hoop,
A moment, by the railway troop,
As o'er some bolder height they speed,—
By circumspect ambition,
By errant gain,
By feasters and the frivolous,—
Recallest us,
And makest sane.
Mute orator! well skilled to plead,
And send conviction without phrase,
Thou dost supply
The shortness of our days,
And promise, on thy Founder's truth,
Long morrow to this mortal youth.

Fable

The mountain and the squirrel
Had a quarrel;
And the former called the latter 'Little Prig.'
Bun replied,
'You are doubtless very big;
But all sorts of things and weather
Must be taken in together,
To make up a year
And a sphere.
And I think it no disgrace
To occupy my place.
If I'm not so large as you,
You are not so small as I,
And not half so spry.
I'll not deny you make
A very pretty squirrel track;
Talents differ; all is well and wisely put;
If I cannot carry forests on my back,
Neither can you crack a nut.'

Ode,

Inscribed to W. H. Channing

Though loath to grieve
The evil time's sole patriot,
I cannot leave
My honied thought
For the priest's cant,
Or statesman's rant.

If I refuse
My study for their politique,
Which at the best is trick,
The angry Muse
Puts confusion in my brain.

But who is he that prates
Of the culture of mankind,
Of better arts and life?
Go, blindworm, go,
Behold the famous States
Harrying Mexico
With rifle and with knife!

Or who, with accent bolder,
Dare praise the freedom-loving mountaineer?
I found by thee, O rushing Contoocook!
And in thy valleys, Agiochook!
The jackals of the negro-holder.

The God who made New Hampshire
Taunted the lofty land
With little men; —
Small bat and wren
House in the oak: —
If earth-fire cleave
The upheaved land, and bury the folk,
The southern crocodile would grieve.

Virtue palters; Right is hence;
Freedom praised, but hid;
Funeral eloquence
Rattles the coffin-lid.

What boots thy zeal,
O glowing friend,
That would indignant rend
The northland from the south?
Wherefore? to what good end?
Boston Bay and Bunker Hill
Would serve things still; —
Things are of the snake.

The horseman serves the horse,
The neatherd serves the neat,
The merchant serves the purse,

The eater serves his meat;
'Tis the day of the chattel,
Web to weave, and corn to grind;
Things are in the saddle,
And ride mankind.

There are two laws discrete,
Not reconciled,—
Law for man, and law for thing;
The last builds town and fleet,
But it runs wild,
And doth the man unking.

'Tis fit the forest fall,
The steep be graded,
The mountain tunnelled,
The sand shaded,
The orchard planted,
The glebe tilled,
The prairie granted,
The steamer built.

Let man serve law for man;
Live for friendship, live for love,
For truth's and harmony's behoof;
The state may follow how it can,
As Olympus follows Jove.

Yet do not I invite
The wrinkled shopman to my sounding woods,
Nor bid the unwilling senator
Ask votes of thrushes in the solitudes.
Every one to his chosen work;—
Foolish hands may mix and mar;
Wise and sure the issues are.
Round they roll till dark is light,
Sex to sex, and even to odd;—
The over-god
Who marries Right to Might,
Who peoples, unpeoples,—

He who exterminates
Races by stronger races,
Black by white faces,—
Knows to bring honey
Out of the lion;
Grafts gentlest scion
On pirate and Turk.

The Cossack eats Poland,
Like stolen fruit;
Her last noble is ruined,
Her last poet mute:
Straight, into double band
The victors divide;
Half for freedom strike and stand;—
The astonished Muse finds thousands at her side.

Astræa

Himself it was who wrote
His rank, and quartered his own coat.
There is no king nor sovereign state
That can fix a hero's rate;
Each to all is venerable,
Cap-a-pie invulnerable,
Until he write, where all eyes rest,
Slave or master on his breast.

I saw men go up and down,
In the country and the town,
With this prayer upon their neck,—
'Judgment and a judge we seek.'
Not to monarchs they repair,
Nor to learned jurist's chair;
But they hurry to their peers,
To their kinsfolk and their dears;
Louder than with speech they pray,—
'What am I? companion, say.'

And the friend not hesitates
To assign just place and mates;
Answers not in word or letter,
Yet is understood the better;
Is to his friend a looking-glass,
Reflects his figure that doth pass.
Every wayfarer he meets
What himself declared repeats,
What himself confessed records,
Sentences him in his words;
The form is his own corporal form,
And his thought the penal worm.

Yet shine forever virgin minds,
Loved by stars and purest winds,
Which, o'er passion throned sedate,
Have not hazarded their state;
Disconcert the searching spy,
Rendering to a curious eye
The durance of a granite ledge
To those who gaze from the sea's edge.
It is there for benefit;
It is there for purging light;
There for purifying storms;
And its depths reflect all forms;
It cannot parley with the mean,—
Pure by impure is not seen.
For there's no sequestered grot,
Lone mountain tarn, or isle forgot,
But Justice, journeying in the sphere,
Daily stoops to harbor there.

Etienne de la Boéce

I serve you not, if you I follow,
Shadowlike, o'er hill and hollow;
And bend my fancy to your leading,
All too nimble for my treading.

When the pilgrimage is done,
And we've the landscape overrun,
I am bitter, vacant, thwarted,
And your heart is unsupported.
Vainly valiant, you have missed
The manhood that should yours resist,—
Its complement; but if I could,
In severe or cordial mood,
Lead you rightly to my altar,
Where the wisest Muses falter,
And worship that world-warming spark
Which dazzles me in midnight dark,
Equalizing small and large,
While the soul it doth surcharge,
That the poor is wealthy grown,
And the hermit never alone,—
The traveller and the road seem one
With the errand to be done,—
That were a man's and lover's part,
That were Freedom's whitest chart.

Suum Cuique

The rain has spoiled the farmer's day;
Shall sorrow put my books away?
    Thereby are two days lost:
Nature shall mind her own affairs;
I will attend my proper cares,
    In rain, or sun, or frost.

Compensation

Why should I keep holiday
    When other men have none?
Why but because, when these are gay,
    I sit and mourn alone?

And why, when mirth unseals all tongues,
  Should mine alone be dumb?
Ah! late I spoke to silent throngs,
  And now their hour is come.

Forbearance

Hast thou named all the birds without a gun?
Loved the wood-rose, and left it on its stalk?
At rich men's tables eaten bread and pulse?
Unarmed, faced danger with a heart of trust?
And loved so well a high behavior,
In man or maid, that thou from speech refrained,
Nobility more nobly to repay?
O, be my friend, and teach me to be thine!

The Park

The prosperous and beautiful
  To me seem not to wear
The yoke of conscience masterful,
  Which galls me everywhere.

I cannot shake off the god;
  On my neck he makes his seat;
I look at my face in the glass,—
  My eyes his eyeballs meet.

Enchanters! enchantresses!
  Your gold makes you seem wise;
The morning mist within your grounds
  More proudly rolls, more softly lies.

Yet spake yon purple mountain,
  Yet said yon ancient wood,
That Night or Day, that Love or Crime,
  Leads all souls to the Good.

Forerunners

Long I followed happy guides,
I could never reach their sides;
Their step is forth, and, ere the day,
Breaks up their leaguer, and away.
Keen my sense, my heart was young,
Right good-will my sinews strung,
But no speed of mine avails
To hunt upon their shining trails.
On and away, their hasting feet
Make the morning proud and sweet;
Flowers they strew,—I catch the scent;
Or tone of silver instrument
Leaves on the wind melodious trace;
Yet I could never see their face.
On eastern hills I see their smokes,
Mixed with mist by distant lochs.
I met many travellers
Who the road had surely kept;
They saw not my fine revellers,—
These had crossed them while they slept.
Some had heard their fair report,
In the country or the court.
Fleetest couriers alive
Never yet could once arrive,
As they went or they returned,
At the house where these sojourned.
Sometimes their strong speed they slacken,
Though they are not overtaken;
In sleep their jubilant troop is near,—
I tuneful voices overhear;
It may be in wood or waste,—
At unawares 'tis come and past.
Their near camp my spirit knows
By signs gracious as rainbows.
I thenceforward, and long after,
Listen for their harp-like laughter,
And carry in my heart, for days,
Peace that hallows rudest ways.

Sursum Corda

Seek not the spirit, if it hide
Inexorable to thy zeal:
Baby, do not whine and chide:
Art thou not also real?
Why shouldst thou stoop to poor excuse?
Turn on the accuser roundly; say,
'Here am I, here will I remain
Forever to myself soothfast;
Go thou, sweet Heaven, or at thy pleasure stay!'
Already Heaven with thee its lot has cast,
For only it can absolutely deal.

Ode to Beauty

Who gave thee, O Beauty,
The keys of this breast, —
Too credulous lover
Of blest and unblest?
Say, when in lapsed ages
Thee knew I of old?
Or what was the service
For which I was sold?
When first my eyes saw thee,
I found me thy thrall,
By magical drawings,
Sweet tyrant of all!
I drank at thy fountain
False waters of thirst;
Thou intimate stranger,
Thou latest and first!
Thy dangerous glances
Make women of men;
New-born, we are melting
Into nature again.

Lavish, lavish promiser,
Nigh persuading gods to err!

Guest of million painted forms,
Which in turn thy glory warms!
The frailest leaf, the mossy bark,
The acorn's cup, the raindrop's arc,
The swinging spider's silver line,
The ruby of the drop of wine,
The shining pebble of the pond,
Thou inscribest with a bond,
In thy momentary play,
Would bankrupt nature to repay.

Ah, what avails it
To hide or to shun
Whom the Infinite One
Hath granted his throne?
The heaven high over
Is the deep's lover;
The sun and sea,
Informed by thee,
Before me run,
And draw me on,
Yet fly me still,
As Fate refuses
To me the heart Fate for me chooses.
Is it that my opulent soul
Was mingled from the generous whole;
Sea-valleys and the deep of skies
Furnished several supplies;
And the sands whereof I'm made
Draw me to them, self-betrayed?
I turn the proud portfolios
Which hold the grand designs
Of Salvator, of Guercino,
And Piranesi's lines.
I hear the lofty pæans
Of the masters of the shell,
Who heard the starry music
And recount the numbers well;
Olympian bards who sung
Divine Ideas below,

Which always find us young,
And always keep us so.
Oft, in streets or humblest places,
I detect far-wandered graces,
Which, from Eden wide astray,
In lowly homes have lost their way.

Thee gliding through the sea of form,
Like the lightning through the storm,
Somewhat not to be possessed,
Somewhat not to be caressed,
No feet so fleet could ever find,
No perfect form could ever bind.
Thou eternal fugitive,
Hovering over all that live,
Quick and skilful to inspire
Sweet, extravagant desire,
Starry space and lily-bell
Filling with thy roseate smell,
Wilt not give the lips to taste
Of the nectar which thou hast.

All that's good and great with thee
Works in close conspiracy;
Thou hast bribed the dark and lonely
To report thy features only,
And the cold and purple morning
Itself with thoughts of thee adorning;
The leafy dell, the city mart,
Equal trophies of thine art;
E'en the flowing azure air
Thou hast touched for my despair;
And, if I languish into dreams,
Again I meet the ardent beams.
Queen of things! I dare not die
In Being's deeps past ear and eye;
Lest there I find the same deceiver,
And be the sport of Fate forever.
Dread Power, but dear! if God thou be,
Unmake me quite, or give thyself to me!

Give All to Love

Give all to love;
Obey thy heart;
Friends, kindred, days,
Estate, good-fame,
Plans, credit, and the Muse,—
Nothing refuse.

'Tis a brave master;
Let it have scope:
Follow it utterly,
Hope beyond hope:
High and more high
It dives into noon,
With wing unspent,
Untold intent;
But it is a god,
Knows its own path,
And the outlets of the sky.

It was not for the mean;
It requireth courage stout,
Souls above doubt,
Valor unbending;
Such 'twill reward,—
They shall return
More than they were,
And ever ascending.

Leave all for love;
Yet, hear me, yet,
One word more thy heart behoved,
One pulse more of firm endeavor,—
Keep thee to-day,
To-morrow, forever,
Free as an Arab
Of thy beloved.

Cling with life to the maid;
But when the surprise,
First vague shadow of surmise
Flits across her bosom young
Of a joy apart from thee,
Free be she, fancy-free;
Nor thou detain her vesture's hem,
Nor the palest rose she flung
From her summer diadem.

Though thou loved her as thyself,
As a self of purer clay,
Though her parting dims the day,
Stealing grace from all alive;
Heartily know,
When half-gods go,
The gods arrive.

To Ellen,

at the South

The green grass is bowing,
   The morning wind is in it;
'Tis a tune worth thy knowing,
   Though it change every minute.

'Tis a tune of the spring;
   Every year plays it over
To the robin on the wing,
   And to the pausing lover.

O'er ten thousand, thousand acres,
   Goes light the nimble zephyr;
The Flowers—tiny sect of Shakers—
   Worship him ever.

Hark to the winning sound!
   They summon thee, dearest,—
Saying, 'We have dressed for thee the ground,
   Nor yet thou appearest.

'O hasten; 'tis our time,
   Ere yet the red Summer
Scorch our delicate prime,
   Loved of bee,—the tawny hummer.

'O pride of thy race!
   Sad, in sooth, it were to ours,
If our brief tribe miss thy face,
   We poor New England flowers.

'Fairest, choose the fairest members
   Of our lithe society;
June's glories and September's
   Show our love and piety.

'Thou shalt command us all,—
   April's cowslip, summer's clover,
To the gentian in the fall,
   Blue-eyed pet of blue-eyed lover.

'O come, then, quickly come!
   We are budding, we are blowing;
And the wind that we perfume
   Sings a tune that's worth the knowing.'

To Eva

O fair and stately maid, whose eyes
Were kindled in the upper skies
    At the same torch that lighted mine;
For so I must interpret still
Thy sweet dominion o'er my will,
    A sympathy divine.

Ah! let me blameless gaze upon
Features that seem at heart my own;
    Nor fear those watchful sentinels,
Who charm the more their glance forbids,
Chaste-glowing, underneath their lids,
    With fire that draws while it repels.

The Amulet

Your picture smiles as first it smiled;
    The ring you gave is still the same;
Your letter tells, O changing child!
    No tidings *since* it came.

Give me an amulet
    That keeps intelligence with you,—
Red when you love, and rosier red,
    And when you love not, pale and blue.

Alas! that neither bonds nor vows
    Can certify possession;
Torments me still the fear that love
    Died in its last expression.

Thine Eyes Still Shined

Thine eyes still shined for me, though far
  I lonely roved the land or sea:
As I behold yon evening star,
  Which yet beholds not me.

This morn I climbed the misty hill,
  And roamed the pastures through;
How danced thy form before my path
  Amidst the deep-eyed dew!

When the redbird spread his sable wing,
  And showed his side of flame;
When the rosebud ripened to the rose,
  In both I read thy name.

Eros

The sense of the world is short, —
Long and various the report, —
  To love and be beloved;
Men and gods have not outlearned it;
And, how oft soe'er they've turned it,
  'Tis not to be improved.

Hermione

On a mound an Arab lay,
And sung his sweet regrets,
And told his amulets:
The summer bird
His sorrow heard,
And, when he heaved a sigh profound,
The sympathetic swallow swept the ground.

'If it be, as they said, she was not fair,
Beauty's not beautiful to me,
But sceptred genius, aye inorbed,
Culminating in her sphere.
This Hermione absorbed
The lustre of the land and ocean,
Hills and islands, cloud and tree,
In her form and motion.

'I ask no bawble miniature,
Nor ringlets dead
Shorn from her comely head,
Now that morning not disdains
Mountains and the misty plains
Her colossal portraiture;
They her heralds be,
Steeped in her quality,
And singers of her fame
Who is their Muse and dame.

'Higher, dear swallows! mind not what I say.
Ah! heedless how the weak are strong,
Say, was it just,
In thee to frame, in me to trust,
Thou to the Syrian couldst belong?

'I am of a lineage
That each for each doth fast engage;
In old Bassora's schools, I seemed
Hermit vowed to books and gloom,—
Ill-bested for gay bridegroom.
I was by thy touch redeemed;
When thy meteor glances came,
We talked at large of worldly fate,
And drew truly every trait.

'Once I dwelt apart,
Now I live with all;
As shepherd's lamp on far hill-side
Seems, by the traveller espied,

A door into the mountain heart,
So didst thou quarry and unlock
Highways for me through the rock.

'Now, deceived, thou wanderest
In strange lands unblest;
And my kindred come to soothe me.
Southwind is my next of blood;
He is come through fragrant wood,
Drugged with spice from climates warm,
And in every twinkling glade,
And twilight nook,
Unveils thy form.
Out of the forest way
Forth paced it yesterday;
And when I sat by the watercourse,
Watching the daylight fade,
It throbbed up from the brook.

'River, and rose, and crag, and bird,
Frost, and sun, and eldest night,
To me their aid preferred,
To me their comfort plight;—
"Courage! we are thine allies,
And with this hint be wise,—
The chains of kind
The distant bind;
Deed thou doest she must do,
Above her will, be true;
And, in her strict resort
To winds and waterfalls,
And autumn's sunlit festivals,
To music, and to music's thought,
Inextricably bound,
She shall find thee, and be found.
Follow not her flying feet;
Come to us herself to meet." '

Initial, Dæmonic, and Celestial Love

I.

The Initial Love

Venus, when her son was lost,
Cried him up and down the coast,
In hamlets, palaces, and parks,
And told the truant by his marks,—
Golden curls, and quiver, and bow.
This befell long ago.
Time and tide are strangely changed,
Men and manners much deranged:
None will now find Cupid latent
By this foolish antique patent.
He came late along the waste,
Shod like a traveller for haste;
With malice dared me to proclaim him,
That the maids and boys might name him.

Boy no more, he wears all coats,
Frocks, and blouses, capes, capotes;
He bears no bow, or quiver, or wand,
Nor chaplet on his head or hand.
Leave his weeds and heed his eyes,—
All the rest he can disguise.
In the pit of his eye 's a spark
Would bring back day if it were dark;
And, if I tell you all my thought,
Though I comprehend it not,
In those unfathomable orbs
Every function he absorbs.
He doth eat, and drink, and fish, and shoot,
And write, and reason, and compute,
And ride, and run, and have, and hold,
And whine, and flatter, and regret,
And kiss, and couple, and beget,
By those roving eyeballs bold.

Undaunted are their courages,
Right Cossacks in their forages;
Fleeter they than any creature,—
They are his steeds, and not his feature;
Inquisitive, and fierce, and fasting,
Restless, predatory, hasting;
And they pounce on other eyes
As lions on their prey;
And round their circles is writ,
Plainer than the day,
Underneath, within, above,—
Love—love—love—love.
He lives in his eyes;
There doth digest, and work, and spin,
And buy, and sell, and lose, and win;
He rolls them with delighted motion,
Joy-tides swell their mimic ocean.
Yet holds he them with tortest rein,
That they may seize and entertain
The glance that to their glance opposes,
Like fiery honey sucked from roses.
He palmistry can understand,
Imbibing virtue by his hand
As if it were a living root;
The pulse of hands will make him mute;
With all his force he gathers balms
Into those wise, thrilling palms.

Cupid is a casuist,
A mystic, and a cabalist,—
Can your lurking thought surprise,
And interpret your device.
He is versed in occult science,
In magic, and in clairvoyance;
Oft he keeps his fine ear strained,
And Reason on her tiptoe pained
For aëry intelligence,
And for strange coincidence.
But it touches his quick heart
When Fate by omens takes his part,

And chance-dropped hints from Nature's sphere
Deeply soothe his anxious ear.
Heralds high before him run;
He has ushers many a one;
He spreads his welcome where he goes,
And touches all things with his rose.
All things wait for and divine him,—
How shall I dare to malign him,
Or accuse the god of sport?
I must end my true report,
Painting him from head to foot,
In as far as I took note,
Trusting well the matchless power
Of this young-eyed emperor
Will clear his fame from every cloud,
With the bards and with the crowd.

He is wilful, mutable,
Shy, untamed, inscrutable,
Swifter-fashioned than the fairies,
Substance mixed of pure contraries;
His vice some elder virtue's token,
And his good is evil-spoken.
Failing sometimes of his own,
He is headstrong and alone;
He affects the wood and wild,
Like a flower-hunting child;
Buries himself in summer waves,
In trees, with beasts, in mines, and caves;
Loves nature like a horned cow,
Bird, or deer, or caribou.

Shun him, nymphs, on the fleet horses!
He has a total world of wit;
O how wise are his discourses!
But he is the arch-hypocrite,
And, through all science and all art,
Seeks alone his counterpart.
He is a Pundit of the East,
He is an augur and a priest,

And his soul will melt in prayer,
But word and wisdom is a snare;
Corrupted by the present toy
He follows joy, and only joy.
There is no mask but he will wear;
He invented oaths to swear;
He paints, he carves, he chants, he prays,
And holds all stars in his embrace,
Godlike,—but 'tis for his fine pelf,
The social quintessence of self.
Well said I he is hypocrite,
And folly the end of his subtle wit!
He takes a sovran privilege
Not allowed to any liege;
For he does go behind all law,
And right into himself does draw;
For he is sovereignly allied,—
Heaven's oldest blood flows in his side,—
And interchangeably at one
With every king on every throne,
That no god dare say him nay,
Or see the fault, or seen betray:
He has the Muses by the heart,
And the Parcæ all are of his part.

His many signs cannot be told;
He has not one mode, but manifold,—
Many fashions and addresses,
Piques, reproaches, hurts, caresses,
Arguments, lore, poetry,
Action, service, badinage;
He will preach like a friar,
And jump like Harlequin;
He will read like a crier,
And fight like a Paladin.
Boundless is his memory;
Plans immense his term prolong;
He is not of counted age,
Meaning always to be young.

And his wish is intimacy,
Intimater intimacy,
And a stricter privacy;
The impossible shall yet be done,
And, being two, shall still be one.
As the wave breaks to foam on shelves,
Then runs into a wave again,
So lovers melt their sundered selves,
Yet melted would be twain.

II.

The Dæmonic and the Celestial Love

Man was made of social earth,
Child and brother from his birth,
Tethered by a liquid cord
Of blood through veins of kindred poured.
Next his heart the fireside band
Of mother, father, sister, stand:
These, like strong amulets preferred,
Throbs of a wild religion stirred;—
Virtue, to love, to hate them, vice;
Till dangerous Beauty came, at last,
Till Beauty came to snap all ties;
The maid, abolishing the past,
With lotus wine obliterates
Dear memory's stone-incarved traits,
And, by herself, supplants alone
Friends year by year more inly known.
When her calm eyes opened bright,
All were foreign in their light.
It was ever the self-same tale,
The first experience will not fail;
Only two in the garden walked,
And with snake and seraph talked.

But God said,
'I will have a purer gift;

There is smoke in the flame;
New flowerets bring, new prayers uplift,
And love without a name.
Fond children, ye desire
To please each other well;
Another round, a higher,
Ye shall climb on the heavenly stair,
And selfish preference forbear;
And in right deserving,
And without a swerving
Each from your proper state,
Weave roses for your mate.

'Deep, deep are loving eyes,
Flowed with naphtha fiery sweet;
And the point is paradise,
Where their glances meet:
Their reach shall yet be more profound,
And a vision without bound;
The axis of those eyes sun-clear
Be the axis of the sphere:
So shall the lights ye pour amain
Go, without check or intervals,
Through from the empyrean walls
Unto the same again.'

Close, close to men,
Like undulating layer of air,
Right above their heads,
The potent plain of Dæmons spreads.
Stands to each human soul its own,
For watch, and ward, and furtherance,
In the snares of Nature's dance;
And the lustre and the grace
Which fascinate each youthful heart,
Beaming from its counterpart,
Translucent through the mortal covers,
Is the Dæmon's form and face.
To and fro the Genius hies,—
A gleam which plays and hovers

Over the maiden's head,
And dips sometimes as low as to her eyes.
Unknown, albeit lying near,
To men, the path to the Dæmon sphere;
And they that swiftly come and go
Leave no track on the heavenly snow.
Sometimes the airy synod bends,
And the mighty choir descends,
And the brains of men thenceforth,
In crowded and in still resorts,
Teem with unwonted thoughts:
As, when a shower of meteors
Cross the orbit of the earth,
And, lit by fringent air,
Blaze near and far,
Mortals deem the planets bright
Have slipped their sacred bars,
And the lone seaman all the night
Sails, astonished, amid stars.

Beauty of a richer vein,
Graces of a subtler strain,
Unto men these moonmen lend,
And our shrinking sky extend.
So is man's narrow path
By strength and terror skirted;
Also, (from the song the wrath
Of the Genii be averted!
The Muse the truth uncolored speaking,)
The Dæmons are self-seeking:
Their fierce and limitary will
Draws men to their likeness still.
The erring painter made Love blind,—
Highest Love who shines on all;
Him, radiant, sharpest-sighted god,
None can bewilder;
Whose eyes pierce
The universe,
Path-finder, road-builder,
Mediator, royal giver;

Rightly seeing, rightly seen,
Of joyful and transparent mien.
'Tis a sparkle passing
From each to each, from thee to me,
To and fro perpetually;
Sharing all, daring all,
Levelling, displacing
Each obstruction, it unites
Equals remote, and seeming opposites.
And ever and forever Love
Delights to build a road:
Unheeded Danger near him strides,
Love laughs, and on a lion rides.
But Cupid wears another face,
Born into Dæmons less divine:
His roses bleach apace,
His nectar smacks of wine.
The Dæmon ever builds a wall,
Himself encloses and includes,
Solitude in solitudes:
In like sort his love doth fall.
He is an oligarch;
He prizes wonder, fame, and mark;
He loveth crowns;
He scorneth drones;
He doth elect
The beautiful and fortunate,
And the sons of intellect,
And the souls of ample fate,
Who the Future's gates unbar, —
Minions of the Morning Star.
In his prowess he exults,
And the multitude insults.
His impatient looks devour
Oft the humble and the poor;
And, seeing his eye glare,
They drop their few pale flowers,
Gathered with hope to please,
Along the mountain towers, —

Lose courage, and despair.
He will never be gainsaid,—
Pitiless, will not be stayed;
His hot tyranny
Burns up every other tie.
Therefore comes an hour from Jove
Which his ruthless will defies,
And the dogs of Fate unties.
Shiver the palaces of glass;
Shrivel the rainbow-colored walls,
Where in bright Art each god and sibyl dwelt,
Secure as in the zodiac's belt;
And the galleries and halls,
Wherein every siren sung,
Like a meteor pass.
For this fortune wanted root
In the core of God's abysm,—
Was a weed of self and schism;
And ever the Dæmonic Love
Is the ancestor of wars,
And the parent of remorse.

III.

Higher far,
Upward into the pure realm,
Over sun and star,
Over the flickering Dæmon film,
Thou must mount for love;
Into vision where all form
In one only form dissolves;
In a region where the wheel
On which all beings ride
Visibly revolves;
Where the starred, eternal worm
Girds the world with bound and term;
Where unlike things are like;
Where good and ill,

And joy and moan,
Melt into one.

There Past, Present, Future shoot
Triple blossoms from one root;
Substances at base divided
In their summits are united;
There the holy essence rolls,
One through separated souls;
And the sunny Æon sleeps
Folding Nature in its deeps:
And every fair and every good,
Known in part, or known impure,
To men below,
In their archetypes endure.
The race of gods,
Or those we erring own,
Are shadows flitting up and down
In the still abodes.
The circles of that sea are laws
Which publish and which hide the cause.

Pray for a beam
Out of that sphere,
Thee to guide and to redeem.
O, what a load
Of care and toil,
By lying use bestowed,
From his shoulders falls who sees
The true astronomy,
The period of peace.
Counsel which the ages kept
Shall the well-born soul accept.
As the overhanging trees
Fill the lake with images,—
As garment draws the garment's hem,
Men their fortunes bring with them.
By right or wrong,
Lands and goods go to the strong.
Property will brutely draw

Still to the proprietor;
Silver to silver creep and wind,
And kind to kind.

Nor less the eternal poles
Of tendency distribute souls.
There need no vows to bind
Whom not each other seek, but find.
They give and take no pledge or oath, —
Nature is the bond of both:
No prayer persuades, no flattery fawns, —
Their noble meanings are their pawns.
Plain and cold is their address,
Power have they for tenderness;
And, so thoroughly is known
Each other's counsel by his own,
They can parley without meeting;
Need is none of forms of greeting;
They can well communicate
In their innermost estate;
When each the other shall avoid,
Shall each by each be most enjoyed.

Not with scarfs or perfumed gloves
Do these celebrate their loves;
Not by jewels, feasts, and savors,
Not by ribbons or by favors,
But by the sun-spark on the sea,
And the cloud-shadow on the lea,
The soothing lapse of morn to mirk,
And the cheerful round of work.
Their cords of love so public are,
They intertwine the farthest star:
The throbbing sea, the quaking earth,
Yield sympathy and signs of mirth;
Is none so high, so mean is none,
But feels and seals this union;
Even the fell Furies are appeased,
The good applaud, the lost are eased.

Love's hearts are faithful, but not fond,
Bound for the just, but not beyond;
Not glad, as the low-loving herd,
Of self in other still preferred,
But they have heartily designed
The benefit of broad mankind.
And they serve men austerely,
After their own genius, clearly,
Without a false humility;
For this is Love's nobility,—
Not to scatter bread and gold,
Goods and raiment bought and sold;
But to hold fast his simple sense,
And speak the speech of innocence,
And with hand, and body, and blood,
To make his bosom-counsel good.
For he that feeds men serveth few;
He serves all who dares be true.

The Apology

Think me not unkind and rude
   That I walk alone in grove and glen;
I go to the god of the wood
   To fetch his word to men.

Tax not my sloth that I
   Fold my arms beside the brook;
Each cloud that floated in the sky
   Writes a letter in my book.

Chide me not, laborious band,
   For the idle flowers I brought;
Every aster in my hand
   Goes home loaded with a thought.

There was never mystery
  But 'tis figured in the flowers;
Was never secret history
  But birds tell it in the bowers.

One harvest from thy field
  Homeward brought the oxen strong;
A second crop thine acres yield,
  Which I gather in a song.

Merlin I

Thy trivial harp will never please
Or fill my craving ear;
Its chords should ring as blows the breeze,
Free, peremptory, clear.
No jingling serenader's art,
Nor tinkle of piano strings,
Can make the wild blood start
In its mystic springs.
The kingly bard
Must smite the chords rudely and hard,
As with hammer or with mace;
That they may render back
Artful thunder, which conveys
Secrets of the solar track,
Sparks of the supersolar blaze.
Merlin's blows are strokes of fate,
Chiming with the forest tone,
When boughs buffet boughs in the wood;
Chiming with the gasp and moan
Of the ice-imprisoned flood;
With the pulse of manly hearts;
With the voice of orators;
With the din of city arts;

With the cannonade of wars;
With the marches of the brave;
And prayers of might from martyrs' cave.

Great is the art,
Great be the manners, of the bard.
He shall not his brain encumber
With the coil of rhythm and number;
But, leaving rule and pale forethought,
He shall aye climb
For his rhyme.
'Pass in, pass in,' the angels say,
'In to the upper doors,
Nor count compartments of the floors,
But mount to paradise
By the stairway of surprise.'

Blameless master of the games,
King of sport that never shames,
He shall daily joy dispense
Hid in song's sweet influence.
Things more cheerly live and go,
What time the subtle mind
Sings aloud the tune whereto
Their pulses beat,
And march their feet,
And their members are combined.

By Sybarites beguiled,
He shall no task decline;
Merlin's mighty line
Extremes of nature reconciled,—
Bereaved a tyrant of his will,
And made the lion mild.
Songs can the tempest still,
Scattered on the stormy air,
Mould the year to fair increase,
And bring in poetic peace.

He shall not seek to weave,
In weak, unhappy times,
Efficacious rhymes;
Wait his returning strength.
Bird, that from the nadir's floor
To the zenith's top can soar,
The soaring orbit of the muse exceeds
    that journey's length.
Nor profane affect to hit
Or compass that, by meddling wit,
Which only the propitious mind
Publishes when 'tis inclined.
There are open hours
When the God's will sallies free,
And the dull idiot might see
The flowing fortunes of a thousand years;—
Sudden, at unawares,
Self-moved, fly-to the doors,
Nor sword of angels could reveal
What they conceal.

Merlin II

The rhyme of the poet
Modulates the king's affairs;
Balance-loving Nature
Made all things in pairs.
To every foot its antipode;
Each color with its counter glowed;
To every tone beat answering tones,
Higher or graver;
Flavor gladly blends with flavor;
Leaf answers leaf upon the bough;
And match the paired cotyledons.
Hands to hands, and feet to feet,
Coeval grooms and brides;
Eldest rite, two married sides
In every mortal meet.

Light's far furnace shines,
Smelting balls and bars,
Forging double stars,
Glittering twins and trines.
The animals are sick with love,
Lovesick with rhyme;
Each with all propitious time
Into chorus wove.

Like the dancers' ordered band,
Thoughts come also hand in hand;
In equal couples mated,
Or else alternated;
Adding by their mutual gage,
One to other, health and age.
Solitary fancies go
Short-lived wandering to and fro,
Most like to bachelors,
Or an ungiven maid,
Not ancestors,
With no posterity to make the lie afraid,
Or keep truth undecayed.
Perfect-paired as eagle's wings,
Justice is the rhyme of things;
Trade and counting use
The self-same tuneful muse;
And Nemesis,
Who with even matches odd,
Who athwart space redresses
The partial wrong,
Fills the just period,
And finishes the song.

Subtle rhymes, with ruin rife,
Murmur in the house of life,
Sung by the Sisters as they spin;
In perfect time and measure they
Build and unbuild our echoing clay,
As the two twilights of the day
Fold us music-drunken in.

Bacchus

Bring me wine, but wine which never grew
In the belly of the grape,
Or grew on vine whose tap-roots, reaching through
Under the Andes to the Cape,
Suffered no savor of the earth to scape.

Let its grapes the morn salute
From a nocturnal root,
Which feels the acrid juice
Of Styx and Erebus;
And turns the woe of Night,
By its own craft, to a more rich delight.

We buy ashes for bread;
We buy diluted wine;
Give me of the true, —
Whose ample leaves and tendrils curled
Among the silver hills of heaven,
Draw everlasting dew;
Wine of wine,
Blood of the world,
Form of forms, and mould of statures,
That I intoxicated,
And by the draught assimilated,
May float at pleasure through all natures;
The bird-language rightly spell,
And that which roses say so well.

Wine that is shed
Like the torrents of the sun
Up the horizon walls,
Or like the Atlantic streams, which run
When the South Sea calls.

Water and bread,
Food which needs no transmuting,
Rainbow-flowering, wisdom-fruiting
Wine which is already man,
Food which teach and reason can.

Wine which Music is, —
Music and wine are one, —
That I, drinking this,
Shall hear far Chaos talk with me;
Kings unborn shall walk with me;
And the poor grass shall plot and plan
What it will do when it is man.
Quickened so, will I unlock
Every crypt of every rock.

I thank the joyful juice
For all I know; —
Winds of remembering
Of the ancient being blow,
And seeming-solid walls of use
Open and flow.

Pour, Bacchus! the remembering wine;
Retrieve the loss of me and mine!
Vine for vine be antidote,
And the grape requite the lote!
Haste to cure the old despair, —
Reason in Nature's lotus drenched,
The memory of ages quenched;
Give them again to shine;
Let wine repair what this undid;
And where the infection slid,
A dazzling memory revive;
Refresh the faded tints,
Recut the aged prints,
And write my old adventures with the pen
Which on the first day drew,
Upon the tablets blue,
The dancing Pleiads and eternal men.

Loss and Gain

Virtue runs before the Muse,
  And defies her skill;
She is rapt, and doth refuse
  To wait a painter's will.

Star-adoring, occupied,
  Virtue cannot bend her
Just to please a poet's pride,
  To parade her splendor.

The bard must be with good intent
  No more his, but hers;
Must throw away his pen and paint,
  Kneel with worshippers.

Then, perchance, a sunny ray
  From the heaven of fire,
His lost tools may overpay,
  And better his desire.

Merops

What care I, so they stand the same,—
  Things of the heavenly mind,—
How long the power to give them name
  Tarries yet behind?

Thus far to-day your favors reach,
  O fair, appeasing presences!
Ye taught my lips a single speech,
  And a thousand silences.

Space grants beyond his fated road
  No inch to the god of day;
And copious language still bestowed
  One word, no more, to say.

The House

There is no architect
   Can build as the Muse can;
She is skilful to select
   Materials for her plan;

Slow and warily to choose
   Rafters of immortal pine,
Or cedar incorruptible,
   Worthy her design.

She threads dark Alpine forests,
   Or valleys by the sea,
In many lands, with painful steps,
   Ere she can find a tree.

She ransacks mines and ledges,
   And quarries every rock,
To hew the famous adamant
   For each eternal block.

She lays her beams in music,
   In music every one,
To the cadence of the whirling world
   Which dances round the sun;

That so they shall not be displaced
   By lapses or by wars,
But, for the love of happy souls,
   Outlive the newest stars.

Saadi

Trees in groves,
Kine in droves,
In ocean sport the scaly herds,
Wedge-like cleave the air the birds,

To northern lakes fly wind-borne ducks,
Browse the mountain sheep in flocks,
Men consort in camp and town,
But the poet dwells alone.

God, who gave to him the lyre,
Of all mortals the desire,
For all breathing men's behoof,
Straitly charged him, 'Sit aloof;'
Annexed a warning, poets say,
To the bright premium,—
Ever, when twain together play,
Shall the harp be dumb.

Many may come,
But one shall sing;
Two touch the string,
The harp is dumb.
Though there come a million,
Wise Saadi dwells alone.

Yet Saadi loved the race of men,—
No churl, immured in cave or den;
In bower and hall
He wants them all,
Nor can dispense
With Persia for his audience;
They must give ear,
Grow red with joy and white with fear;
But he has no companion;
Come ten, or come a million,
Good Saadi dwells alone.

Be thou ware where Saadi dwells;
Wisdom of the gods is he,—
Entertain it reverently.
Gladly round that golden lamp
Sylvan deities encamp,
And simple maids and noble youth
Are welcome to the man of truth.

Most welcome, they who need him most,
They feed the spring which they exhaust;
For greater need
Draws better deed:
But, critic, spare thy vanity,
Nor show thy pompous parts,
To vex with odious subtlety
The cheerer of men's hearts.

Sad-eyed Fakirs swiftly say
Endless dirges to decay,
Never in the blaze of light
Lose the shudder of midnight;
Pale at overflowing noon
Hear wolves barking at the moon;
In the bower of dalliance sweet
Hear the far Avenger's feet;
And shake before those awful Powers,
Who in their pride forgive not ours.
Thus the sad-eyed Fakirs preach:
'Bard, when thee would Allah teach,
And lift thee to his holy mount,
He sends thee from his bitter fount
Wormwood,—saying, "Go thy ways,
Drink not the Malaga of praise,
But do the deed thy fellows hate,
And compromise thy peaceful state;
Smite the white breasts which thee fed;
Stuff sharp thorns beneath the head
Of them thou shouldst have comforted;
For out of woe and out of crime
Draws the heart a lore sublime." '
And yet it seemeth not to me
That the high gods love tragedy;
For Saadi sat in the sun,
And thanks was his contrition;
For haircloth and for bloody whips,
Had active hands and smiling lips;
And yet his runes he rightly read,
And to his folk his message sped.

Sunshine in his heart transferred
Lighted each transparent word,
And well could honoring Persia learn
What Saadi wished to say;
For Saadi's nightly stars did burn
Brighter than Dschami's day.

Whispered the Muse in Saadi's cot:
'O gentle Saadi, listen not,
Tempted by thy praise of wit,
Or by thirst and appetite
For the talents not thine own,
To sons of contradiction.
Never, son of eastern morning,
Follow falsehood, follow scorning.
Denounce who will, who will deny,
And pile the hills to scale the sky;
Let theist, atheist, pantheist,
Define and wrangle how they list,
Fierce conserver, fierce destroyer, —
But thou, joy-giver and enjoyer,
Unknowing war, unknowing crime,
Gentle Saadi, mind thy rhyme;
Heed not what the brawlers say,
Heed thou only Saadi's lay.

'Let the great world bustle on
With war and trade, with camp and town:
A thousand men shall dig and eat;
At forge and furnace thousands sweat;
And thousands sail the purple sea,
And give or take the stroke of war,
Or crowd the market and bazaar;
Oft shall war end, and peace return,
And cities rise where cities burn,
Ere one man my hill shall climb,
Who can turn the golden rhyme.
Let them manage how they may,
Heed thou only Saadi's lay.
Seek the living among the dead, —

Man in man is imprisoned;
Barefooted Dervish is not poor,
If fate unlock his bosom's door,
So that what his eye hath seen
His tongue can paint as bright, as keen;
And what his tender heart hath felt
With equal fire thy heart shall melt.
For, whom the Muses smile upon,
And touch with soft persuasion,
His words like a storm-wind can bring
Terror and beauty on their wing;
In his every syllable
Lurketh nature veritable;
And though he speak in midnight dark,—
In heaven no star, on earth no spark,—
Yet before the listener's eye
Swims the world in ecstasy,
The forest waves, the morning breaks,
The pastures sleep, ripple the lakes,
Leaves twinkle, flowers like persons be,
And life pulsates in rock or tree.
Saadi, so far thy words shall reach:
Suns rise and set in Saadi's speech!'

And thus to Saadi said the Muse:
'Eat thou the bread which men refuse;
Flee from the goods which from thee flee;
Seek nothing,—Fortune seeketh thee.
Nor mount, nor dive; all good things keep
The midway of the eternal deep.
Wish not to fill the isles with eyes
To fetch thee birds of paradise:
On thine orchard's edge belong
All the brags of plume and song;
Wise Ali's sunbright sayings pass
For proverbs in the market-place;
Through mountains bored by regal art,
Toil whistles as he drives his cart.
Nor scour the seas, nor sift mankind,

A poet or a friend to find:
Behold, he watches at the door!
Behold his shadow on the floor!
Open innumerable doors
The heaven where unveiled Allah pours
The flood of truth, the flood of good,
The Seraph's and the Cherub's food:
Those doors are men: the Pariah hind
Admits thee to the perfect Mind.
Seek not beyond thy cottage wall
Redeemers that can yield thee all:
While thou sittest at thy door
On the desert's yellow floor,
Listening to the gray-haired crones,
Foolish gossips, ancient drones,
Saadi, see! they rise in stature
To the height of mighty Nature,
And the secret stands revealed
Fraudulent Time in vain concealed,—
That blessed gods in servile masks
Plied for thee thy household tasks.'

Holidays

From fall to spring the russet acorn,
　Fruit beloved of maid and boy,
Lent itself beneath the forest,
　To be the children's toy.

Pluck it now! In vain,—thou canst not;
　Its root has pierced yon shady mound;
Toy no longer—it has duties;
　It is anchored in the ground.

Year by year the rose-lipped maiden,
　Playfellow of young and old,
Was frolic sunshine, dear to all men,
　More dear to one than mines of gold.

Whither went the lovely hoyden?
   Disappeared in blessed wife;
Servant to a wooden cradle,
   Living in a baby's life.

Still thou playest;—short vacation
   Fate grants each to stand aside;
Now must thou be man and artist,—
   'Tis the turning of the tide.

Painting and Sculpture

The sinful painter drapes his goddess warm,
   Because she still is naked, being dressed:
The godlike sculptor will not so deform
   Beauty, which limbs and flesh enough invest.

From the Persian of Hafiz

The poems of Hafiz are held by the Persians to be allegoric and mystical. His German editor, Von Hammer, remarks on the following poem, that, 'though in appearance anacreontic, it may be regarded as one of the best of those compositions which earned for Hafiz the honorable title of "Tongue of the Secret."'

Butler, fetch the ruby wine
Which with sudden greatness fills us;
Pour for me, who in my spirit
Fail in courage and performance.
Bring this philosophic stone,
Karun's treasure, Noah's age;
Haste, that by thy means I open
All the doors of luck and life.
Bring to me the liquid fire
Zoroaster sought in dust:
To Hafiz, revelling, 'tis allowed

To pray to Matter and to Fire.
Bring the wine of Jamschid's glass,
Which glowed, ere time was, in the Néant;
Bring it me, that through its force
I, as Jamschid, see through worlds.
Wisely said the Kaisar Jamschid,
'The world's not worth a barleycorn:'
Let flute and lyre lordly speak;
Lees of wine outvalue crowns.
Bring me, boy, the veiled beauty,
Who in ill-famed houses sits:
Bring her forth; my honest name
Freely barter I for wine.
Bring me, boy, the fire-water;—
Drinks the lion, the woods burn;
Give it me, that I storm heaven,
And tear the net from the archwolf.
Wine wherewith the Houris teach
Souls the ways of paradise!
On the living coals I'll set it,
And therewith my brain perfume.
Bring me wine, through whose effulgence
Jam and Chosroes yielded light;
Wine, that to the flute I sing
Where is Jam, and where is Kauss.
Bring the blessing of old times,—
Bless the old, departed shahs!
Bring me wine which spendeth lordship,
Wine whose pureness searcheth hearts;
Bring it me, the shah of hearts!
Give me wine to wash me clean
Of the weather-stains of cares,
See the countenance of luck.
Whilst I dwell in spirit-gardens,
Wherefore stand I shackled here?
Lo, this mirror shows me all!
Drunk, I speak of purity,
Beggar, I of lordship speak;
When Hafiz in his revel sings,
Shouteth Sohra in her sphere.

Fear the changes of a day:
Bring wine which increases life.
Since the world is all untrue,
Let the trumpets thee remind
How the crown of Kobad vanished.
Be not certain of the world,—
'Twill not spare to shed thy blood.
Desperate of the world's affair
Came I running to the wine-house.
Bring me wine which maketh glad,
That I may my steed bestride,
Through the course career with Rustem,—
Gallop to my heart's content;
That I reason quite expunge,
And plant banners on the worlds.
Let us make our glasses kiss;
Let us quench the sorrow-cinders.
To-day let us drink together;
Now and *then* will never agree.
Whoso has arranged a banquet
Is with glad mind satisfied,
'Scaping from the snares of Dews.
Woe for youth! 'tis gone in the wind:
Happy he who spent it well!
Bring wine, that I overspring
Both worlds at a single leap.
Stole, at dawn, from glowing spheres
Call of Houris to my sense:—
'O lovely bird, delicious soul,
Spread thy pinions, break thy cage;
Sit on the roof of seven domes,
Where the spirits take their rest.'

In the time of Bisurdschimihr,
Menutscheher's beauty shined.
On the beaker of Nushirvan,
Wrote they once in elder times,
'Hear the counsel; learn from us
Sample of the course of things:
The earth—it is a place of sorrow,

Scanty joys are here below;
Who has nothing has no sorrow.'
Where is Jam, and where his cup?
Solomon and his mirror, where?
Which of the wise masters knows
What time Kauss and Jam existed?
When those heroes left this world,
Left they nothing but their names.
Bind thy heart not to the earth;
When thou goest, come not back;
Fools squander on the world their hearts,—
League with it is feud with heaven:
Never gives it what thou wishest.

A cup of wine imparts the sight
Of the five heaven-domes with nine steps:
Whoso can himself renounce
Without support shall walk thereon;—
Who discreet is is not wise.

Give me, boy, the Kaisar cup,
Which rejoices heart and soul.
Under wine and under cup
Signify we purest love.
Youth like lightning disappears;
Life goes by us as the wind.
Leave the dwelling with six doors,
And the serpent with nine heads;
Life and silver spend thou freely
If thou honorest the soul.
Haste into the other life;
All is vain save God alone.
Give me, boy, this toy of Dæmons:
When the cup of Jam was lost,
Him availed the world no more.
Fetch the wineglass made of ice;
Wake the torpid heart with wine.
Every clod of loam beneath us
Is a skull of Alexander;
Oceans are the blood of princes;

Desert sands the dust of beauties.
More than one Darius was there
Who the whole world overcame;
But, since these gave up the ghost,
Thinkest thou they never were?

Boy, go from me to the shah;
Say to him, 'Shah, crowned as Jam,
Win thou first the poor man's heart,
Then the glass; so know the world.
Empty sorrows from the earth
Canst thou drive away with wine.
Now in thy throne's recent beauty,
In the flowing tide of power,
Moon of fortune, mighty king,
Whose tiara sheddeth lustre,
Peace secure to fish and fowl,
Heart and eye-sparkle to saints; —
Shoreless is the sea of praise;
I content me with a prayer: —
From Nisami's lyric page,
Fairest ornament of speech,
Here a verse will I recite,
Verse more beautiful than pearls:
"More kingdoms wait thy diadem
Than are known to thee by name;
Thee may sovran Destiny
Lead to victory day by day!" '

Ghaselle:

from the Persian of Hafiz

Of Paradise, O hermit wise,
    Let us renounce the thought;
Of old therein our names of sin
    Allah recorded not.

Who dear to God on earthly sod
  No corn-grain plants,
The same is glad that life is had,
  Though corn he wants.

O just fakir, with brow austere,
  Forbid me not the vine;
On the first day, poor Hafiz' clay
  Was kneaded up with wine.

Thy mind the mosque and cool kiosk,
  Spare fast and orisons;
Mine me allows the drinking-house,
  And sweet chase of the nuns.

He is no dervise, Heaven slights his service,
  Who shall refuse
There in the banquet to pawn his blanket
  For Schiraz' juice.

Who his friend's skirt or hem of his shirt
  Shall spare to pledge,
To him Eden's bliss and angel's kiss
  Shall want their edge.

Up! Hafiz, grace from high God's face
  Beams on thee pure;
Shy thou not hell, and trust thou well,
  Heaven is secure.

Xenophanes

By fate, not option, frugal Nature gave
One scent to hyson and to wall-flower,
One sound to pine-groves and to waterfalls,
One aspect to the desert and the lake.
It was her stern necessity: all things

Are of one pattern made; bird, beast, and flower,
Song, picture, form, space, thought, and character,
Deceive us, seeming to be many things,
And are but one. Beheld far off, they differ
As God and devil; bring them to the mind,
They dull its edge with their monotony.
To know one element, explore another,
And in the second reappears the first.
The specious panorama of a year
But multiplies the image of a day,—
A belt of mirrors round a taper's flame;
And universal Nature, through her vast
And crowded whole, an infinite paroquet,
Repeats one note.

The Day's Ration

When I was born,
From all the seas of strength Fate filled a chalice,
Saying, 'This be thy portion, child; this chalice,
Less than a lily's, thou shalt daily draw
From my great arteries,—nor less, nor more.'
All substances the cunning chemist Time
Melts down into that liquor of my life,—
Friends, foes, joys, fortunes, beauty, and disgust.
And whether I am angry or content,
Indebted or insulted, loved or hurt,
All he distils into sidereal wine
And brims my little cup; heedless, alas!
Of all he sheds how little it will hold,
How much runs over on the desert sands.
If a new Muse draw me with splendid ray,
And I uplift myself into its heaven,
The needs of the first sight absorb my blood,
And all the following hours of the day
Drag a ridiculous age.
To-day, when friends approach, and every hour
Brings book, or starbright scroll of genius,

The little cup will hold not a bead more,
And all the costly liquor runs to waste;
Nor gives the jealous lord one diamond drop
So to be husbanded for poorer days.
Why need I volumes, if one word suffice?
Why need I galleries, when a pupil's draught
After the master's sketch fills and o'erfills
My apprehension? why seek Italy,
Who cannot circumnavigate the sea
Of thoughts and things at home, but still adjourn
The nearest matters for a thousand days?

Blight

Give me truths;
For I am weary of the surfaces,
And die of inanition. If I knew
Only the herbs and simples of the wood,
Rue, cinquefoil, gill, vervain, and agrimony,
Blue-vetch, and trillium, hawkweed, sassafras,
Milkweeds, and murky brakes, quaint pipes, and sundew,
And rare and virtuous roots, which in these woods
Draw untold juices from the common earth,
Untold, unknown, and I could surely spell
Their fragrance, and their chemistry apply
By sweet affinities to human flesh,
Driving the foe and stablishing the friend, —
O, that were much, and I could be a part
Of the round day, related to the sun
And planted world, and full executor
Of their imperfect functions.
But these young scholars, who invade our hills,
Bold as the engineer who fells the wood,
And travelling often in the cut he makes,
Love not the flower they pluck, and know it not,
And all their botany is Latin names.
The old men studied magic in the flowers,

And human fortunes in astronomy,
And an omnipotence in chemistry,
Preferring things to names, for these were men,
Were unitarians of the united world,
And, wheresoever their clear eye-beams fell,
They caught the footsteps of the SAME. Our eyes
Are armed, but we are strangers to the stars,
And strangers to the mystic beast and bird,
And strangers to the plant and to the mine.
The injured elements say, 'Not in us;'
And night and day, ocean and continent,
Fire, plant, and mineral say, 'Not in us,'
And haughtily return us stare for stare.
For we invade them impiously for gain;
We devastate them unreligiously,
And coldly ask their pottage, not their love.
Therefore they shove us from them, yield to us
Only what to our griping toil is due;
But the sweet affluence of love and song,
The rich results of the divine consents
Of man and earth, of world beloved and lover,
The nectar and ambrosia, are withheld;
And in the midst of spoils and slaves, we thieves
And pirates of the universe, shut out
Daily to a more thin and outward rind,
Turn pale and starve. Therefore, to our sick eyes,
The stunted trees look sick, the summer short,
Clouds shade the sun, which will not tan our hay,
And nothing thrives to reach its natural term;
And life, shorn of its venerable length,
Even at its greatest space is a defeat,
And dies in anger that it was a dupe;
And, in its highest noon and wantonness,
Is early frugal, like a beggar's child;
With most unhandsome calculation taught,
Even in the hot pursuit of the best aims
And prizes of ambition, checks its hand,
Like Alpine cataracts frozen as they leaped,
Chilled with a miserly comparison
Of the toy's purchase with the length of life.

Musketaquid

Because I was content with these poor fields,
Low, open meads, slender and sluggish streams,
And found a home in haunts which others scorned,
The partial wood-gods overpaid my love,
And granted me the freedom of their state,
And in their secret senate have prevailed
With the dear, dangerous lords that rule our life,
Made moon and planets parties to their bond,
And through my rock-like, solitary wont
Shot million rays of thought and tenderness.
For me, in showers, in sweeping showers, the spring
Visits the valley;—break away the clouds,—
I bathe in the morn's soft and silvered air,
And loiter willing by yon loitering stream.
Sparrows far off, and nearer, April's bird,
Blue-coated,—flying before from tree to tree,
Courageous, sing a delicate overture
To lead the tardy concert of the year.
Onward and nearer rides the sun of May;
And wide around, the marriage of the plants
Is sweetly solemnized. Then flows amain
The surge of summer's beauty; dell and crag,
Hollow and lake, hill-side, and pine arcade,
Are touched with genius. Yonder ragged cliff
Has thousand faces in a thousand hours.

Beneath low hills, in the broad interval
Through which at will our Indian rivulet
Winds mindful still of sannup and of squaw,
Whose pipe and arrow oft the plough unburies,
Here in pine houses built of new fallen trees,
Supplanters of the tribe, the farmers dwell.
Traveller, to thee, perchance, a tedious road,
Or, it may be, a picture; to these men,
The landscape is an armory of powers,
Which, one by one, they know to draw and use.
They harness beast, bird, insect, to their work;
They prove the virtues of each bed of rock,

And, like the chemist mid his loaded jars,
Draw from each stratum its adapted use
To drug their crops or weapon their arts withal.
They turn the frost upon their chemic heap,
They set the wind to winnow pulse and grain,
They thank the spring-flood for its fertile slime,
And, on cheap summit-levels of the snow,
Slide with the sledge to inaccessible woods
O'er meadows bottomless. So, year by year,
They fight the elements with elements,
(That one would say, meadow and forest walked,
Transmuted in these men to rule their like,)
And by the order in the field disclose
The order regnant in the yeoman's brain.

What these strong masters wrote at large in miles,
I followed in small copy in my acre;
For there's no rood has not a star above it;
The cordial quality of pear or plum
Ascends as gladly in a single tree
As in broad orchards resonant with bees;
And every atom poises for itself,
And for the whole. The gentle deities
Showed me the lore of colors and of sounds,
The innumerable tenements of beauty,
The miracle of generative force,
Far-reaching concords of astronomy
Felt in the plants, and in the punctual birds;
Better, the linked purpose of the whole,
And, chiefest prize, found I true liberty
In the glad home plain-dealing nature gave.
The polite found me impolite; the great
Would mortify me, but in vain; for still
I am a willow of the wilderness,
Loving the wind that bent me. All my hurts
My garden spade can heal. A woodland walk,
A quest of river-grapes, a mocking thrush,
A wild-rose, or rock-loving columbine,
Salve my worst wounds.
For thus the wood-gods murmured in my ear:

'Dost love our manners? Canst thou silent lie?
Canst thou, thy pride forgot, like nature pass
Into the winter night's extinguished mood?
Canst thou shine now, then darkle,
And being latent feel thyself no less?
As, when the all-worshipped moon attracts the eye,
The river, hill, stems, foliage are obscure
Yet envies none, none are unenviable.'

Dirge

Knows he who tills this lonely field,
    To reap its scanty corn,
What mystic fruit his acres yield
    At midnight and at morn?

In the long sunny afternoon,
    The plain was full of ghosts;
I wandered up, I wandered down,
    Beset by pensive hosts.

The winding Concord gleamed below,
    Pouring as wide a flood
As when my brothers, long ago,
    Came with me to the wood.

But they are gone,—the holy ones
    Who trod with me this lovely vale;
The strong, star-bright companions
    Are silent, low, and pale.

My good, my noble, in their prime,
    Who made this world the feast it was,
Who learned with me the lore of time,
    Who loved this dwelling-place!

They took this valley for their toy,
    They played with it in every mood;

A cell for prayer, a hall for joy,—
    They treated nature as they would.

They colored the horizon round;
    Stars flamed and faded as they bade;
All echoes hearkened for their sound,—
    They made the woodlands glad or mad.

I touch this flower of silken leaf,
    Which once our childhood knew;
Its soft leaves wound me with a grief
    Whose balsam never grew.

Hearken to yon pine-warbler
    Singing aloft in the tree!
Hearest thou, O traveller,
    What he singeth to me?

Not unless God made sharp thine ear
    With sorrow such as mine,
Out of that delicate lay could'st thou
    Its heavy tale divine.

'Go, lonely man,' it saith;
    'They loved thee from their birth;
Their hands were pure, and pure their faith,—
    There are no such hearts on earth.

'Ye drew one mother's milk,
    One chamber held ye all;
A very tender history
    Did in your childhood fall.

'Ye cannot unlock your heart,
    The key is gone with them;
The silent organ loudest chants
    The master's requiem.'

Threnody

The South-wind brings
Life, sunshine, and desire,
And on every mount and meadow
Breathes aromatic fire;
But over the dead he has no power,
The lost, the lost, he cannot restore;
And, looking over the hills, I mourn
The darling who shall not return.

I see my empty house,
I see my trees repair their boughs;
And he, the wondrous child,
Whose silver warble wild
Outvalued every pulsing sound
Within the air's cerulean round, —
The hyacinthine boy, for whom
Morn well might break and April bloom, —
The gracious boy, who did adorn
The world whereinto he was born,
And by his countenance repay
The favor of the loving Day, —
Has disappeared from the Day's eye;
Far and wide she cannot find him;
My hopes pursue, they cannot bind him.
Returned this day, the south wind searches,
And finds young pines and budding birches;
But finds not the budding man;
Nature, who lost him, cannot remake him;
Fate let him fall, Fate can't retake him;
Nature, Fate, Men, him seek in vain.

And whither now, my truant wise and sweet,
O, whither tend thy feet?
I had the right, few days ago,
Thy steps to watch, thy place to know;
How have I forfeited the right?
Hast thou forgot me in a new delight?

I hearken for thy household cheer,
O eloquent child!
Whose voice, an equal messenger,
Conveyed thy meaning mild.
What though the pains and joys
Whereof it spoke were toys
Fitting his age and ken,
Yet fairest dames and bearded men,
Who heard the sweet request,
So gentle, wise, and grave,
Bended with joy to his behest,
And let the world's affairs go by,
Awhile to share his cordial game,
Or mend his wicker wagon-frame,
Still plotting how their hungry ear
That winsome voice again might hear;
For his lips could well pronounce
Words that were persuasions.

Gentlest guardians marked serene
His early hope, his liberal mien;
Took counsel from his guiding eyes
To make this wisdom earthly wise.
Ah, vainly do these eyes recall
The school-march, each day's festival,
When every morn my bosom glowed
To watch the convoy on the road;
The babe in willow wagon closed,
With rolling eyes and face composed;
With children forward and behind,
Like Cupids studiously inclined;
And he the chieftain paced beside,
The centre of the troop allied,
With sunny face of sweet repose,
To guard the babe from fancied foes.
The little captain innocent
Took the eye with him as he went;
Each village senior paused to scan
And speak the lovely caravan.

From the window I look out
To mark thy beautiful parade,
Stately marching in cap and coat
To some tune by fairies played;—
A music heard by thee alone
To works as noble led thee on.

Now Love and Pride, alas! in vain,
Up and down their glances strain.
The painted sled stands where it stood;
The kennel by the corded wood;
The gathered sticks to stanch the wall
Of the snow-tower, when snow should fall;
The ominous hole he dug in the sand,
And childhood's castles built or planned;
His daily haunts I well discern,—
The poultry-yard, the shed, the barn,—
And every inch of garden ground
Paced by the blessed feet around,
From the roadside to the brook
Whereinto he loved to look.
Step the meek birds where erst they ranged;
The wintry garden lies unchanged;
The brook into the stream runs on;
But the deep-eyed boy is gone.

On that shaded day,
Dark with more clouds than tempests are,
When thou didst yield thy innocent breath
In birdlike heavings unto death,
Night came, and Nature had not thee;
I said, 'We are mates in misery.'
The morrow dawned with needless glow;
Each snowbird chirped, each fowl must crow;
Each tramper started; but the feet
Of the most beautiful and sweet
Of human youth had left the hill
And garden,—they were bound and still.
There's not a sparrow or a wren,

There's not a blade of autumn grain,
Which the four seasons do not tend,
And tides of life and increase lend;
And every chick of every bird,
And weed and rock-moss is preferred.
O ostrich-like forgetfulness!
O loss of larger in the less!
Was there no star that could be sent,
No watcher in the firmament,
No angel from the countless host
That loiters round the crystal coast,
Could stoop to heal that only child,
Nature's sweet marvel undefiled,
And keep the blossom of the earth,
Which all her harvests were not worth?
Not mine,—I never called thee mine,
But Nature's heir,—if I repine,
And seeing rashly torn and moved
Not what I made, but what I loved,
Grow early old with grief that thou
Must to the wastes of Nature go,—
'Tis because a general hope
Was quenched, and all must doubt and grope.
For flattering planets seemed to say
This child should ills of ages stay,
By wondrous tongue, and guided pen,
Bring the flown Muses back to men.
Perchance not he but Nature ailed,
The world and not the infant failed.
It was not ripe yet to sustain
A genius of so fine a strain,
Who gazed upon the sun and moon
As if he came unto his own,
And, pregnant with his grander thought,
Brought the old order into doubt.
His beauty once their beauty tried;
They could not feed him, and he died,
And wandered backward as in scorn,
To wait an æon to be born.

Ill day which made this beauty waste,
Plight broken, this high face defaced!
Some went and came about the dead;
And some in books of solace read;
Some to their friends the tidings say;
Some went to write, some went to pray;
One tarried here, there hurried one;
But their heart abode with none.
Covetous death bereaved us all,
To aggrandize one funeral.
The eager fate which carried thee
Took the largest part of me:
For this losing is true dying;
This is lordly man's down-lying,
This his slow but sure reclining,
Star by star his world resigning.

O child of paradise,
Boy who made dear his father's home,
In whose deep eyes
Men read the welfare of the times to come,
I am too much bereft.
The world dishonored thou hast left.
O truth's and nature's costly lie!
O trusted broken prophecy!
O richest fortune sourly crossed!
Born for the future, to the future lost!

The deep Heart answered, 'Weepest thou?
Worthier cause for passion wild
If I had not taken the child.
And deemest thou as those who pore,
With aged eyes, short way before,—
Think'st Beauty vanished from the coast
Of matter, and thy darling lost?
Taught he not thee—the man of eld,
Whose eyes within his eyes beheld
Heaven's numerous hierarchy span

The mystic gulf from God to man?
To be alone wilt thou begin
When worlds of lovers hem thee in?
To-morrow, when the masks shall fall
That dizen Nature's carnival,
The pure shall see by their own will,
Which overflowing Love shall fill,
'Tis not within the force of fate
The fate-conjoined to separate.
But thou, my votary, weepest thou?
I gave thee sight—where is it now?
I taught thy heart beyond the reach
Of ritual, bible, or of speech;
Wrote in thy mind's transparent table,
As far as the incommunicable;
Taught thee each private sign to raise,
Lit by the supersolar blaze.
Past utterance, and past belief,
And past the blasphemy of grief,
The mysteries of Nature's heart;
And though no Muse can these impart,
Throb thine with Nature's throbbing breast,
And all is clear from east to west.

'I came to thee as to a friend;
Dearest, to thee I did not send
Tutors, but a joyful eye,
Innocence that matched the sky,
Lovely locks, a form of wonder,
Laughter rich as woodland thunder,
That thou might'st entertain apart
The richest flowering of all art:
And, as the great all-loving Day
Through smallest chambers takes its way,
That thou might'st break thy daily bread
With prophet, Savior, and head;
That thou might'st cherish for thine own
The riches of sweet Mary's Son,
Boy-Rabbi, Israel's paragon.

And thoughtest thou such guest
Would in thy hall take up his rest?
Would rushing life forget her laws,
Fate's glowing revolution pause?
High omens ask diviner guess;
Not to be conned to tediousness.
And know my higher gifts unbind
The zone that girds the incarnate mind.
When the scanty shores are full
With Thought's perilous, whirling pool;
When frail Nature can no more,
Then the Spirit strikes the hour:
My servant Death, with solving rite,
Pours finite into infinite.

'Wilt thou freeze love's tidal flow,
Whose streams through nature circling go?
Nail the wild star to its track
On the half-climbed zodiac?
Light is light which radiates,
Blood is blood which circulates,
Life is life which generates,
And many-seeming life is one,—
Wilt thou transfix and make it none?
Its onward force too starkly pent
In figure, bone, and lineament?
Wilt thou, uncalled, interrogate,
Talker! the unreplying Fate?
Nor see the genius of the whole
Ascendant in the private soul,
Beckon it when to go and come,
Self-announced its hour of doom?
Fair the soul's recess and shrine,
Magic-built to last a season;
Masterpiece of love benign;
Fairer that expansive reason
Whose omen 'tis, and sign.
Wilt thou not ope thy heart to know
What rainbows teach, and sunsets show?

Verdict which accumulates
From lengthening scroll of human fates,
Voice of earth to earth returned,
Prayers of saints that inly burned,—
Saying, *What is excellent,*
As God lives, is permanent;
Hearts are dust, hearts' loves remain;
Heart's love will meet thee again.
Revere the Maker; fetch thine eye
Up to his style, and manners of the sky.
Not of adamant and gold
Built he heaven stark and cold;
No, but a nest of bending reeds,
Flowering grass, and scented weeds;
Or like a traveller's fleeing tent,
Or bow above the tempest bent;
Built of tears and sacred flames,
And virtue reaching to its aims;
Built of furtherance and pursuing,
Not of spent deeds, but of doing.
Silent rushes the swift Lord
Through ruined systems still restored,
Broadsowing, bleak and void to bless,
Plants with worlds the wilderness;
Waters with tears of ancient sorrow
Apples of Eden ripe to-morrow.
House and tenant go to ground,
Lost in God, in Godhead found.'

Hymn:

Sung at the Completion of the Concord Monument,
April 19, 1836

By the rude bridge that arched the flood,
   Their flag to April's breeze unfurled,
Here once the embattled farmers stood,
   And fired the shot heard round the world.

The foe long since in silence slept;
   Alike the conqueror silent sleeps;
And Time the ruined bridge has swept
   Down the dark stream which seaward creeps.

On this green bank, by this soft stream,
   We set to-day a votive stone;
That memory may their deed redeem,
   When, like our sires, our sons are gone.

Spirit, that made those heroes dare
   To die, or leave their children free,
Bid Time and Nature gently spare
   The shaft we raise to them and thee.

MAY-DAY AND OTHER PIECES

(1867)

Contents

May-Day

Daughter of Heaven and Earth, coy Spring,
With sudden passion languishing,
Maketh all things softly smile,
Painteth pictures mile on mile,
Holds a cup with cowslip-wreaths,
Whence a smokeless incense breathes.
Girls are peeling the sweet willow,
Poplar white, and Gilead-tree,
And troops of boys
Shouting with whoop and hilloa,
And hip, hip, three times three.
The air is full of whistlings bland;
What was that I heard
Out of the hazy land?
Harp of the wind, or song of bird,
Or clapping of shepherd's hands,
Or vagrant booming of the air,
Voice of a meteor lost in day?
Such tidings of the starry sphere
Can this elastic air convey.
Or haply 't was the cannonade
Of the pent and darkened lake,
Cooled by the pendent mountain's shade,
Whose deeps, till beams of noonday break,
Afflicted moan, and latest hold
Even into May the iceberg cold.
Was it a squirrel's pettish bark,
Or clarionet of jay? or hark,
Where yon wedged line the Nestor leads,
Steering north with raucous cry
Through tracts and provinces of sky,
Every night alighting down

In new landscapes of romance,
Where darkling feed the clamorous clans
By lonely lakes to men unknown.
Come the tumult whence it will,
Voice of sport, or rush of wings,
It is a sound, it is a token
That the marble sleep is broken,
And a change has passed on things.

Beneath the calm, within the light,
A hid unruly appetite
Of swifter life, a surer hope,
Strains every sense to larger scope,
Impatient to anticipate
The halting steps of aged Fate.
Slow grows the palm, too slow the pearl:
When Nature falters, fain would zeal
Grasp the felloes of her wheel,
And grasping give the orbs another whirl.
Turn swiftlier round, O tardy ball!
And sun this frozen side,
Bring hither back the robin's call,
Bring back the tulip's pride.

Why chidest thou the tardy Spring?
The hardy bunting does not chide;
The blackbirds make the maples ring
With social cheer and jubilee;
The redwing flutes his *o-ka-lee*,
The robins know the melting snow;
The sparrow meek, prophetic-eyed,
Her nest beside the snow-drift weaves,
Secure the osier yet will hide
Her callow brood in mantling leaves;
And thou, by science all undone,
Why only must thy reason fail
To see the southing of the sun?

As we thaw frozen flesh with snow,
So Spring will not, foolish fond,

Mix polar night with tropic glow,
Nor cloy us with unshaded sun,
Nor wanton skip with bacchic dance,
But she has the temperance
Of the gods, whereof she is one,—
Masks her treasury of heat
Under east-winds crossed with sleet.
Plants and birds and humble creatures
Well accept her rule austere;
Titan-born, to hardy natures
Cold is genial and dear.
As Southern wrath to Northern right
Is but straw to anthracite;
As in the day of sacrifice,
When heroes piled the pyre,
The dismal Massachusetts ice
Burned more than others' fire,
So Spring guards with surface cold
The garnered heat of ages old:
Hers to sow the seed of bread,
That man and all the kinds be fed;
And, when the sunlight fills the hours,
Dissolves the crust, displays the flowers.

The world rolls round,—mistrust it not,—
Befalls again what once befell;
All things return, both sphere and mote,
And I shall hear my bluebird's note,
And dream the dream of Auburn dell.

When late I walked, in earlier days,
All was stiff and stark;
Knee-deep snows choked all the ways,
In the sky no spark;
Firm-braced I sought my ancient woods,
Struggling through the drifted roads;
The whited desert knew me not,
Snow-ridges masked each darling spot;
The summer dells, by genius haunted,
One arctic moon had disenchanted.

All the sweet secrets therein hid
By Fancy, ghastly spells undid.
Eldest mason, Frost, had piled,
With wicked ingenuity,
Swift cathedrals in the wild;
The piny hosts were sheeted ghosts
In the star-lit minster aisled.
I found no joy: the icy wind
Might rule the forest to his mind.
Who would freeze in frozen brakes?
Back to books and sheltered home,
And wood-fire flickering on the walls,
To hear, when, 'mid our talk and games,
Without the baffled north-wind calls.
But soft! a sultry morning breaks;
The cowslips make the brown brook gay;
A happier hour, a longer day.
Now the sun leads in the May,
Now desire of action wakes,
And the wish to roam.

    The caged linnet in the spring
Hearkens for the choral glee,
When his fellows on the wing
Migrate from the Southern Sea;
When trellised grapes their flowers unmask,
And the new-born tendrils twine,
The old wine darkling in the cask
Feels the bloom on the living vine,
And bursts the hoops at hint of spring:
And so, perchance, in Adam's race,
Of Eden's bower some dream-like trace
Survived the Flight, and swam the Flood,
And wakes the wish in youngest blood
To tread the forfeit Paradise,
And feed once more the exile's eyes;
And ever when the happy child
In May beholds the blooming wild,
And hears in heaven the bluebird sing,
"Onward," he cries, "your baskets bring, —

In the next field is air more mild,
And o'er yon hazy crest is Eden's balmier spring."

   Not for a regiment's parade,
Nor evil laws or rulers made,
Blue Walden rolls its cannonade,
But for a lofty sign
Which the Zodiac threw,
That the bondage-days are told,
And waters free as winds shall flow.
Lo! how all the tribes combine
To rout the flying foe.
See, every patriot oak-leaf throws
His elfin length upon the snows,
Not idle, since the leaf all day
Draws to the spot the solar ray,
Ere sunset quarrying inches down,
And half-way to the mosses brown;
While the grass beneath the rime
Has hints of the propitious time,
And upward pries and perforates
Through the cold slab a thousand gates,
Till green lances peering through
Bend happy in the welkin blue.

   April cold with dropping rain
Willows and lilacs brings again,
The whistle of returning birds,
And trumpet-lowing of the herds.
The scarlet maple-keys betray
What potent blood hath modest May;
What fiery force the earth renews,
The wealth of forms, the flush of hues;
Joy shed in rosy waves abroad
Flows from the heart of Love, the Lord.

   Hither rolls the storm of heat;
I feel its finer billows beat
Like a sea which me infolds;
Heat with viewless fingers moulds,

Swells, and mellows, and matures,
Paints, and flavors, and allures,
Bird and brier inly warms,
Still enriches and transforms,
Gives the reed and lily length,
Adds to oak and oxen strength,
Boils the world in tepid lakes,
Burns the world, yet burnt remakes;
Enveloping heat, enchanted robe,
Wraps the daisy and the globe,
Transforming what it doth infold,
Life out of death, new out of old,
Painting fawns' and leopards' fells,
Seethes the gulf-encrimsoning shells,
Fires gardens with a joyful blaze
Of tulips, in the morning's rays.
The dead log touched bursts into leaf,
The wheat-blade whispers of the sheaf.
What god is this imperial Heat,
Earth's prime secret, sculpture's seat?
Doth it bear hidden in its heart
Water-line patterns of all art,
All figures, organs, hues, and graces?
Is it Dædalus? is it Love?
Or walks in mask almighty Jove,
And drops from Power's redundant horn
All seeds of beauty to be born?

Where shall we keep the holiday,
And duly greet the entering May?
Too strait and low our cottage doors,
And all unmeet our carpet floors;
Nor spacious court, nor monarch's hall,
Suffice to hold the festival.
Up and away! where haughty woods
Front the liberated floods:
We will climb the broad-backed hills,
Hear the uproar of their joy;
We will mark the leaps and gleams
Of the new-delivered streams,

And the murmuring rivers of sap
Mount in the pipes of the trees,
Giddy with day, to the topmost spire,
Which for a spike of tender green
Bartered its powdery cap;
And the colors of joy in the bird,
And the love in its carol heard,
Frog and lizard in holiday coats,
And turtle brave in his golden spots;
We will hear the tiny roar
Of the insects evermore,
While cheerful cries of crag and plain
Reply to the thunder of river and main

 As poured the flood of the ancient sea
Spilling over mountain chains,
Bending forests as bends the sedge,
Faster flowing o'er the plains, —
A world-wide wave with a foaming edge
That rims the running silver sheet, —
So pours the deluge of the heat
Broad northward o'er the land,
Painting artless paradises,
Drugging herbs with Syrian spices,
Fanning secret fires which glow
In columbine and clover-blow,
Climbing the northern zones,
Where a thousand pallid towns
Lie like cockles by the main,
Or tented armies on a plain.
The million-handed sculptor moulds
Quaintest bud and blossom folds,
The million-handed painter pours
Opal hues and purple dye;
Azaleas flush the island floors,
And the tints of heaven reply.

 Wreaths for the May! for happy Spring
To-day shall all her dowry bring,
The love of kind, the joy, the grace,

Hymen of element and race,
Knowing well to celebrate
With song and hue and star and state,
With tender light and youthful cheer,
The spousals of the new-born year.
Lo Love's inundation poured
Over space and race abroad!

Spring is strong and virtuous,
Broad-sowing, cheerful, plenteous,
Quickening underneath the mould
Grains beyond the price of gold.
So deep and large her bounties are,
That one broad, long midsummer day
Shall to the planet overpay
The ravage of a year of war.

Drug the cup, thou butler sweet,
And send the nectar round;
The feet that slid so long on sleet
Are glad to feel the ground.
Fill and saturate each kind
With good according to its mind,
Fill each kind and saturate
With good agreeing with its fate,
Willow and violet, maiden and man.

The bitter-sweet, the haunting air
Creepeth, bloweth everywhere;
It preys on all, all prey on it,
Blooms in beauty, thinks in wit,
Stings the strong with enterprise,
Makes travellers long for Indian skies,
And where it comes this courier fleet
Fans in all hearts expectance sweet,
As if to-morrow should redeem
The vanished rose of evening's dream.
By houses lies a fresher green,
On men and maids a ruddier mien,
As if time brought a new relay

Of shining virgins every May,
And Summer came to ripen maids
To a beauty that not fades.

    The ground-pines wash their rusty green,
The maple-tops their crimson tint,
On the soft path each track is seen,
The girl's foot leaves its neater print.
The pebble loosened from the frost
Asks of the urchin to be tost.
In flint and marble beats a heart,
The kind Earth takes her children's part,
The green lane is the school-boy's friend,
Low leaves his quarrel apprehend,
The fresh ground loves his top and ball,
The air rings jocund to his call,
The brimming brook invites a leap,
He dives the hollow, climbs the steep.
The youth reads omens where he goes,
And speaks all languages the rose.
The wood-fly mocks with tiny noise
The far halloo of human voice;
The perfumed berry on the spray
Smacks of faint memories far away.
A subtle chain of countless rings
The next unto the farthest brings,
And, striving to be man, the worm
Mounts through all the spires of form.

    I saw the bud-crowned Spring go forth,
Stepping daily onward north
To greet staid ancient cavaliers
Filing single in stately train.
And who, and who are the travellers?
They were Night and Day, and Day and Night,
Pilgrims wight with step forthright.
I saw the Days deformed and low,
Short and bent by cold and snow;
The merry Spring threw wreaths on them,
Flower-wreaths gay with bud and bell;

Many a flower and many a gem,
They were refreshed by the smell,
They shook the snow from hats and shoon,
They put their April raiment on;
And those eternal forms,
Unhurt by a thousand storms,
Shot up to the height of the sky again,
And danced as merrily as young men.
I saw them mask their awful glance
Sidewise meek in gossamer lids;
And to speak my thought if none forbids,
It was as if the eternal gods,
Tired of their starry periods,
Hid their majesty in cloth
Woven of tulips and painted moth.
On carpets green the maskers march
Below May's well-appointed arch,
Each star, each god, each grace amain,
Every joy and virtue speed,
Marching duly in her train,
And fainting Nature at her need
Is made whole again.

'T was the vintage-day of field and wood,
When magic wine for bards is brewed;
Every tree and stem and chink
Gushed with syrup to the brink.
The air stole into the streets of towns,
And betrayed the fund of joy
To the high-school and medalled boy:
On from hall to chamber ran,
From youth to maid, from boy to man,
To babes, and to old eyes as well.
'Once more,' the old man cried, 'ye clouds,
Airy turrets purple-piled,
Which once my infancy beguiled,
Beguile me with the wonted spell.
I know ye skilful to convoy
The total freight of hope and joy
Into rude and homely nooks,

Shed mocking lustres on shelf of books,
On farmer's byre, on meadow-pipes,
Or on a pool of dancing chips.
I care not if the pomps you show
Be what they soothfast appear,
Or if yon realms in sunset glow
Be bubbles of the atmosphere.
And if it be to you allowed
To fool me with a shining cloud,
So only new griefs are consoled
By new delights, as old by old,
Frankly I will be your guest,
Count your change and cheer the best.
The world hath overmuch of pain,—
If Nature give me joy again,
Of such deceit I'll not complain.'

   Ah! well I mind the calendar,
Faithful through a thousand years,
Of the painted race of flowers,
Exact to days, exact to hours,
Counted on the spacious dial
Yon broidered zodiac girds.
I know the pretty almanac
Of the punctual coming-back,
On their due days, of the birds.
I marked them yestermorn,
A flock of finches darting
Beneath the crystal arch,
Piping, as they flew, a march,—
Belike the one they used in parting
Last year from yon oak or larch;
Dusky sparrows in a crowd,
Diving, darting northward free,
Suddenly betook them all,
Every one to his hole in the wall,
Or to his niche in the apple-tree.
I greet with joy the choral trains
Fresh from palms and Cuba's canes.
Best gems of Nature's cabinet,

With dews of tropic morning wet,
Beloved of children, bards, and Spring,
O birds, your perfect virtues bring,
Your song, your forms, your rhythmic flight,
Your manners for the heart's delight,
Nestle in hedge, or barn, or roof,
Here weave your chamber weather-proof,
Forgive our harms, and condescend
To man, as to a lubber friend,
And, generous, teach his awkward race
Courage, and probity, and grace!

Poets praise that hidden wine
Hid in milk we drew
At the barrier of Time,
When our life was new.
We had eaten fairy fruit,
We were quick from head to foot,
All the forms we looked on shone
As with diamond dews thereon.
What cared we for costly joys,
The Museum's far-fetched toys?
Gleam of sunshine on the wall
Poured a deeper cheer than all
The revels of the Carnival.
We a pine-grove did prefer
To a marble theatre,
Could with gods on mallows dine,
Nor cared for spices or for wine.
Wreaths of mist and rainbow spanned,
Arch on arch, the grimmest land;
Whistle of a woodland bird
Made the pulses dance,
Note of horn in valleys heard
Filled the region with romance.

None can tell how sweet,
How virtuous, the morning air;
Every accent vibrates well;
Not alone the wood-bird's call,

Or shouting boys that chase their ball,
Pass the height of minstrel skill,
But the ploughman's thoughtless cry,
Lowing oxen, sheep that bleat,
And the joiner's hammer-beat,
Softened are above their will.
All grating discords melt,
No dissonant note is dealt,
And though thy voice be shrill
Like rasping file on steel,
Such is the temper of the air,
Echo waits with art and care,
And will the faults of song repair.

So by remote Superior Lake,
And by resounding Mackinac,
When northern storms the forest shake,
And billows on the long beach break,
The artful Air doth separate
Note by note all sounds that grate,
Smothering in her ample breast
All but godlike words,
Reporting to the happy ear
Only purified accords.
Strangely wrought from barking waves,
Soft music daunts the Indian braves,—
Convent-chanting which the child
Hears pealing from the panther's cave
And the impenetrable wild.

One musician is sure,
His wisdom will not fail,
He has not tasted wine impure,
Nor bent to passion frail.
Age cannot cloud his memory,
Nor grief untune his voice,
Ranging down the ruled scale
From tone of joy to inward wail,
Tempering the pitch of all
In his windy cave.

He all the fables knows,
And in their causes tells,—
Knows Nature's rarest moods,
Ever on her secret broods.
The Muse of men is coy,
Oft courted will not come;
In palaces and market squares
Entreated, she is dumb;
But my minstrel knows and tells
The counsel of the gods,
Knows of Holy Book the spells,
Knows the law of Night and Day,
And the heart of girl and boy,
The tragic and the gay,
And what is writ on Table Round
Of Arthur and his peers,
What sea and land discoursing say
In sidereal years.
He renders all his lore
In numbers wild as dreams,
Modulating all extremes,—
What the spangled meadow saith
To the children who have faith;
Only to children children sing,
Only to youth will spring be spring.

Who is the Bard thus magnified?
When did he sing? and where abide?

Chief of song where poets feast
Is the wind-harp which thou seest
In the casement at my side.

Æolian harp,
How strangely wise thy strain!
Gay for youth, gay for youth,
(Sweet is art, but sweeter truth,)
In the hall at summer eve
Fate and Beauty skilled to weave.
From the eager opening strings

Rung loud and bold the song.
Who but loved the wind-harp's note?
How should not the poet doat
On its mystic tongue,
With its primeval memory,
Reporting what old minstrels said
Of Merlin locked the harp within,—
Merlin paying the pain of sin,
Pent in a dungeon made of air,—
And some attain his voice to hear,
Words of pain and cries of fear,
But pillowed all on melody,
As fits the griefs of bards to be.
And what if that all-echoing shell,
Which thus the buried Past can tell,
Should rive the Future, and reveal
What his dread folds would fain conceal?
It shares the secret of the earth,
And of the kinds that owe her birth.
Speaks not of self that mystic tone,
But of the Overgods alone:
It trembles to the cosmic breath,—
As it heareth, so it saith;
Obeying meek the primal Cause,
It is the tongue of mundane laws.
And this, at least, I dare affirm,
Since genius too has bound and term,
There is no bard in all the choir,
Not Homer's self, the poet sire,
Wise Milton's odes of pensive pleasure,
Or Shakspeare, whom no mind can measure,
Nor Collins' verse of tender pain,
Nor Byron's clarion of disdain,
Scott, the delight of generous boys,
Or Wordsworth, Pan's recording voice,—
Not one of all can put in verse,
Or to this presence could rehearse,
The sights and voices ravishing
The boy knew on the hills in spring,
When pacing through the oaks he heard

Sharp queries of the sentry-bird,
The heavy grouse's sudden whir,
The rattle of the kingfisher;
Saw bonfires of the harlot flies
In the lowland, when day dies;
Or marked, benighted and forlorn,
The first far signal-fire of morn.
These syllables that Nature spoke,
And the thoughts that in him woke,
Can adequately utter none
Save to his ear the wind-harp lone.
And best can teach its Delphian chord
How Nature to the soul is moored,
If once again that silent string,
As erst it wont, would thrill and ring.

Not long ago, at eventide,
It seemed, so listening, at my side
A window rose, and, to say sooth,
I looked forth on the fields of youth:
I saw fair boys bestriding steeds,
I knew their forms in fancy weeds,
Long, long concealed by sundering fates,
Mates of my youth,—yet not my mates,
Stronger and bolder far than I,
With grace, with genius, well attired,
And then as now from far admired,
Followed with love
They knew not of,
With passion cold and shy.
O joy, for what recoveries rare!
Renewed, I breathe Elysian air,
See youth's glad mates in earliest bloom,—
Break not my dream, obtrusive tomb!
Or teach thou, Spring! the grand recoil
Of life resurgent from the soil
Wherein was dropped the mortal spoil.

Soft on the south-wind sleeps the haze:
So on thy broad mystic van

Lie the opal-colored days,
And waft the miracle to man.
Soothsayer of the eldest gods,
Repairer of what harms betide,
Revealer of the inmost powers
Prometheus proffered, Jove denied;
Disclosing treasures more than true,
Or in what far to-morrow due;
Speaking by the tongues of flowers,
By the ten-tongued laurel speaking,
Singing by the oriole songs,
Heart of bird the man's heart seeking;
Whispering hints of treasure hid
Under Morn's unlifted lid,
Islands looming just beyond
The dim horizon's utmost bound; —
Who can, like thee, our rags upbraid,
Or taunt us with our hope decayed?
Or who like thee persuade,
Making the splendor of the air,
The morn and sparkling dew, a snare?
Or who resent
Thy genius, wiles, and blandishment?

There is no orator prevails
To beckon or persuade
Like thee the youth or maid:
Thy birds, thy songs, thy brooks, thy gales,
Thy blooms, thy kinds,
Thy echoes in the wilderness,
Soothe pain, and age, and love's distress,
Fire fainting will, and build heroic minds.

For thou, O Spring! canst renovate
All that high God did first create.
Be still his arm and architect,
Rebuild the ruin, mend defect;
Chemist to vamp old worlds with new,
Coat sea and sky with heavenlier blue,
New-tint the plumage of the birds,

And slough decay from grazing herds,
Sweep ruins from the scarped mountain,
Cleanse the torrent at the fountain,
Purge alpine air by towns defiled,
Bring to fair mother fairer child,
Not less renew the heart and brain,
Scatter the sloth, wash out the stain,
Make the aged eye sun-clear,
To parting soul bring grandeur near.
Under gentle types, my Spring
Masks the might of Nature's king,
An energy that searches thorough
From Chaos to the dawning morrow;
Into all our human plight,
The soul's pilgrimage and flight;
In city or in solitude,
Step by step, lifts bad to good,
Without halting, without rest,
Lifting Better up to Best;
Planting seeds of knowledge pure,
Through earth to ripen, through heaven endure.

The Adirondacs

A Journal.

Dedicated to My Fellow-Travellers in August, 1858.

> Wise and polite,—and if I drew
> Their several portraits, you would own
> Chaucer had no such worthy crew,
> Nor Boccace in Decameron.

We crossed Champlain to Keeseville with our friends,
Thence, in strong country carts, rode up the forks
Of the Ausable stream, intent to reach
The Adirondac lakes. At Martin's Beach
We chose our boats; each man a boat and guide,—
Ten men, ten guides, our company all told.

Next morn, we swept with oars the Saranac,
With skies of benediction, to Round Lake,
Where all the sacred mountains drew around us,
Taháwus, Seaward, MacIntyre, Baldhead,
And other Titans without muse or name.
Pleased with these grand companions, we glide on,
Instead of flowers, crowned with a wreath of hills,
And made our distance wider, boat from boat,
As each would hear the oracle alone.
By the bright morn the gay flotilla slid
Through files of flags that gleamed like bayonets,
Through gold-moth-haunted beds of pickerel-flower,
Through scented banks of lilies white and gold,
Where the deer feeds at night, the teal by day,
On through the Upper Saranac, and up
Père Raquette stream, to a small tortuous pass
Winding through grassy shallows in and out,
Two creeping miles of rushes, pads, and sponge,
To Follansbee Water, and the Lake of Loons.

Northward the length of Follansbee we rowed,
Under low mountains, whose unbroken ridge
Ponderous with beechen forest sloped the shore.

A pause and council: then, where near the head
On the east a bay makes inward to the land
Between two rocky arms, we climb the bank,
And in the twilight of the forest noon
Wield the first axe these echoes ever heard.
We cut young trees to make our poles and thwarts,
Barked the white spruce to weatherfend the roof,
Then struck a light, and kindled the camp-fire.

The wood was sovran with centennial trees,—
Oak, cedar, maple, poplar, beech and fir,
Linden and spruce. In strict society
Three conifers, white, pitch, and Norway pine,
Five-leaved, three-leaved, and two-leaved, grew thereby.
Our patron pine was fifteen feet in girth,
The maple eight, beneath its shapely tower.

'Welcome!' the wood god murmured through the
    leaves,—
'Welcome, though late, unknowing, yet known to me.'
Evening drew on; stars peeped through maple-boughs,
Which o'erhung, like a cloud, our camping fire.
Decayed millennial trunks, like moonlight flecks,
Lit with phosphoric crumbs the forest floor.

Ten scholars, wonted to lie warm and soft
In well-hung chambers daintily bestowed,
Lie here on hemlock-boughs, like Sacs and Sioux,
And greet unanimous the joyful change.
So fast will Nature acclimate her sons,
Though late returning to her pristine ways.
Off soundings, seamen do not suffer cold;
And, in the forest, delicate clerks, unbrowned,
Sleep on the fragrant brush, as on down-beds.
Up with the dawn, they fancied the light air
That circled freshly in their forest dress
Made them to boys again. Happier that they
Slipped off their pack of duties, leagues behind,
At the first mounting of the giant stairs.
No placard on these rocks warned to the polls,

No door-bell heralded a visitor,
No courier waits, no letter came or went,
Nothing was ploughed, or reaped, or bought, or sold;
The frost might glitter, it would blight no crop,
The falling rain will spoil no holiday.
We were made freemen of the forest laws,
All dressed, like Nature, fit for her own ends,
Essaying nothing she cannot perform.

In Adirondac lakes,
At morn or noon, the guide rows bareheaded:
Shoes, flannel shirt, and kersey trousers make
His brief toilette: at night, or in the rain,
He dons a surcoat which he doffs at morn:
A paddle in the right hand, or an oar,
And in the left, a gun, his needful arms.
By turns we praised the stature of our guides,
Their rival strength and suppleness, their skill
To row, to swim, to shoot, to build a camp,
To climb a lofty stem, clean without boughs
Full fifty feet, and bring the eaglet down:
Temper to face wolf, bear, or catamount,
And wit to trap or take him in his lair.
Sound, ruddy men, frolic and innocent,
In winter, lumberers; in summer, guides;
Their sinewy arms pull at the oar untired
Three times ten thousand strokes, from morn to eve.

Look to yourselves, ye polished gentlemen!
No city airs or arts pass current here.
Your rank is all reversed: let men of cloth
Bow to the stalwart churls in overalls:
They are the doctors of the wilderness,
And we the low-prized laymen.
In sooth, red flannel is a saucy test
Which few can put on with impunity.
What make you, master, fumbling at the oar?
Will you catch crabs? Truth tries pretension here.
The sallow knows the basket-maker's thumb;
The oar, the guide's. Dare you accept the tasks

He shall impose, to find a spring, trap foxes,
Tell the sun's time, determine the true north,
Or stumbling on through vast self-similar woods
To thread by night the nearest way to camp?

Ask you, how went the hours?
All day we swept the lake, searched every cove,
North from Camp Maple, south to Osprey Bay,
Watching when the loud dogs should drive in deer,
Or whipping its rough surface for a trout;
Or bathers, diving from the rock at noon;
Challenging Echo by our guns and cries;
Or listening to the laughter of the loon;
Or, in the evening twilight's latest red,
Beholding the procession of the pines;
Or, later yet, beneath a lighted jack,
In the boat's bows, a silent night-hunter
Stealing with paddle to the feeding-grounds
Of the red deer, to aim at a square mist.
Hark to that muffled roar! a tree in the woods
Is fallen: but hush! it has not scared the buck
Who stands astonished at the meteor light,
Then turns to bound away, — is it too late?

Sometimes we tried our rifles at a mark,
Six rods, sixteen, twenty, or forty-five;
Sometimes our wits at sally and retort,
With laughter sudden as the crack of rifle;
Or parties scaled the near acclivities
Competing seekers of a rumored lake,
Whose unauthenticated waves we named
Lake Probability, — our carbuncle,
Long sought, not found.

Two Doctors in the camp
Dissected the slain deer, weighed the trout's brain,
Captured the lizard, salamander, shrew,
Crab, mice, snail, dragon-fly, minnow, and moth;
Insatiate skill in water or in air
Waved the scoop-net, and nothing came amiss;

The while, one leaden pot of alcohol
Gave an impartial tomb to all the kinds.
Not less the ambitious botanist sought plants,
Orchis and gentian, fern, and long whip-scirpus,
Rosy polygonum, lake-margin's pride,
Hypnum and hydnum, mushroom, sponge, and moss,
Or harebell nodding in the gorge of falls.
Above, the eagle flew, the osprey screamed,
The raven croaked, owls hooted, the woodpecker
Loud hammered, and the heron rose in the swamp.
As water poured through hollows of the hills
To feed this wealth of lakes and rivulets,
So Nature shed all beauty lavishly
From her redundant horn.

                    Lords of this realm,
Bounded by dawn and sunset, and the day
Rounded by hours where each outdid the last
In miracles of pomp, we must be proud,
As if associates of the sylvan gods.
We seemed the dwellers of the zodiac,
So pure the Alpine element we breathed,
So light, so lofty pictures came and went.
We trode on air, contemned the distant town,
Its timorous ways, big trifles, and we planned
That we should build, hard-by, a spacious lodge,
And how we should come hither with our sons,
Hereafter,—willing they, and more adroit.

  Hard fare, hard bed, and comic misery,—
The midge, the blue-fly, and the mosquito
Painted our necks, hands, ankles, with red bands:
But, on the second day, we heed them not,
Nay, we saluted them Auxiliaries,
Whom earlier we had chid with spiteful names.
For who defends our leafy tabernacle
From bold intrusion of the travelling crowd,—
Who but the midge, mosquito, and the fly,
Which past endurance sting the tender cit,
But which we learn to scatter with a smudge,
Or baffle by a veil, or slight by scorn?

Our foaming ale we drunk from hunters' pans,
Ale, and a sup of wine. Our steward gave
Venison and trout, potatoes, beans, wheat-bread;
All ate like abbots, and, if any missed
Their wonted convenance, cheerly hid the loss
With hunters' appetite and peals of mirth.
And Stillman, our guides' guide, and Commodore,
Crusoe, Crusader, Pius Æneas, said aloud,
"Chronic dyspepsia never came from eating
Food indigestible": — then murmured some,
Others applauded him who spoke the truth.

Nor doubt but visitings of graver thought
Checked in these souls the turbulent heyday
'Mid all the hints and glories of the home.
For who can tell what sudden privacies
Were sought and found, amid the hue and cry
Of scholars furloughed from their tasks, and let
Into this Oreads' fended Paradise,
As chapels in the city's thoroughfares,
Whither gaunt Labor slips to wipe his brow,
And meditate a moment on Heaven's rest.
Judge with what sweet surprises Nature spoke
To each apart, lifting her lovely shows
To spiritual lessons pointed home.
And as through dreams in watches of the night,
So through all creatures in their form and ways
Some mystic hint accosts the vigilant
Not clearly voiced, but waking a new sense
Inviting to new knowledge, one with old.
Hark to that petulant chirp! what ails the warbler?
Mark his capricious ways to draw the eye.
Now soar again. What wilt thou, restless bird,
Seeking in that chaste blue a bluer light,
Thirsting in that pure for a purer sky?

And presently the sky is changed; O world!
What pictures and what harmonies are thine!
The clouds are rich and dark, the air serene,
So like the soul of me, what if 't were me?

A melancholy better than all mirth.
Comes the sweet sadness at the retrospect,
Or at the foresight of obscurer years?
Like yon slow-sailing cloudy promontory,
Whereon the purple iris dwells in beauty
Superior to all its gaudy skirts.
And, that no day of life may lack romance,
The spiritual stars rise nightly, shedding down
A private beam into each several heart.
Daily the bending skies solicit man,
The seasons chariot him from this exile,
The rainbow hours bedeck his glowing chair,
The storm-winds urge the heavy weeks along,
Suns haste to set, that so remoter lights
Beckon the wanderer to his vaster home.

    With a vermilion pencil mark the day
When of our little fleet three cruising skiffs
Entering Big Tupper, bound for the foaming Falls
Of loud Bog River, suddenly confront
Two of our mates returning with swift oars.
One held a printed journal waving high
Caught from a late-arriving traveller,
Big with great news, and shouted the report
For which the world had waited, now firm fact,
Of the wire-cable laid beneath the sea,
And landed on our coast, and pulsating
With ductile fire. Loud, exulting cries
From boat to boat, and to the echoes round,
Greet the glad miracle. Thought's new-found path
Shall supplement henceforth all trodden ways,
Match God's equator with a zone of art,
And lift man's public action to a height
Worthy the enormous cloud of witnesses,
When linked hemispheres attest his deed.
We have few moments in the longest life
Of such delight and wonder as there grew,—
Nor yet unsuited to that solitude:
A burst of joy, as if we told the fact
To ears intelligent; as if gray rock

And cedar grove and cliff and lake should know
This feat of wit, this triumph of mankind;
As if we men were talking in a vein
Of sympathy so large, that ours was theirs,
And a prime end of the most subtle element
Were fairly reached at last. Wake, echoing caves!
Bend nearer, faint day-moon! Yon thundertops,
Let them hear well! 't is theirs as much as ours.

A spasm throbbing through the pedestals
Of Alp and Andes, isle and continent,
Urging astonished Chaos with a thrill
To be a brain, or serve the brain of man.
The lightning has run masterless too long;
He must to school, and learn his verb and noun,
And teach his nimbleness to earn his wage,
Spelling with guided tongue man's messages
Shot through the weltering pit of the salt sea.
And yet I marked, even in the manly joy
Of our great-hearted Doctor in his boat,
(Perchance I erred,) a shade of discontent;
Or was it for mankind a generous shame,
As of a luck not quite legitimate,
Since fortune snatched from wit the lion's part?
Was it a college pique of town and gown,
As one within whose memory it burned
That not academicians, but some lout,
Found ten years since the Californian gold?
And now, again, a hungry company
Of traders, led by corporate sons of trade,
Perversely borrowing from the shop the tools
Of science, not from the philosophers,
Had won the brightest laurel of all time.
'T was always thus, and will be; hand and head
Are ever rivals: but, though this be swift,
The other slow,—this the Prometheus,
And that the Jove,—yet, howsoever hid,
It was from Jove the other stole his fire,
And, without Jove, the good had never been.

It is not Iroquois or cannibals,
But ever the free race with front sublime,
And these instructed by their wisest too,
Who do the feat, and lift humanity.
Let not him mourn who best entitled was,
Nay, mourn not one: let him exult,
Yea, plant the tree that bears best apples, plant,
And water it with wine, nor watch askance
Whether thy sons or strangers eat the fruit:
Enough that mankind eat, and are refreshed.

We flee away from cities, but we bring
The best of cities with us, these learned classifiers,
Men knowing what they seek, armed eyes of experts.
We praise the guide, we praise the forest life;
But will we sacrifice our dear-bought lore
Of books and arts and trained experiment,
Or count the Sioux a match for Agassiz?
O no, not we! Witness the shout that shook
Wild Tupper Lake; witness the mute all-hail
The joyful traveller gives, when on the verge
Of craggy Indian wilderness he hears
From a log-cabin stream Beethoven's notes
On the piano, played with master's hand.
'Well done!' he cries; 'the bear is kept at bay,
The lynx, the rattlesnake, the flood, the fire;
All the fierce enemies, ague, hunger, cold,
This thin spruce roof, this clayed log-wall,
This wild plantation will suffice to chase.
Now speed the gay celerities of art,
What in the desart was impossible
Within four walls is possible again,—
Culture and libraries, mysteries of skill,
Traditioned fame of masters, eager strife
Of keen competing youths, joined or alone
To outdo each other, and extort applause.
Mind wakes a new-born giant from her sleep.
Twirl the old wheels! Time takes fresh start again,
On for a thousand years of genius more.'

The holidays were fruitful, but must end;
One August evening had a cooler breath;
Into each mind intruding duties crept;
Under the cinders burned the fires of home;
Nay, letters found us in our paradise;
So in the gladness of the new event
We struck our camp, and left the happy hills.
The fortunate star that rose on us sank not;
The prodigal sunshine rested on the land,
The rivers gambolled onward to the sea,
And Nature, the inscrutable and mute,
Permitted on her infinite repose
Almost a smile to steal to cheer her sons,
As if one riddle of the Sphinx were guessed.

OCCASIONAL AND MISCELLANEOUS PIECES

Brahma

If the red slayer think he slays,
   Or if the slain think he is slain,
They know not well the subtle ways
   I keep, and pass, and turn again.

Far or forgot to me is near;
   Shadow and sunlight are the same;
The vanished gods to me appear;
   And one to me are shame and fame.

They reckon ill who leave me out;
   When me they fly, I am the wings;
I am the doubter and the doubt,
   And I the hymn the Brahmin sings.

The strong gods pine for my abode,
   And pine in vain the sacred Seven;
But thou, meek lover of the good!
   Find me, and turn thy back on heaven.

Nemesis

Already blushes in thy cheek
The bosom-thought which thou must speak;
The bird, how far it haply roam
By cloud or isle, is flying home;
The maiden fears, and fearing runs
Into the charmed snare she shuns;
And every man, in love or pride,
Of his fate is never wide.

Will a woman's fan the ocean smooth?
Or prayers the stony Parcæ sooth,
Or coax the thunder from its mark?
Or tapers light the chaos dark?
In spite of Virtue and the Muse,
Nemesis will have her dues,
And all our struggles and our toils
Tighter wind the giant coils.

Fate

Deep in the man sits fast his fate
To mould his fortunes mean or great:
Unknown to Cromwell as to me
Was Cromwell's measure or degree;
Unknown to him, as to his horse,
If he than his groom be better or worse.
He works, plots, fights, in rude affairs,
With squires, lords, kings, his craft compares,
Till late he learned, through doubt and fear,
Broad England harbored not his peer:
Obeying Time, the last to own
The Genius from its cloudy throne.
For the prevision is allied
Unto the thing so signified;
Or say, the foresight that awaits
Is the same Genius that creates.

Freedom

Once I wished I might rehearse
Freedom's pæan in my verse,
That the slave who caught the strain
Should throb until he snapped his chain.
But the Spirit said, 'Not so;
Speak it not, or speak it low;

Name not lightly to be said,
Gift too precious to be prayed,
Passion not to be expressed
But by heaving of the breast:
Yet,—wouldst thou the mountain find
Where this deity is shrined,
Who gives to seas and sunset skies
Their unspent beauty of surprise,
And, when it lists him, waken can
Brute or savage into man;
Or, if in thy heart he shine,
Blends the starry fates with thine,
Draws angels nigh to dwell with thee,
And makes thy thoughts archangels be;
Freedom's secret wilt thou know?—
Counsel not with flesh and blood;
Loiter not for cloak or food;
Right thou feelest, rush to do.'

Ode Sung in the Town Hall,

Concord, July 4, 1857

O tenderly the haughty day
  Fills his blue urn with fire;
One morn is in the mighty heaven,
  And one in our desire.

The cannon booms from town to town,
  Our pulses are not less,
The joy-bells chime their tidings down,
  Which children's voices bless.

For He that flung the broad blue fold
  O'er-mantling land and sea,
One third part of the sky unrolled
  For the banner of the free.

The men are ripe of Saxon kind
  To build an equal state,—
To take the statute from the mind,
  And make of duty fate.

United States! the ages plead,—
  Present and Past in under-song,—
Go put your creed into your deed,
  Nor speak with double tongue.

For sea and land don't understand,
  Nor skies without a frown
See rights for which the one hand fights
  By the other cloven down.

Be just at home; then write your scroll
  Of honor o'er the sea,
And bid the broad Atlantic roll,
  A ferry of the free.

And, henceforth, there shall be no chain,
  Save underneath the sea
The wires shall murmur through the main
  Sweet songs of LIBERTY.

The conscious stars accord above,
  The waters wild below,
And under, through the cable wove,
  Her fiery errands go.

For He that worketh high and wise,
  Nor pauses in his plan,
Will take the sun out of the skies
  Ere freedom out of man.

Boston Hymn

Read in Music Hall, January 1, 1863

The word of the Lord by night
To the watching Pilgrims came,
As they sat by the seaside,
And filled their hearts with flame.

God said, I am tired of kings,
I suffer them no more;
Up to my ear the morning brings
The outrage of the poor.

Think ye I made this ball
A field of havoc and war,
Where tyrants great and tyrants small
Might harry the weak and poor?

My angel,—his name is Freedom,—
Choose him to be your king;
He shall cut pathways east and west,
And fend you with his wing.

Lo! I uncover the land
Which I hid of old time in the West,
As the sculptor uncovers the statue
When he has wrought his best;

I show Columbia, of the rocks
Which dip their foot in the seas,
And soar to the air-borne flocks
Of clouds, and the boreal fleece.

I will divide my goods;
Call in the wretch and slave:
None shall rule but the humble,
And none but Toil shall have.

I will have never a noble,
No lineage counted great;
Fishers and choppers and ploughmen
Shall constitute a state.

Go, cut down trees in the forest,
And trim the straightest boughs;
Cut down trees in the forest,
And build me a wooden house.

Call the people together,
The young men and the sires,
The digger in the harvest field,
Hireling, and him that hires;

And here in a pine state-house
They shall choose men to rule
In every needful faculty,
In church, and state, and school.

Lo, now! if these poor men
Can govern the land and sea,
And make just laws below the sun,
As planets faithful be.

And ye shall succor men;
'T is nobleness to serve;
Help them who cannot help again:
Beware from right to swerve.

I break your bonds and masterships,
And I unchain the slave:
Free be his heart and hand henceforth
As wind and wandering wave.

I cause from every creature
His proper good to flow:
As much as he is and doeth,
So much he shall bestow.

But, laying hands on another
To coin his labor and sweat,
He goes in pawn to his victim
For eternal years in debt.

To-day unbind the captive,
So only are ye unbound;
Lift up a people from the dust,
Trump of their rescue, sound!

Pay ransom to the owner,
And fill the bag to the brim.
Who is the owner? The slave is owner,
And ever was. Pay him.

O North! give him beauty for rags,
And honor, O South! for his shame;
Nevada! coin thy golden crags
With Freedom's image and name.

Up! and the dusky race
That sat in darkness long,—
Be swift their feet as antelopes,
And as behemoth strong.

Come, East and West and North,
By races, as snow-flakes,
And carry my purpose forth,
Which neither halts nor shakes.

My will fulfilled shall be,
For, in daylight or in dark,
My thunderbolt has eyes to see
His way home to the mark.

Voluntaries

I.

Low and mournful be the strain,
Haughty thought be far from me;
Tones of penitence and pain,
Moanings of the tropic sea;
Low and tender in the cell
Where a captive sits in chains,
Crooning ditties treasured well
From his Afric's torrid plains.
Sole estate his sire bequeathed—
Hapless sire to hapless son—
Was the wailing song he breathed,
And his chain when life was done.

What his fault, or what his crime?
Or what ill planet crossed his prime?
Heart too soft and will too weak
To front the fate that crouches near,—
Dove beneath the vulture's beak;—
Will song dissuade the thirsty spear?
Dragged from his mother's arms and breast,
Displaced, disfurnished here,
His wistful toil to do his best
Chilled by a ribald jeer.
Great men in the Senate sate,
Sage and hero, side by side,
Building for their sons the State,
Which they shall rule with pride.
They forbore to break the chain
Which bound the dusky tribe,
Checked by the owners' fierce disdain,
Lured by "Union" as the bribe.
Destiny sat by, and said,
'Pang for pang your seed shall pay,
Hide in false peace your coward head,
I bring round the harvest-day.'

II.

Freedom all winged expands,
Nor perches in a narrow place;
Her broad van seeks unplanted lands;
She loves a poor and virtuous race.
Clinging to a colder zone
Whose dark sky sheds the snow-flake down,
The snow-flake is her banner's star,
Her stripes the boreal streamers are.
Long she loved the Northman well;
Now the iron age is done,
She will not refuse to dwell
With the offspring of the Sun;
Foundling of the desert far,
Where palms plume, siroccos blaze,
He roves unhurt the burning ways
In climates of the summer star.
He has avenues to God
Hid from men of Northern brain,
Far beholding, without cloud,
What these with slowest steps attain.
If once the generous chief arrive
To lead him willing to be led,
For freedom he will strike and strive,
And drain his heart till he be dead.

III.

In an age of fops and toys,
Wanting wisdom, void of right,
Who shall nerve heroic boys
To hazard all in Freedom's fight, —
Break sharply off their jolly games,
Forsake their comrades gay,
And quit proud homes and youthful dames,
For famine, toil, and fray?
Yet on the nimble air benign
Speed nimbler messages,
That waft the breath of grace divine
To hearts in sloth and ease.

So nigh is grandeur to our dust,
So near is God to man,
When Duty whispers low, *Thou must*,
The youth replies, *I can*.

IV.

O, well for the fortunate soul
Which Music's wings infold,
Stealing away the memory
Of sorrows new and old!
Yet happier he whose inward sight,
Stayed on his subtile thought,
Shuts his sense on toys of time,
To vacant bosoms brought.
But best befriended of the God
He who, in evil times,
Warned by an inward voice,
Heeds not the darkness and the dread,
Biding by his rule and choice,
Feeling only the fiery thread
Leading over heroic ground,
Walled with mortal terror round,
To the aim which him allures,
And the sweet heaven his deed secures.

Stainless soldier on the walls,
Knowing this,—and knows no more,—
Whoever fights, whoever falls,
Justice conquers evermore,
Justice after as before,—
And he who battles on her side,
God, though he were ten times slain,
Crowns him victor glorified,
Victor over death and pain;
Forever: but his erring foe,
Self-assured that he prevails,
Looks from his victim lying low,
And sees aloft the red right arm
Redress the eternal scales.

He, the poor foe, whom angels foil,
Blind with pride, and fooled by hate,
Writhes within the dragon coil,
Reserved to a speechless fate.

v.

Blooms the laurel which belongs
To the valiant chief who fights;
I see the wreath, I hear the songs
Lauding the Eternal Rights,
Victors over daily wrongs:
Awful victors, they misguide
Whom they will destroy,
And their coming triumph hide
In our downfall, or our joy:
They reach no term, they never sleep,
In equal strength through space abide;
Though, feigning dwarfs, they crouch and creep,
The strong they slay, the swift outstride:
Fate's grass grows rank in valley clods,
And rankly on the castled steep,—
Speak it firmly, these are gods,
All are ghosts beside.

Love and Thought

Two well-assorted travellers use
The highway, Eros and the Muse.
From the twins is nothing hidden,
To the pair is naught forbidden;
Hand in hand the comrades go
Every nook of nature through:
Each for other they were born,
Each can other best adorn;
They know one only mortal grief
Past all balsam or relief,
When, by false companions crossed,
The pilgrims have each other lost.

Lover's Petition

Good Heart, that ownest all!
I ask a modest boon and small:
Not of lands and towns the gift,—
Too large a load for me to lift,—
But for one proper creature,
Which geographic eye,
Sweeping the map of Western earth,
Or the Atlantic coast, from Maine
To Powhatan's domain,
Could not descry.
Is 't much to ask in all thy huge creation,
So trivial a part,—
A solitary heart?
Yet count me not of spirit mean,
Or mine a mean demand,
For 't is the concentration
And worth of all the land,
The sister of the sea,
The daughter of the strand,
Composed of air and light,
And of the swart earth-might.
So little to thy poet's prayer
Thy large bounty well can spare.
And yet I think, if she were gone,
The world were better left alone.

Una

Roving, roving, as it seems,
Una lights my clouded dreams;
Still for journeys she is dressed;
We wander far by east and west.

In the homestead, homely thought;
At my work I ramble not;
If from home chance draw me wide,
Half-seen Una sits beside.

In my house and garden-plot,
Though beloved, I miss her not;
But one I seek in foreign places,
One face explore in foreign faces.

At home a deeper thought may light
The inward sky with chrysolite,
And I greet from far the ray,
Aurora of a dearer day.

But if upon the seas I sail,
Or trundle on the glowing rail,
I am but a thought of hers,
Loveliest of travellers.

So the gentle poet's name
To foreign parts is blown by fame;
Seek him in his native town,
He is hidden and unknown.

Letters

Every day brings a ship,
Every ship brings a word;
Well for those who have no fear,
Looking seaward well assured
That the word the vessel brings
Is the word they wish to hear.

Rubies

They brought me rubies from the mine,
   And held them to the sun;
I said, they are drops of frozen wine
   From Eden's vats that run.

I looked again,—I thought them hearts
   Of friends to friends unknown;
Tides that should warm each neighboring life
   Are locked in sparkling stone.

But fire to thaw that ruddy snow,
   To break enchanted ice,
And give love's scarlet tides to flow,—
   When shall that sun arise?

Merlin's Song

Of Merlin wise I learned a song,—
Sing it low, or sing it loud,
It is mightier than the strong,
And punishes the proud.
I sing it to the surging crowd,—
Good men it will calm and cheer,
Bad men it will chain and cage.
In the heart of the music peals a strain
Which only angels hear;
Whether it waken joy or rage,
Hushed myriads hark in vain,
Yet they who hear it shed their age,
And take their youth again.

The Test

(Musa loquitur.)

I hung my verses in the wind,
Time and tide their faults may find.
All were winnowed through and through,
Five lines lasted sound and true;
Five were smelted in a pot
Than the South more fierce and hot;
These the siroc could not melt,
Fire their fiercer flaming felt,
And the meaning was more white
Than July's meridian light.
Sunshine cannot bleach the snow,
Nor time unmake what poets know.
Have you eyes to find the five
Which five hundred did survive?

Solution

I am the Muse who sung alway
By Jove, at dawn of the first day.
Star-crowned, sole-sitting, long I wrought
To fire the stagnant earth with thought:
On spawning slime my song prevails,
Wolves shed their fangs, and dragons scales;
Flushed in the sky the sweet May-morn,
Earth smiled with flowers, and man was born.
Then Asia yeaned her shepherd race,
And Nile substructs her granite base, —
Tented Tartary, columned Nile, —
And, under vines, on rocky isle,
Or on wind-blown sea-marge bleak,
Forward stepped the perfect Greek:
That wit and joy might find a tongue,
And earth grow civil, HOMER sung.

Flown to Italy from Greece,
I brooded long, and held my peace,
For I am wont to sing uncalled,
And in days of evil plight
Unlock doors of new delight;
And sometimes mankind I appalled
With a bitter horoscope,
With spasms of terror for balm of hope.
Then by better thought I lead
Bards to speak what nations need;
So I folded me in fears,
And DANTE searched the triple spheres,
Moulding nature at his will,
So shaped, so colored, swift or still,
And, sculptor-like, his large design
Etched on Alp and Apennine.

Seethed in mists of Penmanmaur,
Taught by Plinlimmon's Druid power,
England's genius filled all measure
Of heart and soul, of strength and pleasure,
Gave to the mind its emperor,
And life was larger than before:
Nor sequent centuries could hit
Orbit and sum of SHAKSPEARE's wit.
The men who lived with him became
Poets, for the air was fame.

Far in the North, where polar night
Holds in check the frolic light,
In trance upborne past mortal goal
The Swede EMANUEL leads the soul.
Through snows above, mines underground,
The inks of Erebus he found;
Rehearsed to men the damned wails
On which the seraph music sails.
In spirit-worlds he trod alone,
But walked the earth unmarked, unknown.
The near by-stander caught no sound,—
Yet they who listened far aloof

Heard rendings of the skyey roof,
And felt, beneath, the quaking ground;
And his air-sown, unheeded words,
In the next age, are flaming swords.

In newer days of war and trade,
Romance forgot, and faith decayed,
When Science armed and guided war,
And clerks the Janus-gates unbar,
When France, where poet never grew,
Halved and dealt the globe anew,
GOETHE, raised o'er joy and strife,
Drew the firm lines of Fate and Life,
And brought Olympian wisdom down
To court and mart, to gown and town;
Stooping, his finger wrote in clay
The open secret of to-day.

So bloom the unfading petals five,
And verses that all verse outlive.

NATURE AND LIFE

Nature

I

Winters know
Easily to shed the snow,
And the untaught Spring is wise
In cowslips and anemonies.
Nature, hating art and pains,
Baulks and baffles plotting brains;
Casualty and Surprise
Are the apples of her eyes;
But she dearly loves the poor,
And, by marvel of her own,
Strikes the loud pretender down.
For Nature listens in the rose,
And hearkens in the berry's bell,
To help her friends, to plague her foes,
And like wise God she judges well.
Yet doth much her love excel
To the souls that never fell,
To swains that live in happiness,
And do well because they please,
Who walk in ways that are unfamed,
And feats achieve before they're named.

Nature

II

She is gamesome and good,
But of mutable mood,—
No dreary repeater now and again,
She will be all things to all men.
She who is old, but nowise feeble,
Pours her power into the people,

Merry and manifold without bar,
Makes and moulds them what they are,
And what they call their city way
Is not their way, but hers,
And what they say they made to-day,
They learned of the oaks and firs.
She spawneth men as mallows fresh,
Hero and maiden, flesh of her flesh;
She drugs her water and her wheat
With the flavors she finds meet,
And gives them what to drink and eat;
And having thus their bread and growth,
They do her bidding, nothing loath.
What's most theirs is not their own,
But borrowed in atoms from iron and stone,
And in their vaunted works of Art
The master-stroke is still her part.

The Romany Girl

The sun goes down, and with him takes
The coarseness of my poor attire;
The fair moon mounts, and aye the flame
Of Gypsy beauty blazes higher.

Pale Northern girls! you scorn our race;
You captives of your air-tight halls,
Wear out in-doors your sickly days,
But leave us the horizon walls.

And if I take you, dames, to task,
And say it frankly without guile,
Then you are Gypsies in a mask,
And I the lady all the while.

If, on the heath, below the moon,
I court and play with paler blood,
Me false to mine dare whisper none, —
One sallow horseman knows me good.

Go, keep your cheek's rose from the rain,
For teeth and hair with shopmen deal;
My swarthy tint is in the grain,
The rocks and forest know it real.

The wild air bloweth in our lungs,
The keen stars twinkle in our eyes,
The birds gave us our wily tongues,
The panther in our dances flies.

You doubt we read the stars on high,
Nathless we read your fortunes true;
The stars may hide in the upper sky,
But without glass we fathom you.

Days

Daughters of Time, the hypocritic Days,
Muffled and dumb like barefoot dervishes,
And marching single in an endless file,
Bring diadems and fagots in their hands.
To each they offer gifts after his will,
Bread, kingdoms, stars, and sky that holds them all.
I, in my pleached garden, watched the pomp,
Forgot my morning wishes, hastily
Took a few herbs and apples, and the Day
Turned and departed silent. I, too late,
Under her solemn fillet saw the scorn.

The Chartist's Complaint

Day! hast thou two faces,
Making one place two places?
One, by humble farmer seen,
Chill and wet, unlighted, mean,
Useful only, triste and damp,
Serving for a laborer's lamp?
Have the same mists another side,
To be the appanage of pride,
Gracing the rich man's wood and lake,
His park where amber mornings break,
And treacherously bright to show
His planted isle where roses glow?
O Day! and is your mightiness
A sycophant to smug success?
Will the sweet sky and ocean broad
Be fine accomplices to fraud?
O Sun! I curse thy cruel ray:
Back, back to chaos, harlot Day!

My Garden

If I could put my woods in song,
And tell what's there enjoyed,
All men would to my gardens throng,
And leave the cities void.

In my plot no tulips blow,—
Snow-loving pines and oaks instead;
And rank the savage maples grow
From spring's faint flush to autumn red.

My garden is a forest ledge
Which older forests bound;
The banks slope down to the blue lake-edge,
Then plunge to depths profound.

Here once the Deluge ploughed,
Laid the terraces, one by one;
Ebbing later whence it flowed,
They bleach and dry in the sun.

The sowers made haste to depart,—
The wind and the birds which sowed it;
Not for fame, nor by rules of art,
Planted these, and tempests flowed it.

Waters that wash my garden side
Play not in Nature's lawful web,
They heed not moon or solar tide,—
Five years elapse from flood to ebb.

Hither hasted, in old time, Jove,
And every god,—none did refuse;
And be sure at last came Love,
And after Love, the Muse.

Keen ears can catch a syllable,
As if one spake to another,
In the hemlocks tall, untamable,
And what the whispering grasses smother.

Æolian harps in the pine
Ring with the song of the Fates;
Infant Bacchus in the vine,—
Far distant yet his chorus waits.

Canst thou copy in verse one chime
Of the wood-bell's peal and cry,
Write in a book the morning's prime,
Or match with words that tender sky?

Wonderful verse of the gods,
Of one import, of varied tone;
They chant the bliss of their abodes
To man imprisoned in his own.

Ever the words of the gods resound;
But the porches of man's ear
Seldom in this low life's round
Are unsealed, that he may hear.

Wandering voices in the air,
And murmurs in the wold,
Speak what I cannot declare,
Yet cannot all withhold.

When the shadow fell on the lake,
The whirlwind in ripples wrote
Air-bells of fortune that shine and break,
And omens above thought.

But the meanings cleave to the lake,
Cannot be carried in book or urn;
Go thy ways now, come later back,
On waves and hedges still they burn.

These the fates of men forecast,
Of better men than live to-day;
If who can read them comes at last,
He will spell in the sculpture, 'Stay!'

The Titmouse

You shall not be overbold
When you deal with arctic cold,
As late I found my lukewarm blood
Chilled wading in the snow-choked wood.
How should I fight? my foeman fine
Has million arms to one of mine:
East, west, for aid I looked in vain,
East, west, north, south, are his domain.
Miles off, three dangerous miles, is home;
Must borrow his winds who there would come.
Up and away for life! be fleet! —

The frost-king ties my fumbling feet,
Sings in my ears, my hands are stones,
Curdles the blood to the marble bones,
Tugs at the heart-strings, numbs the sense,
And hems in life with narrowing fence.
Well, in this broad bed lie and sleep,
The punctual stars will vigil keep,
Embalmed by purifying cold,
The winds shall sing their dead-march old,
The snow is no ignoble shroud,
The moon thy mourner, and the cloud.

Softly,—but this way fate was pointing,
'T was coming fast to such anointing,
When piped a tiny voice hard by,
Gay and polite, a cheerful cry,
Chic-chicadeedee! saucy note
Out of sound heart and merry throat,
As if it said, 'Good day, good sir!
Fine afternoon, old passenger!
Happy to meet you in these places,
Where January brings few faces.'

This poet, though he live apart,
Moved by his hospitable heart,
Sped, when I passed his sylvan fort,
To do the honors of his court,
As fits a feathered lord of land;
Flew near, with soft wing grazed my hand,
Hopped on the bough, then, darting low,
Prints his small impress on the snow,
Shows feats of his gymnastic play,
Head downward, clinging to the spray.

Here was this atom in full breath,
Hurling defiance at vast death;
This scrap of valor just for play
Fronts the north-wind in waistcoat gray,
As if to shame my weak behavior;
I greeted loud my little saviour,

'You pet! what dost here? and what for?
In these woods, thy small Labrador,
At this pinch, wee San Salvador!
What fire burns in that little chest
So frolic, stout, and self-possest?
Henceforth I wear no stripe but thine;
Ashes and jet all hues outshine.
Why are not diamonds black and gray,
To ape thy dare-devil array?
And I affirm, the spacious North
Exists to draw thy virtue forth.
I think no virtue goes with size;
The reason of all cowardice
Is, that men are overgrown,
And, to be valiant, must come down
To the titmouse dimension.'

'T is good-will makes intelligence,
And I began to catch the sense
Of my bird's song: 'Live out of doors
In the great woods, on prairie floors.
I dine in the sun; when he sinks in the sea,
I too have a hole in a hollow tree;
And I like less when Summer beats
With stifling beams on these retreats,
Than noontide twilights which snow makes
With tempest of the blinding flakes.
For well the soul, if stout within,
Can arm impregnably the skin;
And polar frost my frame defied,
Made of the air that blows outside.'

With glad remembrance of my debt,
I homeward turn; farewell, my pet!
When here again thy pilgrim comes,
He shall bring store of seeds and crumbs.
Doubt not, so long as earth has bread,
Thou first and foremost shalt be fed;
The Providence that is most large
Takes hearts like thine in special charge,

Helps who for their own need are strong,
And the sky doats on cheerful song.
Henceforth I prize thy wiry chant
O'er all that mass and minster vaunt;
For men mis-hear thy call in spring,
As t'would accost some frivolous wing,
Crying out of the hazel copse, *Phe-be!*
And, in winter, *Chic-a-dee-dee!*
I think old Cæsar must have heard
In northern Gaul my dauntless bird,
And, echoed in some frosty wold,
Borrowed thy battle-numbers bold.
And I will write our annals new,
And thank thee for a better clew,
I, who dreamed not when I came here
To find the antidote of fear,
Now hear thee say in Roman key,
Pæan! Veni, vidi, vici.

Sea-Shore

I heard or seemed to hear the chiding Sea
Say, Pilgrim, why so late and slow to come?
Am I not always here, thy summer home?
Is not my voice thy music, morn and eve?
My breath thy healthful climate in the heats,
My touch thy antidote, my bay thy bath?
Was ever building like my terraces?
Was ever couch magnificent as mine?
Lie on the warm rock-ledges, and there learn
A little hut suffices like a town.
I make your sculptured architecture vain,
Vain beside mine. I drive my wedges home,
And carve the coastwise mountain into caves.
Lo! here is Rome, and Nineveh, and Thebes,
Karnak, and Pyramid, and Giant's Stairs,
Half piled or prostrate; and my newest slab
Older than all thy race.

Behold the Sea,
The opaline, the plentiful and strong,
Yet beautiful as is the rose in June,
Fresh as the trickling rainbow of July;
Sea full of food, the nourisher of kinds,
Purger of earth, and medicine of men;
Creating a sweet climate by my breath,
Washing out harms and griefs from memory,
And, in my mathematic ebb and flow,
Giving a hint of that which changes not.
Rich are the sea-gods:—who gives gifts but they?
They grope the sea for pearls, but more than pearls:
They pluck Force thence, and give it to the wise.
For every wave is wealth to Dædalus,
Wealth to the cunning artist who can work
This matchless strength. Where shall he find, O waves!
A load your Atlas shoulders cannot lift?

I with my hammer pounding evermore
The rocky coast, smite Andes into dust,
Strewing my bed, and, in another age,
Rebuild a continent of better men.
Then I unbar the doors: my paths lead out
The exodus of nations: I disperse
Men to all shores that front the hoary main.

I too have arts and sorceries;
Illusion dwells forever with the wave.
I know what spells are laid. Leave me to deal
With credulous and imaginative man;
For, though he scoop my water in his palm,
A few rods off he deems it gems and clouds.
Planting strange fruits and sunshine on the shore,
I make some coast alluring, some lone isle,
To distant men, who must go there, or die.

Song of Nature

Mine are the night and morning,
The pits of air, the gulf of space,
The sportive sun, the gibbous moon,
The innumerable days.

I hide in the solar glory,
I am dumb in the pealing song,
I rest on the pitch of the torrent,
In slumber I am strong.

No numbers have counted my tallies,
No tribes my house can fill,
I sit by the shining Fount of Life,
And pour the deluge still;

And ever by delicate powers
Gathering along the centuries
From race on race the rarest flowers,
My wreath shall nothing miss.

And many a thousand summers
My apples ripened well,
And light from meliorating stars
With firmer glory fell.

I wrote the past in characters
Of rock and fire the scroll,
The building in the coral sea,
The planting of the coal.

And thefts from satellites and rings
And broken stars I drew,
And out of spent and aged things
I formed the world anew;

What time the gods kept carnival,
Tricked out in star and flower,
And in cramp elf and saurian forms
They swathed their too much power.

Time and Thought were my surveyors,
They laid their courses well,
They boiled the sea, and baked the layers
Of granite, marl, and shell.

But he, the man-child glorious,—
Where tarries he the while?
The rainbow shines his harbinger,
The sunset gleams his smile.

My boreal lights leap upward,
Forthright my planets roll,
And still the man-child is not born,
The summit of the whole.

Must time and tide forever run?
Will never my winds go sleep in the west?
Will never my wheels which whirl the sun
And satellites have rest?

Too much of donning and doffing,
Too slow the rainbow fades,
I weary of my robe of snow,
My leaves and my cascades;

I tire of globes and races,
Too long the game is played;
What without him is summer's pomp,
Or winter's frozen shade?

I travail in pain for him,
My creatures travail and wait;
His couriers come by squadrons,
He comes not to the gate.

Twice I have moulded an image,
And thrice outstretched my hand,
Made one of day, and one of night,
And one of the salt sea-sand.

One in a Judæan manger,
And one by Avon stream,
One over against the mouths of Nile,
And one in the Academe.

I moulded kings and saviours,
And bards o'er kings to rule;—
But fell the starry influence short,
The cup was never full.

Yet whirl the glowing wheels once more,
And mix the bowl again;
Seethe, Fate! the ancient elements,
Heat, cold, wet, dry, and peace, and pain.

Let war and trade and creeds and song
Blend, ripen race on race,
The sunburnt world a man shall breed
Of all the zones, and countless days.

No ray is dimmed, no atom worn,
My oldest force is good as new,
And the fresh rose on yonder thorn
Gives back the bending heavens in dew.

Two Rivers

Thy summer voice, Musketaquit,
Repeats the music of the rain;
But sweeter rivers pulsing flit
Through thee, as thou through Concord Plain.

Thou in thy narrow banks art pent:
The stream I love unbounded goes
Through flood and sea and firmament;
Through light, through life, it forward flows.

I see the inundation sweet,
I hear the spending of the stream
Through years, through men, through nature fleet,
Through passion, thought, through power and dream.

Musketaquit, a goblin strong,
Of shard and flint makes jewels gay;
They lose their grief who hear his song,
And where he winds is the day of day.

So forth and brighter fares my stream,—
Who drink it shall not thirst again;
No darkness stains its equal gleam,
And ages drop in it like rain.

Waldeinsamkeit

I do not count the hours I spend
In wandering by the sea;
The forest is my loyal friend,
Like God it useth me.

In plains that room for shadows make
Of skirting hills to lie,
Bound in by streams which give and take
Their colors from the sky;

Or on the mountain-crest sublime,
Or down the oaken glade,
O what have I to do with time?
For this the day was made.

Cities of mortals woe-begone
Fantastic care derides,
But in the serious landscape lone
Stern benefit abides.

Sheen will tarnish, honey cloy,
And merry is only a mask of sad,
But, sober on a fund of joy,
The woods at heart are glad.

There the great Planter plants
Of fruitful worlds the grain,
And with a million spells enchants
The souls that walk in pain.

Still on the seeds of all he made
The rose of beauty burns;
Through times that wear, and forms that fade,
Immortal youth returns.

The black ducks mounting from the lake,
The pigeon in the pines,
The bittern's boom, a desert make
Which no false art refines.

Down in yon watery nook,
Where bearded mists divide,
The gray old gods whom Chaos knew,
The sires of Nature, hide.

Aloft, in secret veins of air,
Blows the sweet breath of song,
O, few to scale those uplands dare,
Though they to all belong!

See thou bring not to field or stone
The fancies found in books;
Leave authors' eyes, and fetch your own,
To brave the landscape's looks.

And if, amid this dear delight,
My thoughts did home rebound,
I well might reckon it a slight
To the high cheer I found.

Oblivion here thy wisdom is,
Thy thrift, the sleep of cares;
For a proud idleness like this
Crowns all thy mean affairs.

Terminus

It is time to be old,
To take in sail:—
The god of bounds,
Who sets to seas a shore,
Came to me in his fatal rounds,
And said: 'No more!
No farther spread
Thy broad ambitious branches, and thy root.
Fancy departs: no more invent,
Contract thy firmament
To compass of a tent.
There's not enough for this and that,
Make thy option which of two;
Economize the failing river,
Not the less revere the Giver,
Leave the many and hold the few.
Timely wise accept the terms,
Soften the fall with wary foot;
A little while
Still plan and smile,
And, fault of novel germs,
Mature the unfallen fruit.
Curse, if thou wilt, thy sires,
Bad husbands of their fires,
Who, when they gave thee breath,
Failed to bequeath
The needful sinew stark as once,
The Baresark marrow to thy bones,
But left a legacy of ebbing veins,

Inconstant heat and nerveless reins,—
Amid the Muses, left thee deaf and dumb,
Amid the gladiators, halt and numb.'

As the bird trims her to the gale,
I trim myself to the storm of time,
I man the rudder, reef the sail,
Obey the voice at eve obeyed at prime:
'Lowly faithful, banish fear,
Right onward drive unharmed;
The port, well worth the cruise, is near,
And every wave is charmed.'

The Past

The debt is paid,
The verdict said,
The Furies laid,
The plague is stayed,
All fortunes made;
Turn the key and bolt the door,
Sweet is death forevermore.
Nor haughty hope, nor swart chagrin,
Nor murdering hate, can enter in.
All is now secure and fast;
Not the gods can shake the Past;
Flies-to the adamantine door
Bolted down forevermore.
None can re-enter there,—
No thief so politic,
No Satan with a royal trick
Steal in by window, chink, or hole,
To bind or unbind, add what lacked,
Insert a leaf, or forge a name,
New-face or finish what is packed,
Alter or mend eternal Fact.

The Last Farewell

Lines written by the author's brother, Edward Bliss Emerson, whilst sailing out of Boston Harbor, bound for the island of Porto Rico, in 1832.

Farewell, ye lofty spires
That cheered the holy light!
Farewell, domestic fires
That broke the gloom of night!
Too soon those spires are lost,
Too fast we leave the bay,
Too soon by ocean tost
From hearth and home away,
           Far away, far away.

Farewell the busy town,
The wealthy and the wise,
Kind smile and honest frown
From bright, familiar eyes.
All these are fading now;
Our brig hastes on her way,
Her unremembering prow
Is leaping o'er the sea,
           Far away, far away.

Farewell, my mother fond,
Too kind, too good to me;
Nor pearl nor diamond
Would pay my debt to thee.
But even thy kiss denies
Upon my cheek to stay;
The winged vessel flies,
And billows round her play,
           Far away, far away.

Farewell, my brothers true,
My betters, yet my peers;
How desert without you

My few and evil years!
But though aye one in heart,
Together sad or gay,
Rude ocean doth us part;
We separate to-day,
                Far away, far away.

Farewell I breathe again
To dim New England's shore;
My heart shall beat not when
I pant for thee no more.
In yon green palmy isle,
Beneath the tropic ray,
I murmur never while
For thee and thine I pray;
                Far away, far away.

In Memoriam

E. B. E.

I mourn upon this battle-field,
But not for those who perished here.
Behold the river-bank
Whither the angry farmers came,
In sloven dress and broken rank,
Nor thought of fame.
Their deed of blood
All mankind praise;
Even the serene Reason says,
It was well done.
The wise and simple have one glance
To greet yon stern head-stone,
Which more of pride than pity gave
To mark the Briton's friendless grave.
Yet it is a stately tomb;
The grand return
Of eve and morn,
The year's fresh bloom,

The silver cloud,
Might grace the dust that is most proud.

Yet not of these I muse
In this ancestral place,
But of a kindred face
That never joy or hope shall here diffuse.

Ah, brother of the brief but blazing star!
What hast thou to do with these
Haunting this bank's historic trees?
Thou born for noblest life,
For action's field, for victor's car,
Thou living champion of the right?
To these their penalty belonged:
I grudge not these their bed of death,
But thine to thee, who never wronged
The poorest that drew breath.

All inborn power that could
Consist with homage to the good
Flamed from his martial eye;
He who seemed a soldier born,
He should have the helmet worn,
All friends to fend, all foes defy,
Fronting foes of God and man,
Frowning down the evil-doer,
Battling for the weak and poor.
His from youth the leader's look
Gave the law which others took,
And never poor beseeching glance
Shamed that sculptured countenance.

There is no record left on earth,
Save in tablets of the heart,
Of the rich inherent worth,
Of the grace that on him shone,
Of eloquent lips, of joyful wit;
He could not frame a word unfit,
An act unworthy to be done;

Honor prompted every glance,
Honor came and sat beside him,
In lowly cot or painful road,
And evermore the cruel god
Cried, "Onward!" and the palm-crown showed.
Born for success he seemed,
With grace to win, with heart to hold,
With shining gifts that took all eyes,
With budding power in college-halls,
As pledged in coming days to forge
Weapons to guard the State, or scourge
Tyrants despite their guards or walls.
On his young promise Beauty smiled,
Drew his free homage unbeguiled,
And prosperous Age held out his hand,
And richly his large future planned,
And troops of friends enjoyed the tide,—
All, all was given, and only health denied.

I see him with superior smile
Hunted by Sorrow's grisly train
In lands remote, in toil and pain,
With angel patience labor on,
With the high port he wore erewhile,
When, foremost of the youthful band,
The prizes in all lists he won;
Nor bate one jot of heart or hope,
And, least of all, the loyal tie
Which holds to home 'neath every sky,
The joy and pride the pilgrim feels
In hearts which round the hearth at home
Keep pulse for pulse with those who roam.

What generous beliefs console
The brave whom Fate denies the goal!
If others reach it, is content;
To Heaven's high will his will is bent.
Firm on his heart relied,
What lot soe'er betide,
Work of his hand

He nor repents nor grieves,
Pleads for itself the fact,
As unrepenting Nature leaves
Her every act.

   Fell the bolt on the branching oak;
The rainbow of his hope was broke;
No craven cry, no secret tear,—
He told no pang, he knew no fear;
Its peace sublime his aspect kept,
His purpose woke, his features slept;
And yet between the spasms of pain
His genius beamed with joy again.

   O'er thy rich dust the endless smile
Of Nature in thy Spanish isle
Hints never loss or cruel break
And sacrifice for love's dear sake,
Nor mourn the unalterable Days
That Genius goes and Folly stays.
What matters how, or from what ground,
The freed soul its Creator found?
Alike thy memory embalms
That orange-grove, that isle of palms,
And these loved banks, whose oak-boughs bold
Root in the blood of heroes old.

ELEMENTS

Experience

The lords of life, the lords of life,—
I saw them pass,
In their own guise,
Like and unlike,
Portly and grim,—
Use and Surprise,
Surface and Dream,
Succession swift and spectral Wrong,
Temperament without a tongue,
And the inventor of the game
Omnipresent without name;—
Some to see, some to be guessed,
They marched from east to west:
Little man, least of all,
Among the legs of his guardians tall,
Walked about with puzzled look.
Him by the hand dear Nature took,
Dearest Nature, strong and kind,
Whispered, 'Darling, never mind!
To-morrow they will wear another face,
The founder thou; these are thy race!'

Compensation

I.

The wings of Time are black and white,
Pied with morning and with night.
Mountain tall and ocean deep
Trembling balance duly keep.
In changing moon and tidal wave
Glows the feud of Want and Have.

Gauge of more and less through space,
Electric star or pencil plays,
The lonely Earth amid the balls
That hurry through the eternal halls,
A makeweight flying to the void,
Supplemental asteroid,
Or compensatory spark,
Shoots across the neutral Dark.

II.

Man's the elm, and Wealth the vine;
Stanch and strong the tendrils twine:
Though the frail ringlets thee deceive,
None from its stock that vine can reave.
Fear not, then, thou child infirm,
There's no god dare wrong a worm;
Laurel crowns cleave to deserts,
And power to him who power exerts.
Hast not thy share? On winged feet,
Lo! it rushes thee to meet;
And all that Nature made thy own,
Floating in air or pent in stone,
Will rive the hills and swim the sea,
And, like thy shadow, follow thee.

Politics

Gold and iron are good
To buy iron and gold;
All earth's fleece and food
For their like are sold.
Hinted Merlin wise,
Proved Napoleon great,
Nor kind nor coinage buys
Aught above its rate.
Fear, Craft, and Avarice
Cannot rear a State.

Out of dust to build
What is more than dust,—
Walls Amphion piled
Phœbus stablish must.
When the Muses nine
With the Virtues meet,
Find to their design
An Atlantic seat,
By green orchard boughs
Fended from the heat,
Where the statesman ploughs
Furrow for the wheat,—
When the Church is social worth,
When the state-house is the hearth,
Then the perfect State is come,
The republican at home.

Heroism

Ruby wine is drunk by knaves,
Sugar spends to fatten slaves,
Rose and vine-leaf deck buffoons;
Thunder-clouds are Jove's festoons,
Drooping oft in wreaths of dread,
Lightning-knotted round his head;
The hero is not fed on sweets,
Daily his own heart he eats;
Chambers of the great are jails,
And head-winds right for royal sails.

Character

The sun set, but set not his hope:
Stars rose; his faith was earlier up:
Fixed on the enormous galaxy,
Deeper and older seemed his eye;

And matched his sufferance sublime
The taciturnity of time.
He spoke, and words more soft than rain
Brought the Age of Gold again:
His action won such reverence sweet
As hid all measure of the feat.

Culture

Can rules or tutors educate
The semigod whom we await?
He must be musical,
Tremulous, impressional,
Alive to gentle influence
Of landscape and of sky,
And tender to the spirit-touch
Of man's or maiden's eye:
But, to his native centre fast,
Shall into Future fuse the Past,
And the world's flowing fates in his own mould recast.

Friendship

A ruddy drop of manly blood
The surging sea outweighs,
The world uncertain comes and goes,
The lover rooted stays.
I fancied he was fled,—
And, after many a year,
Glowed unexhausted kindliness,
Like daily sunrise there.
My careful heart was free again,
O friend, my bosom said,
Through thee alone the sky is arched,
Through thee the rose is red;
All things through thee take nobler form,

And look beyond the earth,
The mill-round of our fate appears
A sun-path in thy worth.
Me too thy nobleness has taught
To master my despair;
The fountains of my hidden life
Are through thy friendship fair.

Beauty

Was never form and never face
So sweet to SEYD as only grace
Which did not slumber like a stone,
But hovered gleaming and was gone.
Beauty chased he everywhere,
In flame, in storm, in clouds of air.
He smote the lake to feed his eye
With the beryl beam of the broken wave;
He flung in pebbles well to hear
The moment's music which they gave.
Oft pealed for him a lofty tone
From nodding pole and belting zone.
He heard a voice none else could hear
From centred and from errant sphere.
The quaking earth did quake in rhyme,
Seas ebbed and flowed in epic chime.
In dens of passion, and pits of woe,
He saw strong Eros struggling through,
To sun the dark and solve the curse,
And beam to the bounds of the universe.
While thus to love he gave his days
In loyal worship, scorning praise,
How spread their lures for him in vain
Thieving Ambition and paltering Gain!
He thought it happier to be dead,
To die for Beauty, than live for bread.

Manners

Grace, Beauty, and Caprice
Build this golden portal;
Graceful women, chosen men,
Dazzle every mortal.
Their sweet and lofty countenance
His enchanted food;
He need not go to them, their forms
Beset his solitude.
He looketh seldom in their face,
His eyes explore the ground, —
The green grass is a looking-glass
Whereon their traits are found.
Little and less he says to them,
So dances his heart in his breast;
Their tranquil mien bereaveth him
Of wit, of words, of rest.
Too weak to win, too fond to shun
The tyrants of his doom,
The much deceived Endymion
Slips behind a tomb.

Art

Give to barrows, trays, and pans
Grace and glimmer of romance;
Bring the moonlight into noon
Hid in gleaming piles of stone;
On the city's paved street
Plant gardens lined with lilacs sweet;
Let spouting fountains cool the air,
Singing in the sun-baked square;
Let statue, picture, park, and hall,
Ballad, flag, and festival,
The past restore, the day adorn,
And make to-morrow a new morn.

So shall the drudge in dusty frock
Spy behind the city clock
Retinues of airy kings,
Skirts of angels, starry wings,
His fathers shining in bright fables,
His children fed at heavenly tables.
'T is the privilege of Art
Thus to play its cheerful part,
Man on earth to acclimate,
And bend the exile to his fate,
And, moulded of one element
With the days and firmament,
Teach him on these as stairs to climb,
And live on even terms with Time;
Whilst upper life the slender rill
Of human sense doth overfill.

Spiritual Laws

The living Heaven thy prayers respect,
House at once and architect,
Quarrying man's rejected hours,
Builds therewith eternal towers;
Sole and self-commanded works,
Fears not undermining days,
Grows by decays,
And, by the famous might that lurks
In reaction and recoil,
Makes flame to freeze, and ice to boil;
Forging, through swart arms of Offence,
The silver seat of Innocence.

Unity

Space is ample, east and west,
But two cannot go abreast,
Cannot travel in it two:

Yonder masterful cuckoo
Crowds every egg out of the nest,
Quick or dead, except its own;
A spell is laid on sod and stone,
Night and Day were tampered with,
Every quality and pith
Surcharged and sultry with a power
That works its will on age and hour.

Worship

This is he, who, felled by foes,
Sprung harmless up, refreshed by blows:
He to captivity was sold,
But him no prison-bars would hold:
Though they sealed him in a rock,
Mountain chains he can unlock:
Thrown to lions for their meat,
The crouching lion kissed his feet:
Bound to the stake, no flames appalled,
But arched o'er him an honoring vault.
This is he men miscall Fate,
Threading dark ways, arriving late,
But ever coming in time to crown
The truth, and hurl wrong-doers down.
He is the oldest, and best known,
More near than aught thou call'st thy own,
Yet, greeted in another's eyes,
Disconcerts with glad surprise.
This is Jove, who, deaf to prayers,
Floods with blessings unawares.
Draw, if thou canst, the mystic line
Severing rightly his from thine,
Which is human, which divine.

QUATRAINS

S. H.

With beams December planets dart
His cold eye truth and conduct scanned,
July was in his sunny heart,
October in his liberal hand.

A. H.

High was her heart, and yet was well inclined,
Her manners made of bounty well refined;
Far capitals, and marble courts, her eye still seemed to see,
Minstrels, and kings, and high-born dames, and of the best
    that be.

"Suum Cuique"

Wilt thou seal up the avenues of ill?
Pay every debt, as if God wrote the bill.

Hush!

Every thought is public,
Every nook is wide;
Thy gossips spread each whisper,
And the gods from side to side.

Orator

He who has no hands
Perforce must use his tongue;
Foxes are so cunning
Because they are not strong.

Artist

Quit the hut, frequent the palace,
Reck not what the people say;
For still, where'er the trees grow biggest,
Huntsmen find the easiest way.

Poet

Ever the Poet *from* the land
Steers his bark, and trims his sail;
Right out to sea his courses stand,
New worlds to find in pinnace frail.

Poet

To clothe the fiery thought
In simple words succeeds,
For still the craft of genius is
To mask a king in weeds.

Botanist

Go thou to thy learned task,
I stay with the flowers of spring:
Do thou of the ages ask
What me the hours will bring.

Gardener

True Bramin, in the morning meadows wet,
Expound the Vedas of the violet,
Or, hid in vines, peeping through many a loop,
See the plum redden, and the beurré stoop.

Forester

He took the color of his vest
From rabbit's coat or grouse's breast;
For, as the wood-kinds lurk and hide,
So walks the woodman, unespied.

Northman

The gale that wrecked you on the sand,
It helped my rowers to row;
The storm is my best galley hand,
And drives me where I go.

From Alcuin

The sea is the road of the bold,
Frontier of the wheat-sown plains,
The pit wherein the streams are rolled,
And fountain of the rains.

Excelsior

Over his head were the maple buds,
And over the tree was the moon,
And over the moon were the starry studs,
That drop from the angels' shoon.

Borrowing

From the French

Some of your hurts you have cured,
And the sharpest you still have survived,
But what torments of grief you endured
From evils which never arrived!

Nature

Boon Nature yields each day a brag which we now first
    behold,
And trains us on to slight the new, as if it were the old:
But blest is he, who, playing deep, yet haply asks not why,
Too busied with the crowded hour to fear to live or die.

Fate

Her planted eye to-day controls,
Is in the morrow most at home,
And sternly calls to being souls
That curse her when they come.

Horoscope

Ere he was born, the stars of fate
Plotted to make him rich and great:
When from the womb the babe was loosed,
The gate of gifts behind him closed.

Power

Cast the bantling on the rocks,
Suckle him with the she-wolf's teat,
Wintered with the hawk and fox,
Power and speed be hands and feet.

Climacteric

I am not wiser for my age,
Nor skilful by my grief;
Life loiters at the book's first page,—
Ah! could we turn the leaf.

Heri, Cras, Hodie

Shines the last age, the next with hope is seen,
To-day slinks poorly off unmarked between:
Future or Past no richer secret folds,
O friendless Present! than thy bosom holds.

Memory

Night-dreams trace on Memory's wall
Shadows of the thoughts of day,
And thy fortunes, as they fall,
The bias of the will betray.

Love

Love on his errand bound to go
Can swim the flood, and wade through snow,
Where way is none, 't will creep and wind
And eat through Alps its home to find.

Sacrifice

Though love repine, and reason chafe,
There came a voice without reply,—
' 'T is man's perdition to be safe,
When for the truth he ought to die.'

Pericles

Well and wisely said the Greek,
Be thou faithful, but not fond;
To the altar's foot thy fellow seek,
The Furies wait beyond.

Casella

Test of the poet is knowledge of love,
For Eros is older than Saturn or Jove;
Never was poet, of late or of yore,
Who was not tremulous with love-lore.

Shakspeare

I see all human wits
Are measured but a few,
Unmeasured still my Shakspeare sits,
Lone as the blessed Jew.

Hafiz

Her passions the shy violet
From Hafiz never hides;
Love-longings of the raptured bird
The bird to him confides.

Nature in Leasts

As sings the pine-tree in the wind,
So sings in the wind a sprig of the pine;
Her strength and soul has laughing France
Shed in each drop of wine.

'ΑΔΑΚΡΥΝ ΝΕΜΟΝΤΑΙ ΑΙΩΝΑ

'A new commandment,' said the smiling Muse,
'I give my darling son, Thou shalt not preach'; —
Luther, Fox, Behmen, Swedenborg, grew pale,
And, on the instant, rosier clouds upbore
Hafiz and Shakspeare with their shining choirs.

TRANSLATIONS

Sonnet of Michel Angelo Buonaroti

Never did sculptor's dream unfold
A form which marble doth not hold
In its white block; yet it therein shall find
Only the hand secure and bold
Which still obeys the mind.
So hide in thee, thou heavenly dame,
The ill I shun, the good I claim;
I alas! not well alive,
Miss the aim whereto I strive.

Not love, nor beauty's pride,
Nor Fortune, nor thy coldness, can I chide,
If, whilst within thy heart abide
Both death and pity, my unequal skill
Fails of the life, but draws the death and ill.

The Exile

From the Persian of Kermani

In Farsistan the violet spreads
Its leaves to the rival sky;
I ask how far is the Tigris flood,
And the vine that grows thereby?

Except the amber morning wind,
Not one salutes me here;
There is no lover in all Bagdat
To offer the exile cheer.

I know that thou, O morning wind!
O'er Kernan's meadow blowest,
And thou, heart-warming nightingale!
My father's orchard knowest.

The merchant hath stuffs of price,
And gems from the sea-washed strand,
And princes offer me grace
To stay in the Syrian land;

But what is gold *for*, but for gifts?
And dark, without love, is the day;
And all that I see in Bagdat
Is the Tigris to float me away.

From Hafiz

I said to heaven that glowed above,
O hide yon sun-filled zone,
Hide all the stars you boast;
For, in the world of love
And estimation true,
The heaped-up harvest of the moon
Is worth one barley-corn at most,
The Pleiads' sheaf but two.

———

If my darling should depart,
And search the skies for prouder friends,
God forbid my angry heart
In other love should seek amends.

When the blue horizon's hoop
Me a little pinches here,
Instant to my grave I stoop,
And go find thee in the sphere.

Epitaph

Bethink, poor heart, what bitter kind of jest
Mad Destiny this tender stripling played;
For a warm breast of maiden to his breast,
She laid a slab of marble on his head.

———

They say, through patience, chalk
Becomes a ruby stone;
Ah, yes! but by the true heart's blood
The chalk is crimson grown.

Friendship

Thou foolish Hafiz! Say, do churls
Know the worth of Oman's pearls?
Give the gem which dims the moon
To the noblest, or to none.

———

Dearest, where thy shadow falls,
Beauty sits, and Music calls;
Where thy form and favor come,
All good creatures have their home.

———

On prince or bride no diamond stone
Half so gracious ever shone,
As the light of enterprise
Beaming from a young man's eyes.

From Omar Chiam

Each spot where tulips prank their state
Has drunk the life-blood of the great;
The violets yon field which stain
Are moles of beauties Time hath slain.

He who has a thousand friends has not a friend to spare,
And he who has one enemy will meet him everywhere.

On two days it steads not to run from thy grave,
The appointed, and the unappointed day;
On the first, neither balm nor physician can save,
Nor thee, on the second, the Universe slay.

From Ibn Jemin

Two things thou shalt not long for, if thou love a mind
    serene;—
A woman to thy wife, though she were a crowned queen;
And the second, borrowed money,—though the smiling
    lender say,
That he will not demand the debt until the Judgment Day.

The Flute

From Hilali

Hark what, now loud, now low, the pining flute complains,
Without tongue, yellow-cheeked, full of winds that wail and
    sigh;
Saying, Sweetheart! the old mystery remains,—
If I am I; thou, thou; or thou art I?

To the Shah

From Hafiz

Thy foes to hunt, thy enviers to strike down,
Poises Arcturus aloft morning and evening his spear.

To the Shah

From Enweri

Not in their houses stand the stars,
But o'er the pinnacles of thine!

To the Shah

From Enweri

From thy worth and weight the stars gravitate,
And the equipoise of heaven is thy house's equipoise.

Song of Seid Nimetollah of Kuhistan

[*Among the religious customs of the dervishes is an astro-
nomical dance, in which the dervish imitates the movements
of the heavenly bodies, by spinning on his own axis, whilst at
the same time he revolves round the Sheikh in the centre,
representing the sun; and, as he spins, he sings the Song of
Seid Nimetollah of Kuhistan.*]

Spin the ball! I reel, I burn,
Nor head from foot can I discern,
Nor my heart from love of mine,
Nor the wine-cup from the wine.
All my doing, all my leaving,

Reaches not to my perceiving;
Lost in whirling spheres I rove,
And know only that I love.

I am seeker of the stone,
Living gem of Solomon;
From the shore of souls arrived,
In the sea of sense I dived;
But what is land, or what is wave,
To me who only jewels crave?
Love is the air-fed fire intense,
And my heart the frankincense;
As the rich aloes flames, I glow,
Yet the censer cannot know.
I'm all-knowing, yet unknowing;
Stand not, pause not, in my going.

Ask not me, as Muftis can,
To recite the Alcoran;
Well I love the meaning sweet,—
I tread the book beneath my feet.

Lo! the God's love blazes higher,
Till all difference expire.
What are Moslems? what are Giaours?
All are Love's, and all are ours.
I embrace the true believers,
But I reck not of deceivers.
Firm to Heaven my bosom clings,
Heedless of inferior things;
Down on earth there, underfoot,
What men chatter know I not.

from SELECTED POEMS

(1876)

Contents

The Harp

One musician is sure,
His wisdom will not fail,
He has not tasted wine impure,
Nor bent to passion frail.
Age cannot cloud his memory,
Nor grief untune his voice,
Ranging down the ruled scale
From tone of joy to inward wail,
Tempering the pitch of all
In his windy cave.
He all the fables knows,
And in their causes tells,—
Knows Nature's rarest moods,
Ever on her secret broods.
The Muse of men is coy,
Oft courted will not come;
In palaces and market-squares
Entreated, she is dumb;
But my minstrel knows and tells
The counsel of the gods,
Knows of Holy Book the spells,
Knows the law of Night and Day,
And the heart of girl and boy,
The tragic and the gay,
And what is writ on Table Round
Of Arthur and his peers,
What sea and land discoursing say
In sidereal years.
He renders all his lore
In numbers wild as dreams,
Modulating all extremes,—
What the spangled meadow saith

To the children who have faith;
Only to children children sing,
Only to youth will spring be spring.

  Who is the Bard thus magnified?
When did he sing? and where abide?

  Chief of song where poets feast
In the wind-harp which thou seest
In the casement at my side.

  Æolian harp,
How strangely wise thy strain!
Gay for youth, gay for youth,
(Sweet is art, but sweeter truth,)
In the hall at summer eve
Fate and Beauty skilled to weave.
From the eager opening strings
Rung loud and bold the song.
Who but loved the wind-harp's note?
How should not the poet dote
On its mystic tongue,
With its primeval memory,
Reporting what old minstrels told
Of Merlin locked the harp within,—
Merlin paying the pain of sin,
Pent in a dungeon made of air,—
And some attain his voice to hear,—
Words of pain and cries of fear,
But pillowed all on melody,
As fits the griefs of bards to be.
And what if that all-echoing shell,
Which thus the buried Past can tell,
Should rive the Future, and reveal
What his dread folds would fain conceal?
It shares the secret of the earth,
And of the kinds that owe her birth.
Speaks not of self that mystic tone,
But of the Overgods alone:
It trembles to the cosmic breath,—

As it heareth, so it saith;
Obeying meek the primal Cause,
It is the tongue of mundane laws.
And this, at least, I dare affirm,
Since genius too has bound and term,
There is no bard in all the choir,
Not Homer's self, the poet sire,
Wise Milton's odes of pensive pleasure,
Or Shakspeare, whom no mind can measure,
Nor Collins' verse of tender pain,
Nor Byron's clarion of disdain,
Scott, the delight of generous boys,
Or Wordsworth, Pan's recording voice,—
Not one of all can put in verse,
Or to this presence could rehearse,
The sights and voices ravishing
The boy knew on the hills in spring,
When pacing through the oaks he heard
Sharp queries of the sentry-bird,
The heavy grouse's sudden whir,
The rattle of the kingfisher;
Saw bonfires of the harlot flies
In the lowland, when day dies;
Or marked, benighted and forlorn,
The first far signal-fire of morn.
These syllables that Nature spoke,
And the thoughts that in him woke,
Can adequately utter none
Save to his ear the wind-harp lone.
Therein I hear the Parcæ reel
The threads of man at their humming-wheel,
The threads of life, and power, and pain,
So sweet and mournful falls the strain.
And best can teach its Delphian chord
How Nature to the soul is moored,
If once again that silent string,
As erst it wont, would thrill and ring.

    Not long ago, at eventide,
It seemed, so listening, at my side

A window rose, and, to say sooth,
I looked forth on the fields of youth:
I saw fair boys bestriding steeds,
I knew their forms in fancy weeds,
Long, long concealed by sundering fates,
Mates of my youth,—yet not my mates,
Stronger and bolder far than I,
With grace, with genius, well attired,
And then as now from far admired,
Followed with love
They knew not of,
With passion cold and shy.
O joy, for what recoveries rare!
Renewed, I breathe Elysian air,
See youth's glad mates in earliest bloom,—
Break not my dream, obtrusive tomb!
Or teach thou, Spring! the grand recoil
Of life resurgent from the soil
Wherein was dropped the mortal spoil.

April

The April winds are magical,
And thrill our tuneful frames;
The garden-walks are passional
To bachelors and dames.
The hedge is gemmed with diamonds,
The air with Cupids full,
The clews of fairy Rosamonds
Guide lovers to the pool.
Each dimple in the water,
Each leaf that shades the rock,
Can cozen, pique, and flatter,
Can parley and provoke.
Goodfellow, Puck, and goblins
Know more than any book;
Down with your doleful problems,

And court the sunny brook.
The south-winds are quick-witted,
The schools are sad and slow,
The masters quite omitted
The lore we care to know.

Wealth

Who shall tell what did befall,
Far away in time, when once,
Over the lifeless ball,
Hung idle stars and suns?
What god the element obeyed?
Wings of what wind the lichen bore,
Wafting the puny seeds of power,
Which, lodged in rock, the rock abrade?
And well the primal pioneer
Knew the strong task to it assigned,
Patient through Heaven's enormous year
To build in matter home for mind.
From air the creeping centuries drew
The matted thicket low and wide,
This must the leaves of ages strew
The granite slab to clothe and hide,
Ere wheat can wave its golden pride.
What smiths, and in what furnace, rolled
(In dizzy æons dim and mute
The reeling brain can ill compute)
Copper and iron, lead and gold?
What oldest star the fame can save
Of races perishing to pave
The planet with a floor of lime?
Dust is their pyramid and mole:
Who saw what ferns and palms were pressed
Under the tumbling mountain's breast,
In the safe herbal of the coal?
But when the quarried means were piled,

All is waste and worthless, till
Arrives the wise selecting will,
And, out of slime and chaos, Wit
Draws the threads of fair and fit.
Then temples rose, and towns, and marts,
The shop of toil, the hall of arts;
Then flew the sail across the seas
To feed the North from tropic trees;
The storm-wind wove, the torrent span,
Where they were bid the rivers ran;
New slaves fulfilled the poet's dream,
Galvanic wire, strong-shouldered steam.
Then docks were built, and crops were stored,
And ingots added to the hoard.
But, though light-headed man forget,
Remembering Matter pays her debt:
Still, through her motes and masses, draw
Electric thrills and ties of Law,
Which bind the strength of Nature wild
To the conscience of a child.

Maiden Speech of the Æolian Harp

Soft and softlier hold me, friends!
Thanks if your genial care
Unbind and give me to the air.
Keep your lips or finger-tips
For flute or spinnet's dancing chips;
I await a tenderer touch,
I ask more or not so much:
Give me to the atmosphere,—
Where is the wind my brother,—where?
Lift the sash, lay me within,
Lend me your ears, and I begin.
For gentle harp to gentle hearts
The secret of the world imparts;
And not to-day and not to-morrow

Can drain its wealth of hope and sorrow;
But day by day, to loving ear
Unlocks new sense and loftier cheer.
I've come to live with you, sweet friends,
This home my minstrel journeying ends.
Many and subtle are my lays,
The latest better than the first,
For I can mend the happiest days,
And charm the anguish of the worst.

Cupido

The solid, solid universe
Is pervious to Love;
With bandaged eyes he never errs,
Around, below, above.
His blinding light
He flingeth white
On God's and Satan's brood,
And reconciles
By mystic wiles
The evil and the good.

The Nun's Aspiration

The yesterday doth never smile,
To-day goes drudging through the while,
Yet in the name of Godhead, I
The morrow front, and can defy;
Though I am weak, yet God, when prayed,
Cannot withhold his conquering aid.
Ah me! it was my childhood's thought,
If He should make my web a blot
On life's fair picture of delight,
My heart's content would find it right.
But O, these waves and leaves, —

When haply stoic Nature grieves,—
No human speech so beautiful
As their murmurs mine to lull.
On this altar God hath built
I lay my vanity and guilt;
Nor me can Hope or Passion urge
Hearing as now the lofty dirge
Which blasts of Northern mountains hymn,
Nature's funeral, high and dim,—
Sable pageantry of clouds,
Mourning summer laid in shrouds.
Many a day shall dawn and die,
Many an angel wander by,
And passing, light my sunken turf
Moist perhaps by ocean surf,
Forgotten amid splendid tombs,
Yet wreathed and hid by summer blooms.
On earth I dream;—I die to be:
Time! shake not thy bald head at me.
I challenge thee to hurry past,
Or for my turn to fly too fast.
Think me not numbed or halt with age,
Or cares that earth to earth engage,
Caught with love's cord of twisted beams,
Or mired by climate's gross extremes.
I tire of shams, I rush to Be,
I pass with yonder comet free,—
Pass with the comet into space
Which mocks thy æons to embrace;
Æons which tardily unfold
Realm beyond realm,—extent untold;
No early morn, no evening late,—
Realms self-upheld, disdaining Fate,
Whose shining sons, too great for fame,
Never heard thy weary name;
Nor lives the tragic bard to say
How drear the part I held in one,
How lame the other limped away.

Hymn

*Sung at the Second Church, Boston, at the Ordination of
Rev. Chandler Robbins.*

We love the venerable house
   Our fathers built to God; —
In heaven are kept their grateful vows,
   Their dust endears the sod.

Here holy thoughts a light have shed
   From many a radiant face,
And prayers of humble virtue made
   The perfume of the place.

And anxious hearts have pondered here
   The mystery of life,
And prayed the eternal Light to clear
   Their doubts, and aid their strife.

From humble tenements around
   Came up the pensive train,
And in the church a blessing found
   That filled their homes again;

For faith and peace and mighty love
   That from the Godhead flow,
Showed them the life of Heaven above
   Springs from the life below.

They live with God; their homes are dust;
   Yet here their children pray,
And in this fleeting lifetime trust
   To find the narrow way.

On him who by the altar stands,
   On him thy blessing fall,
Speak through his lips thy pure commands,
   Thou heart that lovest all.

Boston

Sicut patribus, sit Deus nobis.

*Read in Faneuil Hall, on December 16, 1873, on the Centennial
Anniversary of the Destruction of the Tea in Boston Harbor.*

The rocky nook with hill-tops three
  Looked eastward from the farms,
And twice each day the flowing sea
  Took Boston in its arms;
    The men of yore were stout and poor,
    And sailed for bread to every shore.

And where they went on trade intent
  They did what freemen can,
Their dauntless ways did all men praise,
  The merchant was a man.
    The world was made for honest trade,—
    To plant and eat be none afraid.

The waves that rocked them on the deep
  To them their secret told;
Said the winds that sung the lads to sleep,
  "Like us be free and bold!"
    The honest waves refuse to slaves
    The empire of the ocean caves.

Old Europe groans with palaces,
  Has lords enough and more;—
We plant and build by foaming seas
  A city of the poor;—
    For day by day could Boston Bay
    Their honest labor overpay.

We grant no dukedoms to the few,
  We hold like rights and shall;—
Equal on Sunday in the pew,

On Monday in the mall.
   For what avail the plough or sail,
   Or land or life, if freedom fail?

The noble craftsman we promote,
   Disown the knave and fool;
Each honest man shall have his vote,
   Each child shall have his school.
     A union then of honest men,
     Or union nevermore again.

The wild rose and the barberry thorn
   Hung out their summer pride
Where now on heated pavements worn
   The feet of millions stride.

Fair rose the planted hills behind
   The good town on the bay,
And where the western hills declined
   The prairie stretched away.

What care though rival cities soar
   Along the stormy coast,
Penn's town, New York, and Baltimore,
   If Boston knew the most!

They laughed to know the world so wide;
   The mountains said, 'Good day!
We greet you well, you Saxon men,
   Up with your towns and stay!'
     The world was made for honest trade,—
     To plant and eat be none afraid.

"For you," they said, "no barriers be,
   For you no sluggard rest;
Each street leads downward to the sea,
   Or landward to the West."

O happy town beside the sea,
　Whose roads lead everywhere to all;
Than thine no deeper moat can be,
　No stouter fence, no steeper wall!

Bad news from George on the English throne:
　"You are thriving well," said he;
"Now by these presents be it known,
　You shall pay us a tax on tea;
　　'T is very small,—no load at all,—
　　Honor enough that we send the call."

"Not so," said Boston, "good my lord,
　We pay your governors here
Abundant for their bed and board,
　Six thousand pounds a year.
(Your Highness knows our homely word,)
　　Millions for self-government,
　　But for tribute never a cent."

The cargo came! and who could blame
　If *Indians* seized the tea,
And, chest by chest, let down the same
　Into the laughing sea?
　　For what avail the plough or sail,
　　Or land or life, if freedom fail?

The townsmen braved the English king,
　Found friendship in the French,
And Honor joined the patriot ring
　Low on their wooden bench.

O bounteous seas that never fail!
　O day remembered yet!
O happy port that spied the sail
　Which wafted Lafayette!
　　Pole-star of light in Europe's night,
　　That never faltered from the right.

Kings shook with fear, old empires crave
   The secret force to find
Which fired the little State to save
   The rights of all mankind.

But right is might through all the world;
   Province to province faithful clung,
Through good and ill the war-bolt hurled,
   Till Freedom cheered and the joy-bells rung.

The sea returning day by day
   Restores the world-wide mart;
So let each dweller on the Bay
   Fold Boston in his heart,
     Till these echoes be choked with snows,
     Or over the town blue ocean flows.

Let the blood of her hundred thousands
   Throb in each manly vein;
And the wit of all her wisest,
   Make sunshine in her brain.
     For you can teach the lightning speech,
     And round the globe your voices reach.

And each shall care for other,
   And each to each shall bend,
To the poor a noble brother,
   To the good an equal friend.

A blessing through the ages thus
   Shield all thy roofs and towers!
God with the fathers, so with us,
   Thou darling town of ours!

OTHER PUBLISHED
POEMS AND TRANSLATIONS

Contents

William Rufus and the Jew

"May it please my lord the king,—there's a Jew at the
    door."
—"Let him in," said the king, "what's he waiting there
    for?"
—"I wot, Sir, you come from Abraham's loins,
Love not Christ, eat no pork, do no good with your
    coins."
"My lord the king! I do as Moses bids;
 Eschewing all evil, I shut my coffer lids;
From the law of my fathers, God forbid I should swerve;
The uncircumcised Nazarite, my race must not serve;
But Isaac my son to the Gentiles hath gone over,
And no means can I find my first-born to recover.
I would give fifty marks, and my gabardine to boot,
To the Rabbi that would bring him from the Christian faith
    about;
But phylacteried Rabbins live far over sea,
I cannot go to them, and they will not come to me.
Will it please my lord the king, from the house of Magog,
To bring my son back to his own synagogue."
—"Why I'll be the Rabbi,—where's a fitter Pharisee?
Count me out the fifty marks, and go send your son to me."
The king filled his mouth with arguments and jibes,
To win the boy back to the faith of the tribes,
But Isaac the Jew was so hard and stiff-necked,
That by no means could the king come to any effect;
So he paid the Jew back twenty marks of his gains;
Quoth he, "I think I'll keep the thirty for the payment of
    my pains."

Fame

Ah Fate! cannot a man
    Be wise without a beard?
From East to West, from Beersheba to Dan,
    Say, was it never heard,
That wisdom might in youth be gotten,
Or wit be ripe before 't was rotten?

He pays too high a price
    For knowledge and for fame,
Who gives his sinews, to be wise,
    His teeth and bones, to buy a name,
And crawls through life a paralytic,
To earn the praise of bard and critic.

Is it not better done,
    To dine and sleep through forty years,
Be loved by few, be feared by none,
    Laugh life away, have wine for tears,
And take the mortal leap undaunted,
Content that all we asked was granted?

But Fate will not permit
    The seed of gods to die,
Nor suffer Sense to win from Wit
    Its guerdon in the sky,
Nor let us hide, whate'er our pleasure,
The world's light underneath a measure.

Go then, sad youth, and shine!
    Go, sacrifice to fame;
Put love, joy, health, upon the shrine,
    And life to fan the flame!
Thy hapless self for praises barter,
And die to Fame an honored martyr.

Silence

They put their finger on their lip,—
   The Powers above;
The seas their islands clip,
The moons in Ocean dip,—
   They love but name not love.

Mottoes to "History"

There is no great and no small
To the Soul that maketh all:
And where it cometh, all things are;
And it cometh everywhere.

———————

I am owner of the sphere,
Of the seven stars and the solar year,
Of Cæsar's hand, and Plato's brain,
Of Lord Christ's heart, and Shakspeare's strain.

Grace

How much, Preventing God! how much I owe
To the defences thou hast round me set:
Example, custom, fear, occasion slow,—
These scorned bondmen were my parapet.
I dare not peep over this parapet
To guage with glance the roaring gulf below.
The depths of sin to which I had descended,
Had not these me against myself defended.

The Three Dimensions

"Room for the spheres!"—then first they shined,
  And dived into the ample sky;
"Room! room!" cried the new mankind,
  And took the oath of liberty.
  Room! room! willed the opening mind,
  And found it in Variety.

Motto to "The Poet"

A moody child and wildly wise
Pursued the game with joyful eyes,
Which chose, like meteors, their way,
And rived the dark with private ray:
They overleapt the horizon's edge,
Searched with Apollo's privilege;
Through man, and woman, and sea, and star,
Saw the dance of nature forward far;
Through worlds, and races, and terms, and times,
Saw musical order, and pairing rhymes.

Motto to "Gifts"

Gifts of one who loved me,—
'T was high time they came;
When he ceased to love me,
Time they stopped for shame.

Motto to "Nature"

The rounded world is fair to see,
Nine times folded in mystery:
Though baffled seers cannot impart
The secret of its laboring heart,
Throb thine with Nature's throbbing breast,
And all is clear from east to west.
Spirit that lurks each form within
Beckons to spirit of its kin;
Self-kindled every atom glows,
And hints the future which it owes.

Motto to "Nominalist and Realist"

In countless upward-striving waves
The moon-drawn tide-wave strives;
In thousand far-transplanted grafts
The parent fruit survives;
So, in the new-born millions,
The perfect Adam lives.
Not less are summer-mornings dear
To every child they wake,
And each with novel life his sphere
Fills for his proper sake.

My Thoughts

Many are the thoughts that come to me
In my lonely musing;
And they drift so strange and swift,
There's no time for choosing
Which to follow, for to leave
Any, seems a losing.

When they come, they come in flocks,
    As on glancing feather,
Startled birds rise one by one
    In autumnal weather,
Waking one another up
    From the sheltering heather.

Some so merry that I laugh,
    Some are grave and serious,
Some so trite, their least approach
    Is enough to weary us:—
Others flit like midnight ghosts,
    Shrouded and mysterious.

There are thoughts that o'er me steal,
    Like the day when dawning;
Great thoughts winged with melody
    Common utterance scorning,
Moving in an inward tune,
    And an inward morning.

Some have dark and drooping wings,
    Children all of sorrow;
Some are as gay, as if today
    Could see no cloudy morrow,—
And yet, like light and shade, they each
    Must from the other borrow.

One by one they come to me
    On their destined mission;
One by one I see them fade
    With no hopeless vision;
For they've led me on a step
    To their home Elysian.

Motto to "Prudence"

Theme no poet gladly sung,
Fair to old and foul to young,
Scorn not thou the love of parts,
And the articles of arts.
Grandeur of the perfect sphere
Thanks the atoms that cohere.

Motto to "Circles"

Nature centres into balls,
And her proud ephemerals,
Fast to surface and outside,
Scan the profile of the sphere;
Knew they what that signified,
A new genesis were here.

Motto to "Intellect"

Go, speed the stars of Thought
On to their shining goals; —
The sower scatters broad his seed,
The wheat thou strew'st be souls.

Motto to "Nature"

A subtle chain of countless rings
The next unto the farthest brings;
The eye reads omens where it goes,
And speaks all languages the rose;
And, striving to be man, the worm
Mounts through all the spires of form.

Motto to "New England Reformers"

In the suburb, in the town,
On the railway, in the square,
Came a beam of goodness down
Doubling daylight everywhere:
Peace now each for malice takes,
Beauty for his sinful weeds,
For the angel Hope aye makes
Him an angel whom she leads.

Motto to "Fate"

Delicate omens traced in air
To the lone bard true witness bare;
Birds with auguries on their wings
Chanted undeceiving things
Him to beckon, him to warn;
Well might then the poet scorn
To learn of scribe or courier
Hints writ in vaster character;
And on his mind, at dawn of day,
Soft shadows of the evening lay.
For the prevision is allied
Unto the thing so signified;
Or say, the foresight that awaits
Is the same Genius that creates.

Motto to "Power"

His tongue was framed to music,
And his hand was armed with skill,
His face was the mould of beauty,
And his heart the throne of will.

Motto to "Considerations by the Way"

Hear what British Merlin sung,
Of keenest eye and truest tongue.
Say not, the chiefs who first arrive
Usurp the seats for which all strive;
The forefathers this land who found
Failed to plant the vantage-ground;
Ever from one who comes to-morrow
Men wait their good and truth to borrow.
But wilt thou measure all thy road,
See thou lift the lightest load.
Who has little, to him who has less, can spare,
And thou, Cyndyllan's son! beware
Ponderous gold and stuffs to bear,
To falter ere thou thy task fulfil, —
Only the light-armed climb the hill.
The richest of all lords is Use,
And ruddy Health the loftiest Muse.
Live in the sunshine, swim the sea,
Drink the wild air's salubrity:
Where the star Canope shines in May,
Shepherds are thankful, and nations gay.
The music that can deepest reach,
And cure all ill, is cordial speech:
Mask thy wisdom with delight,
Toy with the bow, yet hit the white.
Of all wit's uses, the main one
Is to live well with who has none.
Cleave to thine acre; the round year
Will fetch all fruits and virtues here:
Fool and foe may harmless roam,
Loved and lovers bide at home.
A day for toil, an hour for sport,
But for a friend is life too short.

Motto to "Illusions"

Flow, flow the waves hated,
Accursed, adored,
The waves of mutation:
No anchorage is.
Sleep is not, death is not;
Who seem to die live.
House you were born in,
Friends of your spring-time,
Old man and young maid,
Day's toil and its guerdon,
They are all vanishing,
Fleeing to fables,
Cannot be moored.
See the stars through them,
Through treacherous marbles.
Know, the stars yonder,
The stars everlasting,
Are fugitive also,
And emulate, vaulted,
The lambent heat-lightning,
And fire-fly's flight.

When thou dost return
On the wave's circulation,
Beholding the shimmer,
The wild dissipation,
And, out of endeavor
To change and to flow,
The gas become solid,
And phantoms and nothings
Return to be things,
And endless imbroglio
Is law and the world,—
Then first shalt thou know,
That in the wild turmoil,
Horsed on the Proteus,
Thou ridest to power,
And to endurance.

———————

The cup of life is not so shallow
That we have drained the best,
That all the wine at once we swallow,
And lees make all the rest.

Maids of as soft a bloom shall marry
As Hymen yet hath blessed,
And fairer forms are in the quarry
Than Angelo released.

———————

Where is Skrymir? Giant Skrymir?
Come transplant the woods for me!
Scoop up yonder aged ash,
Centennial pine, mahogany beech,
Oaks that grew in the dark ages
Heedful, bring them, set them straight,
In sifted soil, before my porch;
Now turn the river on their roots,
So the new top shall not droop
His tall erected plume, nor a leaf wilt.

———————

There are beggars in Iran and Araby,
Said was hungrier than all;
Men said he was a fly
That came to every festival,
Also he came to the mosque
In trail of camel and caravan,
Out from Mecca to Isphaban; —
Northward he went to the snowy hills, —
At court he sat in the grave divan.

His music was the south wind's sigh,
His lamp the maiden's downcast eye,
And ever the spell of beauty came
And turned the drowsy world to flame.
By lake and stream and gleaming hall,
And modest copse, and the forest tall,
Where'er he went the magic guide
Kept its place by the poet's side.
Tell me the world is a talisman,
To read it must be the art of man;
Said melted the days in cups like pearl,
Served high and low, the lord and the churl;
Loved harebells nodding on a rock,
A cabin hung with curling smoke,
And huts and tents, nor loved he less
Stately lords in palaces,
Fenced by form and ceremony.

———————

Quoth Saadi, when I stood before
Hassan the camel-driver's door,
I scorned the fame of Timour brave,—
Timour to Hassan was a slave.
In every glance of Hassan's eye
I read great years of victory;
And I, who cower mean and small
In the frequent interval
When Wisdom not with me resides,
Worship toil's wisdom that abides;
I shunned his eye,—the faithful man's,
I shunned the toiling Hassan's glance.

South Wind

In the turbulent beauty
Of a gusty autumn day,
Poet in a wood-crowned headland
Sighed his soul away.
Farms the sunny landscape dappled,
Swan-down clouds dappled the farms,
Cattle lowed in hazy distance
Where far oaks outstretched their arms.
Sudden gusts came full of meaning,
All too much to him they said;—
Southwinds have long memories,
Of that be none afraid.
I cannot tell rude listeners
Half the telltale Southwind said,
T'would bring the blushes of yon maples
To a man and to a maid.

TRANSLATIONS

Sunshine was he
In the winter day;
And in the midsummer
Coolness and shade.

(*Arabian*)

Go boldly forth, and feast on being's banquet;
Thou art the called,—the rest admitted with thee.

(*Arabian*)

The principle of all things; entrails made
Of smallest entrails; bone, of smallest bone;
Blood, of small sanguine drops reduced to one;
Gold, of small grains; earth, of small sands compacted;
Small drops to water, sparks to fire contracted:

Lucretius

The secret that should not be blown
Not one of thy nation must know;
You may padlock the gate of a town,
But never the mouth of a foe.

(*Persian*)

On earth's wide thoroughfares below
Two only men contented go:
Who knows what's right and what's forbid,
And he from whom is knowledge hid.

Omar Khayyám

———

Color, taste, and smell, smaragdus, sugar, and musk,—
Amber for the tongue, for the eye a picture rare,—
If you cut the fruit in slices, every slice a crescent fair,—
If you leave it whole, the full harvest-moon is there.

Adsched of Meru

———

I batter the wheel of heaven
    When it rolls not rightly by;
I am not one of the snivellers
    Who fall thereon and die.

Hafiz

———

See how the roses burn!
    Bring wine to quench the fire!
Alas! the flames come up with us,—
    We perish with desire.

Hafiz

———

Alas! till now I had not known
My guide and Fortune's guide are one.

Hafiz

The understanding's copper coin
Counts not with the gold of love.

Hafiz

'Tis writ on Paradise's gate,
"Wo to the dupe that yields to Fate!"

Hafiz

The world is a bride superbly dressed;—
Who weds her for dowry must pay his soul.

Hafiz

Loose the knots of the heart; never think on thy fate:
No Euclid has yet disentangled that snarl.

Hafiz

There resides in the grieving
A poison to kill;
Beware to go near them
'Tis pestilent still.

Hafiz

I will be drunk and down with wine;
Treasures we find in a ruined house.

Hafiz

———————

To be wise the dull brain so earnestly throbs,
Bring bands of wine for the stupid head.

Hafiz

———————

The Builder of heaven
    Hath sundered the earth,
So that no footway
    Leads out of it forth.

On turnpikes of wonder
    Wine leads the mind forth,
Straight, sidewise, and upward,
    West, southward, and north.

Stands the vault adamantine
    Until the Doomsday;
The wine-cup shall ferry
    Thee o'er it away.

Hafiz

———————

I am: what I am
My dust will be again.

Hafiz

What lovelier forms things wear,
Now that the Shah comes back!

Hafiz

Take my heart in thy hand, O beautiful boy of Schiraz!
I would give for the mole on thy cheek Samarcand and
  Buchara!

Hafiz

Out of the East, and out of the West, no man understands
  me;
Oh, the happier I, who confide to none but the wind!
This morning heard I how the lyre of the stars resounded,
"Sweeter tones have we heard from Hafiz!"

Hafiz

Fit for the Pleiads' azure chord
The songs I sung, the pearls I bored.

Hafiz

I have no hoarded treasure,
  Yet have I rich content;
The first from Allah to the Shah,
  The last to Hafiz went.

Hafiz

High heart, O Hafiz! though not thine
    Fine gold and silver ore;
More worth to thee the gift of song,
    And the clear insight more.

Hafiz

———————

O Hafiz! speak not of thy need;
    Are not these verses thine?
Then all the poets are agreed,
    No man can less repine.

Hafiz

———————

Oft have I said, I say it once more,
I, a wanderer, do not stray from myself.
I am a kind of parrot; the mirror is holden to me;
What the Eternal says, I stammering say again.
Give me what you will; I eat thistles as roses,
And according to my food I grow and I give.
Scorn me not, but know I have the pearl,
And am only seeking one to receive it.

Hafiz

The Phoenix

My phœnix long ago secured
  His nest in the sky-vault's cope;
In the body's cage immured,
  He is weary of life's hope.

Round and round this heap of ashes
  Now flies the bird amain,
But in that odorous niche of heaven
  Nestles the bird again.

Once flies he upward, he will perch
  On Tuba's golden bough;
His home is on that fruited arch
  Which cools the blest below.

If over this world of ours
  His wings my phœnix spread,
How gracious falls on land and sea
  The soul-refreshing shade!

Either world inhabits he,
  Sees oft below him planets roll;
His body is all of air compact,
  Of Allah's love his soul.

Hafiz

Come!—the palace of heaven rests on aëry pillars,—
Come, and bring me wine; our days are wind.
I declare myself the slave of that masculine soul
Which ties and alliance on earth once forever renounces.
Told I thee yester-morn how the Iris of heaven
Brought to me in my cup a gospel of joy?
O high-flying falcon! the Tree of Life is thy perch;
This nook of grief fits thee ill for a nest.
Hearken! they call to thee down from the ramparts of
    heaven;
I cannot divine what holds thee here in a net.
I, too, have a counsel for thee; oh, mark it and keep it,
Since I received the same from the Master above:
Seek not for faith or for truth in a world of light-minded
    girls;
A thousand suitors reckons this dangerous bride.
This jest of the world, which tickles me, leave to my
    vagabond self.
Accept whatever befalls; uncover thy brow from thy locks;
Neither to me nor to thee was option imparted;
Neither endurance nor truth belongs to the laugh of the
    rose.
The loving nightingale mourns;—cause enow for
    mourning;—
Why envies the bird the streaming verses of Hafiz?
Know that a god bestowed on him eloquent speech.

Hafiz

By breath of beds of roses drawn,
    I found the grove in the morning pure,
In the concert of the nightingales
    My drunken brain to cure.

With unrelated glance
    I looked the rose in the eye;
The rose in the hour of gloaming
    Flamed like a lamp hard-by.

She was of her beauty proud,
    And prouder of her youth,
The while unto her flaming heart
    The bulbul gave his truth.

The sweet narcissus closed
    Its eye, with passion pressed;
The tulips out of envy burned
    Moles in their scarlet breast.

The lilies white prolonged
    Their sworded tongue to the smell;
The clustering anemones
    Their pretty secrets tell.

Hafiz

All day the rain
Bathed the dark hyacinths in vain,
The flood may pour from morn till night
Nor wash the pretty Indians white.

Hafiz

O'er the garden water goes the wind alone
   To rasp and to polish the cheek of the wave;
The fire is quenched on the dear hearth-stone,
   But it burns again on the tulips brave.

Enweri

———————

Whilst I disdain the populace,
I find no peer in higher place.
Friend is a word of royal tone,
Friend is a poem all alone.
Wisdom is like the elephant,
Lofty and rare inhabitant:
He dwells in deserts or in courts;
With hucksters he has no resorts.

Ibn Jemin

———————

A friend is he, who, hunted as a foe,
   So much the kindlier shows him than before;
Throw stones at him, or ruder javelins throw,
   He builds with stone and steel a firmer floor.

Dschami

———————

The chemist of love
   Will this perishing mould,
Were it made out of mire,
   Transmute into gold

Hafiz

And since round lines are drawn
   My darling's lips about,
The very Moon looks puzzled on,
   And hesitates in doubt
If the sweet curve that rounds thy mouth
Be not her true way to the South.

                              Hafiz

———————

Ah, could I hide me in my song,
To kiss thy lips from which it flows!

                              Hafiz

———————

Fair fall thy soft heart!
   A good work wilt thou do?
Oh, pray for the dead
   Whom thine eyelashes slew!

                              Hafiz

———————

They strew in the path of kings and czars
   Jewels and gems of price;
But for thy head I will pluck down stars,
   And pave thy way with eyes.

I have sought for thee a costlier dome
   Than Mahmoud's palace high,
And thou, returning, find thy home
   In the apple of Love's eye.

                              Hafiz

I know this perilous love-lane
　No whither the traveller leads,
Yet my fancy the sweet scent of
　Thy tangled tresses feeds.

In the midnight of thy locks,
　I renounce the day;
In the ring of thy rose-lips,
　My heart forgets to pray.

Hafiz

———

Plunge in yon angry waves,
　Renouncing doubt and care;
The flowing of the seven broad seas
　Shall never wet thy hair.

Is Allah's face on thee
　Bending with love benign,
And thou not less on Allah's eye
　O fairest! turnest thine.

Hafiz

While roses bloomed along the plain,
The nightingale to the falcon said,
"Why, of all birds, must thou be dumb?
With closed mouth thou utterest,
Though dying, no last word to man.
Yet sitt'st thou on the hand of princes,
And feedest on the grouse's breast,
Whilst I, who hundred thousand jewels
Squander in a single tone,
Lo! I feed myself with worms,
And my dwelling is the thorn."—
The falcon answered, "Be all ear:
I, experienced in affairs,
See fifty things, say never one;
But thee the people prizes not,
Who, doing nothing, say'st a thousand.
To me, appointed to the chase,
The king's hand gives the grouse's breast;
Whilst a chatterer like thee
Must gnaw worms in the thorn. Farewell!"

Nisami

Body and Soul

A painter in China once painted a hall;—
Such a web never hung on an emperor's wall;—
One half from his brush with rich colors did run,
The other he touched with a beam of the sun;
So that all which delighted the eye in one side,
The same, point for point, in the other replied.

In thee, friend, that Tyrian chamber is found;
Thine the star-pointing roof, and the base on the ground:
Is one half depicted with colors less bright?
Beware that the counterpart blazes with light!

Enweri

I read on the porch of a palace bold
   In a purple tablet letters cast,—
"A house, though a million winters old,
   A house of earth comes down at last;
Then quarry thy stones from the crystal All,
And build the dome that shall not fall."

Ibn Jemin

The eternal Watcher, who doth wake
   All night in the body's earthen chest,
Will of thine arms a pillow make,
   And a bolster of thy breast.

Feisi

from "Bird Conversations"

The bird-soul was ashamed;
Their body was quite annihilated;
They had cleaned themselves from the dust,
And were by the light ensouled.
What was, and was not,—the Past,—
Was wiped out from their breast.
The sun from near-by beamed
Clearest light into their soul;
The resplendence of the Simorg beamed
As one back from all three.
They knew not, amazed, if they
Were either this or that.
They saw themselves all as Simorg,
Themselves in the eternal Simorg.
When to the Simorg up they looked,
They beheld him among themselves;
And when they looked on each other,
They saw themselves in the Simorg.
A single look grouped the two parties,

The Simorg emerged, the Simorg vanished,
This in that, and that in this,
As the world has never heard.
So remained they, sunk in wonder,
Thoughtless in deepest thinking,
And quite unconscious of themselves.
Speechless prayed they to the Highest
To open this secret,
And to unlock *Thou* and *We*.
There came an answer without tongue. —
"The Highest is a sun-mirror;
Who comes to Him sees himself therein,
Sees body and soul, and soul and body:
When you came to the Simorg,
Three therein appeared to you,
And, had fifty of you come,
So had you seen yourselves as many.
Him has none of us yet seen.
Ants see not the Pleindes.
Can the gnat grasp with his teeth
The body of the elephant?
What you see is He not;
What you hear is He not.
The valleys which you traverse,
The actions which you perform,
They lie under our treatment
And among our properties.
You as three birds are amazed,
Impatient, heartless, confused:
Far over you am I raised,
Since I am in act Simorg.
Ye blot out my highest being,
That ye may find yourselves on my throne;
Forever ye blot out yourselves,
As shadows in the sun. Farewell!"

Ferideddin Attar

MANUSCRIPT POEMS
AND TRANSLATIONS

Contents

Manuscript poems are presented in their approximate order of composition; some poems cannot be dated. Translations are arranged by author.

No. 13 Hymn Written in Concord Sept. 1814

Come heavenly Muse my voice inspire
Teach me to tune the poet's lyre
In feeble notes that I may sing
And let Religion guide the string.
The works of God demand a song
From spirits and the angelic throng
O then let mortals also raise
In humbler strains their songs of praise
My soul O look around and see
How many things are made for thee
For thee the fields are cover'd o'er,
For thee the harvest yields its store,
Speech, reason, sight, and every sense
Is given thee by Providence
God's praise is sung by every rill
O then let not my tongue be still
Let morn, and noon, and shady night
Hear praise to him who made the light
And to his Son who willing came
To save mankind from death and shame.

On the Death of Mr. John Haskins

See the calm exit of the aged Saint,
Without a murmur, and without complaint,
Whil'st round him gathered his dear children stand
And some one holds his withered pallid hand.
He bids them trust in God, nor mourn nor weep;
He breathes Religion, and then falls asleep.
Then on angelic wings he flies to God,
Rejoiced to leave this earthly mortal clod.
His head is covered with a crown of gold.
A golden harp his hands immortal hold.

Lines on the Death of Miss. M. B. Farnham

Come heavenly Muse a suppliant asks thine aid,
No common theme his feeble pen pursues,
Where the blue grave-stone marks the silent dead,
There would he go and there in silence muse.

Here let unhallowed feet ne'er bend their way,
Here where decaying, youth & Beauty sleeps,
Here where cold Death holds his imperious sway,
And fond affection clad in mourning weeps.

Lowly beneath this green and nameless sod,
Rests the frail body of departed worth;
Her happy soul has mounted to her GOD,
And gone forever from this narrow Earth.

Her's was the brightness of the noonday Sun
Her fancy brilliant as his golden rays,
Judgement & Reason, mounted on the throne,
And pure Religion shone in all her ways.

Long as the life blood flows within the veins,
Long as the throbbing heart persists to move,
So long shall thought of Mary lessen pains,
And bring to Memory all her cares, and love.

Her brilliant taste, and manners well refined,
Shone with bright splendor on this lower earth,
Her graceful form, and modesty combined,
Proclaimed her value, excellence, and worth.

Farewel thou dear departed! ah farewel,
Peace to thine ashes in their clay cold bed,
Till the last trump shalt burst thy narrow cell,
And bid thee leave the mansions of the dead.

Poem on Eloquence by R. W. Emerson

When oer the world the son of genius rose
And woke mankind from indolent repose
When Science first diffused her genial rays
And Learning fair enlightened elder days
Then Eloquence descending from above
Left the high palace of Olympian Jove
To earth's fair field she bent her airy way
Guided by Hermes from the realms of day
Thrice happy Greece her lighting footsteps bore
When first the Goddess on earthly shore
In thy fair realm Polymnia fix'd her throne
And raised her sacred fane,—nor there alone—
Where to bright knowledge Ignorance gave way
Where Superstition fled the dawn of day
There in the temple of the Muses shone
Polymnia star by radiant lustre known.
First mid the band that sought her courts for fame
Stood cloth'd in light the great Athenian name
Hail great Demosthenes! thine ardent soul
Could nature's arts and nature's self controul
Thy speech inspired with accents clear and loud
Flash'd like the lightning from the thunder cloud
As the fierce flame that rends the rumbling ground
With sudden blaze throws dire destruction round
From Etna's top with mad resistless force
In liquid fire precipitates its course
Nor shepherd's hut nor prince's stately tower
Can save the tenant from the torrents power
Thus from thy lips the fire of Hermes flow'd
And from a mortal almost made a God
Gave thee the power the hearts of men to bind
The magic springs to know that actuate the mind
The strong in war thy strength resist in vain
The great and brave obey thy guiding vein
Twas with that power endued each sep'rate clause

Drew from the listening crowds the loud applause.
When Freedom from thy lips in thunder spoke
And all her spirit flash'd in every look.
When Phillip vainly tried each subtle art
To tempt with venal gold each patriot's heart
Rous'd by their "last great man" they tried the field
But not those Greeks unknowing how to yield—
One mercy more oh! had the Gods bestow'd
Courage on him whose lips with ardour glow'd
Then had led their armies to the plain
And falling Greece had conquered once again
The dubious field of battle's strife been won
And set majestic had their falling sun
But time forbids that more the muse should name
Of Grecian orators well known to fame
Farewell to Greece of liberal arts the nurse
Turn now Oh Muse to Rome direct thy course
See where with awful majesty arise
Her mighty leaders eloquent & wise
See great Hortentius to a greater yield
And stript of laurels quit the long-fought field

Original—"Apropos"

Night slowly stretches o'er the changing skies
And killing darkness shrouds the rolling Earth
Up to her well-known rock the night-owl hies
And wizard hags begin their cursed mirth.

A misty cloud bedims the rising moon
Few are the stars that cheer the evening sky
And dark and gloomy is the night; and soon
The light that issues from those stars will die.

This night, I deem, the moon is in her spell
And fiends have mutter'd incantations dire
This night in revelry, the hags of hell
Dance in deep cave, around th'infernal fire

Ah! bleakly blows the Ocean's stormy blast
Grim Water-Sprites bestride the foaming wave,
Woe to the hapless bark, the towering mast
The careworn sailor finds tonight his Grave!

On Ballans lonely moor what sounds were heard!
When the chill night brought on the darkness drear
And in thy lofty towers lone Villagird!
What startling noise came sudden on the ear.

I passed at eve the foot of Ben-lide's hill
I heard a voice as the sad breeze blew by
Starting I listened—all again was still
Nought through the mist could mortal sight descry.

———————

William does thy frigid soul,
The charms of poetry deny,
And think thy heart beyond controul,
Of each Parnassian Deity?

This I suspect from that cold look,
Quenching like ice Apollo's fire,
With which each vagrant verse you took,
When offer'd from my humble lyre.

Not that in truth I mean to say,
I ever had a lyre—not I—
Rhymers you know have got a way,
To Tell a *bumper*, alias *lie*.—

—I love quotations—Dr Gibbs—
Or some one else perhaps—has said,
—Poets have leave to publish fibs,
And t'is a portion of their trade—

But to return—ti's wrong to say,
That I should not have leave to write,
My maxim is—write while it's day,—
For soon, forsooth it will be night,

That is—poor Ralph must versify,
Through College *like a thousand drums*
But when well *through* then then oh my
The dark dull *night* of *Business* comes

While this my letter you peruse,
Frown no long-faced *apostrophe*,
Dare not to blame the wayward muse,
Nor scowl the *scrof'lous* brow at me—

Song
Tune "Scots wha hae wi' Wallace bled"

Shout for those whose course is done,—
Bow you to their setting sun,
—Souls of patriots who won
                    Noble Liberty.

Fell Brittania's tyrant power
Quailed in combats fearful hour;
Lowly did the Lion cower
                    To their victory.

Stars of Freedom's spangled banner!
Burst ye forth in loud hosanne,
While the morning breezes fan her
                    Passing cheerfully.

Celebrate with song today,
Feats of eras far away
Ruin to the British sway
                    O'er Columbia

———————

Perhaps thy lot in life is higher
   Than the fates assign to me
While they fulfil thy large desire
   And bid my hopes as visions flee
But grant me still in joy or sorrow
   In grief or hope to claim thy heart
And I will then defy the morrow
   Whilst I fulfil a loyal part.

———————

Valedictory Poem

Gambol and song and jubilee are done,
Life's motley pilgrimage must be begun;—
Another scene is crowding on the last,—
Perhaps a darkened picture of the past;
And we, who leave Youth's fairy vales behind,
Where Joy hath hailed us on the summer wind,
Would fain, with fond delay, prolong the hour,
Which sternly strikes at Friendship's golden power.
Then chide us not, though idly we may strew
Some blooming chaplets in the way we view.
We cannot weep—while Hope is dancing nigh,—
We may not smile at Sorrow's withering eye.
On Youth's last threshold, while we doubtful stand,
What crowded scenes of various hues expand,—
A thousand fears the fields of Time deform,
Hope's gilded rainbows resting on the storm.

Oh long ago, while Freedom yet was young,
Her wreaths ungathered, and her praise unsung,
While Europe languished in barbaric night,
And young Columbus kindled life and light,—
Fate's finger pointed to the brooding cloud
Which wrapped a new world in its ponderous shroud.

On three full ages has the seal been set
Since, o'er this land, Fate's awful Angels met;—
This land,—the scene of glory unrevealed,
Pregnant with powers her Genius woke to wield.
Here stood those Angels, on our mountain strand,
And looked through Time, and waved their charmed wand,
Hailed the full hour when God proclaims its birth,
A new and blissful paradise on earth.
Thrice oer the clime they flapped their dusky wings,
To lodge rich virtues in its secret springs,
And ere its gale and mortal banner furled,
Charm bound its shores, the asylum of the World.
Then bade the breezes waft Columbus on,
To crown the triumph which the hero won.
Columbus comes;—far *land* bedims the sky,
And rapture kindled in his eagle eye.
With awe struck soul, the trembling sailor feels
What man dishonoured, & what God reveals;
Found the first Eden's pomp of hills and woods,
Lost in vast Ocean's watery solitudes.
Like that rare bird the enamoured Ethiop praised
Whose peerless beauty all unworshipped blazed,
Gift of the Sun, his golden plumage shone,
In Afric's boundless solitudes,—alone.

Back to the crowded multitudes of men,
Swelled with glad tidings, came the sail again;
Europe's loud welcome bade the wanderers hail,
Delighted Wonder listened to their tale.
The eyes of men were fastened on the scene,
Whose distant beauty charmed with light serene.
Adventurous hosts, from Europe's tower-crowned shore,
Claimed boundless realms unvisited before;
But 'mid the shouts of rushing nations,—came,
And louder than the trumpet voice of fame,
Prophetic sounds, in solemn murmur heard,
The oracles of Fate breathed out the thrilling word.

—'When dying Europe mourns her lost renown,
'Her wasted honour, and her broken crown;
'When Vice and Ruin rend the earth with sin,
'And pour the deluge of destruction in,
'Corruption scorches with his tainted breath,
'And hundred-handed Havoc rides on death;—
'Be thou—fair land! their refuge, and their stay,
'The pillared gate to Glory's narrow way.
The sound had ceased, the unearthly host retired
Dark in the North,—and men, with awe, admired.

Time rolls away, but Nature stands the same;
Her starry host, her mountain wrapped in flame,
Earth, air, and heaven, which smiled benignant then
On those far travellers from the haunts of men,
With equal lustre now look calmly on
This youthful band,—this goal which they have won;
Perhaps bear with them, in their counsels high,
The *near* fulfilment of old prophecy;
And *we*, perchance, may claim with joy to be
The Ministers of Fate, the priests of Destiny.

Here, in the halls of Fate, we proudly stand,
Youth's holy fires by Hope's broad pinion fanned;
And while we wait what Destiny betides,
Gaze on the forms which fairy Fancy guides;
Bright apparitions floating on the air,
Which soft approaching claim a guardian care.
Shall I see *FORTUNE* wave her silken robe,
Or strong *AMBITION* comprehend the globe?
Shall warbling *MUSES* steal the soul away
To the rich stores of legendary lay?
Shall *HONOUR* trace the heraldry of Fame,
Or *BEAUTY* come, as Cleopatra came?—
—Not to dull sense shall forms like these appear,
But conscious feeling finds them hovering near.
These are the living principles, which weave

Lifes treacherous web, to flatter and deceive;
Through every age, they lead the lot of life,
And grasp the Urn with human fortunes rife
The early minstrel, when his kindling eye
Marked the bright stars illuminate the sky,
Saw these wild phantoms, in those planets, roll
The tides of fortune to their fearful goal.
There, robed in light, the Genii of the stars
Launch, in refulgent space, their diamond cars;
Or, in pavilions of celestial pride,
Serene above all influence beside,
Vent the bold joy, which swells the glorious soul,
Rich with the rapture of secure controul.
They read the silent mysteries of fate,
The slow revealings of the future state;
Trace the colossal shades of coming time,
Pregnant with unknown prodigies of crime,
While passing on, to ill-omened birth,
Low in the hapless atmosphere of earth.
—These were proud visions, and though part were feigned,
Enough of Truth's sweet union remained.

We may not stoop dull folly's round to creep,
And we must climb *Ambitions* rugged steep;
What though the toil should vex the soul with pain,—
Beyond its woes, there is a crown to gain.
We look for days of joy, and groves of peace,
Where all the turmoils of ambition cease;
We love that garland, which the scholar wears,
Who wreaths new blossoms with successive years,
Crouched in his cot, amid romantic bowers,
Domestic visions wing the happy hours,
When mellow eve shall paint the saffron sky,
And light the star of Hesperus on high,
Hush the wild warble of the lonely grove,
And charm the hamlet with the tales of love,
Then, the glad sire shall gather round his door,
His ruddy boys, to list his fairy lore;
By every soothing spell to Nature known
She courts him willing to her sylvan throne;

While, oer his sense, her bright enchantment steals,
Enamoured Memory all her stores reveals;
The star oft seen in youth's rejoicing prime
Rolls back his soul along the tides of time;
Recalls the spring-time of his health and pride,
His gay companions bounding at his side;
The reckless shout which shook the college hall, —
The classic lesson potent to appal, —
The gorgeous dreams which ardent fancy wove
To gild the blushing morning of his love; —
All these shall rise for Memory's brilliant theme,
And float in beauty, like an angel's dream.
The old man's fearless gaze salutes the sky,
Ere savage death hath shut his glazing eye.
When the grave closed oer Athens' laurelled son,
The fair-haired Muses wept in Helicon;
Be our's that tear, — fair Nature's holiest gem,
That song, for aye, shall be our requiem.

   But let not eager fancy roam so far,
Whose tale should now remind us what we are.
In this bright age, with seeds of glory sown,
The hand of fate hath placed us, — not our own.
When the old world is crumbling with decay,
And empires unregarded, pass away,
When the world's days of infancy are told,
And Nature's crowded destinies unfold,
Perhaps tis our's — when strength and grandeur fail,
And pride and power confess that man is frail,
When vanquished Virtue's reign is fully past,
And stern Corruption climbs the throne at last,
And men kneel down beneath that wasting sway, —
Perhaps tis our's to rend the veil away;
To bid men see their honour, and their bliss,
The proud connection of that world and this;
To shew the triumphs of a loftier scene,
Than on this humble ball hath ever been,
Ourselves, heavens honoured instruments prepared,
Whose little band even savage Death has spared.

Let not the censure of presumption blot
The venial boldness of aspiring thought;
For proudest deeds, the lowliest means are made,
Where the dark schemes of Providence are laid,
So when, of old, to strike a lawless sway,
The arm of Nemesis was shrined in clay,
When the black host of earthborn giants strove
To rend Olympus from the might of Jove,
When Terror reddened on the Almighty's cheek,
And even Jove's thunders whispered they were weak,
Then was the might, which blessed high heaven with peace,
Found in the arm of youthful Hercules;
So heaven may bid this young unhonoured land
Lead the long changes which mankind demand.

I seek no pardon if my wayward lays
Flow too profusely with my country's praise;
Shall a vain taunt proscribe my love of home,
Bid the heart sicken, sacred feeling roam?
Shall paltry ridicule assail the name,
Which twines its honours with Columbia's fame?
The man whose soul, with patriot ardor thrills
To scorn the proud world from his native hills?

But what be these but idle dreams of hope
Which soon shall fade, and leave the blind to grope?
Ah! what be these, amid the night of life,
The certain, near, inevitable strife?
We stand on slippery paths; the Ocean's roar
Is loud around us,—and the world, before;—
Thousands have crossed the gulf,—but few can tell
Of all that countless multitude—how well.
No glorious lustre gathers round their name,
Or gives their virtues to the trump of Fame.
As if men bless them with a brief renown,
Oh think how sadly purchased was that crown,
How malice blights the name it would destroy,
—Think on *Columbus chained*,—canst *thou* be crowned
    with joy?

When mighty thoughts come crowding on the soul,
And Fancy's dreams in sparkling lustre roll,
Let not the dreamer heed her baneful charms,
Perfidious smiles and Folly's winning arms;
Fancy and Hope in chill Despair shall end,
He clasps a viper whom he thought a *friend*,
And when he finds the rapture of renown,
—That crown of glory is a thorny crown.

We meet to part; then haste, no more delay
To bid farewell, and stretch our sail away;
And if a kindred sympathy shall rise
Here in the hearts, and friendships, which we prize,
Our heartfelt wish shall gratefully respond,
And God will sanction this fraternal bond.
And we shall cherish long this parting day,
When *Beauty* smiled to cheer us on our way.
Think not that heart, and feeling's vital glow
Part from the little pageant which we show,—
No; brightly shrined in Memory's hallowed cell,
All that we leave, and weep to leave, shall dwell.
    One debt of gratitude remains unpaid
To those who led us through Minerva's shade;
The thanks we offer, not by words expressed,
Let future years of grateful toil attest;
Be this our pride and boast to offer here
A freewill homage, grateful & sincere.

    There is no joy to tear ourselves away
From scenes endeared by life's young holiday.
When many days have dimmed the eye with tears,
And darkening round, the sky of life appears,
How will our hearts rejoice to look behind
On these old halls, and call the past to mind.
Spots, where while studies, friends, & pleasures bless,
We dreamed the dreams of youthful happiness;
Or learned to venerate the guardian care
Enthroned in Learning's consecrated Chair;
Where ancient Science, with a frown severe,
Appalled the trifler, as he ventured near;

Here where we learned to wield the *gun* and *quill*,
Recite in sections, and in sections drill:
Here where we learned, still studious to excel
In arts and arms, to cheer, and to *rebel*;
Recall the pleasant faces which we knew,
Which oft put on a sombre colouring too;
The strange vicissitudes of life, which speak
In anxious paleness, on the sufferer's cheek,
Who, while cold terror shakes his frame throughout,
Asks, with a ghastly smile, 'Are the *parts* out?'

And many a one, whose sorrow, & whose fears,
Like Arethusa, melt himself to tears,
Short youth; disaster trembles in his eye,
An inch too *short* to join "the Company."
In whom both art & nature joined to strive
To reach the lofty limit,—"five feet, five";
Perchance, in Commons Hall too sparely fed,
His hopes, alas! proved higher than his head.

Enough;—Affection may not linger here,
Repeating fond farewells, and vows sincere;
Impatient Time doth knit his sullen brow,
Gird up your loins for fates dread mandate now!
May Glory wait you on your proudest ways,
The wise applaud you, while the world obeys,
May Joy attend the journey which we fear,
And may God speed our perilous career!

From Frodmer's Drama "The Friends"

Malcolm, I love thee more than women love
And pure and warm and equal is the feeling
Which binds us and our destinies forever
But there are seasons in the change of times
When strong excitement kindles up the light
Of ancient memories

———————

Dedication

Quem fugis? Aut quis te nostris complexibus arcet?
Haec memorans, cinerem et sopitos suscitat ignes.
                                        Virgilian lot.

*This song to one whose unimproved talents and unattained
friendship have interested the writer in his character & fate.*

> By the unacknowledged tie
> Which binds us to each other
> By the pride of feeling high
> Which friendship's name can smother
>
> By the cold encountering eyes
> Whose language deeply thrilling
> Rebelled against the prompt surmise
> Which told the heart was willing;
>
> By all which you have felt and feel
> My eager gaze returning
> I offer to this silent zeal
> On youthful altars burning,
>
> All the classic hours which fill
> This little urn of honour;
> Minerva guide & pay the pen
> Your hand conferred upon her.

———————

Idealism

Deep in the soul a strong delusion dwells,
A curious round of fairly fashioned dreams;
Yet quietly, the pleasant vision swells
Its gay proportions far around; the streams
Of the wide universe their wealth supply,
Their everlasting sources furnish forth
The fabled splendours, whose immortal dye

Colours the scene with hues which mock the summer sky
And oh how sweetly, in youth's seraph soul,
That vision, like the light of heaven, doth rest
Its name is Life; its Hours their circle roll
Like angels in the robes of morning drest;
And every phantom of the train is blest
Who shakes his plumes upon the odorous air,
Or lights a star upon his azure crest
And while the lovely beam reposes there
Joy in the guileless heart his welcome will prepare

I spread my gorgeous sail
Upon a starless sea
And oer the deep with a chilly gale
My painted bark sailed fast & free—

Old Ocean shook his waves
Beneath the roaring wind,
But the little keel of the mariner braves
The foaming abyss, & the midnight blind.

The firmament darkened overhead,
Below, the surges swelled,—
My bark ran low in the watery bed,
As the tempest breath its course compelled.

I took my silver lyre,
And waked its voice on high;—
The wild blasts were hushed to admire,
And the stars looked out from the charmed sky.

Bear me then, ye wild waters,
To Apollo's Delphian isle,
My name is *Music*, in Castalie known,
Where bowers of joy the Nine beguile.—

A Shout to the Shepherds

Freshly, gaily, the rivulet flows
Beside its emerald bank
Each silver bubble in beauty goes
Adown the stream & briefly glows
Till it reach the broad flags & the alders dank.
   Shepherds, who love the lay
Of untaught bards in oaken shades
Brighteyed Apollos of the forest glades
   Hither, hither, turn your way.
Come to the grassy border of the brook
Here where the ragged hawthorn dips
His prickly buds of perfume in the wave
And thence again a costly fragrance sips
Drinking with each balmy floweret's lips
Pure from the Naiad's welling urn
While overhead the embowering elms
Bow their broad branches & keep out the day.
   Hither, hither, turn your way.
     Good bye.

I wear no badge; no tinsel star
Glitters upon my breast;
Nor jewelled crown nor victor's car
Rob me of rest.

I am not poor, but I am proud
Of one inalienable right,
Above the envy of the crowd—
Thought's holy light.

Better it is than gems or gold,
And oh! it cannot die,
But thought will glow when the Sun grows cold,
And mix with Deity.

———————

I love thy music, mellow bell,
I love thine iron chime,
To life or death, to heaven or hell,
Which calls the Sons of Time.

Thy voice upon the deep
The homebound sea-boy hails,
It charms his cares to sleep,
It cheers him as he sails.

To house of God & heavenly joys
Thy summons called our sires,
And good men thought thy sacred voice
Disarmed the thunder's fires.

And soon thy music, sad death-bell!
Shall lift its notes once more,
And mix my requiem with the wind
That sweeps my native shore.

———————

I rake no coffined clay, nor publish wide
The resurrection of departed pride
Safe in their ancient crannies dark & deep
Let kings & conquerors saints & soldiers sleep.
Late in the world too late perchance for fame
Just late enough to reap abundant blame
I choose a novel theme, a bold abuse
Of critic charters, an unlaurelled muse.

Old mouldy men & books & names & lands
Disgust my reason & defile my hands
I had as lief respect an ancient shoe
As love Old things *for age*, & hate the new.

I spurn the Past, my mind disdains its nod
Nor kneels in homage to so mean a god.
I laugh at those who while they   & gaze
The bald antiquity of China praise.
Youth is (whatever Cynic tubs pretend)
The fault that boys & nations soonest mend.

———————

O What have I to do
With merriment & jollities
Youths golden hair & sparkling eyes?
And deafening games that children prize

I am not made to tune a lute
Nor amble in a soft saloon
Nor mine the grace of kind salute
To mien of pride & heart of stone

My pulse is slow my blood is cold
My stammering tongue is rudely tuned

I care not who shall kiss the cup
That Fashion holds to Beauty up
Nor who shall slip thro' the smiling throng
With honied lyes upon his tongue
The swift hours that go singing by
Tell not the triflers they must die

Man to his work the merry to their wine
Friend to his friend folly to festivals
All hopes & humors to their several ends
Sages to schools, young Passion to its love
Ambition to its task and me to mine.
I am not charged with dallying messages
That thus I mingle in this glittering crowd
Seeing with strange eyes their buffooneries

I am not tangled in the cobweb net
That wanton Beauty weaves for youth so knit
To some fair maid he follows with his eye
A sterner errand to the silken troop
Has quenched the uneasy blush that warmed my cheek
I am commissioned in my day of joy
To leave my woods & streams & the sweet sloth
Of prayer & song that were my dear delight
To leave the rudeness of my woodland life
Sweet twilight walks and midnight solitude
And kind acquaintance with the morning stars
& the smooth passage of my household hours
The innocent mirth which sweetens daily bread
Railing in love at those who rail again by mind's industry
          sharpening the love of life
Books, Muses, study, fireside, friends, & love,
I loved ye with true love, so fare ye well.

    I was a boy; boyhood slid gaily by
And the impatient years that trod on it
Taught me new lessons in the lore of life.

I've learned the burthen of that sad history
All woman born do know, that hoped for days
Days that come dancing on fraught with delights
Dash our blown hopes as they limp heavily by
But I—the bantling of a country Muse
Abandon all those toys with speed to obey
The King whose meek ambassador I go.

———————

Have ye seen the caterpillar
Foully warking in his nest?
Tis the poor man getting siller,
Without cleanness, without rest.

Have you seen the butterfly
In braw claithing drest?
Tis the poor man gotten rich,
In rings & painted vest.

The poor man crawls in web of rags,
And sore bested with woes,
But when he flees on riches' wings,
He laugheth at his foes.

———————

The panoply of Paradise is mine
No armourer wrought it on Eteian forge
No dear luxurious maiden brought the gift
By lying bards profanely deemed divine
I am clad in mail of celestial proof
I brandish Michael's sword of flame
And I come to quell the pride of the world
But avaunt these toys of poesy Why wrap
The fiery truths in riddles dark
Truth treads on the pride of Plato
Truth treads on lovesick rhymes
The fashion of riddling priests
The trick of Delphos & Dodona
The cunning of Homer & Hesiod
Mischievous polytheists who deceived mankind
These delusions are overpast.
The altar of the Capitoline god is crushed
The spindle of ancient Fate is broken
The sisters do not spin the eternal thread
There is no fire glowing on Persic mountains
Where the sun was greeted with fragrant spikenard
The Nile breeds crocodiles in his slime

And the pyramids are by great Alcairo
But the swarthy votary will not adore the reptile
And the dead oppressor is not entombed in the piles
The immortal Gods are deceased
Go let your fabled muses chant their obituary.
    Do you see how the world slides away
How its huge pomps dwindle to unsubstantial things
Tho' they were dear to the heart & solid to the eye
There is a sentence on the lip of Tully
That Truth shall last tho' the fabrics of imagination decay.
Many incidents up & down in the world shall verify
The simple oracle.
The proud hieroglyphic shall be the child's bauble alphabet
The spectral tale that blanched the forefather's cheek
Makes merriment for vermillion maids.
Fools judge by outside show, for while
The champion vanquishes in vain
And armed kings are met unprofitably
(Great things that have no harvest home)
The unconscious wit scratches his paper in a corner
And the words that are writ
Burn like pains in ten thousand memories
And are chanted in thunder to the four winds.
And the pillars of social fabrics are shaken at the sound like
    bulrushes.

————

No fate, save by the victim's fault, is low,
For God hath writ all dooms magnificent,
So guilt not traverses his tender will.

————

When success exalts thy lot
God for thy virtue lays a plot;
And all thy life is for thy own
Then for mankind's instruction shewn;
And, tho' thy knees were never bent,
To heaven thy hourly prayers are sent,
And whether formed for good or ill,
Are registered & answered still.

———————

The spirits of the wise, sit on the clouds
And mock the ambition of man
For his breath is vapour; his beauty the colour of a cloud
And his body & soul are parted by a sun, a storm
Or the feeble fork of a poor worm
And who shall tell his household
Whither the soul of the dead man is gone.
Is it gone to live in torture
Enduring a dread resurrection into pain
And perceive mortal plagues in an immortal body
Sighing to the heavy centuries, that bring
No light no hope in their immeasurable train?
Is it gone to farther regions of unequal lot
To a land where the colours of love & disgust
Are blended anew in the texture of the web
And the web is stained with black & bloody clouds.
Is it gone to harmonies of joy
To the ardour of virtue & the wealth of truth
Is it gone to blank oblivion
The mockery of hope & virtue & the death of God.
Alas! Alas! Alas!
Wo is me! for the sad survivor
Tho' Fortune threw good not evil in his way
Showering the roses of pleasure & the laurel of Fame
Whilst his brother breasted the driving snows
Alas for the sad survivor.
He walks the long streets of his native City

But the peopled street is like the desolate sea.
Men study his face and its lofty lines
And love the graceful tones of pride & power
Rolled with rich thunder of eloquent words.
In the bosom of his own land.
They love him and they honour him
And they think his heart leaps at the voice of their praise.
But their thoughts are dark & their eyes are dim
And they cannot see that a noble nature
Must pine or be matched with noble things.
It is ill with the living, it is well with the dead.
It is better with the dead who live
Than it is with the living who die daily.
Oh Life, thou art a house wherein Fears inhabit
And when Man, poor pilgrim, enters the doors
They flock unto him with icy hands
They lead him in their shivering company
And if he come to a shining room
They tell him it leads to a dungeon tower.

―――――――

Let not conceited sages laugh aloud
Because another ventures from the crowd
And all unblushing in the sun assumes
The bard's derided bays—ridiculous to grooms.
I know a rabble of misguided men
Have seized with untaught hand the poet's pen
And alien born to morals & to mind
Usurped the laureate pomp & mocked mankind.
I know the Muses kept their shells unstrung
And hid their starcrowned heads while Dulness sung
Men of vain hearts but uninstructed souls
Talk out the madness of their midnight bowls

―――――――

My days roll by me like a train of dreams
A host of joyless undistinguished forms
Cloud after cloud my firmament deforms
While the sweet Eye of Heaven his purple gleams
Pour in rich rivers of Promethean beams
On all his ample family beside
On me on me the day forgets to dawn
Encountering darkness clasps me like a bride
Tombs rise around and from each cell forlorn
Starts with an ominous cry some ghastly child
Of death & darkness, summoning me to mourn
Companion of the clod brother of worms—
The future has no hope and memory mild
Gives not the blessed light that once my woes beguiled.

One hand washes the other.
I'll not pilfer a victory.
I'll not be a moth of peace
I'll turn my plumed helm into a skillet.

Whoso alas is young
And being young is wise
And deaf to saws of gray advice
Hath listened when the Muses sung
And heard with joy when on the wind the shell of Clio rung

In tender youth if he was proud
Nor would his gentle soul profane
And loathed the arts of gain
Assorted with the rabble crowd
But shared his soul with few, or sauntered lone & proud

When thy soul
Is filled with a just image fear not thou
Lest halting rhymes or unharmonious verse
Cripple the fair Conception Leave the heart
Alone to find its language. In all tongues
It hath a sovereign instinct that doth teach
An eloquence which rules can never give.
In the high hour when Destiny ordains
That thou bear testimony to its dooms
That hour a guiding spirit shall impart
The fervid utterance art could never find
Wait then, stern friend, wait in majestic peace.

The blackbird's song the blackbird's song
Still still it warbles in my ear
Tho' I have travelled many a mile
From the sweet woods where the bird is found.

The sound rings shrilly in my ear
It vibrates strong on every nerve
Impels the blood in a swifter tide
And riots thro' all the house of life.

It hurries me back my sense my eye
My ear, my heart, to the dusky lake
Whose silent margin I trod alone
When the morn sent me on my way.

The sun was veiled in summer clouds
Nor spared one beam to welcome me
The wind in the chambers of the mount
Lay couched nor breathed his gay good morrow.

But where the chestnut & the oak
Fringed the smooth lake with leaves
And on the slender boughs of the birch
And amid the berries of the cedar tree

There tilting & shaking down the dew
Sang his good song the merry blackbird
Quoth he, I hope you like music young man—
For I'm determined to be heard.

And straightway as he sang, the sound
Woke every bird in the silent woods
On a thousand sprays, above around
They poured their notes to the sylvan gods.

Then the shy ducks that were swimming there
Skirred along the lake to a distant cove
And the pelican started from the reeds
And poised his broad wings on the morning air.

And I am here
On the green earth contemplating the moon
Much marvelling what may betide tomorrow
I love my life

———————

I am an exile from my home; heavily
And all alone I walk the long sea shore
And find no joy. The trees the bushes talk to me
And the small fly that whispers in my ear.
    Ah me I do not love the look
       Of foreign men
    And wo is me that I forsook
    My little home my lamp my book
    To find across the foaming seas
       This cheerless fen.

———————

He must have
Droll fancies sometimes cross his quiet thoughts,
Who in my vagrant verse shall look to find
A holiday from study or from toil,
And consolation to his mortal care.
Such idler will not be a man of name,
But must be, & therein resembles me,
A little liable to ridicule,
Because he cares a particle too much
For the opinion of the fickle world;
And notes how Merit does not swim to place
In th' tides of this world,—& feels the scandal oft
Of low salute to men of meaner mould;
And yet has felt, albeit with scorn the while,
A kind of justice in the Seneschal,
The uncivil fate, that made his fortunes vile.
I am frank, my friend, your eye has found
A gipsy muse that reads your lineaments
To tell the faithful fortunes of your life.
Go to, I'll feed my humour to the full,
And still expand the pleasant commentary.
    Who loves my verse is one whose roving eye
Detects more beauty than his tongue will own
In art & nature. Nay his traitor tongue
Sometimes consenting to the coxcomb's jest,
Derides the beauty which delights his soul.
He is a man, who, though he told it not,
Mourned in the hour of manhood whilst he saw
The rich imagination which had tinged
Each earthly thing with hues from paradise
Forsake forever his instructed eye,
Bewailed its loss & felt how dearly bought
Is wisdom at the price of happiness.
Ah me, sometimes in
And sometimes when the dainty southwind blew
Its soft luxurious airs, & called the clouds
Mustering their hosts from all the sunny bays,—
Then when the piping wind & sounding sea
And tossing boughs combined their cadences,
The sweet & solemn melody they made

Enticed him oft in heady wantonness
To scoff at knowledge, mock the forms of life,
Cast off his years & be a boy again.
Then has he left his books, & vulgar cares,
And sallied forth across the freshened fields
With all the heart of highborn cavalier
In quest of forest glades hid from the sun,
And dim enchantments that therein abide.

I had rather follow him than talk to him;
Fast fast he leaves the villages behind,
As one who loathed them, yet he loathes them not,
And snuffs the scents which on the dallying gale
The woods send out as gentle harbingers
Bro't from their inmost glens to lure the step
Of the pleased pilgrim to their alleys green.
I know the pleasures of this humour well
And, please you, reader, I'll remember them.
First the glad sense of solitude, the sure
The absolute deliverance from the yoke
Of social forms, that are as tedious
Oft to a fretful & romantic man
As a musquito's song at summer eve.
In the wood he is alone, & for the hollow chat
Of men that do not love, & will not think,
He has the unpretending company
Of birds & squirrels & the fine race of flowers.
He forms his friendships with the flowers
Whose habits or whose hue may please him best,
Goes by the red & yellow populace
That with their vulgar beauty spot the plain
To find the honoured orchis—seldom seen,
The low pyrola with a lilac's smell,
Or the small cinque-foil, the wild strawberry's friend.
He speculates with love on Natures forms
Admires a calyx much as Winkelmann
The architecture of a Doric Pile
Not more he doated on the [   ]
Of frieze or triglyph or on architrave,
Than doth this dreamer, on the slender shaft

With awns & stipules graced, that lifts in air
The lily or the loosestrife, tapestried with leaves.
And close below
The faithful capsule to transmit its race
Like from its like to another year of flowers,
Once more to be the food of tuneful bird
Low stooping on swift wing, or busy bee,
Or the small nameless eaters that can find
A country in a leaf. —

St. Augustine

For fifteen winter days
I sailed upon the deep, & turned my back
Upon the Northern lights, & burning Bear,
On the twin Bears fast tethered to the Pole
And the cold orbs that hang by them in heaven,
Till star by star they sank into the sea.
Full swelled the sail before the driving wind,
Till the stout pilot turned his prow to land,
Where peered, mid orange groves & citron boughs,
The little city of Saint Augustine.

Slow slid the vessel to the fragrant shore,
Loitering along Matanzas' sunny waves,
And under Anastasia's verdant isle.
I saw Saint Mark's grim bastions, piles of stone
Planting their deep foundations in the sea,
And speaking to the eye a thousand things
Of Spain, a thousand heavy histories.
Under these bleached walls of old renown
Our ship was moored.
                    —An hour of busy noise,
And I was made a quiet citizen,
Pacing my chamber in a Spanish street.
An exile's bread is salt, his heart is sad, —
Happy, he saith, the eye that never saw
The smoke ascending from a stranger's fire!

        Yet much is here
Than can beguile the months of banishment
To the pale travellers whom Disease hath sent
Hither for genial air from Northern homes.
Oh many a tragic story can be read,—
Dim vestiges of a romantic past,
Within the small peninsula of sand.
Here is the old land of America
And in this sea-girt nook, the infant steps
First foot-prints of that Genius giant-grown
That daunts the nations with his power today.

Inquisitive of such, I walk alone
Along the narrow streets, unpaved & old,
Among few dwellers, and the jealous doors
And windows barred upon the public way.

                I explored
The castle & the ruined monastery
Unpeopled town, ruins of streets of stone,
Pillars upon the margin of the sea,
With worn inscriptions oft explored in vain,
Then with a keener scrutiny, I marked
The motley population. Hither come
The forest families, timid & tame
Not now as once with stained tomahawk
The restless red man left his council fire,
Or when, with Mexique art, he painted haughtily
On canvas woven in his boundless woods
His simple symbols for his foes to read.
Not such an one is yon poor vagabond
Who in unclean & sloven apathy
Brings venison from the forest,—silly trade.
Alas! red men are few, red men are feeble,
They are few & feeble, & must pass away.—
                — — And here,
The dark Minorcan, sad & separate,
Wrapt in his cloak, strolls with unsocial eye:
By day, basks idle in the sun, then seeks his food
All night upon the waters, stilly plying

His hook & line in all the moonlit bays.
Here steals the sick man with uncertain gait
Looks with a feeble spirit at things around
As if he sighing said, "What is't to me?
"I dwell afar;—far from this cheerless fen
"My wife, my children strain their eyes to me
"And oh! in vain. Wo, wo is me! I feel
"In spite of hope, these wishful eyes no more
"Shall see New England's wood-crowned hills again."

   x   x   x   x   x

(Here is a chasm very much to be regretted in the original
    manuscript.)

   x   x   x   x   x   x

There liest thou, little city of the deep,
And alway hearest the unceasing sound
By day & night in summer & in frost,
The roar of waters on thy coral shore.
But softening southward in thy gentle clime
Even the rude sea relents to clemency,
Feels the kind ray of that benignant sun
And pours warm billows up the beach of shells.
Farewell; & fair befall thee, gentle town!
The prayer of those who thank thee for their life,
The benison of those thy fragrant airs,
And simple hospitality hath blest,
Be to thee ever as the rich perfume
Of a good name, & pleasant memory!

Awed I behold once more
My old familiar haunts; here the blue river
The same blue wonder that my infant eye
Admired, sage doubting whence the traveller came,—
Whence brought his sunny bubbles ere he washed
The fragrant flag roots in my father's fields,
And where thereafter in the world he went.

Look, here he is unaltered, save that now
He hath broke his banks & flooded all the vales
With his redundant waves.

Here is the rock where yet a simple child
I caught with bended pin my earliest fish,
Much triumphing,—And these the fields
Over whose flowers I chased the butterfly,
A blooming hunter of a fairy fine.
And hark! where overhead the ancient crows
Hold their sour conversation in the sky.
        These are the same, but I am not the same
But wiser than I was, & wise enough
Not to regret the changes, tho' they cost
Me many a sigh. Oh call not Nature dumb;
These trees & stones are audible to me,
These idle flowers, that tremble in the wind,
I understand their faery syllables,
And all their sad significance. This wind,
That rustles down the well-known forest road—
It hath a sound more eloquent than speech.
The stream, the trees, the grass, the sighing wind,
All of them utter sounds of admonishment
And grave parental love.

They are not of our race, they seem to say,
And yet have knowledge of our moral race,
And somewhat of majestic sympathy,
Something of pity for the puny clay,
That holds & boasts the immeasureable mind.

I feel as if I were welcome to these trees
After long months of weary wandering,
Acknowledged by their hospitable boughs;
They know me as their son, for side by side,
They were coeval with my ancestors,
Adorned with them my country's primitive times,
And soon may give my dust their funeral shade.

———————

An ancient lady who dwelt in Rome
Bro't Tarquin the King her Album from home
Nine ponderous volumes conveyed in a cart
And mentioned that this was only a part
And requested the monarch to buy the nine tomes
At a price he thought might buy nine Romes.
The unmannerly king refused to buy
A lady's Album appraised so high,
And she, to show her honest ire,
Threw the three first volumes into the fire,
And offered the king the rest of her lore
At the price she had fixed for the nine before.
The king was amazed at the lady's story,
But the argument now was an *a fortiori*,
And he flatly refused to redeem the volumes,
Whatever might be or might not in their columns.
The lady departed, & straightway burned
Three more of the six, & then returned

———————

Be of good cheer, brave spirit; steadfastly
Serve that low whisper thou hast served; for know,
God hath a select family of Sons
Now scattered wide thro' earth, & each alone,
Who are thy spiritual kindred, & each one
By constant service to that inward law,
Is rearing the sublime proportions
Of a true monarch's soul. Beauty & Strength
The riches of a spotless memory,
The eloquence of truth, the wisdom got
By searching of a clear & loving eye
That seeth as God seeth   These are their gifts
And Time who keeps God's word brings on the day
To seal the marriage of these minds with thine
Thine everlasting lovers. Ye shall be
The salt of all the elements, world of the world

The winds are cold, the days are dark,
In this unlovely land
The East wind rises with the tide
To chill the populous strand

Above me shines no Syrian moon
With warm luxurious glow,
Nor golden orange groves at noon
Perfume the world below.

Yet more I prize this frozen land,
This iron soil of ours,
Than fields by Indian breezes fanned
And crimsoned oer with flowers

Written in Sickness

I bear in youth the sad infirmities
That use to undo the limb & sense of age:
It hath pleased Heaven to break the dream of bliss
Which lit my onward way with bright presage,
And my unserviceable limbs forego
The sweet delight I found in fields & farms,
On windy hills, whose tops with morning glow,
And lakes, smooth mirrors of Aurora's charms.
Yet I think on them in the silent night,
Still breaks that morn, though dim, to Memory's eye
And the firm soul does the pale train defy
Of grim Disease, that would her peace affright.
Please God, I'll wrap me in mine innocence
And bid each awful Muse drive the damned harpies hence.

———————

Oil & Wine,
Sparkling gems, & rich attire,
House & lands that men desire,
 —Ye may seek at Plutus' shrine.

High renown,
Plaudits from desiring throngs,
Echoed far by poets songs
 Are dowry to the Victors crown.

Royal state,
Diamond star, & cap of gold,
Bedizened throne, how hard to hold!
 —Are got by force, or fraud, or fate.

Man must learn—.
In haunts of care, in fields of strife,
Are bought the glittering goods of life,
 These to ashes turn.

But go thou home,
Home to the mansion of the mind,
If solid good thy search would find,
 In the bright bower of Joy, & Thought's
 immortal dome.

———————

All that thy virgin soul can ask be thine
Beautiful Ellen   Let this prayer be mine
The first devotion that my soul has paid
To mortal grace it pays to thee fair maid
I am enamoured of thy loveliness
Lovesick with thy sweet beauty which shall bless
With its glad light my path of life around
Which now is joyless where thou art not found
Now am I stricken with the sympathy
That binds the whole world in electric tie
I hail love's birth within my hermit breast
And welcome the bright ordinance to be blest
I was a hermit whom the lone Muse cheers,
I sped apart my solitary years,
I found no joy in woman's meaning eye
When Fashion's merry mob were dancing by;
Yet had I read the law all laws above,
—Great Nature hath ordained the heart to love—
Yet had I heard that in this mortal state
To every mind exists its natural mate,
That God at first did marry soul to soul
Tho' lands divide & seas between them roll.
Then eagerly I searched each circle round
I panted for my mate, but no mate found
I saw bright eyes, fair forms, complexions fine,
But not a single soul that spoke to mine.
At last the star broke thro' the hiding cloud,
At last I found thee in the silken crowd
I found thee, Ellen, born to love & shine,
And I who found am blessed to call thee mine.

———

That wandering fire to me appears
Albeit a tiny spark
Older than the oldest spheres
That glow in the heavens dark

———

Though her eye seek other forms
And a glad delight below
Yet the love the world that warms
Bids for me her bosom glow

She must love me till she find
Another heart as large & true
Her soul like mine is unconfined
And the world has only two

If Nature hold another heart
That knows a purer flame than we
I too therein would challenge part
And learn of love a new degree

———————

Dear Ellen, many a golden year
May ripe, then dim, thy beauty's bloom
But never shall the hour appear
In sunny joy, in sorrow's gloom,
When aught shall hinder me from telling
My ardent love, all loves excelling.

The spot is not in the rounded earth,
In cities vast, in islands lone,
Where I will not proclaim thy worth,
And glory that thou art mine own;
Will you, nill you, I'll say I love thee,
Be the moon of June or of March above thee.

And when this porcelain clay of thine
Is laid beneath the cold earth's flowers,
And close beside reposes mine,
Prey to the sun & air & showers,
I'll find thy soul in the upper sphere,
And say I love thee in Paradise here.

———————

I call her beautiful; — she says
Go to; your words are idle;
My lips began to speak her praise,
My lips she tried to bridle.
But, Ellen, I must tell you this,
Your prohibition wasted is,
Unless among your things you find
A little jail to hold the mind;
If you should dazzle out mine eyes,
As dimmer suns sometimes have done,
My sleepless ears, those judges wise,
Would say, Tis the *voice* of the Peerless one.
And if your witchery decree
That my five senses closed should be,
The little image in my soul
Is Ellen out of Ellen's controul,
And whilst I live in the Universe
I will say tis my beauty, for better, for worse.

I've found the dainty malice out
Of Ellen's hypocritic eye
She's wound her gipsy nets about

I thought it was no harm to watch
The features of an artless maid

And do I waste my time
Scribbling of love to my beautiful queen
And is it idle to talk in prose & rhyme
Of one who at midnight & morning's prime
In daylight is fancied, in visions seen?
And do I forget the burning crown
That Glory should weave of light for me

———

And though he dearly prized the bards of fame
His sweetest poem was one maiden's name

———

And Ellen, when the greybeard years
Have brought us to life's Evening hour
And all the crowded Past appears
A tiny scene of sun & shower.——

Then, if I read the page aright
Where Hope the soothsayer reads our lot,
Thyself shalt own the page was bright
Well that we loved wo had we not.

When Mirth is dumb & Flattery's fled
And thy mute music's dearest tone
When all but Love itself is dead,
And all but deathless Reason gone

———

The brave Empedocles defying fools
Pronounced the word that mortals hate to hear
"I am divine I am not mortal made
I am superior to my human weeds"
Not sense but Reason is the Judge of truth
Reason's twofold; part human part divine
That human part may be described & taught
The other portion language cannot speak

———

Dear brother, would you know the life
Please God, that I would lead?
On the first wheels that quit this weary town
Over yon western bridges I would ride
And with a cheerful benison forsake
Each street & spire & roof incontinent.
Then would I seek where God might guide my steps,
Deep in a woodland tract, a sunny farm,
Amid the mountain counties, Hants Franklin Berks,
Where down the rock ravine a river roars,
Even from a brook, & where old woods
Not tamed & cleared, cumber the ample ground
With their centennial wrecks.
Find me a slope where I can feel the sun
And mark the rising of the early stars.
There will I bring my books, my household gods,
The reliquaires of my dead saint, & dwell
In the sweet odor of her memory.
There, in the uncouth solitude, unlock
My stock of art, plant dials, in the grass,
Hang in the air a bright thermometer,
And aim a telescope at the inviolate Sun.

———

Dost thou not hear me Ellen
Is thy ear deaf to me
Is thy radiant eye
Dark that it cannot see

In yonder ground thy limbs are laid
Under the snow
And earth has no spot so dear above
As that below

And there I know the heart is still
And the eye is shut & the ear is dull

But the spirit that dwelt in mine
The spirit wherein mine dwelt
The soul of Ellen the thought divine
From God, that came—for all that felt

Does it not know me now
Does it not share my thought
Is it prisoned from Waldo's prayer
Is its glowing love forgot

———————

Teach me I am forgotten by the dead
And that the dead is by herself forgot
And I no longer would keep terms with me.
I would not murder, steal, or fornicate,
Nor with ambition break the peace of towns
But I would bury my ambition
The hope & action of my sovereign soul
In miserable ruin. Not a hope
Should ever make a holiday for me
I would not be the fool of accident
I would not have a project seek an end
That needed aught
Beyond the handful of my present means
The sun of Duty drop from his firmament
To be a rushlight for each petty end
I would not harm my fellow men
On this low argument, *'twould harm myself*

———————

Why should I live
The future will repeat the past
Yet cannot give
Again the Vision beautiful too beautiful to last
And o perhaps the welcome stroke
That severs forever this fleshly yoke
Shall restore the vision to the soul
In the great Vision of the Whole.

———————

Shall the Muse sing for thousands & not sing
For thee a Muse thyself of sweetest lay
I would forget my
What is life for & what is Memory
If it wants room for thee Is it a curse
Can it contain all painful circumstance
Each dull degrading fact & make life stale
With its street calendar its tavern roll
And can it not sanctify itself with thee
Yea fill the soul with odoriferous thought
By limning there thy lineaments in the serene
& Spiritual beauty God drest thee withal
And write the story of an angel's life
And all thy ministry to thine & mine
And me

Shalt thou go to thy grave unsung
Shall no flower be plucked for thee
Shall no rites be paid no death bell rung
When the desire of all eyes is gone

'Tis well for we
Are on the outside of that world
Wherein thou enterest fair & free
And all the rites we pay
Are symbols bodily
Gropings in the dark
Around the door

Thou art gone in to God
Thou walkest in heaven's day
Thou talkest with the seraphim
The select sons of truth
Thou addest a verse to their hymn
And curious speculation occupies
Thy radiant eyes
Every thought fresh wonders brings
On his planetary wings
And every thought is a chapel where
Thou perfumest heaven with prayer
And the eldest born of Godhead say
What star beams new on us today
And yet thou hast a bond on earth
Which thou wilt keep in heaven
The nearer to the throne thou goest
The more place it will have in thy holy breast.

For I know that the Universe cannot blot
From a holy soul its true record
And so on a cherub's wings I fly
To the Holy of Holies of the Lord

If the heart is raised by heavenly choirs
That which here made heaven is not lost
And so I rise on her risen desires
Amid the pure martyrs' host.

If there is joy when a sinner comes
There's sympathy when
The dust lies on thy head
In the dark sepulchre
Thou hast gone alone to thy bed
Peace calm peace to her,
But oh what funeral is thine
My holy wife
Sad thoughts in every kindred breast
That knew thou hadst passed from life
And in the breast you loved

In the Soul that was dear to you
Dark hopeless visions roved
And a perpetual yew

And every day renews
The unrepaired regret

What from this barren being do we reap
And what shall hinder the wise
From lying down to sleep in the earth
The innocent child is dead
The blushing cheek of youth is cold
Genius hath untimely fled
Nor hath the world a face
To fill thy vacant place
O radiant daughter of light & love
Too rich in the graces that dwell above
To be lent long to the sinful earth
God had garnished with thy birth.
Thou wert pure as they are not
Who dwell upon this murky spot
And every thing that's fair below.

Dust unto dust! and shall no more be said
Ellen for thee, and shall a common fate
Blend thy last hour with the last hours of all?
Of thee my wife, my undefiled, my dear?
The muse thy living beauty could inspire
Shall spare one verse to strew thy urn
Or be forever silent. Ellen is dead
She who outshone all beauty yet knew not
That she was beautiful, she who was fair

After another mould than flesh & blood.
Her beauty was of God—The maker's hand
Yet rested on his work,
And cast an atmosphere of sanctity
Around her steps that pleased old age & youth.
Yea that not won the eye, but did persuade
The soul by realizing human hopes,
Teaching that faith & love were not a dream,
Teaching that purity had yet a shrine,
And that the innocent & affectionate thoughts
That harbour in the bosom of a child
Might live embodied in a riper form,
And dwell with wisdom never bought by sin.
Blessed, sweet singer, were the ears that heard
To her, the eye that saw, bare witness.
The holy light of her eye did prophesy
The impatient heaven that called her hence.

———————

The days pass over me,
And I am still the same;
The aroma of my life is gone
With the flower with which it came.

———————

Why fear to die
And let thy body lie
Under the flowers of June
Thy body food
For the groundworm's brood
And thy grave smiled on by the visiting moon

Amid great Nature's halls,
Girt in by mountain walls,
And washed with waterfalls,

It would please me to die,
Where every wind that sweeps my tomb
Goes loaded with a free perfume,
Dealt out with a God's charity.

I should like to lie in sweets,
A hill's leaves for winding sheets,
And the searching sun to see
That I'm laid with decency
And the commissioned wind to sing
His mighty Psalm from fall to spring
And annual tunes commemorate
Of nature's child the common fate.

———————

I am alone. Sad is my solitude.
O thou sweet daughter of God, my angel wife,
Why dost thou leave me thus in the great stranger world
Without one sign or token, one remembrancer
Sent o'er the weary lands that sunder us
To say I greet thee with a beating heart.
Does thy heart beat with mine? does thy blue eye
Ever look northward with desire, O do thy prayers
Remember me when thou hallowest thy maker's name,
Remember him
Who never failed to grace his orison
With thy dear name, believes it acceptable
And prays, that he may pray for thee—

———————

On thee has God conferred
A bodily presence mean as Paul's
Yet made thee bearer of a word
That sleepy nations as with trumpet calls

O noble heart accept
With equal thanks the talent & disgrace
The splendid town unwept
Nourish thy power in a private place.

Think not that unattended
By heavenly Powers thou steal'st to solitude
Nor even on earth all unbefriended
Tho no sweet rabble shouts on thee intrude

Let Webster's lofty face
Ever on thousands shine
A beacon set that Freedoms race
Might gather omens from that radiant sign.

————————

All the great & good,
And all the fair,
As if in a disdainful mood,
Forsake the world, & to the grave repair.

Is there a sage
Needed to curb the unruly times; —
He hastes to quit the stage,
And blushing leaves his country to its crimes.

Is there an angel drest
In weeds of mortal beauty, whom high Heaven
With all sweet perfections doth invest; —
It hastes to take what it hath given.

And, as the delicate snow
Which latest fell, the thieving wind first takes
So thou, dear wife, must go,
As frail, as spotless, as those new fallen flakes.

Let me not fear to die,
But let me live so well,
As to win this mark of death from on high,
That I with God, & thee, dear heart, may dwell.

———————

Seemed to me—never maid
Wore the poor weeds of hapless womanhood
With such a brave sustained purity.
She felt no shame that she was mortal

———————

Where art thou
Thou beautiful dream
Whom every grace & every joy
Clothed in sunbeams dearest, best
Whom every fleeting hour in new graces drest
And every wondering eye that saw thee blest

Where art thou now
Sad I miss thy beaming brow
I miss thy radiant eye
The joyful noon of my life is past
My sun is set my moon is gone
Each star of hope sunk one by one
And in this cold, damp, silent eve of life
I walk alone oh Ellen, oh my wife.

One by one those graces come
Day by day to memory's eye
Which thou worest as a robe
And I live over thy history
Thy thots were wove in beauty
Wisdom drest in dewbright flowers;
And sad & sportive hours
Had swelled alike the potent melody

———

I live among ideal men
I know graces
I cannot find in human faces
And I would gladly know
Where I got my vision,
If the earth does not hold its archetype

With open eye & ear
I move thro all this world of men
And well their various gifts discern
What I cannot do, they do
If I do not covet their powers
Not less do I mark & prize them

Yet still from all its journeys wide
The eye comes back unsatisfied
No living man can yet pretend
To earn the sacred name of Friend.

And that wherein alike all fail
Is the easiest part of virtue
To wit, simplicity & truth
The native ornaments of human youth.

———

What avails it me
That I have many friends
If when my walking ends
I come back to a lonely house

What boots it that I dwell
In a city free and rich and old
If the long streets never hold
The only form I love

What avails it I have bread
Raiment and books and leisure
Access to wisdom and to pleasure
If Ellen still is dead

In my chamber she is not
From my parlour joy is gone
Round the house I roam and groan
The glory of my house is fled

What avails it me
That I have many thoughts
That the nimble brain can run
Through all lands that see the sun
Hath a record of each race
That have had a dwelling place

If only I have right of seeing
In this wilderness of being
And from the vision glorious
Must come back to my lonely house.

———————

She never comes to me
She promised me a thousand times
That she would dearly dearly love me
That in sickness & in health
Others present others absent
Whilst air was round & heaven above me
She would be present as my life
My holy gentle tender wife

She promised in my secret ear
When none but God & I could hear
That she would cleave to me forever

There was one will between us
There was one heart within us
And God upon his children smiled
As we the hours with love beguiled

And now I am alone
Unheard I moan
She never comes to me
Sits never by my side
I never hear her voice
She comes not even to my dreams
O Ellen

And comes she not
Ask thy heart, Waldo.
Doth she break her word
Doth not her love embrace thee yet
Even from the Spirits' land?

———————

Leave me, Fear! thy throbs are base,
Trembling for the body's sake.
Come, Love! who dost the spirit raise,
Because for others thou dost wake.
O it is beautiful in death
To hide the shame of human nature's end
In sweet & wary serving of a friend.
Love is true Glory's field, where the last breath
Expires in troops of honorable cares.
The wound of Fate the hero cannot feel
Smit with the heavenlier smart of social zeal.
It draws immortal day
In soot & ashes of our clay.
It is the virtue that enchants it.
It is the face of God that haunts it.

Γνωθι Σεαυτον

If thou canst bear
Strong meat of simple truth
If thou durst my words compare
With what thou thinkest in the soul's free youth

Then take this fact unto thy soul—
God dwells in thee.—
It is no metaphor nor parable
It is unknown to thousands & to thee
Yet there is God.

He is in thy world
But thy world knows him not
He is the mighty Heart
From which life's varied pulses part

Clouded & shrouded there doth sit
The Infinite
Embosomed in a man
And thou art stranger to thy guest
And know'st not what thou dost invest.
The clouds that veil his light within
Are thy thick woven webs of sin
Which his glory struggling through
Darkens to thine evil hue

Then bear thyself, o man!
Up to the scale & compass of thy guest
Soul of thy soul.
Be great as doth beseem
The ambassador who bears
The royal presence where he goes.
Give up to thy soul—
Let it have its way—
It is, I tell thee, God himself,
The selfsame One that rules the Whole
Tho' he speaks thro' thee with a stifled voice
And looks thro' thee shorn of his beams

But if thou listen to his voice
If thou obey the royal thought
It will grow clearer to thine ear
More glorious to thine eye
The clouds will burst that veil him now
And thou shalt see the Lord.

Therefore be great
Not proud, too great to be proud
Let not thine eyes rove
Peep not in corners; let thine eyes
Look straight before thee as befits
The simplicity of Power.
And in thy closet carry state
Filled with light walk therein
And as a King
Would do no treason to his own empire
So do not thou to thine.

This is the reason why thou dost recognize
Things now first revealed
Because in thee resides
The Spirit that lives in all
And thou canst learn the laws of Nature
Because its author is latent in thy breast.
And in the Word
A wise man, Daniel, is the man
In whom the Spirit of the mighty gods abides
His goodness doth permit the deity within
To appear in his own light

Therefore o happy youth
Happy if thou dost know & love this truth
Thou art unto thyself a law
And since the Soul of things is in thee
Thou needest nothing out of thee.
The law, the gospel, & the Providence,
Heaven, Hell, the Judgment, & the stores
Immeasurable of Truth & Good
All these thou must find

Within thy single mind
Or never find.
Thou art the *law*;
The *gospel* has no revelation
Of peace or hope until there is response
From the deep chambers of thy mind thereto
The rest is straw
It can reveal no truth unknown before.
The *Providence*
Thou art thyself that doth dispense
Wealth to thy work Want to thy sloth
Glory to goodness to Neglect the Moth
Thou sow'st the wind, the whirlwind reapest
Thou payest the wages
Of thy own work, through all ages.
The almighty energy within
Crowneth Virtue curseth Sin
Virtue sees by its own light
Stumbleth Sin in selfmade night.

Who approves thee doing right?
God in thee
Who condemns thee doing wrong?
God in thee
Who punishes thine evil deed?
God in thee
What is thine evil meed?
Thy worse mind, with error blind
And more prone to evil
That is, the greater hiding of the God within
The loss of peace
The terrible displeasure of this inmate
And next the consequence
More faintly as more distant wrought
Upon our outward fortunes
Which decay with vice
With virtue rise.

The selfsame God
By the same law

Makes the souls of angels glad
And the souls of devils sad

There is nothing else but God
Where e'er I look
All things hasten back to him
Light is but his shadow dim.

Shall I ask wealth or power of God who gave
An image of himself to be my Soul
As well might swilling Ocean ask a wave
Or the starred firmament a dying coal
For that which is in me lives in the whole

————

A dull uncertain brain
But gifted yet to know
That God has Seraphim who go
Singing an immortal strain
Immortal here below
I know the mighty bards
I listen when they sing
And more I know
The Secret store
Which these explore
When they with torch of genius pierce
The tenfold clouds that cover
The riches of the Universe
From God's adoring lover.
And if to me it is not given
To bring one ingot thence
Of that unfading gold of heaven
His merchants may dispense
Yet well I know the royal mine
And know the sparkle of its ore
Celestial truths from lies that shine
Explored they teach us to explore.

There is in all the sons of men
A love that in the spirit dwells
That panteth after things unseen
And tidings of the Future tells

And God hath built his altar here
To keep this fire of faith alive
And set his priests in holy fear
To speak the truth—for truth to survive.

And hither come the pensive train
Of rich & poor of young & old,
Of ardent youths untouched by pain
Of thoughtful maids & manhood bold

They seek a friend to speak the word
Already trembling on their tongue
To touch with prophet's hand the Chord
Which God in human hearts hath strung

To speak the plain reproof of sin
That sounded in the soul before
And bid them let the angels in
That knock at humble Sorrow's door.

They come to hear of faith & hope
That fill the exulting soul
They come to lift the curtain up
That hides the mortal goal

O thou sole source of hope assured
O give thy servant power
So shall he speak to us the word
Thyself dost give forevermore

———————

I will not live out of me
I will not see with others' eyes
My good is good, my evil ill
I would be free—I cannot be
While I take things as others please to rate them
I dare attempt to lay out my own road
That which myself delights in shall be Good
That which I do not want,—indifferent,
That which I hate is Bad. That's flat
Henceforth, please God, forever I forego
The yoke of men's opinions. I will be
Lighthearted as a bird & live with God.
I find him in the bottom of my heart
I hear continually his Voice therein
And books, & priests, & worlds, I less esteem
Who says the heart's a blind guide? It is not.
My heart did never counsel me to sin
I wonder where it got its wisdom
For in the darkest maze amid the sweetest baits
Or amid horrid dangers never once
Did that gentle Angel fail of his oracle
The little needle always knows the north
The little bird remembereth his note
And this wise Seer never errs
I never taught it what it teaches me
I only follow when I act aright.
Whence then did this Omniscient Spirit come?
From God it came. It is the Deity.

———————

Hard is it to persuade the public mind of its plain duty &
  true interest
And hard to find a straight road to renown
And hard for young men to get honest gold
And hard to find a perfect wife
And mid the armies of imperfect men
To find a friend hardest of all
All good is hard to come by
Yet all these are easilier done
Than to live well one day—to be a Man.
Who speaks the truth outspeaks our Everett
Who acts his thought takes place of Washington
And who prefers music of his Reason
Above the thunder of all men's example
Embraces the beatitude of God.
Alas! that evermore the worldly hands
Hang back behind the charitable Will.

————

Always day & night
Day before me
Night behind me

This I penned
Sitting on two stakes
Under the apple tree
Down in the swamp
To guard a friend

————

Hearst thou, sweet spirit, thou hast heard before—
In heaven perchance
The heavy tidings had a golden sound
Thy dear sister, sharer of thy thots

While yet, dear Ellen, thou didst linger here,
Meekly receives the death blows, one by one,
And as thou, blessed wife, didst wither once in February's
    cold eye,
From month to month,
Passing from earth an angel into heaven
So, in her turn, she hastes upon thy steps,
And leaves two mourners following presently.

———————

None spares another yet it pleases me
That none to any is indifferent
No heart in all this world is separate
But all are cisterns of one central sea
All are mouthpieces of the Eternal Word

———————

Written in Naples, March, 1833

We are what we are made; each following day
Is the Creator of our human mould
Not less than was the first; the all wise God
Gilds a few points in every several life
And as each flower upon the fresh hill-side,
And every coloured petal of each flower,
Is sketched and dyed each with a new design,
Its spot of purple, & its streak of brown,
So each man's life shall have its proper lights,
And a few joys, a few peculiar charms,
For him round in the melancholy hours,
And reconcile him to the common days.
Not many men see beauty in the fogs
Of close low pine-woods in a river town:
Yet unto me not morn's magnificence,
Nor the red rainbow of a summer eve,

Nor Rome, nor joyful Paris, nor the halls
Of rich men blazing hospitable light,
Nor wit, nor eloquence, no, nor even the song
Of any woman that is now alive,
Hath such a soul, such divine influence,
Such resurrection of the happy past,
As is to me when I behold the morn
Ope in such low moist road-side, & beneath
Peep the blue violets out of the black loam,
Pathetic silent poets that sing to me
Thine elegy, sweet singer, sainted wife!

———————

What is it to sail
Upon the calm blue sea
To ride as a cloud
Over the purple floor
With golden mists for company?

And Day & Night are drest
Ever in their jocund vest,
And the water is warm to the hands,
And far below you see motes of light
By day, & streams of fire by night.

What is it to sail
Upon the stormy sea,
To drive with naked spars
Before the roaring gale,
Hemmed round with ragged clouds,
Foaming & hissing & thumping waves
The reeling cabin is cold & wet,
The masts are strained, & the sail is torn,
The gale blows fiercer as the night sets in
Scarce can the seaman aloft master his struggling reef,
Even the stout captain in his coat of storms
Sighs as he glances astern at the white, white combs

And the passenger sits unsocial
And puts his book aside
And leans upon his hand.
  Yet is the difference less
Between this gray sea & that golden one
Than twixt the moods of the man that sails upon it
  Today & yesterday.

———

Alone in Rome! Why Rome is lonely too,
Virtue alone is sweet society.
It keeps the key to all heroic hearts,
And opens you a welcome when you dare.
You must be like them, if you challenge them,
Scorn trifles, & embrace a better aim
Than wine, or sleep, or praise,
Hunt knowledge, as the lover woos a maid,
And ever, in the strife of your own tho'ts,
Obey the nobler impulse. That is Rome.
That shall command a senate to your side
For there is no force in the universe
That can contend with love.
Wait then, sad friend, wait in majestic peace
The hour of Heaven

———

At Sea, September 1833

  Oft as I paced the deck,
My thought recurred on the uncertain sea
To what is faster than the solid land.
My Country! can the heart clasp realm so vast
As the broad oceans that wash thee inclose?

Is not the charity ambitious
That meets its arms about a continent?
And yet the sages praise the preference
Of my own cabin to a baron's hall.
Chide it not then, but count it honesty
The insidious love & hate that curl the lip
Of the frank Yankee in the tenements
Of ducal & of royal rank abroad;
His supercilious ignorance
Of lordship, heraldry, & ceremony;
Nor less, his too tenacious memory,
Amid the particolored treasuries
That deck the Louvre & the Pitti House,
Of the brave steamboats puffing by New York,
Boston's half-island, & the Hadley Farms
Washed by Connecticut's psalm-loving stream.
Yea, if the ruddy Englishman speak true,
In Rome's basilica, and underneath
The frescoed sky of its audacious dome,
Dauntless Kentucky chews, & counts the cost,
And builds the shrine with dollars in his head.
Arrived in Italy, his first demand,—
'Has the star-bearing squadron left Leghorn?'

———

I will not hesitate to speak the word
Committed to me. It is not of men
It is not of myself—no vain discourse
Empty oration, tinkling soulless talk
My heart lies open to the Universe
I read only what there is writ I speak
The sincere word that's whispered in my ear
I am an organ in the mouth of God
My prophecy the music of his lips.
Tho' harsh in evil ears 'tis harmony
To patient wise & faithful hearts whose love
Cooperates with his

Concord of heaven & earth. Author divine
Of what I am & what I say, vouchsafe
To cleanse me that my folly may not hide
Thy truth nor my infirmity disguise
The Omnipotence that animates my clay.
Thou Lord dost clothe thy attributes with flesh
And named it man a morning spectacle
Unto the universe exhibiting
A manifold & mystic lesson

———————

The Sun is the sole inconsumable fire
And God is the sole inexhaustible Giver.

———————

Poem, Spoken Before the ϕβκ Society, August, 1834

Is not this house a harp whose living chords,
Touched by a Poet with electric words,
Would vibrate with a harmony more true
Than Handel's married thunders ever knew?
But I,—mere lover of the Bards' sweet speech,
A simple seeker of the truth they teach,
Having no skill to play, must touch a string
That even to fumbling hands may music bring.
For who can love AMERICA, but seems
Clothed with some favor from its woods and streams?

His hand who hung in space this sun-burnt ball
Made Man the Heart in harmony with all
And each man to his native country tied
With the twin ligaments of love & pride.
And shall it be by antique men alone
In petty states can patriot zeal be shown
They vaunt their pastures at a kingdom's worth
And we be dumb, whose lands balance the earth.

What purpose to man friendly hid so long
Columbia from the subtle & the strong,
Almost from pole to pole its green extent
Yet measured—only by the firmament.
Along the enormous tract in every belt
Of latitude, a several climate felt:
Under the arctic morn, red snow and moss,
Flora's cold elements, the rocks emboss.
Southward, the rose, the apple, and the corn,
Thank the sweet influence of night and morn;
The palm-tree shakes its feathers on the Line,
And round the cane and plantain, curls the vine.

Thou shalt not covet; leave those lands alone,
Content to speculate within thine own.
As the stars shine in heaven, so genial shine
Thy stars, my country, to all lands a sign!
The little traveller from Britain's isle
Lost in these far-spread states, may chirp and smile
At unbred men; because his dinner cools,
The country's naught,—the countrymen are fools.
For him an ill-served soup hath disenchanted
The mighty hemisphere his fathers planted;
He sees not, by the famous pilgrims won,
A hundred Englands opening to the sun.

These northern fields, once the bear's range and den
Bread, iron, oak, and coal, they yield to men.
Richer than purple hills of oil & wine,
Our barren mountains give their son, the Pine;
Borne on whose planks, the hardy fishers float
Round earth, wherever waves will bear a boat.

Angels might lean to see man going forth
With axe & plough to tame the savage earth;
The builder's saw and hammer never rest;
A village climbs each hill with whitening crest;
Lowell, Bangor, & Rochester express
To pleased God the redeemed wilderness:
See the green line of culture westward run

Oer hill, swamp, prairie, to the setting sun:
Yon wagon, disappearing in the woods,
Transplants the Saxon germ to lovelier solitudes,
Bearing the wife, the babes,—basket & store—
To greet with English tongue Pacific's shore.
What's Italy? What's England; Flanders France
That may compare with this inheritance
Prisons of cooped up millions born too late
Whose loss were gain to the oerburdened state
Here shall a man be rated at his worth
And nature's freshest roses hail his birth.

Best name that Time can in his annals find
Columbia styled the Asylum of mankind
Blest office! to the exile to dispense
With open hand a God's munificence
Say to him there is room for us and him
In the deep woods & by the Ocean's brim;
Yes greet sad Europe's exile to your shores
Let love unbar to him the mountain doors
Bid homeless Poland prove this side the main
The freedom she hath perilled all to gain
Give Erin's starving outcast, wholesome meat;
And England's haggard weaver slumber sweet.

Ah thou poor orphan! did the pitiless bed
Of feudal earth that bare thee grudge thee bread?
Was man so cheap in yon preserves of game
That thou must bend thy body as in shame
At being man; in Want, did life begin;
Thy only happiness the joys of sin;
Was it thine added crime some shame to feel,
To be for life the treadle of a wheel?
Come, clear thy brow; the hospitable Hours
Shall weave thy future web with healing flowers.
Welcome! in this continent thou shalt see
God's blessing broad enough to cover thee.
Come, teach thy lip to smile; that hopeless brow
Ill fits the firmament that shades thee now.
Go climb the Allegany's strait defiles;

Speed up Missouri twice a thousand miles,
Traverse the unplanted forest floor, whereon
The allseeing sun for ages hath not shone;
Build where thou wilt thy home in Freedoms soil,
And bare thy strong arms to a freeman's toil;
Plenty shall fill for thee her laughing horn,
And fields be jocund when thy son is born;
Go rear,—for truth the British gibe prevents,—
A race of captains, judges, presidents.

Small praise I deem it that this continent
Provides the beggar bread, clothing, content;
But greater praise no lands have claimed or can
Than this,—we make the vagabond a man.
Him for whom Thought & Freedom were but words
Whose substance was monopolized by lords
Open in him that inward eye whose view
Doth re-create the Universe anew
Is the rose fair? behold it glows for him;
For him the sea shells blush; the dolphins swim;
The perfumed morning sheds her diamond dews;
All sights and sounds in him their spirit infuse;
The keen October's air, when trees are gay
With rainbow plumage, deepening day by day;
The midnights pomp when yonder horned moon
Rivals days golden with a silver moon;
But more than all, he was for Virtue born,
Though thrown neglected on his country's scorn
And every gift benignant heaven let fall
On Man, the exile *here* is heir of all.

Yes, ope the hospitable forest wide
Unto poor men from all the realms of pride
So shall the New World pay the old its debt
For the great pair,—Columbus,—Lafayette;
From yon serene heaven leaning they shall see
The land which one would find, and one would free.

Alas for France! her truest heart is fled:
Her long-descended noble lieth dead
—The best of heroes in the worst of times
His spotless life relieves his country's crimes
Permit the vagrant muse to grace her verse
Borrowing a garland from his recent hearse

Ten years are flown since this great heir of fame
Stood here among us—to his children came
In his clear atmosphere of honor stood
And warmed us with the glory of the good
You know Who knows it not in any clime
The jubilee & triumph of that time
The nation followed him with eyes of love
As if he were some Genius from above
Uprose the farmer by his apple-tree
Tarried the sailor ere he put to sea.
The story of his life through all mouths ran
And swelling crowds hemmed in the heroic man
They pored insatiate on his seamed face
As if to search therein the spirit's grace
In calm simplicity the old man stood
As one on sights of joy unused to brood
Seemed his great heart more easily would brave
A martyr for man's liberty—the grave
He wore no badge—no mark the eye could see
Adorned only with his history.

So seemed to us; but envious Carlists prate
He was a good man but was never great;
His simple figure in the rich saloons
And halting foot displeased the court buffoons
He had a fixed smile, a farmers face,
Nor looked like marquis of the ancient race.
Ah! could these worshippers of ribbons read
In mortal features an immortal meed!
That smile has braved Bourbon's & Orleans' frown,
That farmer's face outfaced Napoleon.
That patient worshipper of right was known
Where gayer lineaments might not be shown

In war's red lines, & in the popular shock
When foaming thousands bellowed, 'To the block!'
A tower immovable in Factions sea,
The patriarch, 'mid the nations, of the free.
Smile did he? twas for Freedoms livelong hope
When all but he quailed at her horoscope;
Write on his tomb—'He never failed to smile
Gainst death, for freedom & for man the while.'
    But when a man to noble place pretends
Take the old touchstone Judge him by his friends
There were two men in this our latter age
Might challenge greatness on a Roman page
One had a patriot's, one a monarch's heart,—
Both soldiers—Washington and Bonaparte.
On Lafayette in arms leaned Washington,
—When saw the world such pair?—father and son.
Napoleon, when all Europe knelt around him,
Sought Lafayette,—fain with his love had bound him,
And he whom Europe served, proud of its chain,
Sued to the great republican in vain.

    Rich is the living map the eagle sees
Sailing oer Auburn in the harvest breeze;
Bright streams, white towns, & man sustaining farms,
And Boston folded in the Ocean's arms;
—O'er town & suburb broods her public dome,
And speaks to countless eyes of Law & Home.—
And farther than that wind-borne eagle flies
Beyond the Southern Horn, or northern ice,
The errands of the pleasant land are done,
As shod with winds oer seas her envoys run.
Fair heritage! only by Virtue strong,
Be thou the tower of right, abolisher of wrong.
What charms the man that views from hill or tower
These gathered symbols of a people's power.
Is it that round him six score thousand men
Feed fat each day to sleep out night again.
If there to grudge, to rob, to mob, they dwell,
The wolf, the wild cat might be there as well.

If ancient Virtue's fire is gone & spent,
Perish these piles of Art & ornament!
Burn church & schoolhouse, which our license mock,
And let the gallant vessel rot in the dock.
The world-encircling merchant sink his goods
And with his babes pick berries in the woods:
Nay let the rotten land suck in the seas,
And the whales pasture mid our college trees!

But if the children of New England feel
With their high lifted fate an even zeal
If to be native of this law-ruled earth
Shall be in the world synonimous with worth;
Who eats his bread by Massachusett' streams
Shall steadfast aim to be the thing he seems
Shall love the country that him bore & bred
Revere the memory of her worthy dead
Feel his heart beat with throbs no sneer withstands
At Concord, Bunker's height, and Plymouth sands
And, his debt owned to God & to good men,
Cannot lay down his dust in dust again
Till he, by studious thought, or deed of love,
Have sealed his kindred with the blest above;
—Enamoured of such worthiness shall Fate
Concede the commonwealth a longer date.
And when remotest times together view
Acts of the elder England & the New
One self same genius shall shine through them all
From ancient Runnimede to Faneuil Hall.

That genius is the Saxon love of Law
And Freedom, whence our daily peace we draw.
For see how Heaven preserves us; when, of late,
Ill omened birds screamed shipwreck to the state,
Then, to redeem the law from the law's foes,
An unexpected strength at once arose;
Thundered from lips long silent, voices wise,
And patriot anger flamed in quiet eyes.

Ill fits the abstemious muse a crown to weave
For living brows;—ill fits them to receive:
And yet, if Virtue abrogate the law,
One portrait,—fact or fancy—we may draw:
A form which nature cast in the heroic mould
Of them who rescued liberty of old;
He, when the rising storm of party roared,
Brought his great forehead to the council board:
There, when hot heads perplexed with fears the state,
Calm as the morn, the manly patriot sate;
Seemed, when at last his clarion accents broke,
As if the conscience of the country spoke.
Not on its base Monadnoc surer stood
Than he to common sense and common good
No mimic;—from his breast his counsel drew
Believed the eloquent was aye the true;
He bridged the gulf from the alway good & wise,
To that within the vision of small eyes.
Self centred; when he launched the genuine word
It shook or captivated all who heard;
Ran from his mouth to mountains & the sea,
And burned in noble hearts proverb & prophecy.
Not old but wise,—for justice born to strive,—
God keep New England's WEBSTER long alive!

Yet even this day of hope may be o'ercast
And future months resemble months now past
O countrymen! though every cheek may burn
With crimson shame from time this lesson learn
The towers that generations did combine
To build & grace, a rat may undermine.

I speak unto the generous & the good
Unto New England's choicest brotherhood
Trust not the guarding sea, the fertile land
Nor fleets, nor hosts, nor law's unsure command;
Build in the soul your citadel apart,—
The true New England is the patriots heart.
The day of elder states may come to us
When public faith shall be ridiculous.

When times are changed, and the old cement gone,
Nor longer laws can yield protection;
Even then, when justice is put up to sale,
Shall one resource redress the unequal scale
For, the true man, as long as earth shall stand,
Is to himself a state, a law, a land;
In his own breast shall read the righteous laws,
His own heart argue injured Virtues cause,
With cheerful brow undauntedly shall face
Or frowning kings, or roaring populace;
And, spending in man's cause his latest breath,
Shall greet with joy sublime the Angel Death.

———————

O what is Heaven but the fellowship
Of minds that each can stand against the world,
By its own meek but incorruptible will?

———————

Ah strange strange strange
The Dualism of man
That he can enlist
But half his being in his act

———————

See yonder leafless trees against the sky,
How they diffuse themselves into the air,
And ever subdividing separate,
Limbs into branches, branches into twigs,
As if they loved the element, & hasted
To dissipate their being into it.

———

Do that which you can do
The world will feel its need of you.

———

Few are free
All might be
Tis the height
Of the soul's flight

———

Van Buren

The towers that generations did combine
To build & grace, a rat may undermine.

———

The Future

How many big events to shake the earth,
Lie packed in silence waiting for their birth.

———

Rex

The bard & mystic held me for their own
I filled the dream of sad poetic maids
I took the friendly noble by the hand
I was the trustee of the handcartman
The brother of the fisher, porter, swain,—
And these from the crowd's edge well pleased beheld
The honor done to me as done to them.

Written in a Volume of Goethe

Six thankful weeks,—& let it be
A metre of prosperity,—
In my coat I bore this book,
And seldom therein could I look,
Each morning brought too much to think,
Heaven & earth to eat & drink.
Is he hapless, who can spare
In his plenty things so rare?

———————

I left my dreamy page & sallied forth
Received the fair inscriptions of the night
The moon was making amber of the world
Glittered with silver every cottage pane
The trees were rich yet ominous with gloom
        the meadows broad
From ferns & grasses & from folded flowers
Sent a nocturnal fragrance
        the harlot flies
Flashed their small fires in air or held their court
In fairy groves of herds grass

———————

S. R.

Demure apothecary
Whose early reverend genius my young eye
With wonder followed, & undoubting joy,
Believing in that cold & modest form

Brooded alway the everlasting mind.
And that thou faithful didst obey the soul,
So should the splendid favour of the God
From thine observed lips shower words of fire,
Pictures that cast before the common eye,

I know for mine, & all men know for theirs.
How is the fine gold dim! the lofty low!
And thou, reputed speaker for the soul,
Forgoest the matchless benefit, & now,
Sleek deacon of the New Jerusalem,

Thou hast defied the offering world to be
A blind man's blind man.
Was it not worth ambition
To be the bard of nature to these times
With words like things,

An universal speech that did present
All natural creatures, and the eye beheld
A lake, a rose tree, when he named their names?

    And better was it to cower before the phantoms
One self deceiving mystic drew in swarms
Wherever rolled his visionary eye,
The Swedish Pluto of a world of ghosts,
Eyes without light, men without character,
Nature a cave of theologions?——

And lo! the young men of the land
Decline the strife of virtue, fail to be
The bringers of glad thought, preferring Ease
Ease & irresolution & the wine
Of placid rich men, they consent to be
Danglers & dolls. With these, not thou, not thou,
O noblest youth, not thou wilt there remain!
Up! for thy life, & for thy people's life!
And be the sun's light & the rainbow's glow,
And by the power of picture, to the eye
Show wherefore it was made. Unlock
The world of sound to the astonished ear,
And thus by thee shall man be twice a man.
Were it not better than to boast thyself
Father of fifty sons, flesh of thy flesh,
Rather to live earth's better bachelor
Planting ethereal seed in souls,

Spreading abroad thy being in the being
Of men whom thou dost foster & inform,
Fill with new hopes, & shake with grand desire?

———————

Philosophers are lined with eyes within
And being so the sage unmakes the man
He is in love he cannot therefore cease his trade
Scarce the first blush has overspread his cheek
He feels it, introverts his learned eye
To catch the unconscious heart in the very act
His mother died, the only friend he had
Some tears escaped but his philosophy
Couched like a cat sat watching close behind
And throttled all his passion. Is't not like
That devil-spider that devours her mate
Scarce freed from her embraces

———————

The simple people each with basket or tool
Had left the young & resolute to rule
But strange disorder in the councils crept
Whilst they in farm & orchard toiled & slept
The farmer & the merchant missed their mart
And no reward attends the craftsman's art
Awaking from their lethargy they hear
Rude words which neither land nor sea will bear
A great concourse surrounds a single man
And waits obsequious
Watches his words, & predicates his will
Uprose the farmer by his apple tree
Tarried the sailor ere he put to sea
And who is he & who are ye he said
And what care I if ye are tail or head
Shall I who know not of the trade of state

Who know not, care not for the statesmans fate
Scarce hold the name of parties & of banks
Measures or leaders, officers or ranks
Shall I descend so low to ask or hear
What one man does or says with hope or fear
Follow the chance direction of his eye
Find his smile Fortune his frown poverty
God made these eyes: fear's watch they cannot keep
God made this frame erect, it cannot creep.

On bravely through the sunshine & the showers
Time hath his work to do & we have Ours.

Let me go where e'er I will
I hear a skyborn music still
It sounds from all things old
It sounds from all things young
From all that's fair from all that's foul
Peals out a cheerful song
  It is not only in the Rose
  It is not only in the bird
  Not only where the Rainbow glows
  Nor in the song of woman heard
But in the darkest meanest things
Theres alway alway something sings.

Tis not in the high stars alone
Nor in the cups of budding flowers
Nor in the redbreast's mellow tone
Nor in the bow that smiles in showers
But in the mud & scum of things
Theres alway alway something sings.

———

And when I am entombed in my place,
Be it remembered of a single man,
He never, though he dearly loved his race,
For fear of human eyes, swerved from his plan.

———

Bard or dunce is blest, but hard
Is it to be half a bard.

———

It takes philosopher or fool
To build a fire or keep a school.

———

Tell men what they knew before
Paint the prospect from their door.

———

I use the knife
To save the life.

———

There is no evil but can speak,
If the wheel want oil t'will creak.

———————

The sea reflects the rosy sky,
The sky doth marry the blue main.

———————

In this sour world, o summerwind
Who taught thee sweet to blow
Who should not love me, summerwind,
If thou canst flatter so

———————

Look danger in the eye it vanishes
Anatomize that roaring populace
Big dire & overwhelming as they seem
Piecemeal t'is nothing. Some of them scream
Fearing the others some are lookers on
One of them hectic day by day consumes
And one will die tomorrow of the flux
One of them has already changed his mind
And falls out with the ringleader and one
Has seen his creditor amidst the crowd
And flees. And there are heavy eyes
That miss their sleep & meditate retreat.
A few malignant heads keep up the din
The rest are idle boys.

———————

As I walked in the wood
The silence into music broke
Sang the thrush in the dark oak
I unwilling to intrude
Slink into nigh solitude
Till warned by a scout of a jay
That flying courier so gay
That he sees me if I see not him
His eyes are bright if mine are dim

———

I sat upon the ground
I leaned against an ancient pine
The pleasant breeze
Shook the forest tops like waves of ocean
I felt of the trunk the gentle motion

———

Good Charles the springs adorer
True worshipper of Flora
Knows't thou the gay Rhodora
    That blossoms in the May
It blooms in dark nooks
By the wood loving brooks
    And makes their twilight gay

———

Around the man who seeks a noble end
Not angels but divinities attend.

———

In the deep heart of man a poet dwells
Who all the day of life his summer story tells
Scatters on every eye dust of his spells
Scent form & color to the flowers & shells
Wins the believing child with wondrous tales
Touches a cheek with colors of romance
And crowds a history into a glance
Gives beauty to the lake & fountain
Spies over sea the fires of the mountain
When thrushes ope their throat, tis he that sings
And he that paints the oriole's fiery wings
The little Shakspeare in the maidens heart
Makes Romeo of a ploughboy on his cart
Opens the eye to Virtues starlike meed
And gives persuasion to a gentle deed.

———————

O what are heroes prophets men
But pipes through which the breath of Pan doth blow
A momentary music. Being's tide
Swells hitherward & myriads of forms
Live, robed with beauty, painted by the Sun:
Their dust pervaded by the nerves of God
Throbs with an overmastering energy
Knowing & doing. Ebbs the tide, they lie
White hollow shells upon the desart shore.
But not the less the eternal wave rolls on
To animate new millions, & exhale
Races & planets its enchanted foam.

———————

Yet sometime to the sorrow stricken
Shall his own sorrow seem impertinent
A thing that takes no more root in the world
Than doth the traveller's shadow on the rock

———————

When thou sittest moping
Nor seeing nor hoping
Thy thought is none
But being freed
By action & deed
Thy thoughts come in bands
Sisters hand in hand
Them thou canst not dispart
From the worlds that be
They reach to the stars
From the bed of the sea.

———————

Woods
A Prose Sonnet

Wise are ye, O ancient woods! wiser than man. Whoso goeth in your paths or into your thickets where no paths are, readeth the same cheerful lesson whether he be a young child or a hundred years old. Comes he in good fortune or bad, ye say the same things, & from age to age. Ever the needles of the pine grow & fall, the acorns on the oak, the maples redden in autumn, & at all times of the year the ground pine & the pyrola bud & root under foot. What is called fortune & what is called Time by men—ye know them not. Men have not language to describe one moment of your eternal life. This I would ask of you, o sacred Woods, when ye shall next give me somewhat to say, give me also the tune wherein to say it. Give me a tune of your own like your winds or rains or brooks or birds; for the songs of men grow old when they have been often repeated, but yours, though a man have heard them for seventy years, are never the same, but always new, like time itself, or like love.

———————

I have supped with the gods tonight
Shall I come under wooden roofs?
   As I walked on the hills
The great stars did not shine aloof
But they hurried down from their deep abodes
And hemmed me in their glittering troop

———————

   Once the priest
Lived in an age
   Of narrow & strait experience
   Narrow & strait it cut his cowl
Narrow & strait it pinched his soul
The times are changed, the ball is known
The lands are found, the forest shown,
The woods are felled, the cities rise,
Swift fly the ships, the letter flies,
The train along the railroad skates
It leaves the land behind like ages past
The foreland flows to it in river fast
Missouri is the merchant's mart
Iowa learns the Saxon Art
What should the old priest in a world like this
The new time will have a new priest I wis
He must know the house where he belongs
His ear must catch its many tongues
On the Bourse in Louvre walk
In Lloyd's in Wall Street talk
His fine ear judge in the theater
In Caucus know the ballots go
And what the Barroom gossips so
What books the people write & read
What Reforms the restless breed
What the loghut thinks of the White House

He should know all things, all things see
And present at their secret be

———

Natures web star broidered
Of animated fibre woven

———

For that a man is a mark
Shows not that he has done
What he is charged withal;
But that some flaw
The censurer knows not what
Has cracked his crystal vase

———

The Bohemian Hymn

In many forms we try
To utter God's infinity
But the boundless hath no form
And the Universal Friend
Doth as far transcend
An angel as a worm.

The great Idea baffles wit
Language falters under it
It leaves the learned in the lurch
Nor art nor power nor toil can find
The measure of the eternal Mind
Nor hymn nor prayer nor church.

———

Kind & holy were the words—
O how trustingly they fell!
Music wants such sweet accords—
Sister, this thy perfect spell.
All the woman now was dropt,
All the friend came forth to me,
The beauty I had pictured oft
Was vanished utterly
Before the dearer emanation
Of undefiled affection,
Of earnest, wistful, ancient love,
With clear & liquid eye,
Older than the gods above,
Fountain of their deity.
Yet thou showed me no love
For the sake of love,
That for meaner souls was made
To whom passion is their bread.
Thou didst wrap thy love in thought
It to me in wisdom taught
In the rapid utterance
Of thy noble aim & hope
In the clear deliverance
Of the will's & wisdoms scope.
Now pleasant fall the blinding snows,
And gay to me the darkest night,
A merry catch the cold wind blows,
And Pain can yield its own delight,
Whilst thou to me & I to thee belong
By the high kin of thought, O Sister of my song!

———

Bluebeard. Let the gentle wife prepare
With housewife's pride her utmost feast
I know with granite glance
And one or two bitter words
How to spoil her relish for it.

Divine Inviters! I accept
The courtesy ye have shown & kept
From ancient ages for the bard,
To modulate
With finer fate
A fortune harsh & hard.
With aim like yours
I watch your course,
Who never break your lawful dance
By error or intemperance.
O birds of ether without wings!
O heavenly ships without a sail!
O fire of fire! o best of things!
O mariners who never fail!
Sail swiftly through your amber vault
An animated law, a presence to exalt

Go if thou wilt ambrosial Flower
Go match thee with thy seeming peers
I will wait Heaven's perfect hour
Through the innumerable years

In Walden wood the chickadee
Runs round the pine & maple tree,
Intent on insect slaughter:
O tufted entomologist!
Devour as many as you list,
Then drink in Walden Water.

———

Star seer Copernicus
Only could earn a curse
A slip of a fellow to show men the stars
What a scandalous slip of a fellow was he
Presuming to show what men wished not to see
Misunderstood—Misunderstood
How dared the old graybeard be misunderstood

———

At last the poet spoke
The richest gifts are vain
As lightning in yon dark clouds grain
A poison in the worlds veins creeps
A devil in celestial deeps

———

The Discontented Poet: a Masque

Lonely he sat, the men were strange
The women all forbidden
Too closely pent in narrow range
Between two sleeps a short day's stealth
Mid many ails a brittle health
Counts his scant stock of native wealth
By conscience sorely chidden

His loves were sharp sharp pains
Outlets to his thoughts were none
A wandering fire within his veins
His soul was smouldered & undone
A cripple of God, half true, half formed,
And by great sparks Promethean warmed

Constrained by impotence to adjourn
To infinite time his eager turn,
His lot of action from the Urn.

He by false usage pinned about
No breath therein, no passage out,
Cast wishful glances at the stars
And wishful hailed the Ocean stream,
"Merge me in the brute Universe
Or lift to some diviner dream."

Beside him sat enduring love:
Upon him noble eyes did rest,
Which for the genius that there strove
The follies bore that it invest:
They spoke not: for their earnest sense
Outran the craft of eloquence:

The holy lovers peaceful sate
Through extacy inanimate
As marble statues in a hall,
Yet was their silence musical;
The only plaints, the sole replies,
Were those long looks of liquid eyes.

Chorus   Yon waterflags, yon sighing osier,
A drop can shake, a breath can fan
Maidens laugh & weep: Composure
Is the pudency of man.

Chorus   Means,—dear brother, ask them not;
Soul's desire is means enow;
Pure content is angels lot;
Thine own theatre art thou.

Poet   I see your forms with deep content
I know that ye are excellent;
But will ye stay?
I hear the rustle of wings
Ye meditate what to say
When ye go to quit me forever & aye.

Chorus   Brother, we are no phantom band,
        Brother accept this fatal hand
        Aches thy unbelieving heart
        With the fear that we must part?
        See all we are rooted here
        By one thought to one same sphere;
        From thyself thou canst not flee,
        From thyself no more can we.

Poet   Suns & stars their courses keep,
        But not angels of the deep;
        Day & night their turn observe,
        But the day of day may swerve.
        Is there warrant that the waves
        Of thought from their mysterious caves
        Will heap in me their highest tide
        In me therewith beatified?
        Unsure the ebb & flow of thought,—
        The moon comes back, the spirit not.

Chorus   Brother, sweeter is the Law
        Than all the grace Love ever saw
        We are its suppliants. By it we
        Draw the breath of eternity:
        Serve thou it not for daily bread
        Serve it for pain & fear & dread.
        Love it, though it hide its light;
        By love behold the Sun at night;
        If the Law should thee forget,
        More enamoured serve it yet:
        Though it hate thee,—suffer long,—
        Put the Spirit in the wrong,—
        That were a deed to sing in Eden,
        By the waters of life to Seraphs heeding.

— — Love
Asks nought his brother cannot give
Asks nothing but does all receive
Love calls not to his aid events
He to his wants can well suffice
Asks not of others soft consents
Nor kind Occasion without eyes
Nor plots to ope or bolt a gate
Nor heeds Condition's iron walls
Where he goes, goes before him Fate;
Whom he uniteth God instals;
Instant & perfect his access
To the dear object of his thought,
Though foes & lands & seas between
Himself & his love intervene.

———————

Hold of the Maker, not the made,
Sit with the Cause, or grim or glad.

———————

He walked the streets of great New York
Full of men, the men were full of blood
Signs of power, signs of worth,
Yet all seemed trivial
As the ceaseless cry
Of the newsboys in the street
Now men do not listen after
The voice in the breast
Which makes the thunder mean
But the Great God hath departed
And they listen after Scott & Byron
I met no gods—I harboured none,
As I walked by noon & night alone

The crowded ways
And yet I found in the heart of the town
A few children of God nestling in his bosom
Not detached as all the crowd appeared
each one a sutlers boat
Cruising for private gain
But these seemed undetached united
Lovers of Love, of Truth,
And as among Indians they say
The One the One is known
So under the eaves of Wall Street
Brokers had met the Eternal
In the city of surfaces
Where I a swain became a surface
I found & worshipped Him.
Always thus neighbored well
The two contemporaries dwell
The World which by the world is known
And Wisdom seeking still its own
I walked with men
Who seemed as if they were chairs or stools
Tables or shopwindows or champagne baskets
For these they loved & were if truly seen
I walked with others of their wisdom gave me proof
Who brought the starry heaven
As near as the house roof

The Archangel Hope
Looks to the azure cope
Waits through dark ages for the morn
Defeated day by day but unto victory born

Atom from atom yawns as far
As moon from earth, or star from star.

———————

I grieve that better souls than mine
Docile read my measured line
High destined youths & holy maids
Hallow these my orchard shades
Environ me & me baptize
With light that streams from gracious eyes,
I dare not be beloved or known,
I ungrateful, I alone.

———————

Nantasket

Lobster-car, boat, or fishbasket,
Peeps, noddies, oldsquaws, or quail,
To Musketaquid what from Nantasket,
What token of greeting & hail?

Can we tie up & send you our thunder,—
Pulse-beat of the sea on the shore?
Or our Rainbow, the daughter of Wonder,
Our rock Massasoit's palace-door.

White pebbles from Nantasket beach,
Whereon to write the maiden's name;
Shells, sea-eggs, sea flowers, could they teach
Thee the fair haunts from whence they came!

———————

Water

The Water understands
Civilization well—
It wets my foot, but prettily,
It chills my life, but wittily,
It is not disconcerted,
It is not broken-hearted,
Well used, it decketh joy,
Adorneth, doubleth joy;
Ill-used it will destroy
In perfect time and measure,
With a face of golden pleasure,
Elegantly destroy.

———————

Where the fungus broad & red
Lifts its head
Like poisoned loaf of elfin bread
Where the aster grew
With the social goldenrod
In a chapel which the dew
Made beautiful for God
The maple street
In the houseless wood
O what would nature say
She spared no speech today
The fungus & the bulrush spoke
Answered the pinetree & the oak
The wizard South blew down the glen
Filled the straits & filled the wide,
Each maple leaf turned up its silver side.
All things shine in his damp ray
And all we see are pictures high
Many a high hill side

Which oaks of pride
Climb to their tops
And boys run out upon their leafy ropes

In the houseless wood
Voices followed after
Every shrub & grapeleaf
Rang with fairy laughter
I have heard them fall
Like the strain of all
King Oberons minstrelsy
   Would hear the everlasting
And know the only strong
You must worship fasting
You must listen long
Words of the air
Which birds of the air
Carry aloft below around
To the isles of the deep
To the snow capped steep
To the thundercloud
To the loud bazaar
To the haram of Caliph & Kremlin of Czar
Is the verse original
Let its numbers rise & fall
As the winds do when they call
One to another

Come search the wood for flowers
Wild tea & wild pea
Grape vine & succory
Coreopsis
And liatris
Flaunting in their bowers
Grass with greenflag halfmast high
Succory to match the sky
Columbine with horn of honey
Scented fern & agrimony
Forest full of essences

Fit for fairy presences,
Peppermint & sassafras
Sweet fern, mint, & vernal grass,
Panax, black birch, sugar maple,
Sweet & scent for Dian's table,
Elder-blow, sarsaparilla,
Wild-rose, lily, dry vanilla.

———————

The Skeptic

Madness, madness,
Madness from the gods!
To every brain a several vein
Of madness from the gods!
Their heads they toss each one aloft
They toss their heads with pride,
Though to break free they struggle oft
And shoulder each aside
What boots it, though their arms stretch out,
And wings behind their shoulders sprout,
If as at first, also at last,
Their planted feet like trees are fast,
Rooted in the slime of Fate,
Sepulchre predestinate:
As if their feet were flint, & soon
All the trunk will grow to stone.
Not one has surmounted
The Destiny yet:
Not one has accounted
To Conscience his debt.
Many in the dark have groped,
Many for the dawn have hoped,
And some more brave, or else more blind,
The freedom all desire, pretend to find.
Of all past men
Not one has snapped the chain

All enter life, each one the dupe
Of the arch-deceiver Hope:
Each hears the Siren whisper; 'he,
Though first of men, shall yet be free;'
That one of their own stem,
Man of Ur, or Bethlehem,
Jove or Alcides,
Mahmoud or Moses,
From their eye shall pluck the beam
And their heart from death redeem.
But Destiny sat still,
And had her will.
Know thou surely
That there is yet no prophet's ken,
No seer in the sons of men,
Those in whom thou dost confide,
Whom thy love has deified,
With a superabundant trust,—
Their words are wind, their forms are dust.
O thousand blossomed but barren tree!
Much-pretending, helped they thee?
Merchant & statesman
Poet & craftsman
Prophet & judge
Pirate & drudge
One fortune levels
Human angels human devils
For ever when a human brain
Its perfect purpose will attain
Then suddenly the pitiless
Performance-hating Nemesis
Withdraws the prize like a painted slide
And a new bauble is supplied
He that threatens is threatened
Who terrifieth is afraid

When Jane was absent Edgar's eye
Roved to the door incessantly
But when she came he went away
For the poor youth could nothing say
Yet hated to appear unwise
Before those beatific eyes

I have found a nobler love
Than the sordid world doth know
Above its envy or belief
My flames of passion glow

Fine presentiments controlled him,
As one who knew a day was great,
And freighted with a friendly fate,
Ere whispered news or couriers told him;
When first at morn he read the face
Of Nature from his resting place
He the coming day inspired
Was with its rare genius fired,
And, in his bearing & his gait,
Calm expectancy did wait

We sauntered amidst miracles
We were the fairies in the bells
The summer was our quaint bouquet
The winter eve our Milky Way
We played in turn with all the slides
In Natures lamp of suns & tides
We pierced all books with criticism
We plied with doubts the Catechism
The Christian Fold
The Bible Old

———

This world is tedious
Shingled with lies
Reform's as bad as vice
Reformer as complier
And I as much a coward
As any he I blame

———

What are all the flowers
And all the rainbows of the skies
To the lights that rain from Eva's eyes
She turned on me those azure orbs
And steeped me in their lavish light
All thot, all things, that joy absorbs.
Yet had no hint of vain delight
Yet tho I spend my days in love
I never have known aught good thereof

———

A pair of crystal eyes will lead me
All about the rounded globe
Averted oft, if once they heed me
I will follow follow follow
To kiss the hem of her robe

———

Knows he who tills this lonely field
To reap its scanty corn
What mystic fruit his acres yield
At midnight & at morn

That field by spirits bad & good
By Hell & Heaven is haunted
And every rood in the hemlock wood
I know is ground enchanted

In the long sunny afternoon
The plain was full of ghosts
I wandered up I wandered down
Beset by pensive hosts

For in those lonely grounds the sun
Shines not as on the town
In nearer arcs his journeys run
And nearer stoops the moon

There in a moment I have seen
The buried Past arise
The fields of Thessaly grew green
Old gods forsook the skies

I cannot publish in my rhyme
What pranks the greenwood played
It was the Carnival of time
And Ages went or stayed

To me that spectral nook appeared
The mustering Day of doom
And round me swarmed in shadowy troop
Things past & things to come

The darkness haunteth me elsewhere
There I am full of light
In every whispering leaf I hear
More sense than sages write

There is no mystery
But tis figured in the flowers
There is no history
But tis calendared in the bowers

Underwoods were full of pleasance
All to each in kindness bend
And every flower made obeisance
As a man unto his friend.

————————

Far seen the river glides below
Tossing one sparkle to the eyes
I catch thy meaning wizard wave
The River of my Life replies

————————

From the stores of eldest Matter
The deepeyed flame obedient water
Transparent air allfeeding earth
He took the flower of all their worth
And best with best in sweet consent
Combined a new temperament

————————

And the best gift of God
Is the love of superior souls

————————

Stout Sparta shrined the god of Laughter
In a niche below the rafter,
Visible from every seat
Where the young men carve their meat.

———————

Brother, no decrepitude
Cramps the limbs of Time;
As fleet his feet, his hands as good,
His vision as sublime.
As when at first Jehovah hurled
The Sun & each revolving world.

———————

Who knows this or that
Hark in the wall to the rat
Since the world was, he has gnawed;
Of his wisdom of his fraud
What dost thou know
In the wretched little beast
Is life & heart
Child & parent
Not without relation
To fruitful field & sun & moon
What art thou? his wicked eye
Is cruel to thy cruelty

———————

Saadi loved the new & old
The near & far the town & wold
Him when Genius urged to roam
Stronger Custom brot him home

———————

But if thou do thy best
Without remission without rest
And invite the sunbeam
And abhor to feign or seem
Even to those who thee shd. love
And thy behavior approve
If thou go in thine own likeness
Be it health or be it sickness
If thou go as thy fathers son
If thou wear no mask or lie
Dealing purely & nakedly

An ancient drop of feudal blood
From the high line of Bulkeley-Mere
Mixed with the democratic flood
Of sires to Yankee freedom dear.

These trees like tho'ts that to visions congeal
Gleamed out on my sight like the gleaming of steel
These woodlands how grand & how sacred they seem
And the air of my house but a pestilent steam
My eyes were bewitched O Nature but thou
Hast with woodland perfumes disenchanted them now

Vain against him were hostile blows
He did their weapons decompose
Aimed at him the blushing blade
Healed as fast the wounds it made
On whomsoever fell his gaze
Power it had to blind & craze

———————

Like vaulters in the circus round
Who step from horse to horse but never touch the ground

———————

If he go apart
And tear the foible from his heart
And with himself content
Live in the deed & not the event
He shall thus himself erect
Into a tower of intellect
Farseen farseeing circumspect
Star specular high & clear
And to thyself more justly dear
Than if thy heart with soft alarms
Did palpitate within his arms

———————

Nature will not lose
In any ends she doth propose
But if thou thy debt decline
Will mulct thee with a fine
If thou refuse to bring forth men

———————

The crowning hour when bodies vie with souls
And bifold essence rushes to its poles

———————

And as the light divided the dark
Thorough with living swords
So shalt thou pierce the distant age
With adamantine words.

———————

When devils bite
A damned parasite
Strikes at their throat & stings them home

———————

Comfort with a purring cat
Prosperity in a white hat

———————

I cannot find a place so lonely
To harbour thee & me only
I cannot find a nook so deep
So sheltered may suffice to keep
The ever glowing festival
When thou & I to each are all

———————

He whom God had thus preferred
To whom sweet angels ministered
Wrapped him in love as in a cloud
Their gifts bestowed, their love avowed,
Saluted him each morn as Brother
[   ] to each other

———

Bended to fops who bent to him
Surface with surfaces did swim
And in the fashionable crowd
None more obsequious heartless bowed
"Sorrow! Sorrow!" the Angels cried
"Is this dear nature's manly pride!
Call hither thy mortal enemy
Make him glad thy fall to see."

———

On that night the poet went
From the lighted halls
Beneath the darkling firmament
To the sea shore to the old sea walls
Dark was night upon the seas
Darker was the poet's mind
For his shallow suppleness
Black abyss of penitence
The wind blew keen, the poet threw
His cloak apart to feel the cold
The wind he said is free & true
But I am mean and sold.
Out shone a star between the clouds
The constellation glittered soon,
"You have no lapse! so have ye glowed
But once in your dominion.
And I to whom your light has spoke
I pining to be one of you
I fall, my faith is broken
Ye scorn me from your deeps of Blue
And yet dear stars I know ye shine
Only by needs & loves of mine
Light loving light asking Life in me
Feeds those eternal lamps I see

Ye have Grace
With swiftness to abolish space
Alike your tiny arrows work
On Schiraz Cairo & New York

The Dervish whined to *Said*,
"Thou didst not tarry while I prayed."
Beware the fires which Eblis burned.
But Saadi coldly thus returned,
"Once, with manlike love & fear,
I gave thee for an hour my ear,
I kept the sun & stars at bay,
And love, for words thy tongue could say;
I cannot sell my heaven again
For all that rattles in thy brain.

Life is great
Men are small
Were it not for the Power
To which each testifies
We could not suppress a titter.
The Soul is in eternity.
As a man stands in the landscape
He is very small,
But he is apprised that the other is large
And being so apprized
Partakes of its scope.
When once he has believed
And become doubly alive
Threescore & ten orbits of the sun

To him short term appears
And he finds it not unworthy
To live long only for a few lessons
Assured he shall pass through a million forms
And in each acquire the appropriate facts
So that one day he will emerge
Armed at all points a god,
A demigod, a chrystal soul
Sphered & concentred to the whole.

The husband has the nearest acres
The poet has the far

From a far mountain creeping down
Music floats up from the town
As we nearer come
We hear only noise & hum

In dreamy woods, what forms abound
That elsewhere never poet found!
Here voices ring, & pictures burn,
And grace on grace, wheree'er I turn.

But O to see his solar eyes
Like meteors which chose their way
And rived the dark like a new day
Not lazy gazing on all they saw

Each chimney pot & cottage door
Farmgear & every picket fence
But feeding on magnificence
They bounded to the horizon's edge
And searched with the sun's privilege
Landward they reached the mountains old
Where pastoral tribes the flocks infold
Saw rivers run seaward from forest high
And the seas wash the low hung sky
Saw the endless rack of the firmament
And the sailing moon where the cloud was rent
And thro' man & woman & sea & star
Saw the dance of nature go
Thro' worlds & races & terms & times
Saw musical order & pairing rhymes.

   Who saw the hid beginnings
When Chaos & Order strove?
Or who can date the morning prime
And purple flame of love?

I saw the hid beginnings
When Chaos & Order strove,
And I can date the morning prime
And purple flame of Love.

Song breather from all the forest,
The total air was fame;
It seemed the world was all torches
That suddenly caught the flame.

Is there never a retroscope mirror
In the realms & corners of space,
That can give us a glimpse of the battle
And the soldiers face to face?

Sit here on the basalt ranges,
Where twisted hills betray
The feet of the world-old Forces
Who wrestled here on a day.

When the purple flame shoots up,
And Love ascends his throne,
I cannot hear your songs, o birds,
For the witchery of my own.

And every human heart
Still keeps that golden day,
And rings the bells of jubilee
On its own First of May.

———————

What never was not, & still will be,
Weighs in sand, grows in tree
Burns in fire primaeval Force
Lodged they say in Chaos once
Shooting thence it runs its course
Filling Space with moons & suns
Now it binds, & now it rives,
Feigns to perish yet revives
To bud & breed, to cling & hold,
Never wanes by waxing old,
The decaying of the fruit
Feeding fat the younger root
Nor less in souls
The subtle potentate controls
Pours thro mans tyrannic will
Fatal streams of empire still

———————

Enough is done highminded friend go sleep
And leave me here to weep
With joy & envy at thy vestibule
And kneel to be admitted of thy school
Go sleep serene, for now thy deeds will wake
And other slumberers will rudely shake
Sleep, for thy deed will answer for thee loud
And crown thee absent to the wishful crowd
Actions are sons & daughters. O who need
In action sweat who's father to a deed?
Who longer pines or hoards, that once hath won
Engine or art a frigate or a town?
Thy genius which still drave thee as a ghost
Comes forth in actions that are uppermost
And that which rent thee with unkindly throes
Born is more sweet than apple or the rose
Henceforth our easy faith will grant thee all
    Undone as done will thee the Master call
    In thee the arts revive; the spritely seer
    That looked thro Phidias has found a peer
    We shall not fear the loss of arts again
    Forgive us bards of Judah & of Greece
    If we seem heedless of your memories
    He has reinstated man on his own heart
    And we shall rightly read the hint you gave
    And henceforth leave your graveclothes in the grave

    Cheered us with plenty
For now we see the niggard cowardice
Ended so quick the inventory of arts
And six or seven branches could comprize
All the fine arts all the humanities

On a few plants & stones our commerce waits
Corn cotton cane vine iron opium wheat
Hemp flax as these grow or fade
The wealth of states is stablished or unmade
There's not a weed waves in the wind
But is the girdle that will empires bind
As many arts & circles radiant

Of handmaid crafts & callings adjutant
With all their pensioners & appanage
As are the stuffs our chemistry engage

———————

Thou shalt make thy house
The temple of a nation's vows
Spirits of a higher strain
Who sought thee once shall seek again
I detected many a god
Forth already on the road
Ancestors of beauty come
In thy breast to make a home

———————

The gods walk in the breath of the woods
They walk by the sounding pine,
And fill the long reach of the old seashore
With colloquy divine
And the poet who overhears
Each random word they say
Is the prophet without peers
Whom kings & lords obey.

———————

Would you know what joy is hid
In our green Musketaquid
And for travelled eyes what charms
Draw us to these meadow farms
Come & I will show you all
Makes each day a festival
Stand upon this pasture hill
Face the eastern star until
The slow eye of heaven shall show
The world above the world below

The mottled clouds like scraps of wool
Steeped in the light are beautiful
And what majestic stillness broods
Over those colored solitudes
Sleeps the vast East in pleased peace
Whilst up behind yon mountain walls
The silent river flows

———————

Tell me maiden dost thou use
Thyself thro nature to diffuse
All the angles of the coast
Were tenanted by thy sweet ghost
Bore thy colours every flower
Thine each leaf & berry bore
All wore thy badges & thy favours
In their scent or in their savours
Every moth with painted wing
Every bird in caroling
The woodboughs with thy manners waved
The rocks uphold thy name engraved
The sod throbbed friendly to my feet
And the sweet air with thee was sweet
The saffron cloud that floated warm
Studied thy motion, took thy form,
And in his airy road benign
Recalled thy skill in bold design
Or seemed to use his privilege
To gaze over the horizon's edge
To search where now thy beauty glowed
Or made what other purlieus proud?

———————

I have no brothers & no peers
And the dearest interferes
When I would spend a lonely day
Sun & moon are in my way

———

Solar insect on the wing
In the garden murmuring
Soothing with thy summer horn
Swains by winter pinched & worn

———

And man of wit & mark
Repair to men of wit
It cannot be society
In one saloon to sit.

———

I know the appointed hour,
I greet my office well,
Never faster, never slower
Revolves the fatal wheel.

I am neither faint nor weary,—
Fill thy will, O faultless Heart!
Here from youth to age I tarry,
Count it flight of bird or dart.

My heart at the heart of things
Heeds no longer lapse of time,
Ages vainly fan their wings,
Me shall keep thy love sublime.

———

You shall not love me for what daily spends,
You shall not know me in the noisy street
Where I as others follow petty ends,

Nor when in fair saloons we chance to meet,
Nor when I'm jaded, sick, perplexed, or mean:
But love me then & only when you know
Me for the channel of the rivers of God,
From deep, ideal, fontal heavens that flow,
Making the shores, making their beauty broad,
Which birds & cattle drink, drink too the roots of the grove,
And animating all it feeds with love.

Elizabeth Hoar

Almost I am tempted to essay
For sympathetic eyes the portraiture
Of the good angels that environ me.
My sister is a Greek in mind & face
And well embodies to these latest years
The truth of those high sculptors old who drew
In marble or in bronze, on vase or frieze
The perfect forms of Pallas or the Muse;
Forms in simplicity complete
And beauty of the soul disdaining art.
So bright, so positive, so much itself,
Yet so adapted to the work it wrought
It drew true love, but was complete alone.
She seemed to commune with herself, & say,
I cannot stoop to custom & the crowd,
For either I will marry with a star,
Or I will pick threads in a factory.
So perfect in her action, one would say,
She condescended if she added speech.
Her look was sympathy, & though she spoke
Better than all the rest, she did not speak
Worthy of her. She read in many books,
And loved the Greek as t'were her mother tongue
She knew the value of the passing day
Thought it no mark of virtue to be scornful
Or cry for better company, but held

Each day a solid good; never mistook
The fashionable judgment for her own.
So keen perception that no judge or scribe
Could vie with her unerring estimate.
When through much silence & delay she spoke,
It was the Mind's own oracle, through joy
And love of truth or beauty so perceived:
Never a poor return on self.

Proteus

Poet bred in Saadi's school
Can wind the world off any spool,
Knows the lore of more & less.
Brahma stooped from the sky
& made the sun of the slime.
He made, of a toad, an archangel,
Of bats & bugs, a god as well,
If he should wash your eyes with rue,
You would remember
How hated were the forms you clasp,
And that once you adored the mummies,
Trust nothing that you see
It changes while you look
Do not think him a dunce
Who wore bells & foolscap once
He is the teacher of ages
For there is no wise man
Men are vascular only,
Constructive men only,
Pipes or channels, clay or crystal
Thro' them rolls the stream today
To roll tomorrow otherwheres
And leave these dry & mean
As high as thy perception goes,
Thou canst not overpraise the great
Yet grander heroes shine beyond.

We tread the ladder's lowest round
And before the Deity
Thy gods are pismires

    Flow flow the waves hated
    Accursed adored!
    The waves of mutation;
    No anchorage is.
    Sleep is not, death is not,
    Who seem to die, live.
    House you were born in
    Friends of your youth
    Old man & young maid
    Early toil & its gains
    They are all vanishing
    Fleeing to fables
    Cannot be moored
    See the stars through them,
    The treacherous marbles
    Know, the stars yonder
    The stars everlasting
    Are fugitive also
    And emulate, vaulted,
    The passing heat-lightning
    or fireflys flight

When thou dost return
On the wave's circulation
Beholding the shimmer
The wild dissipation,
And out of endeavor
To change & to flow,
The gas become solid
And phantasms & nothings
Return to be things
And endless imbroglio
Is law & the world,
Then first shalt thou know
That in the wild turmoil

Horsed on the Proteus
Only canst thou ride to power.
    And to Endurance.

Much thou must suffer
Be shocked & derided
Lose faith to gain faith,
Ah worse! must I say it?
Lose thy virtue, lose thy soul,
To gain the incorruptible.
    The scale in this world
    Of greatness & height
    Is reversed in the other.
Crown of power, is fashioned
Of dust of abasement.

———————

    To every creature
Adam gave its name
Let each to all unmask its feature
And cognizance
Moth or bug or worm or snail
Mite or fly or atomy
Nor each nor any fail
Its lineage to proclaim
Not a plant obscure
But some bright morn its flowers unfold
And tell the Universe
Its family & fame.
No fly or aphis bites the leaf
But comes a chance
When egg or fretted path betray
The petty thief,
And his small malfaisance.
Many things the garden shows
And pleased I stray
From tree to tree
Watching the white pear bloom

Bee infested quince or plum.
I could walk days, years, away
Till the slow ripening secular tree
Had reached its fruiting time
Nor think it long

———

Cloud upon cloud
The world is a seeming,
Feigns dying, but dies not,
Corpses rise ruddy,
Follow their funerals.
Seest thou not brother
Drops hate detachment,
And atoms disorder,
How they run into plants,
And grow into beauties.
The darkness will glow,
The solitude sing

———

Since the devil hopping on
From bush to vine from man to dame
Marshals temptations
A million deep
And ever new beauties rise
And with what faults soever
The stock of illusion
Is inexhaustible
I meantime depreciate
Every hour in the market
But the wares I would buy
Are enhanced every hour
I see no other way
Than to run violently from the market

———

Samson stark at Dagon's knee
Gropes for column strong as he
When his ringlets grew & curled
Groped for axle of the world

———————

Pour the wine! pour the wine!
As it changes to foam,
So flashes the day-god
Rushing abroad,
Ever new & unlooked for,
In furthest & smallest
Comes royally home.
In spider wise
Will again geometrize,
Will in bee & gnat keep time
With the annual solar chime;
Aphides like emperors
Sprawl & play their pair of hours

For Fancys gift
Can mountains lift;
The Muse can knit
What is past & what is done
With the web that's just begun,
Making free with time & size,
Dwindles here, there magnifies
Swells a rain-drop to a tun;
So to repeat
No word or feat,
Crowds in a day the sum of ages,
And blushing Love outwits the sages.

———————

Heartily heartily
Nothing be false
Men ocular jocular

Work with the fingertips
Speak no deeper than the lips
Blow, good northwind, I grow nervous
Good wind, blow away all trace
Of the spectral populace.

———————

Poets are colorpots
Dovesnecks & opaline
Exquisite daintiness
Vapors of wine
Delicate gloom
Barrel of opium
Blowing simoom
Cloud-collecting, dissipating
Brain relaxing enervating
Put your body on your word
Man & sonnet at accord
Set your foot upon the scales
My foot weighs just a pound
Said the cruel Yankee captain
Trucking for his precious bales
Of ermine skin & silver fur
With the painted islander.

———————

Thanks to those who go & come
Bringing Hellas, Thebes, & Rome,
As near to me as is my home:
Careful husbands of the mind
Who keep decaying history good,
And do not suffer Tyre or Troy
To know decrepitude.

———————

Is Jove immortal
So is Cerberus at his portal
Nothing but lying is mean
Never let thy banner down
Rat & worm & wolverine
Have the old dazzle of God's crown
And in the Zodiack are seen
Health & Power become the wise
Fill the gaps with charities
Scatter this vetch everywhere
It will take root in the air
But he the dreaded Fates will please
Who has no eye or time for pease
God having shaped him like a wedge
And driven him to his forepledge
Forth as from a gun.

———————

Heartily heartily sing
Ever be true in town or grove
Bears & men must have their swing
Of berries, & honey, & love.
There's no ideot like the wise
And most virtue's cowardice
What each is born to let him do
Let the devil himself be true
And he has an open track
And all planets at his back
Bare good meaning is an ass
Virtue brings its will to pass
He is wise who marries his end
Makes heaven & earth & hell his friend
Rushes to his deed
Will crack nature or succeed
Values in the issue had
Tis all one
What feat is done
Alike to build an iron way
From Montreal to Boston Bay
Or make a shanty glad.

———

Thank the gods thy governors
Many painful ancestors
Wore away successive lives
To sun & mellow a stock
Which neither Rome nor Antioch
China nor Egypt could forestal
Ripe in thee now last of all.

———

If thy body pine,
Tis the Genius's retreat
To the chambers from the street,
Magnifying the coming vaunt
Of his flowering aloe plant
Starves the florets due today

———

Scholar is a ball thats spent,
Or the barrel that it sent,
Twas fired ere he came into hall,
Here is neither charge nor ball.

———

Ask not treasures from his store,—
For he lies in wait for more;
Nor what dawneth in his brain,—
That to whisper were profane.

———

King.   If farmers make my land secure,
        If pedlers use their craft for me,
        How can I other than endure
        Once in a year their company

Intellect

Rule which by obeying grows
Knowledge not its fountain knows
Wave removing whom it bears
From the shores which he compares
Adding wings thro things to range
Makes him to his own blood strange

Chladni strewed on glass the sand
Then struck the glass its music sweet
The sand flew into symmetry
Then with altered hand
drew discords, & the sand scattered formless,
We cannot find a foreign land
Into new laws we never come
Tho we run along the diameter
Of sidereal space.
Sing, & the rock will crystallize
Sing, & the plant will grow.

Obey one law above, below,
light, heat, & sound, each a liquid wave
And Beauty for the guide I gave
To lead where you should go.

The motes of the stream shall prate
Of the current that floats them on.

———————

I must not borrow light
From history trite
But from friends whom God gave
And the destiny I have

———————

Go into the garden,
Feed thine eyes & ears,
And every sense;
But do not touch a weed,
nor cut off a twig
Be not tempted.
If thou wilt not be a garden tool

———————

But as this fugitive sunlight
Arrested & fixed
And with the primal atoms mixed
Is plant & man & rock
So a fleeing thought
Taken up in act & wrought
Makes the air & the sun
And hurls new systems out to run

———————

Comrade of the snow & wind
He left each civil scale behind
Him woodgods fed with honey wild
And of his memory beguiled
In caves & hollow trees he crept
And near the wolf & panther slept

He came to the green ocean's rim
And saw the sea birds skim
Summer & winter oer the wave
Like creatures made of skiey mould
Impassible to heat or cold.
He stood beside the main
Beautiful but insane
He felt himself as if the sky walked
Or the son of the wind
There was no man near
To mete himself withal

———————

God only knew how Saadi dined
Roses he ate, & drank the wind

———————

Friends to me are frozen wine
I wait the sun shall on them shine

———————

That each should in his house abide,
Therefore was the world so wide

———————

New England Capitalist

What are his machines
Of steel, brass, leather, oak, & ivory,
But manikins & miniatures,
Dwarfs of one faculty, measured from him,
As nimbly he applies his bending self
Unto the changing world, thus making that
Another weapon of his conquering will?

He built the mills, & by his polities, made
The arms of millions turn them.

Stalwart New Hampshire, mother of men,
Sea-dented Maine, reluctant Carolina,
Must drag his coach, & by arts of peace
He, in the plenitude of love & honor,
Eats up the poor,—poor citizen poor state.
                    Much has he done,
Has made his telegraph,
Propeller, car, postoffice, phototype,
His coast survey, vote by majority,
His life assurance, & star registry,
Preludes & hints of what he meditates;—
Now let him make a harp!

———————

On a raisin stone
The wheels of nature turn,
Out of it the fury comes
Wherewith the spondyls burn.
And, because the seed of the vine
Is creation's heart,
Wash with wine those eyes of thine
To know the hidden part.
Wine is translated wit,
Wine is the day of day,
Wine from the veiled secret
Tears the veil away.

———————

Go out into Nature and plant trees
That when the southwind blows
You shall not be warm in your own limbs
but in ten thousand limbs & ten million leaves
Of your blossoming trees of orchard & forest

————

But God will keep his promise yet
Trees & clouds are prophets sure
And new & finer forms of life
Day by day approach the pure.

————

Poet of poets
Is Time, the distiller,
Chemist, refiner:

Time hath a vitriol
Which can dissolve
Towns into melody,
Rubbish to gold.
        Burn up the libraries!
        Down with the colleges!
        Raze the foundations!
        Drive out the doctors!
        Rout the philosophers!
        Exile the critics!
        Men of particulars,
        Narrowing niggardly
        Something to nothing.
All their ten thousand ways
End in the Néant.

        All through the countryside
Rush locomotives:
Prosperous grocers
Poring on newspapers
Over their shop fires
Settle the State.
But, for the Poet,—
Seldom in centuries

Comes the well-tempered
Musical man.
He is the waited-for,
He is the complement,
One man of all men.
The random wayfarer
Counts him of his kin.
This is he that should come
The tongue of the secret,
The key of the casket,
Of Past & of Future.
Sudden the lustre
That hovered round cities,
Round bureaus of Power,
Or Chambers of Commerce,
Round banks, or round beauties,
Or state-rending factions,
Has quit them, & perches
Well pleased on his form.
True bard never cared
To flatter the princes
Costs time to live with them.
Ill genius affords it,
Preengaged to the skies.
Foremost of all men
The Poet inherits
Badge of nobility,
Charter of Earth;
Free of the city,
Free of the meadows,
Knight of each order,
Sworn of each guild,
Fellow of monarchs,
And, what is better,
Mate of all men.

Pan's paths are wonderful.
Subtile his counsel.
Wisdom needs circumstance,
Many concomitants,

Goes not in purple,
Steals along secretly,
Shunning the eye;
Has the dominion
Of men & the planet,
On this sole condition,—
She shall not assume it.
When the crown first incloses
The brows of her son,
The Muse him deposes
From kingdom & throne.

———

See the spheres rushing,—
Poet that tracks them
With emulous eye,
What lovest thou?
Planet, or orbit?
Whether the pipe,
Or the lay, it discourses?
In heaven, up yonder,
All the astronomy,
Sun-dance & star blaze,
Is Emblem of love.

Nought is of worth
In earth or in sky
But Love & Thought only.
Fast perish the mankind,
Firm bideth the thought,
Clothes it with Adam-kind,
Puts on a new suit
Of earth & of stars.
He will come one day
Who can articulate
That which unspoken
Vaults itself over us,
Globes itself under us,
Looks out of lovers' eyes,
Dies, & is born again;—
He who can speak well;

Men hearing delighted
Shall say, *'that is ours.'*
Trees hearing shall blossom,
Rocks hearing shall tremble,
And range themselves dreamlike
In new compositions,
Architecture of thought.
Then will appear
What the old centuries,
Aeons were groping for,
Times of discomfiture,
Bankrupt millenniums.

———————

The patient Pan,
Drunken with nectar
Sleeps or feigns slumber
Drowsily humming
Music to the march of Time.
This poor tooting creaking cricket,
Pan half asleep, rolling over
His great body in the grass,
Tooting, creaking,
Feigns to sleep, sleeping never:
Tis his manner,
Well he knows his own affair,
Piling mountain-chains of phlegm
On the nervous brain of man,
As he holds down central fires
Under Alps & Andes cold.
Haply else we could not live
Life would be too wild an ode
Sun & planet would explode
Ah! the poor Adamkind
Fault of supplies
From the fire fountains
We busybodies
Ever experiment

See what will come of it
Prove the quaint substances
Prove our bodies, prove our essence
Fortunes, genius, elements,
Try a foot, try a hand,
Then plunge the body in
Then our wits characters
And our gods if we can
Analysing analysing
As the chemist his new stone
Puts to azote, puts to chlorine,
Puts to vegetable blues.
Ah my poor apothecaries,
Can ye never wiselier sit,
Meddle less & more accept,
With dignity not overstepped
Skies have their etiquette

We are faithful to time
Time measured in moments
Only so many
Share of Methusalem
Share of the babe
Hundredhanded, hundredeyed,
Fussy & anxious
We would so gladly
Serve an apprenticeship
Day by day faithfully
Learn the use of Adam's tools
Fire & water, azote, carbon,
Gravity levity
Hatred attraction
Animals chemistry
Botany land
Have a right to our flesh
Know the honest earth by heart

    Do the feat of Archimedes
If the earth reject her sons
Till theyve learned her alphabeta
None but Hooke & Newton dare

Cross the threshold when it thunders.
Life is all too short for farming
All too short for architecture
All too short to learn the tongues
And for philosophy
Life's done ere weve begun to think.
Solid farming haw & geeing
Drive uphill the loaded team
Bud the pear & dig potatoes
What time Lyra's in the Zenith
That is wholesome as it makes
Man as massive as the glebe
Pricks dropsical pretension
Tames the infinite romance
Underpins the falcon turrets
High as fly falcons, fancy builds

———————

To transmute crime to wisdom, & to stem
The vice of Japhet by the thought of Shem.

———————

Pale Genius roves alone,
No scout can track his way,
None credits him till he have shown
His diamonds to the day.

Not his the feaster's wine,
Nor land, nor gold, nor power,
By want & pain God screeneth him
Till his elected hour.

Go, speed the stars of Thought
On to their shining goals; —
The sower scatters broad his seed,
The wheat thou strew'st be souls.

———

Burn your literary verses
Give us rather the glib curses
Of the truckmen in the street
Songs of the forecastle
To the caboose

———

Intellect
Gravely broods apart on joy,
And truth to tell, amused by pain

———

What all the books of ages paint, I have.
What prayers & dreams of youthful genius feign,
I daily dwell in, & am not so blind
But I can see the elastic tent of day
Belike has wider hospitality
Than my few needs exhaust, & bids me read
The quaint devices on its mornings gay.
Yet nature will not be in full possessed,
And they who trueliest love her, heralds are
And harbingers of a majestic race,
Who, having more absorbed, more largely yield,
And walk on earth as the sun walks in the sphere.

———

The civil world will much forgive
To bards who from its maxims live
But if, grown bold, the poet dare
Bend his practice to his prayer,

And, following his mighty heart
Shame the time, & live apart,
Vae solis!
I found this,—
That of goods I could not miss
If I fell within the line,
Once a member, all was mine,
Houses, banquets, gardens, fountains,
Fortune's delectable mountains;
But if I would walk alone,
Was neither cloak nor crumb my own

———

Mask thy wisdom with delight,
Toy with the bow, yet hit the white.
The lesson which the Muses say
Was sweet to hear & to obey.
He loved to round a verse, & play,
Without remoter hope, or fear,
Or purpose, than to please his ear.
And all the golden summer-time
Rung out the hours with happy rhyme.
Meantime every cunning word
Tribes & ages overheard:
Those idle catches told the laws
Holding nature to her Cause.

———

Roomy Eternity
Casts her schemes rarely,
And an aeon allows
For each quality and part
In the multitudinous
And many-chambered heart.

—————

Dark Flower of Cheshire garden
Red Evening duly dyes
Thy sombre head with rosy hues
To fix fargazing eyes.
Well the planter knew how strongly
Works thy form on human thought:
I muse what secret purpose had he
To draw all fancies to this spot.

—————

Terminus

For thought & not praise;
Thought is the wages
For which I sell days,
Will gladly sell ages,
And willing grow old,
Deaf, & dumb, & blind, & cold,
Melting matter into dreams,
Panoramas which I saw
And whatever glows or seems
Into substance into Law

—————

I to my garden went
To the unplanted woods

———

More sweet than my refrain
Was the first drop of April rain

———

Wisp & meteor nightly falling
But the stars of God remain.

———

God The Lord save Massachusetts
Without chivalry or slave
We are ignorant of stealing
Quite too stupid to be knave
And to perjure and to poison
Not our way our souls to save

———

A poet is at home
He does not follow the old & dead
Ruins & mummies
But cities & heroes come to him
One [   ] will serve
As well as another
For he fills them
From his own winepress
In the village he can find.

———

O Boston city lecture-hearing,
O unitarian God-fearing,
But more, I fear, bad men-revering;
Too civil by half, thine evil guest
Makes thee his byword & his jest,
And scorns the men that honeyed the pest,
Piso & Atticus, with the rest.
Thy fault is much civility,
Thy bane, respectability.
And thou hadst been as wise, & wiser,
Lacking the Daily Advertiser.
Ah, gentlemen,—for you are gentle,—
And mental maids, not sentimental.

———————

A patch of meadow & upland
Reached by a mile of road,
Soothed by the voice of waters,
With birds & flowers bestowed.

This is my book of Chronicles,
Code, Psalter, lexicon,
My Genesis & calendar
I read it as I run.

It is my consolation
In mild or poignant grief,
My park & my gymnasium,
My out-of-door relief.

I come to it for strength,
Which it can well supply,
For Love draws might from terrene force
And potences of sky.

The tremulous battery, earth,
Responds to touch of man,
It thrills to the antipodes,
From Boston to Japan.

The planets' child the planet knows
And to his joy replies;
To the lark's trill unfolds the rose,
Clouds flush their gayest dyes.

When Ali prayed & loved
Where Syrian waters roll,
Upward the ninth heaven thrilled & moved
At the tread of the jubilant soul.

———————

And he like me is not too proud
To be the poet of the crowd

———————

Parks & ponds are good by day,
But where's the husband doth delight
In black acres of the night?
Not my unseasoned step disturbs
The sleeps of trees or dreams of herbs

———————

Cloud upon cloud.
Clouds after rain
Value standeth in success,
But the same value
Hideth in failure,
In poverty, mourning,
In solitude, crime;

The value adhesive
Sticks to them all
Refuses to sunder
From man, from man.
Differ servitude & rank
As chains that clank not, chains that clank

The last shall be first
The first be postponed
The latest promoted
At the end of the day
It first will appear
Who never surrendered
Who combated stoutly,
Where God was the while
We strutted we coxcombs
So condescendingly
Bowing & giving
Affecting to give
Virtue is a cockney grown

———————

For Lyra yet shall be the pole
And grass grow in the Capitol

———————

A score of airy miles will smooth
Rough Monadnock to a gem.

———————

All things rehearse
The meaning of the universe

Webster

Why did all manly gifts in Webster fail?
He wrote on Nature's grandest brow, *For Sale*.

———

The atom displaces all atoms beside
And Genius unspheres all souls that abide

———

I have an arrow that can find its mark,
A mastiff that will bite without a bark.

———

From high to higher forces
The scale of power uprears,
The heroes on their horses,
The gods upon the spheres.

———

All day the waves assailed the rock,
I heard no church-bell chime;
The sea-beat scorns the minister clock,
And breaks the glass of Time.

———

Honor bright o muse
Muses keep your faith with me
Give me some audacious hours
Draw to a just close
The poem ye begun

———————

Such another peerless queen
Only could her mirror show

———————

See how Romance adheres
To the deer, the lion,
    and every bird,
Because they are free
And have no master but Law
On the wild ice   in depths of sea
On Alp or Andes side
In the vast abyss of air
The bird, the flying cloud,
The fire   the wind   the element
These have not manners coarse or cowed
And no borrowed will
But graceful as cloud & flame
All eyes with pleasure fill

———————

With the key of the secret he marches faster
From strength to strength, and for night brings day,
While classes or tribes too weak to master
The flowing conditions of life give way.

———————

For what need I of book or priest
Or Sibyls from the mummied East
When every star is Bethlehem's star
I count as many as there are
Cinquefoils or violets in the grass;
So many saints & saviors,
So many high behaviors,
Salute the boy of years thrice five
Who only sees what he doth give

———————

And rival Coxcombs with enamored stare
Perused the mysteries of her coiled hair

———————

For joy & beauty planted it
With faerie lustres cheered,
And boding Fancy haunted it,
With men & women weird.

———————

Papas Blondine
Grew tall & wise
Eschewing vanities
And loved the truth
Can Truth suffice?
The years shall show:
Truth is put upon its trial
Her judgment will not brook denial
In her large memory
Is never fact forgotten

And she will know
If Truth's as true as she
In action & in word
If the false world can afford
That any sterling be

And if it prove that things are rotten
She will frankly call them so
She who is real,
She who cannot aught conceal,
She that hypocrisy disdains,
Never palters, never feigns,
But well believes
That she may dare
Confess her faith in any air
That honest meaning will not fail
Over falsehood to prevail
She will launch her thought nor fear it
Speak the truth to who will hear it.
But still as now
With pure good will

 And Bounty sculptured on thy brow
Give the downhearted world
Hints of Eternal cheer.

Brave maid obey thy heart
Accept what rule it shall impart
Nor heed one word of all the voices gay
Which in their manifolded quire
Stoop to Fashion & stoop to please
Flatter worthless ease

In every house a welcome guest
For her good heart & searching eye
Though she bring this sunlike test
In lieu of a polished lie.
She can weave & embroider
Can write & draw
And like a mirror report

Orderly beautiful all she sees
But when she signs her name
With plain verity content
Never prefixed a compliment
And in whatever circle came
Never stooped to utter one
Who if polite society
Did not exist, would it invent,
By her practice show its laws,
Grace without compliment.
Grace that grows from pure intent
Grace that fascinates & draws
Advance life as now
Bearer of good news
Or if disaster come
Evil news were not allowed
To dim her eye, her aspect cloud
Or choke her cheerful voice
Tell ill news as thou tellest good
Nor mar thy quiet in the broil
Adorn thy self with hardihood
With ice bath fortify the blood,
    arctic winds blew round her bed
Hard fare & charitable toil

———

The Asmodaean feat be mine
To spin my sand heaps into twine.

———

A puff of air or dry or damp
Shall burn the town or quench the lamp
    As the babe to the mothers breast
    We are tied to the element
    By hands no Will can circumvent

Through the world east & west
Pupils & children of the wind
Since our forefather Adam sinned
And as sinks or mounts the song
We are impotent or strong
A whiff of air will make the odds
Between the victim & the gods
As blows from divers points the gale
The man shall prosper or shall fail

———————

Coin the daydawn into lines
In which its proper splendor shines;
Coin the moonlight into verse
Which all its marvels shall rehearse

———————

He loved to watch & wake
When the wing of the southwind whipt the lake
And the glassy surface in ripples brake
And fled in pretty darkness away
Like the flitting boreal lights
Rippling roses in northern nights
Or like the thrill of Aeolian strings
On which the sudden wind-god rings

———————

She walked in flowers around my field
As June herself around the sphere

———————

The bird was gone   the ghastly trees
Heard the wind sing with in the breeze
Was this her funeral that I see
Did that asking eye ask me?

———————

Pedants all
They would be original
The mute pebble shames their wit
The echo is ironical
And wiser silence swallows speech

———————

If bright the sun, he tarries;
All day his song is heard;
And when he goes, he carries
No more baggage than a bird.

———————

Teach me your mood, O patient stars!
Who climb each night the ancient sky,
Leaving on space no shade, no scars,
No trace of age, no fear to die.

———————

O sun! take off thy hood of clouds,
O land! take off thy chain,
And fill the world with happy mood
And love from main to main.

Ye shall not on this charter day
Disloyally withhold
Their household rights from captive men
By pirates bought & sold.

Ah little knew the innocent
In throes of birth forlorn,
That wolves & foxes waited for
Their victim to be born.

———————

As the drop feeds its fated flower,
As finds its Alp the snowy shower,
Child of the omnific Need
Hurled into life to do a deed,
Man drinks the water, drinks the light

———————

I leave the book, I leave the wine,
I breathe freer by the pine:
In houses, I am low & mean,
Mountain waters wash me clean,
And by the seawaves I am strong,
I hear their medicinal song,
No balsam but the breeze I crave,
And no physician but the wave.

———————

Gentle Spring has charmed the earth
Where an April sunbeam fell,
Let no glacier from the north
Floating by undo the spell.

———————

The coral worm beneath the sea
Mason planter spreads
Its rock vegetable threads
Foundation of the isles to be
His colossal flowers
Home of imperial powers
And nobler life

———————

Easy to match what others do,
Perform the feat as well as they;
Hard to outdo the wise, the true,
And find a loftier way.
The school decays, the learning spoils,
Because of the sons of wine:—
How snatch the stripling from their toils?
Yet can one ray of truth divine
The banquet's blaze outshine.

———————

If wishes would carry me over the land,
I would ride with free bridle today,
I would greet every tree with a grasp of my hand,
I would drink of each river, & swim in each bay.

———————

Maia

Illusion works impenetrable,
Weaving webs innumerable,
Her gay pictures never fail,
Crowds each on other, veil on veil,
Charmer who will be believed
By Man who thirsts to be deceived.

———————

Seyd planted where the deluge ploughed,
His hired hands were wind & cloud
His eyes could spy the gods concealed
In each hummock of the field

———————

For every god
Obeys the hymn, obeys the ode,
Obeys the holy ode.

———————

For Genius made his cabin wide
And Love brought gods therein to bide
Better he thought no god could bring
And basked in friendship all the days of Spring.
And though he found his friendships meet
His quarrels too had somewhat sweet.

———————

He lives not who can refuse me,
All my force saith, 'Come & use me.'
A little sun, a little rain,
And all the zone is green again

———————

Forbore the ant hill, shunned to tread,
In mercy, on one little head

———————

By art, by music, overthrilled
The wine cup shakes, the wine is spilled

———————

Borrow Urania's subtile wings
Chasing with words fast-flowing things:
Cling to the sacred fact, nor try
To plant thy shrivelled pedantry
On the shoulders of the sky.

———————

The comrade or the book is good
That puts me in a working mood:
Unless to thought be added will,
Apollo is an imbecile.
What parts, what truth, what fancies shine!
—Ah! but I miss the just design.

———————

Is the pace of nature slow?
Why not from strength to strength
From miracle to miracle
And not as now with retardation
As with sprained foot

———————

Why honor the new men
Who never understood the old

———————

I never knew but one
Could do what thou hast done
Give me back the song of birds
Into plainest English words
Or articulate
The sough of the wind as I sate

———————

Think not the gods receive thy prayer
In ear & heart, but find it there.

———————

Turtle in swamp
wader on beaches
camel in sand
goat on mountain
fish in sea
eyes in light
Every Zone its flora & fauna
animals hybernate, or wake when dinner is ready
food, parasite, enemy, census,
Same fitness between a man & his time & event
Man comes when world is ready for him.
And things ripen, new men
Hercules comes first, & St John afterwards.
& Shakspeare at last.

———————

Inspired we must forget our books,
To see the landscape's royal looks.

———————

She had wealth of mornings in her year
And planets in her sky,
She chose the best thy heart to cheer
Thy beauty to supply.—
Now younger lovers find the stream
The willow & the vine
But aye to me the happiest seem
To draw the dregs of wine

———

When wrath & terror changed Jove's regal port,
And the rashleaping thunderbolt fell short.

———

Softens the air so cold & rude
What can the heart do less?
If Earth puts off her savage mood,
We should learn gentleness.

———

Spices in the plants that run
To bring their firstfruits to the sun
Earliest heats that follow frore
Nerved leaf of hellebore
Sweet willow, checkerberry red,
With its savory leaf for bread
Silver birch & black
With the selfsame spice
Found in polygala root & rind
    Sassafras & fern
        Benzoin
Mouse ear cowslip wintergreen
Which by aroma may compel
The frost to spare what scents so well

———

She paints with white & red the moors
To draw the nations out of doors

———

The Earth

Our eyeless bark sails free
Tho' rough with boom & spar
—Andes, Alp or Himmalee,—
Strikes never moon or star

———

The sun athwart the cloud thought it no sin
To use my land to put his rainbow in.

———

October woods, wherein
The boy's dream comes to pass,
And nature squanders on the boy her pomp
And crowns him with a more than royal crown
And unimagined splendor waits his steps
The urchin walks thro tents of gold
Thro crimson chambers porphyry & pearl
Pavilion on pavilion garlanded
Incensed & starred with lights & airs & shapes
And sounds, music
Beyond the best conceit of pomp or power

———————

How drearily in College hall
The Doctor stretched the hours!
But in each pause we heard the call
Of robins out of doors.

The air is wise, the wind thinks well,
And all through which it blows,
If plant or brain, if egg or cell,
To joyful beauty grows.

And oft at home 'mid tasks I heed
I heed how wears the day—
We must not halt while fiercely speed
The spans of life away.

Who asketh here of Thebes or Rome
Or lands of eastern day?
In forests joy is still at home,
And there I cannot stray.

———————

If curses be the wage of love
Hide in thy skies thou fruitless Jove
Not to be named
It is clear
Why the gods will not appear
They are ashamed

———————

The land was all electric
  There was no need of trumpets
  As they float by coast & crag
There was no need of banners
Every zephyr was a bugle
Every maple was a flag
Each steeple was a rallying sign
The tocsin was its bell
Sharp steel was the lieutenant
And powder was his men.

The mountain echoes roar,
Every crutch became a pike,
The woods & meadows murmured war,
And the valleys shouted, Strike!

———————

  For Nature true & like in every place
Will hint her secret in a garden patch,
or in lone corners of a doleful heath,
As in the Andes watched by fleets at sea
or the sky-piercing horns of Himmaleh
or Europe's pilgrims at Niagara
And when I would recall the scenes I dreamed
On Adirondac steeps I know
Small need have I of Turner or Daguerre,
Assured to find the token once again
In silver lakes that unexhausted gleam,
And peaceful woods beside my cottage door.

————

History & prophecy are alike
It matters little if thou read
Backward or forth a frivolous creed
Alike unworthy thou hast learned
The world was drowned & shall be burned
As if man's Spirit were some cat
Loved its old barn to end with that

————

The coil of space the cones of light
Starry orbits
Where they end, begin & enlarge
And the worlds of God
Are a dot on its marge

Ah waste & ocean, fold on fold,
And doubled ever more by Thought
Which nothing bounds which all can hold

————

The heavy blue chain
Of the boundless main
Lock up their prison door,
And the cannon's wrath
Forbid their path
On Ocean's azure floor.

————

This shining hour is an edifice
Which the Omnipotent cannot rebuild

———

He could condense cerulean ether
Into the very best sole leather

———

The sparrow is rich in her nest
The bee has her desire
The lover in his love is blest
The poet in his brain of fire

———

James Russell Lowell

As I left my door,
The muse came by,
Said, "Whither away?"
I, well-pleased to praise myself,
And in such presence raise myself,
Replied, 'To keep thy bards birthday'
—"O happy morn! o happy eve!"—
The muse rejoined, "And dost thou weave
For noble night a noble rhyme,
And up to song through friendship climb?
For every guest
Ere he can rest
Plucks for my son or flower or fruit
In sign of Nature's glad salute."

—'Alas! thou know'st,
Dearest muse, I cannot boast
Of any grace from thee:
To thy spare bounty, queen, thou ow'st,
No verse will flow from me.

Beside, the bard himself, profuse
In thy accomplishment,
Does Comedy & Lyric use,
And to thy sisters all too dear,
Too gifted, than that he can chuse
To raise an eyebrow's hint severe
On the toiling good intention
Of ill-equipped incomprehension.'

"The bard is loyal,"
  Said the queen
  With haughtier mien,
"And hear thou this, my mandate royal:
  Instant to the Sibyl's chair,
  To the Delphic maid repair,
  He has reached the middle date
  Stars tonight that culminate
  Shed beams fair & fortunate:
  Go inquire his horoscope,
  Half of memory, half of hope."

———

From Paques to Noel,
Prophets & Bards,
Merlin, Llewellyn,
Highborn Hoel,
Wellborn Lowell,
What said the Sibyl?
What was the fortune
She sung for him? —
"Strength for the hour."

Man of marrow, man of mark,
Virtue lodged in sinew stark,
Rich supplies & never stinted,
More behind at need is hinted,
Never cumbered with the morrow,
Never knew corroding sorrow,
Too well gifted to have found
Yet his opulence's bound,

Most at home in mounting fun,
Broadest joke, & luckiest pun,
Masking in the mantling tones
Of his rich laugh-loving voice,
In speeding troops of social joys,
And in volleys of wild mirth,
Purer metal, rarest worth,
Logic, passion, cordial zeal,
Such as bard & hero feel.

Strength for the hour,—
For the day sufficient power,
Well advised, too easily great
His large fleece to antedate.

But, if another temper come,
If on the sun shall creep a gloom,
A time & tide too exigent,
When the old mounds are torn & rent,
More proud, more strong competitiors
Marshal the lists for Emperors,
—Then, the pleasant bard will know
To put this frolic masque behind him,
Like an old summer cloak,
And in sky-born mail to bind him,
And single-handed cope with Time,
And parry & deal the thunderstroke.

———

Ever the Rock of Ages melts
Into the mineral air,
To be the quarry whence is built
Thought & its mansion fair.

———

But never yet the man was found
Who could the mystery expound
Tho' Adam born when oaks were young
Endured, the Bible says, as long,
But when at last the patriarch died
The Gordian noose was not untied.
He left, though goodly centuries old,
Meek natures secret still untold.

From Nature's beginning
Sin blunders & brags,
True making, true winning
Go hidden in rags.

Wit has the creation
Of worlds & their fame
On one stipulation,
—Renouncing the same.

What wilt thou? the Forces?
Or skies which they breed?
The strain it discourses
Or Pan? or his reed?

If the crown once incloses
The brows of her son,
The Muse him deposes
From kingdom & throne

A queen rejoices in her peers,
And wary Nature knows her own,
By court & city, dale & down,
And like a lover volunteers,
And to her son will treasures more
And more to purpose freely pour
In one woodwalk than learned men
Will find with glass in ten times ten.

By kinds I keep my kinds in check,
I plant the oak, the rose I deck.

But Nature whistled with all her winds,
Did as she pleased, & went her way.

Dear are the pleasant memories
Of unreturning years,
And griefs recalled delight not less,—
Youth's terrors & its tears

The genial spark the poet felt
Flamed till every barrier melt,
He poured his heart out like a bird,
And as he spoke, so was he heard.

One night he dreamed of a palace fair,—
Next year, it stood in marble strong,
Sheltered a nation's proudest throne,
There sate the fathers of the state,
There echoed freedom's shrill debate
A thousand years it will stand the same
Enacting laws & breathing Fame.

———————

The low December vault in June be up-lifted high
And largest clouds be flakes of down in that enormous sky.

———————

At Plymouth in the friendly crowd
Mamma was not a little proud
To see her beaming candlesticks
Almost outshine their lighted wicks
Why not? since shafts of solid silver
Might tempt the Plymouth saints to pilfer
But Time, a more relentless thief
Betrayed Mamma & these to grief
He stole the silver grain by grain
Nothing but copper would remain
But when Aladdin came to town
Hiding his famed lamp in his gown
Touched the old sticks with fingers new
As if with starshine riddled through
And now they beam like her own feats
Of mercy in the Concord streets.

———————

Old Age

The brook sings on the selfsame strain
But finds no echo in my brain

To the Clock

Hail requiem of departed time
Never was richman's funeral
Followed behind the pall
By the heir's eager feet,
With resignation more complete
Yet not his hope is mine

Thou diggst the grave of each day
Not mine, Dig it thou shalt;
I defy thee to forbear it

O Time thou loiterer
Thou whose might
Laid low Enceladus & crushed the moth
Rest on thy hoary throne forgetting
Alike thy agitations & thy graves

Arachnean webs decoying & destroying
Webs whereat the Gorgons ply
But lo! thy web's motheaten
The shuttles quiver as the loom's beams are shaken

———————

Nature says,
　　　These craggy hills that front the dawn
　　Man-bearing granite of the North
　　Shall fiercer forms & races spawn
　　Charged with my genius forth

———————

Shun passion, fold the hands of thrift,
Sit still, and Truth is near;
Suddenly it will uplift
Your eye-lids to the sphere,
Wait a little, you shall see
The portraiture of things to be.

———————

To the mizen, the main, & the fore,
Up with it once more,
The old tricolor,
The ribbon of power,
The white, blue, & red, which the nations adore.

———————

The rules to men made evident
By Him who built the day,
The columns of the firmament
Not firmer based than they.

———————

Too late the anxious fire came
The Express had mounted his pot of flame
No gift tho' urged by Ediths voice
No bugler can the rider bring
Only this paper scrap can make amends
Tomorrow rides with equal fire
And brings the haughty horseman home
He well can wait
This horse forever bounds
This horn to fancy ever sounds
The warcloud hints what bursts behind

———————

His instant thought the Poet spoke
And filled the age his fame;
An inch of earth the wild bolt strook
But lit the sky with flame.

———————

Try the might the Muse affords,
And the balm of thoughtful words.
Bring music to the desolate
Hang roses on the stony fate

———————

Saadi held the Muse in awe
She was his mistress & his law
A twelvemonth he could silence hold
Nor ran to speak till she him told
He felt the flame, the fanning wings,
Nor offered words till they were things.
Glad when the solid mountain swims
In Music & uplifting hymns

———————

No song so tuneful, quoth the fox,
As the rich crowing of the cocks.

———————

Life

A train of gay and clouded days
Dappled with joy and grief & praise,
Beauty to fire us, saints to save,
Escort us to a little grave.

Song of Taliesin

Vain Bards! I can discover all,
What befel or shall befal.
I come seeking what is lost,
And my aim shall not be crossed.
Strong am I who this demand,
More strong my tongue than Arthur's hand
Three hundred potent songs & more
Are hidden in the strain I pour:
No foemen in these mountains dwell
On whom I cannot cast a spell;
Nor stone nor brass, nor iron ring
Can fetter Elphin when I sing;
All that I seek this hand can find,
All Gates unbar, all bonds unbind.

———

Seemed, tho' the soft sheen all enchants,
Cheers the rough crag & mournful dell,
As if on such stern forms & haunts,
A wintry storm more fitly fell.

———

Nature saith,
I am not infinite,
But imprisoned & bound,
Tool of mind,
Tool of the being I feed & adorn.

Twas I did soothe
Thy thorny youth;
I found thee placed
In my most leafless waste;
I comforted thy little feet

On the forlorn errand bound;
I fed thee, with my mallows fed,
On the first day of failing bread.

———————

Illusions like the tints of pearl,
Or changing colors of the sky,
Or ribbons of a dancing girl
That mend her beauty to the eye.

———————

Inscription on a Well in Memory of the Martyrs of the War

Fall stream from Heaven to bless: return as well;
So did our sons; Heaven met them as they fell.

———————

Letters

My tongue is prone to lose the way,
Not so my pen, for in a letter
We have not better things to say,
But surely put them better.

———————

May

When all their blooms the meadows flaunt
To deck the morning of the year,
Why tinge thy lustres jubilant
With forecast or with fear?

Softens the air so sharp and rude,
What can the heart do less?
If Earth put off her savage mood,
Let us learn gentleness.

The purple flame all bosoms girds,
And Love ascends his throne;
I cannot hear your songs, O birds!
For the witchery of my own.

Each human heart this tide makes free
To keep the golden day,
And ring the bells of jubilee
On its own First of May.

The Miracle

I have trod this path a hundred times
With idle footsteps, crooning rhymes,
I know each nest & web-worms tent;
The fox-hole which the woodchucks rent
Maple & oak, the old "divan,"
Self-planted twice like the banian;
I know not why I came again
Unless to learn it ten times ten.
To read the sense the woods impart,
You must bring the throbbing heart;
Love is aye the counterforce,
Terror, & Hope, & wild Remorse.
Newest knowledge, fiery thought,
Or Duty to grand purpose wrought.

Wandering yester-morn the brake,
I reached the margin of the lake,
And oh! the wonder of the power,
The deeper secret of the hour!—

Nature, the supplement of Man,
His hidden sense interpret can,—
What friend to friend cannot convey
Shall the dumb bird instructed say.
Passing yonder oak, I heard
Sharp accents of my woodland bird,—
I watched the singer with delight,—
But mark what changed my joy to fright,
When that bird sang, I gave the theme,—
That wood-bird sang my last night's dream,
A brown wren was the Daniel
That pierced my trance its drift to tell;
It knew my quarrel, how and why,
Published it to lake and sky,—
Told every word and syllable
In his flippant chirping babble,
All my wrath, & all my shames,
Nay, Heaven be witness,—gave the names.

———————

A dangerous gift & grace is mine
Closely dame your ear incline
A word my merits shall unlock
Behold me here a whispering clock
I both time & silence keep
Will not wake you when you sleep
Yet count as true the balmy hours
As truly as
The thunderer from the steeple towers

———————

And hungry Debt beseiged my door
And still held out his hundred hands

———

Use will in man new grace reveal
The gleam which Labor adds to steel.

———

Put in, drive home the sightless wedges,
Exploding burst the crystal ledges.

———

What flowing central forces, say,
Make up thy splendor, matchless day!

———

The best of life is presence of a muse
Who does not wish to wander, comes by stealth,
Divulging to the heart she sets a flame
No popular tale, no bauble for the mart.
When the wings grow that draw the gazing crowd,
Ofttimes poor Genius fluttering near the earth
Is wrecked upon the turrets of the town:
But, lifted till he meets the steadfast gales
Calm blowing from the Everlasting West

———

The Pilgrims

Behold I make partition
In this new world I have built,
For slavery differs from freedom
As honor is wide from guilt.

Lo now to Freedom I assign
And make partition fair,
All space above the waterline
All ground below the air.

And what's beside may slavery claim
Her residue & share,
Within the earth to hide her shame,
Or climb above the air.

Firm to the pole he knots the cord,
And to the tropics drew,
About the round globe's quarter broad,
Along the welkin blue.

Hills clapped their hands, the rivers shined,
The seas applauding roar,
The elements were of one mind,
As they had been of yore.

———————

I care not whither I may go,
Or if my task be high or low,
Work to hide or proudly show,
Or if my mates shall be my peers
Or only rare-met travellers,
Whether I pace the shop-lined street
And scan the city at my feet
With secret pride to rule the town
And shire on which the dome looks down.

———————

I am not black in my mind
But born to make black fair:
   On the battlefield my master find, —
      His white corpse taints the air.

Eve roved in Paradise, I've heard,
With no more baggage than a bird;
Exiled, she soon found necessary
More garments than she liked to carry;
Adam devised valise & sack,
And trunk & tray her weeds to pack,
But when the hatbox he invented,
Dear Eve declared herself contented;
Eden was well—Angels prefer it—
She thought the outworld had its merit;
And now transmits to Ellen dear
This sable cube of comfort here.

Trimountain

Sicut cum patribus sit Deus nobis

The land that has no song
Shall have a song today,
The granite ledge is dumb too long,
The vales have much to say.
Its men can teach the lightning speech,
And round the globe their voices reach.

—

The rocky Nook with hilltops three
Looked eastward from the farms,
And twice a day the flowing sea
Took Boston in its arms:
   The men of yore were stout & poor,
   And sailed for bread to every shore.

The waves that rocked them on the deep
To them their secret told,

Said the winds that sung the lads to sleep,
"Like us be free & bold.
    The honest waves refuse to slaves
    The empire of the Ocean caves."

And where they went, on trade intent,
They did what freemen can;
Their dauntless ways did all men praise,
The merchant was a man.
    The world was made for honest trade,
    To plant & eat be none afraid.

    Old Europe groans with palaces
Has lords enough & more
We plant & build by foaming seas
A city of the poor.
    For what avail the plough & sail,
    Or land, or life, if freedom fail?

The noble craftsman we promote,
Disown the knave & fool;
Each honest man shall have his vote,
Each child shall have his school.

We grant no dukedoms to the few,
We hold like rights & shall,
Equal on Sunday in the pew,
On Monday in the mall.

    Fair rose the planted hills behind
The good town on the Bay,
And where the western slopes declined
The prairie stretched away.

Out from the many-fountained earth
The rivers gushed & foamed,
Sweet airs from every forest forth
Around the mountains roamed.

What rival towers majestic soar
Along the stormy coast,—
Penn's town, New York, & Baltimore,
If Boston knew the most!

They laughed to know the world so wide,
The mountains said, "Good-day!
We greet you well, you Saxon men,
Up with your towns, & stay."

"For you," they said, "no barriers be,
For you no sluggard's rest;
Each street leads downward to the Sea,
Or land-ward to the West."

The townsmen braved the English King,
Found friendship in the French,
And Honor joined the patriot ring
Low on their wooden bench.

O bounteous seas that never fail!
O day remembered yet!
O happy port that spied the sail
Which wafted Lafayette!
    Abdiel bright, in Europe's night,
    That never faltered from the right.

O pity that I pause,—
The song disdaining shuns
To name the noble sires, because
Of the unworthy sons:
For what avail the plough & sail,
Or land, or life, if freedom fail?

But there was chaff within the flour,
And one was false in ten;
And reckless clerks in lust of power
Forgot the rights of men;
Cruel & blind did file their mind,
And sell the blood of human kind.

Your town is full of gentle names
By patriots once were watchwords made;
Those war-cry names are muffled shames
On recreant sons mislaid.
What slave shall dare a name to wear
Once Freedom's passport everywhere?

O welaway! if this be so,
And man cannot afford the right,
And if the wage of love is woe,
And honest dealing yield despite.
  For what avail the plough & sail,
  Or land, or life, if freedom fail?

Hie to the woods, sleek citizen!
Back to the sea, go landsmen down!
Climb the White Hills, sleek aldermen,
And vacant leave the town:
Ere these echoes be choked with snows,
Or over the roofs blue Ocean flows.

The sea returning day by day
Restores the world-wide mart,
So let each dweller on the Bay
Fold Boston in his heart.
For what avail the plough & sail,
Or land or life, if freedom fail?

Let the blood of her hundred thousands
Throb in each manly vein
And the wit of all her wisest
Make sunshine in his brain.
A union then of honest men,
Or Union nevermore again.

And each shall care for other,
And each to each shall bend,
To the poor a noble brother,
To the good an equal friend.

A blessing through the ages thus
Shield all thy roofs & towers!
God with the fathers, So with us!
Thou darling town of ours!

———————

For Lucifer, that old athlete,
Tho' flung from Heaven falls on his feet

———————

Traitors tho' plumed & steel equipped
Are born to be betrayed & whipped
Born to be caught & to be whipped

———————

The Muse
Can at pleasure use
Every syllable men have heard
And can move with every word
Need not mimic, plot or veer
But speak right onward without fear
She need not turn aside
Or half convey & half suppress
New meaning in a worn-out phrase
She will not walk in crooked ways
But bend the language to her
Make the language bend to her
Not unable not afraid
To say what never yet was said
She need not stray from her path
To find the words of love or wrath
The world is as rich in nouns & verbs
As in sea sand or in herbs

————————

In my garden three ways meet,
Thrice the spot is blest;
Hermit thrush comes there to build
Carrier doves to rest.

The broad armed oaks, the copse's maze
The cold sea-wind detain;
And sultry summer overstays
When autumn chills the plain.

Self-sown my stately garden grows,
The winds and wind-blown seed,
Cold April rain, and colder snows
My hedges plant and feed.

From mountains far and valleys near,
The harvests sown to-day,
Thrive in all weathers without fear,—
Wild planters plant away!

In cities high the careful crowd
Of woe-worn mortals darkling go,
But in these sunny solitudes
My quiet roses blow.

Methought the sky looked scornful down
On all was base in man,
And airy tongues did taunt the town,
Achieve our peace who can!

What need I holier dew
Than Walden's haunted wave,
Distilled from heaven's alembic blue,
Steeped in each forest cave.

If Thought unlock her mysteries,
If Friendship on me smile,
I walk in marble galleries,
I talk with kings the while.

And chiefest thou, whom Genius loved,
Daughter of sounding seas,
Whom Nature pampered in these groves,
And lavished all to please.

What wealth of mornings in her year,
What planets in her sky!
She chose her best thy heart to cheer,
Thy beauty to supply.

Now younger pilgrims find the stream,
The willows and the vine,
But aye to me the happiest seem
To draw the dregs of wine.

Thermometer

Mine to watch the sun at work
Or if he hide in clouds & shirk
I test the force of wood & bark,
And keep the pitcoal to the mark
On my white enamelled scale
The warning numbers never fail
From sixty up to seventy one
The grades of household comfort run
If they climb a hairsbreadth higher
Fling wide the door, put out the fire,
Each year will have its holidays
Which I report nor blame nor praise
Twice I dive twenty below zero
Twice climb to heat would blacken Nero
But health & heart will prosper more
At the mean point of 54

———————

Nature

Day by day for her darlings to her much she added more,
In her hundred-gated Thebes every chamber was a door,
A door to something grander,—loftier walls, & vaster floor.

———————

Seashore

Here chimes no clock, no pedant calendar,
My waves abolish time, dwarf days to hours,
And give my guest eternal afternoon.

———————

Things oft miscalling, as the hen-
Fever raged not in fowls but men.

———————

On the chamber, on the stairs,
  Lurking dumb,
  Go and come
The Lemurs and the Lars.

———————

Ah! not to me these dreams belong,
A better voice sings through my song.

———————

"For deathless powers to verse belong
And they like demigods are strong
    On whom the Muses smile."

———————

Upon a rock yet uncreate
Amid a Chaos inchoate
An uncreated being sate
Beneath him rock
Above him cloud
And the cloud was rock
And the rock was cloud
The rock then growing soft & warm
The cloud began to take a form
A form chaotic vast & vague
Which issued in the cosmic egg
Then the being uncreate
Upon the egg did incubate
And thus became an incubator
And of the egg did allegate
And thus became an alligator
And the incubate was potentate
But the alligator was potentator

———————

TRANSLATIONS

Boy bring the bowl full of wine
Bring me two bowls of the purest wine
I take wine to be the love-potion
This stuff for old & young, bring
Sun & moon are the wine & the glass
In the midst of the moon bring me the sun
How the understanding strives so earnestly
Bring bands made of wine for the stupid head
Fan this dissolving glow,
That is, instead of water bring wine
Goes the rose by, say gladly:
Nectar of pearls & blood of the rose, bring.
Sounds not the nightingale it is right
Sound of glass & sound of wine, bring.
Mourn for nothing, since past is past
Harp & lute tones therefore bring
Only in dreams enjoy I my love
Then bring wine for wine brings sleep
Am I drunken   What is to do
That I may be well drunken bring one glass more
One two cups bring to Hafiz
Be it now well or ill done, bring.

Hafiz

Who royally bedded
On ermine lies
Knows not the stone pillow
Of the pilgrims thorn bed

Hafiz

Desire no bread, forsake the guest hall of the earth,
The earth is a host who murders his guests

Hafiz

The red rose blooms
The nightingale is drunken
Now leave free course to drinking
Ye reverencers of wine

The building of Sorrow it seemed so firm
Piled of granite gray
O see how the crystal glass
Has already shattered it & broke

Bring wine; before the Throne
Which hears our wishes
Drunkard & sage are one
And prince & groom

Since I must one day leave
This two-ported guest house
It is all one whether my lifes course
Be high or humble

It is not possible without sorrow
And without grief to live
Since on the day of Destiny was
Sorrow assigned to us

For being & not-being cumber thee not
Be ever of glad heart
The end of every excellence
Is the Chaos & the Night

Pomp, Asaph, the East-wind-horse,
The knowledge of the bird language,
Is all gone to the winds
And profits not the king

Mount not from the straight way
In to the air with wings
The arrow flies into the air & falls
Again to earth

How can the tongue of thy quill
Thank Hafiz therefor
That thy words steadily from mouth
to mouth fly.

Hafiz

———

Many our needs, yet we spare prayers
Since thro' thy nature have we no need of praying
The Nature of my beloved is the world-showing mirror
Ah it has taught me that thy need is no need
Long time I endured the torments of the ship
Since the pearls are mine, what do I want of the sea
Beggar! the soul-squandering life of the beloved
Knows thy petition. She has no need of explanation
Prince of beauty, by God! I am burned up by love.
Ask me finally still, Have the beggars really need?
Thou importunate flee   I have nothing to do with thee
My friends are there   Is there need of enemies
Thy word conquers Hafiz, of itself appears virtue
Envy & empty strife with the adversary are not needful

Hafiz

———

Early after the night long revel
Took I lyre plectrum & bowl
Bridled the horse of Reason
Drove it with spurs to the town of revellers

See the host flatters me
That I fear not the blinding of Destiny

Thou the aim of the arrow of speech
Said the host with bows of brows

Little profits it thee
Tho thou embrace me like a belt
Spread the net for others
Over the net the Auka soars

Host & trusted are one
Every difference is only a pretence
Reach us the boats of Sohra
That we save us out of these waters

Ah how enjoyed the Shah
Who in himself is constantly enamoured
All is riddle Hafiz
To explain it to us is mere talk.

Hafiz

———

Thou who with thy long hair
As with thy chains art come
Thine be opportunity
Since to capture slaves thou comest

O show thyself benign
And change thy mood
Since they to resign
Thou to ask & claim comest

Be it in peace be it in war
To yield to thee it is my doom
Since in every event thou art
With entrancing kisses come

Fire & water mingled are
In thy swelling ruby lip
Evil eyes be far!
As a juggler thou art come

Honor to thy soft heart
And a good work wouldst thou do
Pray for all the dead
Whom thine eyelashes slew

Say what boots my virtue
Since thou intent to steal the heart's treasures
All drunken & confused
To my still chamber art come

See Hafis said he to me
Thy coat with spots soiled
Wert thou safe from this company
Once home again?

Hafiz

Art thou wise, four things resign,—
Love, & loneness, sloth, and wine.

Hafiz

Knowst thou the luck the friends face to see
Rather to beg near him than a prince to bee
Tis easy out of the soul to banish lust
Not easy the friend from the soul to thrust
With my own heart go I like a flower
There tear I the garment of good name
Now kiss I secretly with the roses, as the East wind,
Now hearken I the secrets of the nightingale
Kiss the friends lips when thou canst
Otherwise wilt thou in the lips bite full of sorrow
  Seize the chance of talking with thy friend
  Who knows if we meet again on the way.

Hafiz

Untruth is become the mode
And no man knows of friendship & truth
The worthy nears now the worthless
And stretch out their hands for a gift
Whoso in the world is virtuous & wise
Is no moment free from care & sorrow
On the other side the dunce lives in plenty
With gold & honour overlaid
And if a poet fluent as water
Full of heart speaking to mind & to soul
So yields him avarice no shilling
Tho his songs were worthy of Abusina
Yesterday said Reason to the Understanding
Go forth suffer & complain not
In satisfaction seek thy kingdom
And drink wine instead of other potions
Hafiz follow thou this good counsel
Then tho thy foot fall thy head shall rise

Hafiz

Novice, hear me what I say
So shalt thou be purified
Whilst thou dost not tread the way,
Thou canst not be a guide.

Pride of the gazing school,
Lord of thy companions,
Mark, hear boy thou too shalt be
One day the sire of sons

Sleeping, eating, drinking,
The spark of love withstood,
Eat not, sleep not, love in thinking
Will come rushing like a flood.

A beam of the love of Allah
Once fall thy soul upon,
By God I know thou then wilt be
More brilliant than the sun.

As learned magians do,
Thy hand from brass withhold,
That thou in life true alchemist
May turn all stones to gold.

From thy footsole to thy head
A beam of God thou burnest,
So [   ]thout foot or head
To the hest of God thou turnest

Go leap into the waves,
And have no doubt or care,
And the flowing of the seven broad seas
Shall never wet thy hair.

If Allah's face on thee
Look down with love benign,
Who disbelieves that thou also
To his face turnest thine?

And though thy form & fortune
Were broken waste & void
Dream not of thy eternal root
A fibre is destroyed

Hafiz

Lament not, o Hafiz, the distribution
Thy nature & thy verse, which flow like water, let them
content you.

Hafiz

Hafiz thou art from Eternity
By God created for a man
Who abhors hypocrisy

Hafiz

———

Hafiz since on the world
Sorrows & joys pass away
So it is better that thou ever
Of glad spirit art

Hafiz

———

I said to the East wind
On the tulip-enriched plain,
Of what martyrs are these the bloody corpse-cloths?
He said, Dear Hafiz, to you & me
Has no one told this.
Tell thou of wine-ruby, of silver-chin,
Seize the skirt of thy friend,
Care not for the enemy,
Be God's man & fear not the Devil.

Hafiz

———

We wish like the glass
All clean to be; who wishes it not
The East wind breathes out in scents
Spices & perfumes
Why changes not the inner mind
Violet earth into musk?

Hafiz

———

When in eternity the light
Of thy beauty glistened, *Love was,*
Which set the worlds on fire

Beams trickled from thy cheeks,
Angels saw them & remained cold
Indignant turned they then to men

See, the Understanding prayed
for a spark his light to kindle.
Jealousy was the dazzling spark

Hafiz

Secretly to love & to drink, what is it? tis a dissolute
    day's work.
I side with the open drunkards, be it as it may.
Loose the knots of the heart & cumber thee no farther
    for the lot
No geometer has yet disentangled this confusion.
At the trade & changes of Time wonder not;
The like enchantments keeps Destiny ready.
Hold the glass discreetly, it was put together
Of the skulls of Jamschid, Keikobad, & Behmen,
Who teaches us where Kai was & Nimrod are gone
How the throne of Jamschid fell in pieces at last
See Ferhad, how he longs for the lips of Schirin
Out of the flood of tears sprang tulips before him.
Come I will be riotous & wasted by wine
Who knows but I shall find treasures in a desolate
    house

Hafiz

This effervescing gentleman who despises a secret
Scorns me since I am riotous & enamoured,
Look at the virtues of lovers not at their faults
Since who is not virtuous himself, sees faults.

People of heart have the key to the treasure of the heart
Let none henceforth doubt of this refined truth
Shepherd in the vale of Rest thy wish will then be first
    fulfilled.
When thou several years hast served the Jethro of the heart
Blood trickles from the eye of Hafiz as if he were enchanted
When he as old man remembers the days of youth

Hafiz

————

Stand up, that we may sacrifice the soul
Before the pencil of the Master
Who the picture of this world
So masterly has painted

Hafiz

————

O friend blame not Hafiz,
While his glances so follow you,
I have in him all the time
Only your friend seen.

Hafiz

————

The way of love is unlimited
The soul is there sacrificed
　There is no other way.

Scare me not with reason
Bring wine. Since Reason as watchman
　Has nothing here to do

When thou givest thy heart to love
Tis good time tis a good thing
　Use no counsel first

Who smote me? Ask thine eye,
O sweet child, let this not lie
　As guilt against my Destiny

As the new moon needs a sharp eye
So thou an intelligent one; not every one
　Sees the young crescent

Use drinking with wisdom
The way to it as to a treasure is not
　Open to every man

Hafiz

———————

His learning truly lifted Hafiz to Heaven
But his love of thee has brot him to the dust

Hafiz

———————

Thousand dangers of ruin has the street of love
Believe not that death frees thee from all

Hafiz

———————

Bring wine release me
From care
Only with wine they drive
Sorrow away

There are no other lamps
In society
Than wine & the face
Of the handsome cupbearer

Be not proud of the Enchantment
Of thy eyelashes
Since pride profits not
Oft have I proved.

Master thou oft well advisest me
Not to love
But this lesson is
No law for me

Love befouls only the heart
Of great men
Since thou hast no love
Thou art excused

To a wink sacrificed I
My virtue
Ah therein is all my store
Of good works

The luck of enjoyment is there
Bating separation
And the land of the heart is now
Again arable

Hafiz

Blame me not thou hoarse preacher
Did not the Creator know
Who set me on fire with this flame
Whom I ought to love?

Hafiz

———————

I never went out of my country
In all my life

Hafiz

———————

For his constant dwelling place has Hafiz
Once for all chosen the wine-house
So chooses the lion the wood for his abode
And the bird the plain

Hafiz

———————

Our Shah's counsel is the efflux
Of higher light
See thou have, if thou draw nigh him,
Clear vision.
Take the wish for his greatness
Into thy prayer
Since the ear of his heart
Converses with angels

Hafiz

———————

If thy darling favor thee
Both worlds thou mayest defy
Let fortune stand thy friend
Armies encamp against thee in vain

Hafiz

No physician has a balsam for my wo
I am only sound or sick thro my friend

Hafiz

Spare thou neither time nor blood for thy friend
Sacrifice also a hundred souls for one drink

Hafiz

It is certain that who his mind
In his friend concentered has
Has good luck to his handmaid
Higher than the Understanding
Is the cabinet of love,
Who has his soul in his own sleeve
Kisses only the door.
The mouth of the friend perchance
Is the seal of Solomons hand
Which under the power of a ruby
Has the world at command
My friend has a musk down
And lips like fireglow
I will flatter the beauty finely
Who has this & that.
As long as thou art in the earth
Use occasion, work & climb

Since the Grave has a plenty
of unprofitable time.
Happy who sees the poor
Without contempt
While the first place of honour
Has many poor sitters
It screens from harms body & soul
The hearts prayer of the poor;
Whilst he who is ashamed of the poor
Has no good end.

Hafiz

Who dedicates himself to the glass
Wherein the world mirrors itself
Lifts securely the veil
Which separates the worlds

Hafiz

Wine resembles the Lord Jesus
It wakes the dead to life

Hafiz

Drink till the turbans are all unbound
Drink till the house like the world turns round

Hafiz?

So long as there's a trace
Of wine & banquet house
My head will lie in the dust
Of the threshold of the winehouse
Ask thou for grace hereafter
At my gravestone
That will be the pilgrim city
Of all the drinkers of wine
The ring of mine host hangs
Forever in my ear.
I am; what I was
My dust will be again.
Go, blind hermit, go,
Since to thee & me alike
The secret is hidden,
And always will be.
My well beloved went
Abroad today to hunt
Whomsoever the lot had doomed
To bleed at the heart.
A place on which the sole
Of thy foot falls
Will be the resort
Of all reasonable men.
From the day when by love
I am laid as in the grave
Until the Judgment, my eye
Will be by thine
So long the luck of Hafiz
Will be no better
The hair of his love
Will be in the hands of another.

Hafiz

To whom a glass full of red wine
Was given in the morning
To him was a place in heaven
By the Lord given.
Be no saint; look not
Too closely after drunkards
To them was on the day of lots
The love-bias given.

Hafiz

In bounding youth the night & rain
Shut toys out vex the brain
But later, dark & rainy skies
Give not the cheer the sun supplies

Hafiz?

The ninefold table of Heaven
Its gold & silver bread
Compared with the table of thy grace
Are but a morsel

Hafiz

Should I shed my tears
Into the Sinderud,
Irak would in a moment
Be watered through & through

Hafiz

Prince the ball of heaven should
Under thy bat be
And the field of time of space
Should be thy playground

Hafiz

———————

Since you set no worth on the heart
Will I on the way instead of small coin
Strew eyes.

Hafiz

———————

Now tells the flower
Histories of May
Who fetters himself with gold
He is not wise.

Cheer thy heart with wine:
The Earth is only
A house to which our bones
Give the mortar.

Seek not in thy friend, truth;
Truth is dead;
Holy fire comes not
Out of Church lamps.

Blacken thou not my name
For my riot;
Who knows what the lot
Inscribed on the brow?

Turn not thy steps
From the grave of Hafiz,
Since though in sins sunken
He expects Heaven

Hafiz

Good is what goes on the road of Nature
On the straight way never yet erred man

Hafiz

Reach me wine   No counsel weakens the conclusion of
      the lot,
None alters what Destiny determines for him.

Hafiz

Has thine enemy slandered thy house
He shall find his sin in his childs child

Hafiz

Yet all comes out of this, that one door
Opens, when another shuts.

Hafiz

Hear what the glass will tell thee
This again-married world
Has had many husbands mighty & glorious
Jam & Keikobad

Hafiz

Free thyself from wo
Thou drinkest blood when thou enviest others their luck

Hafiz

———————

And had Hafiz
Ten tongues like the lily,
He would be silent
Like the rosebud,
While thro love his mouth is sealed.

Hafiz

———————

Thy songs O Hafiz
Are erst in Paradise
On the leaves of the jasmin
And the rose bush written

Hafiz

———————

Who compares a poem
Of others to mine
Compares gold
With rush-plaits

Hafiz

———————

Thy poems Hafiz shame the rose leaves
Since they breathe the praise of the rosier cheeks of thy love

Hafiz

———————

In the kingdom of Poesy Hafiz waves like a banner
Thro' the Shah's defending favor

Hafiz

———

Where o where is the message which today
brought us tidings of joy
That instead of silver & gold I on the earth
Might strew souls.

Hafiz

———

    Come let us strew roses
And pour wine in the cup
Break up the roof of heaven
And throw it into new forms

So soon the army of cares
Shed the blood of the true
So will I with the cupbearer
Shatter the building of woe

We will rosewater
In winecups pour
And sugar in the censer
Full of musksmell throw

Thy harping is lovely
O play sweet airs
That we may sing songs
And shake our heads

Bring Eastwind the dust of the body
To that great lord
That we also may cast our eyes
On his beauty

Hafiz

Who gave thy cheek the mixed tint
Of tulip & rose
Is also in state to give
Patience & rest to me poor
Who taught cruelty
To thy dark hair
Is also in state to give
The right against myself
I gave up hope of Ferhad
Once for all on the day
When I learned he had given
His heart to Schirin
Surely I have no treasure
Yet am I richly satisfied
God has given that to the Shah
And this to the beggar
The bride of the world is truly
Outwardly richly dressed
Who enjoys her must give
His soul for a dowry.
At the cedar's foot by the brook
Lift I freer my hands
When now the blowing of the East
Gives tidings of May

Hafiz

Drink, hear my counsel, my son, that the world fret thee
    not.
Tho' the heart bleed, let thy lips laugh, like the wine cup:
Is thy soul hurt, yet dance with the viol-strings:
Thou learnest no secret, until thou knowest friendship,
Since to the unsound no heavenly knowledge comes in.

Hafiz

———

Ruler after word & thought
Which no eye yet saw
Which no ear yet heard
Remain, until thy young destiny
From the old greybeard of the sky
His blue coat takes.

Hafiz

———

O follow the sonnet's flight
Thou seest a fleet career
A child begot in a night
That travels a thousand year

Hafiz

———

O Hafiz, give me thought
In fiery figures cast;
For all beside is naught,—
All else is din & blast.

Hafiz

———

In thy holiday of life,
Use occasion, work & climb,
The sepulchre has overmuch
Unprofitable time.

Hafiz

———

The roguish wind and I
Are truly an amorous pair;
Me burns the sparkle of thine eye,
He fans thy scented hair.

Hafiz

———————

The treacherous wind pipes a lewd song,
Makes saints perverse, & angels bad;
Shall we sit & see such wrong,
And not cry out like mad!
Fie! what flute pants in the North?
What viol in the west?
Steals Virtue not from men of worth?
Corrupts he not the best?
Shall this pass in silence by?
Shall we not make hue & cry?

Hafiz

———————

We would do nought but good,
Else shall dishonor come
On the day when the flying soul
Hies backward to its home.

Hafiz

———————

Lo! where from Heaven's high roof
Misfortune staggers down;
We, just from harm to stand aloof,
Will to the wineshop run.

Hafiz

———

Drink wine, and the heaven
New lustre diffuses,
And doubt not that sinning
Has also its uses.

The builder of Heaven
Has sundered the earth,
So that no footway
Leads out of it forth:

On turnpikes of wonder
Wine leads the mind forth,
Straight, sidewise & upward
Southward and north.

Stands the vault adamantine
Until the last day;
The wine-cup shall ferry
Thee o'er it away.

Hafiz

———

A stately bride is the shining world,
Yet none can woo that maid to wife.

Hafiz

———

Who ever suffered as I from separation?
Ah I will punish separation by separation.

Hafiz

I shall go from my sickbed to heaven
If, on my last march, thou holdest a torch for me
The wind-borne dust is heavy from thy attraction
Think on me, I am an older servant.
Not every poet sings inspired songs
My sly falcon grasps firmly the partridge of song.
Believest me not? Go ask the pictures of Sina
Whether Mani did not wish a stroke from my ink?
The nightingale says, Up cupbearer, good morning,
Still rings in my head the lute-tone of yesterday,
Ask not Hafiz, ask me, of revelry & love,
Since flask & cups are to me the moon & pleiads.

Hafiz

See & hear the fraud, the malice of the change of fortune,
Every eye is blind, every ear is deaf.
Many whom the sun & the moon had served for a bolster
Lay down their head at last in ashes & dust.
Will thy thumb-ring span the bow of Fate?
Will a shield ward off the strokes of Destiny?
Though thou screen thyself with iron walls, & brazen gates,
Ever the hand of your Fate crashes in.
Never mind the trembling light in the lamp of life,
Night follows on light, sugar only conceals poison.

Hafiz

Who loves his friend with his heart of hearts
Bends not his head though the sky rain darts,
O, our lifetime wastes to no lofty end
Till the hero is matched with an equal friend.
Poison from the hand of my love were food,
The sweet & the bane do the heart good.
Knowst thou shy Saadi sits ever alone?
Because he cannot part from the darling one.

Saadi

Had I the world for my enemy
Yet kept the treasure of a true friend,
Never should I ask whether things were
Or were not, in this world.
A ship on the high seas
Doth the state of a lover resemble.
Overboard cast they the cargo
If so they can save their lives.

Saadi

Salve senescentem

Saadi's poem on Old Age

Now is the time when weakness comes,—& strength goes
The magic of sweet words—I lose
The harvest wind cuts keen: the tender sheen and shade
And pink & purple light upon thy garland fade
To my foot fails the power—of manly stride in streets;
Happy he who soonest to his orchard hut—retreats.
Saadi's whole power lies—in sweet words
Keep this   all the rest may go to beast & birds

Saadi

The pain of love's a better fate
Than the body's best estate.

Saadi

In Senahar, my first born sleeps;
Stunned with the blow, poor Saadi weeps;
Tho' youth more fresh than Jussuf blooms,
The charnelworm his cheek consumes.
Where is the palm, star-topped, earth-footed,
Which the brute storm has not uprooted?
I muttered,—"Perish God on high,
Since pure youth dies as greybeards die!"
I staggered to my darling's tomb,
And tore the sealed stone therefrom,
Then frantic, tottering, void of wit,
Groped down into that marble pit.
When grief was spent, & reason came,
Methought I heard my son exclaim
'If my dark house thy heart affright
'Saadi strive upwards to the light
'Wilt thou give graves the blaze of noon
'High hearts can work that wonder soon
The crowd believe that harvests grow
Where never man did barley sow.
But Saadi saw the fruit enchanted
By bending sower truly planted.

Saadi

Unbar the door, since thou the Opener art,
Show me the forward way, since thou art guide,
I put no faith in pilot or in chart,
Since they are transient, & thou dost abide.

Omar Khayyám

———————

For two rewards, & nought beside,
A prudent man the world would ride;
His friend with benefits to crown,
And put his adversary down.

Ibn Jemin

———————

Shah Sandschar, whose lowest slave
Is on this earth a king;
The mole of his despotic command
Adorns men & daemons.
When his wrath burns on earth,
Nothing in heaven is secure.
Looks he on the world with power,
Life mounts in it.
Where his name is named,
Is the love of gold unknown.
Death, out of fear of him, clatters his dry bones.
The deep-hid secret is discovered by thy wit;
Unrest is stilled by thee, unrest which know no limits.
When thy wrath glowed
The wolves become tame in the wood,
The world would not stand, if thy foot held it not firm,
In the desert, his breath restores the equipoise of the air.
The Lion of the Zodiack is a picture of the lions of his
        banner.
Hope leads his light bridle,
His heavy stirrup leads death.
Ambush of destiny lies
For all, behind his arrow.
When his bow moves,
It is already the Last Day.
Whom his onset marks out,
To him is life not appointed:
And the ghost of the Holy Ghost

Were not sure of its time.
None holds himself once firm in the stirrup, save Victory.
A hundred conquerors heaven strikes dead
Before thee, as thy right.
O Lord, take him into thy pay. It is his only wish.
Is he not of thy circle? Stands he yet at thy door?
Buy him, ere thou yet knowest him,
Or instantly his price will rise.
Once every ten years let him kiss thy hand,
Only one day let him stand in thy Forecourts.

Suffer in thy lands, o Shah! a poet, tho' rough & rude,
But in thy praise is he finer than a hair.
Steadily so long as the tongue speaks, sounds thy name in
    prayer.
As long as there is gold, will thy name be coined on it.
Of thee, Time stands in need, as Space stands in need of
    Time;
So long as men give & take, Thou shalt give & take
    lordship.
Rule thou forever, so will rule subsist.

Enweri

———

Wilt thou life's best elixir drain?
Be lowliest of the lowly found;
The sweetest drop of the sugar-cane
Grows nearest to the ground.

Feisi

———

The Soul

I am the falcon of the spirit world,
  Escaped out of highest heaven
Who out of desire of the hunt,
  Am fallen into earthly form
Of the Mount Kaf am I the Simorg,
  Whom the net of Being holds imprisoned
Of Paradise am I the Peacock,
  Who has escaped from his nest.

(Persian)

Teach your child to earn his meal,
Or you bring him up to steal.

Jean Chardin

Only three things lengthen life,—
Fine clothes, fine house, & comely wife.

Jean Chardin

For pearls, plunge in the sea
For greatness, wake all night

Jean Chardin

Arabian Ballad

1   Under the rock   on the trail
    He lies slain
    Into whose blood
    No dew falls

2   A great load laid he on me
    And died;
    God knows, this load
    Will I lift.

3   Heir of my revenge
    Is my sister's son,
    The warlike,
    The irreconcileable.

4   Mute sweats he poison,
    As the otter sweats;
    As the snake breathes venom
    Against which no enchantment avails

5   The stern message came to us
    Of the heavy woe;
    The stoutest had they
    Overpowered.

6   Me had Destiny plundered
    Striking down my friend,
    Whose dearest friend
    Was left unhurt.

7   Sunshine was he
    On the cold day,
    And when the dogstar burned
    He was shade & coolness.

8   Dry were his hips
Not slow;
Moist his hand,
Bold & strong.

9   With firm mind
Followed he his aim
Until he rested,
Then rested also the firm mind.

10   The rain cloud was he
Imparting gifts;
And, when he attacked,
The terrible lion.

11   Stately before men,
Black haired, long-robed,
When rushing on the foe
A lean wolf.

———

12   Two cups offered he,
Honey and wormwood;
Fare of such kind
Tasted each.

13   Terrible rode he alone;
No man accompanied him;
Like the sword of Yemen,
With teeth adorned.

14   At noon we young men set forth
On the war trail
Rode all night
Like sweeping clouds   without rest

15   Every one was a sword
Girt with a sword;
Out of the sheath drawn
A glancing lightning

16 They sipped the spirit of sleep,
    But, when they nodded their heads,
    We smote them,
    And they were away

17 Our vengeance was complete.
    There escaped of two tribes
    Quite little,
    The least.

18 And when the Hudselite
    Had broken his lance to kill his man
    The man with his lance
    Slew the Hudselite.

19 On a rough resting place
    They laid him, —
    On a sharp rock, where the very camels
    Broke their paws.

20 When the morning greeted him there,
    The murdered, on the grim place,
    Was he robbed,
    The booty carried away.

21 But now are murdered by me
    The Hudseleites with deep wounds;
    Pity makes me not unhappy
    Itself is murdered.

22 The spear's thirst was assuaged
    With the first drink;
    To it was not denied
    Repeated drinks.

23 Now is wine again permitted
    Which first was forbidden:
    With much toil
    I won this permission.

24   To sword & spear,
      And to horse, gave I
      This favor,
      Which is now the good of all.

25   Reach then the bowl,
      O Sawab Ben Amre!
      Since my body, at the command of my uncle
      Is now one great wound.

26   And the cup of death
      Reached we to the Hudseleites
      Whose working is wo,
      Blindness, & ruin.

27   Then laughed the hyenas
      At the death of the Hudseleites;
      And thou sawest the wolves
      Whose faces shone.

28   The noblest vultures flew thither
      They stepped from corpse to corpse
      And from the richly prepared feast
      They could not rise into the air.

                                              Goethe

——————

      Fortune and Hope! I've made my port,
Farewell ye twin deceivers!
You've trained me many a weary chase,
Go cozen new believers.

                                   Prudentius

——————

Alas, Alas, that I am betrayed
By my flying days, it is then the looking glass,
Not the mind, if self love do not tarnish it
Alas that he who foolish frets in desire
Not heeding the flying time
Finds himself, like me, at one instant, old.
Nor know I how to repent, nor do I make myself ready,
Nor advise myself with death at the door.
   Enemy of myself
Vainly I pour out plaints & sighs
Since there is no harm equal to lost time

Michelangelo

———————

Wo is me woe's me when I think
Of my spent years I find not one
Among so many days; not one was mine.
Hopes which betrayed me, vain longing,
Tears, love, fiery glow, & sigh,
For not one mortal affection is longer new to me
Held me fast, & now, I know it, & learn it,
And from goodness & truth ever severed,
Go I forth, from day to day, further;
Ever the shadows grow longer; ever deeper
Sinks for me the sun;
And I am ready to fall infirm & outworn.

Michelangelo

———————

Sweet, sweet, is sleep, — Ah! sweeter, to be stone,
Whilst wrong & shame exist & grow;
Not to see, not to feel, is a boon;
Then, not to wake me, pray speak low!

Michelangelo

———————

The power of a beautiful face lifts me to heaven
Since else in earth is none that delights me
And I mount living among the elect souls,
A grace which seldom falls to a mortal.

So well with its Maker the work consents,
That I rise to him through divine conceptions
And here I shape all thoughts & words,
Burning, loving, through this gentle form:

Whence, if ever from two beautiful eyes
I know not how to turn my look, I know in them
The light which shows me the way which guides me
    to God.

And if, kindled at their light, I burn,
In my noble flame sweetly shines
The eternal joy which smiles in heaven.

Michelangelo

———————

Dante's Vita Nuova

The New Life of Dante Alighieri

I

In that part of the book of my memory before which little could be read, is found this title, The New Life begins. Under which rubric, I find written the words which it is my purpose to copy in this book, and if not all, at least their sense.

II

Nine times already after my birth was the heaven of light returned to the same point in its proper gyration, when to my eyes first appeared the gracious lady of my mind, who was called Beatrice by many who did not know her name. She had then been so long in this life that in her time the starry heaven had moved towards the East one of the twelve parts of a degree, so that she appeared to me as at the beginning of her ninth year, & I saw her about the end of mine and she appeared to me clothed in a very noble lowly colour and becoming red, girt & adorned in the mode which belonged to her tender youth. At that moment, I say verily the spirit of life which dwells in the secretest chamber of the heart did so quake that it appeared violently in my least pulses, and trembling said,

> Ecce deus fortior me; veniens dominabitur mihi.
>
> Behold a god stronger than I who cometh to rule me.

At that moment, the animal spirit which dwells in the chamber into which all the sensuous spirits carry their perceptions, began to marvel much, &, speaking specially to the spirits of sight, said,

> Now hath appeared our Supreme Good.
>
> Apparuit jam Beatitudo nostra.

At that moment, the natural spirit which dwells in that part where our nourishment is supplied, began to weep & weeping said,

Heu miser, quia frequenter impeditus ero deinceps.

Wo is me I am henceforth to have my way no longer.

From that hour forth, I say, that, Love ruled my soul, which was so much disposed by him & he began to take over me so much lordship & governance, through the strength which my imagination gave to him, that it behoved me to do all his pleasure to the utmost, & he commanded me many times that I should seek to see this youngest angel; wherefore I in my boyhood many times went seeking her, & I saw her with such new & such praiseworthy manners that certainly those words of the Poet Homer might be spoken of her,

> "She seemed not the daughter of a mortal, but
> of a god."

And it was so that her image which continually abode with me, (was it the presumption of Love to subdue me) was always of so noble virtue that it never suffered Love to rule me without the faithful counsel of reason in matters wherein such counsel were good to hear. But since the controuling the passions & manners of so much youth may seem to some fabulous, I will quit these, & passing over many things which might be taken from the book where these lie hidden, I will come to those words which are written in my memory under longer paragraphs.

III

When so many days were past that nine years were exactly completed after the forewritten appearance of this most gentle maid, — in the last of these days, it happened, that this wonderful lady appeared to me clothed in the purest white, in the middle between two gentlewomen who were of maturer age; & passing through a road turned her eyes towards that part where I was, very fearful, and by her ineffable courtesy which is today requited in the other world, saluted me virtuously, so that it appeared to me then that I saw all the limits of happiness. The hour when her sweetest salute arrived at me, was precisely the ninth of that day, and inasmuch as it was the first time that her words turned to arrive at my ears, I took so much sweetness, that, like one intoxicated, I departed from the company & withdrew to a solitary place of my chamber, & set myself to think on this most courteous one. And thinking of her, there came to me a sweet sleep in which appeared to me a marvellous vision, wherein I seemed to see in my chamber a cloud of the colour of fire, within which I discerned a figure of a signor of aspect fearful to the beholder. And he appeared to have so much joy in himself, that it was wonderful, and he said many things, which I did not understand, except a few, among which I heard these words;

I am thy lord.

In his arms appeared to me to sleep a person naked save that she was lightly infolded in a blood-red cloth, whom I beholding very attentively knew that she was the lady of peace, who had the day before deigned to salute me, & in one of his hands it appeared that he held something which burned wholly, & it seemed to me that he said to me these words;

Vide cor tuum.

And when he had remained some time it appeared to me that he waked her who slept, and so prevailed by his genius that he made her eat that thing which burned in her hand which she eat doubtfully. After a little while his joy turned into bitterest lamentation, and thus complaining he took again this lady in his arms, and with her he seemed to me to go towards heaven. Whence I suffered so great anguish that my weak sleep could not bear, so it broke, & I awaked. And immediately I began to reflect, & found that the hour in which this dream had appeared to me was the fourth of the night, so that it appeared plainly that it was the first hour of the nine last hours of the night. I thinking of this which had appeared to me proposed to make it known to many who were the famous poets (trovatori) in that time. And because I had already seen by myself the art of saying words in rhyme, I proposed to make a sonnet, in which I should salute all the faithful of love, & praying them that they would judge my vision, I should write them what I had seen in my dream, & I then begun this sonnet.

To each taken soul & gentle heart,
To whose sight comes the present word,
To the end that they may write again their thought
Greeting in the name of their lord, that is, Love.
Already was it the third hour
Of the time when every star is most bright,
When Love appeared to me suddenly
Whose substance seen made me tremble.
Glad seemed Love, holding
My heart in his hand, & in his arms had
My lady asleep rolled in a garment;
Then he waked her, and with that burning heart
Fed he her lowly trembling;
Then bewailing it, he seemed to go away.

This sonnet was answered by many & with different meanings; among which respondents was he whom I call first among my friends (Guido Cavalcanti). And he wrote this sonnet.

You have seen, in my judgment, every valour,
And every game, & every good which man feels,
As if you were in proof of a mighty lord
Who ruled the world of honour.
Then live in places where grief dies,
And hold reason in your pious mind
Yes go gently in dreams to the race
Who carry their heart without pain.
Seeing her carry the heart of you,
Death demands your lady,
Feeds on the living heart of her timid.
When it appeared to you that she went away grieving
It was the sweet dream which was completed
That its contrary came conquering it.

And this was the beginning of the friendship between me & him, when he knew that it was I that had sent this to him. The true meaning of the said sonnet was not seen then by any one, but now is manifest to the most simple.

IV

And after this vision my natural spirit began to be impeded in its operation because the soul was all given up to thinking of this most gentle one, whence I became in a little time after, of so frail & weak a condition, that many friends grieved at my face, and many full of envy persisted to know of me that which I wished to conceal altogether, from others, and I becoming sensible of the evil demand which they made me, through the will of love which commanded me according to the counsel of reason, answered them, that love was that which had governed me thus. I spoke of love because I carried in my face so many of his ensigns which could not be covered & when they asked on whose account this love had thus destroyed me I smiling looked at them & said nothing to them.

V

One day it happened that this most gentle one sat in a place where were heard words of the Queen of Glory, & I was in a place from whence I could see my chief joy, and in the midst between her & me in a right line sat a gentlewoman of very pleasant aspect who beheld many times with wonder my glances which appeared to terminate on her, whence many were informed of her looking. And so much was this regarded, that, on leaving that place I heard some one say near me, See how such a lady destroys the person of this man. And naming her, I heard that they spoke of her who was placed midway in the right line which begun from the most gentle Beatrice & terminated in my eyes. Then I comforted myself much, assuring myself that my secret was not communicated to others that day by my face, & immediately I thought of making of this gentlewoman a screen of the truth, and I carried this so well in a little time that my secret was believed to be known by many persons who spoke to me of it. Through this gentlewoman I concealed myself some years & months & to make it more credible to others, I made for her certain little pieces in rhyme, which it is not my purpose to write here, except insofar as they concern the most gentle Beatrice;

and therefore I will leave them all, only I shall write one which appears to be in praise of her.

VI

I say that in the time when this gentlewoman was the screen of so much love, there arose on my part a wish to record the name of the most gentle, and to accompany it with many names of ladies, & specially with the name of this gentlewoman, and having taken the names of sixty the fairest women of the city, where my lady was placed by the most High Lord, I composed an epistle under the form of service, which I will not copy, & should not have mentioned except to say this, that composing it, it strangely happened that in no other number would the name of my lady stand, except in the *ninth*, among the names of these ladies.

VII

The gentlewoman through whom I had for some time concealed my inclination, happened to quit the abovementioned city & went into a distant country; I as it were frightened from my fine defence, greatly discomforted myself more than I should have believed beforehand, & thinking that if I should not speak somewhat dolorously of her departure, people would very soon become aware of my secret, I proposed to make a lament, in a sonnet which I will copy, because my lady was the immediate cause of certain words which are in the sonnet as appears to whoso understands it; and then I wrote this sonnet;

> O ye who pass by the way of Love,
> Attend & behold,
> If any sorrow be great as mine.
> And I pray only that you will hear me
> And then imagine
> If I am the lodging & the key of every grief.
> Love, not truly by my small goodness
> But by his own nobility
> Placed me in a life so sweet & gentle

That I heard myself say secretly many times
Ah! by what worth
Does the heart so lightly possess this treasure?
Now have I lost all my presumption
Which arose out of the amorous treasure
Wherefore I remain poor
In a fashion, which to speak, breeds doubt.
So that wishing to do as those
Who through shame conceal their want,
I outwardly show a gladness
And within from the heart I pine & bewail.

VIII

After the departure of this gentlewoman, it was the plea-
sure of the Lord of the Angels to call to his glory a lady of
very gentle countenance who was a great favourite in this city,
whose body I saw lie without life in the midst of many ladies
who lamented her. I also lamenting, proposed to myself to
say some words of her death in guerdon of this, that I had
once seen her with my lady; &, on that, I touched in the last
part of the words which I wrote of her, as appears plainly to
whoso understands it; and I said then these two sonnets; of
which the first begins;

Lament lovers, since Love laments,
Seeing what cause he had to weep.
Love hears with pity ladies cry
Showing bitter grief in their eyes,
Because rough Death in gentle heart
Hath wrought his cruel work,
Spoiling that which the world praises
In a gentle dame, out of honour.
Hear how much horror Love felt,
Since I saw him lament in true form
Over the beautiful dead image;
And I looked toward the Heaven often
Where the gentle soul was already placed,
Who was a lady of so gay an aspect.

and the second;

Rough Death, enemy of pity,
Ancient mother of grief,
Indisputable heavy judgment
Thou hast given matter of grief to the heart;
Wherefore I go sad.
The tongue wearies of blaming thee
And if thou wouldst make request for grace
It behoves that I tell
Your offence with every cruel injury;
Not because it is hidden from people
But to make angry at it
Whoso nourishes himself with Love henceforth.
From the world thou hast divided courtesy,
And that which in a lady is virtue to prize.
In gay youth
Thou hast destroyed amorous beauty
I will no more discover what dame she is
Except by her known virtues.
Whoso does not merit salvation
Let her never hope to have her company.

IX

Some days after the death of this lady, something occurred which required me to leave the city abovementioned, & to go towards those parts where was the gentlewoman who had been my defence. It chanced that my journey did not reach so far as to where she was, and although I was in the company of many according to the appearance, the going displeased me so that my sighs could not exhale the anguish which the heart felt, because I was departing from my felicity. And yet my sweetest lord who ruled me through the virtue of the most gentle lady, in my imagination appeared like a pilgrim lightly clad, & with coarse clothes, He seemed to me astonished & looked on the ground, except that sometimes his eyes turned to a beautiful running river, very clear, which ran along the road in which I walked. It seemed to me that Love called me, & said to me these words; "I come from that lady who has long been thy defence, & I know that her return will not be.

And therefore this heart which I made thee to have from her, I have with me & I carry it to a lady who shall be thy defence as this one was, (and he named her to me so that I knew her well) but notwithstanding if of these words I have spoken to thee, thou speakest anything, tell it in a fashion that by them may not be discerned the feigned love which thou hast shown to this one, & which it will behove thee to show to others." And having said these words, this my imagination disappeared very suddenly through the large part which it appeared to me that Love had given me of himself. And, as if changed in countenance, I rode that day very thoughtful, &, attended by many sighs, on the next day I began thus this sonnet.

> Riding the other day through a road
> Sad at going where it displeased me
> I found Love in the midst of the way
> In the light dress of a pilgrim.
> His semblance appeared mean
> As if he had lost his lordship,
> And sighing thoughtful came
> So as not to see the people, his head down;
> When he saw me, he called me by name,
> And said, I come from the distant place
> Where was your heart by my will,
> And I bring it back to serve a new pleasure.
> Then I took of him so great part
> That he disappeared & I knew not how.

X

After my return I set myself to seek this lady whom my lord had named to me in the road of sighs &, that my story may be short, I say, that in a little time I made her my defence so much, that too many people spoke of her, beyond all the limits of courtesy, whereat I often was sorely grieved. And for this cause, that is, of this excessive fame, which appeared as if I had viciously defamed myself, that most gentle one who was the destroyer of all vices, & queen of the virtues, passing in some place, denied to me her sweetest salute, in which consisted all my peace. And digressing somewhat from the present argument, I wish to explain what her salutation operated virtuously in me.

XI

I say that when she appeared from any part, through the hope of her wonderful sweetness no enemy remained to me; also there was added to me a flame of charity, which made me pardon whoever had offended me. And if any one had demanded aught of me, my answer would have been only Love, with a face clothed in humility; and when she was at hand ready to salute, a spirit of Love destroying all the other sensuous spirits, advanced forth the weak spirits of sight and said to them, Go to honour your lady, & he remained in the place of them; and whoso had wished to know Love, could do so, beholding the tremor of my eyes. And when this gentlest lady saluted me, not that Love was such a medium that he could shade from me the intolerable clearness, but he, as by excess of sweetness became such that my body, which now was all under his regiment, often moved itself as something heavily inanimate, so that it plainly appeared that in her salute dwelt my peace, which many times filled & overran my capacity.

XII

Now returning to the argument, I say, that when this joy was denied me, there came to me so much grief, that withdrawing from all company, I went into a lonely place to bathe the ground with bitterest tears. And, after some time, this weeping being stopped, I went into my chamber, where I could lament without being heard, and there calling pity from the Lady of all courtesy, & saying, O Love, aid thy faithful servant,—I slept like a beaten child worn out with crying. It happened in the midst of my sleep, that I seemed to see in my chamber beside me a youth clothed in whitest vestments & thinking much how much he looked at me there where I lay, & when he had looked at me some time, it seemed to me, that, sighing he called me; & he said to me these words.

Fili mi, tempus est ut pretermictantur simulacra nostra.

Then it appeared to me that I knew him who called me thus, as many times in my sighs he had called me and considering him I thought that he wept piteously & he seemed to expect some word from me, whence taking courage began to speak thus with him. Lord of nobleness, why weepest thou? and he said to me these words;

> "I am, as it were, the centre of the circle, to whom all the parts of the circumference are alike. But not so, thou."

Then thinking on his words, it seemed to me that he had spoken very obscurely, so that I forced myself to speak, & said these words to him, "What is that, my Lord, which you say with so much obscurity?" And he replied to me in the vulgar speech. "Do not ask more than is useful to you." And yet I begun to speak with him of the salute which had been denied me. And asking the cause, it was answered in this manner. "This our Beatrice heard from certain persons that the lady whom I named to thee in the road of sighs received some displeasure from you. And therefore this most gentle one who is the contrary of all annoys, did not deign to salute your person, fearing lest it should be hurtful. Wherefore to the end that she may truly know something of the secret you have kept through so long a consuetude, I wish that you should say certain words, first, in which you comprise the power which I hold over you through her, & how you were hers, so early, from her infancy & of this call as witness him who knows it and pray him that he tell her it, & I who know this, willingly will converse with her of it, & by this she shall know your will, knowing which, she will understand the words of those deceived persons. Make these words as a means, so that thou shalt not speak to her immediately, which is not fit nor send them into any place without me where they can be heard by her, but adorn them with sweet harmony in which I will be in all parts where it behoves;" and, having said these words, he disappeared, & my dream was broken. Wherefore recollecting myself I found that this vision had appeared to me in the ninth hour of the day. And before I went out of the chamber, I proposed to make a ballad in which that was done which my lord had imposed on me, and I made this Ballad;

Ballad, I wish that you should find Love
And with him go before my lady
So that my excuse which thou shalt sing
My lord may reason with her,
Thou ballad goest so courteously
That without company
Thou shouldest have courage in all parts;
But if thou wouldst go securely,
Find Love again first,
Who perhaps it is not good sense to leave
Because she who ought to hear thee
If she is, as I believe, in truth angry with me
If thou by him be not attended
Easily may do you a dishonour.
With sweet sound, when thou art with him,
Begin these words;
After thou hast sought pity,
Lady, he who sent me to you
If it please you
If there be excuse would that you should hear it of me
Love is here who through your beauty
Makes him, as he will, change face,
Then because he made him look at another
Think you not that his heart is changed.
Tell her; lady his heart is set
With such firm faith
That to serve you he has every thought ready;
Early was yours & he never swerved.
If she do not believe you
Tell her to ask Love whether it be true;
And at last make to her a humble prayer
(To pardon it if it were a trouble to her)
That she would command me by messenger that I
        should die.
And she shall see her good servant obey.

And say to her who is the key of all pity
Before I become free
That I shall know how to tell my good reason
Through the grace of my sweet notes;
Remain thou here with her
And tell of thy servant what you will.
And if she by thy prayer pardon him,
Cause that she announce to him a fair seeming peace.
My gentle ballad, when it pleases thee
Move in such form that you have honor.

Should any man confront me & say that he knew not to what purpose was this speaking in the second person, since the ballad is nothing else than these words which I speak, then I say, that this doubt I intend to solve & clear up in this little book, in part even more doubtful, and then he may here understand who doubts more than one who should confront me in the manner proposed.

XIII

After the abovementioned vision, having already spoken the words which Love had charged me to say, many & diverse thoughts began to combat & to try me, each, as it were, irresistible; among which thoughts, four hindered most the repose of life. One of them was this. Good is the lordship of Love since it draws the mind of the faithful from all vile matters. Another was this. The lordship of love is not good, since by how much faith the faithful yields, by so much the more sharp & grievous crises it requires him to pass. Another was this; The name of love is so sweet to hear, that it appears to me impossible that its proper operation should be in most things other than sweet, because names follow the things named, as it is written, Names are the consequences of things *Nomina sunt consequentia rerum.* The fourth was this; The lady through whom Love binds thee thus, is not like other ladies, that she may lightly be removed from the heart. — And each assaulted me so long, that it made me stand like one who knows not by what way he shall take his road, who wishes to go & knows not his path. And if I thought of wishing to seek a common passage for them, that is, one in which they should

all agree, this was very unpleasing to me, that is, to cry out &
to throw myself into the arms of pity. And remaining in this
state, there came to me a willingness to write rhymes and, I
then said this sonnet;

> All my thoughts speak of Love
> And have in them so great variety,
> That one makes me wish his power,
> Another foolish talks of his valour,
> Another hopeful brings me grief,
> Another makes me complain often,
> And they agree only in asking pity.
> Trembling with fear which is in the heart.
> Therefore I know not what theme to take.
> And I would speak; and I know not what to say;
> Thus I find myself in amorous errour
> And if with all I would make agreement
> It would need that I should call my enemy
> My lady Pity who defends me

XIV

After the battle of these different thoughts it happened that
this most gentle one was in a place where many gentle ladies
were assembled, to which place I was conducted by a friendly
person thinking to do me a great pleasure, inasmuch as he led
me where so many ladies displayed their beauties, wherefore
I, not knowing whither I was led, & confiding in the person
who was one that had led his friend to the end of life, said to
him, Why are we come to these ladies? Then he said, that he
did thus that they should be worthily served. It is true that
here they were gathered to the company of a gentlewoman
who was that day married, and, therefore, according to the
custom in that city, it behoved that they should give her their
company in the first sitting down at table in the house of her
bridegroom. So that I, believing that I did this friend a plea-
sure, made myself ready to stand at the service of these ladies
in his company; and in the end of my making ready, it ap-
peared to me that I felt a strange tremor begin on the left side
of my breast, & extend itself suddenly through all parts of
my body. Then I say that I turned my person feignedly to a

picture which surrounded this house, & fearing lest others should be aware of my trembling, I lifted my eyes, & beholding the ladies, I saw among them the most gentle Beatrice. Then were my spirits destroyed through the force with which Love took me, seeing himself in such nearness to the most gentle lady, that there did not remain in life any but the spirits of sight, & even these remained outside of their organs, because Love wished to stand in their most noble place to see the wonder of this lady. And as soon as I was other than at first, I was much grieved for these *little spirits* (spiritelli) who lamented aloud, & said, If this one had not dazzled us out of our places, we could have remained to see the marvel of this dame, as our peers also remain. I say that many of these ladies becoming aware of my transfiguration, began to wonder, &, discoursing, bantered concerning me and that most gentle one. Therefore the friend of good faith took me by the hand & leading me out of the sight of these ladies, asked me what ailed me? Then I answered somewhat, & rallied my dead-like spirits, & these fugitives being returned to their seats, I said to my friend these words,—"I have had my feet in that part of the life beyond, from which there is no more power in the understanding to return." And having parted with him, I returned to my chamber of tears, where, weeping & ashamed, I said to myself, If this lady knew my condition, I do not believe that she would so mistake my person; rather would she surely have much pity on me. And remaining in this grief, I proposed to speak some words, in which, addressing her, I might signify to her the cause of my transfiguration; & I would say that I know well that she knows me not, & that if she knew me, I believe that pity of it would come to others, & I proposed to tell her them (the words or verses) desiring that they would come by chance into her audience, & then I said this sonnet;

> With the other dames you deride my sight
> And do not know the lady who moves me
> That I assumed to you a strange face
> When I beheld your beauty.
> If you knew it, your compassion could not
> Hold out longer against me the accustomed trial

That when Love found me so near to you
He took courage & so much security
That haughtily among my tremulous spirits,
Some he slew, & some he drove out,
So that he alone remained to see you.
Wherefore I change myself into the form of another
But not so that I do not well taste now
The woes of the tormented fugitives.

XV

After the new transfiguration, there came to me a strong thought, which rarely left me, nay which was always with me; since you came to so ridiculous appearance, when you were near this lady, why then do you seek to see her? If you were asked anything by her, what wouldst thou have to answer? Granting that thou shouldest have each of thy powers liberated, in as much as thou shouldest answer her. And to this replied another humble thought, & said, I would tell her that so soon as I imagine her wonderful beauty, so soon have I the desire to behold her, which is of so much force that it kills & destroys in my memory all which can rise against it, & therefore these past sufferings do not restrain me from seeking the view of her. Therefore, I, moved by such thoughts, proposed to say certain words in which excusing myself to her with such passion, I described also how it was with me in her presence; & I said then this sonnet;

Whatever in the mind hinders dies
When I come to behold you, o beautiful joy,
And when I am near you, I hear Love
Who says, Fly, if you are loath to die.
The face shows the colour of the heart
Fainting where it leans;
And through the drunkenness of great fear
The stones seem to cry, Die, die;
It were a sin in whom should then see me
If he should not comfort the astonished soul
Only showing that he grieved for me
For pity which shall kill your contempt

Which cries in the sad expression
Of the eyes which desire their own death

XVI

After that which I had said in this sonnet I had an inclination to say also words in which I might say the four things also abovementioned concerning my state, which it did not seem to me I had yet made known. The first of which is, that, often I grieved when my memory moved the fancy to imagine what Love had made me become. The second is, that, Love often suddenly assailed me so strongly that there remained no other life in me except the thought which spoke of this lady. The third; that, when this battle of love so assaulted me, I moved myself, as it were, all discoloured, to see this lady, believing that the sight of her would defend me from this array, forgetting all which had befallen me through approaching so much gentleness. The fourth is, how such a sight not only did not defend me, but finally discomfited the little life I had; and therefore I said this sonnet;

> Often comes to mind
> The dark quality Love gives me
> And such pity rises, that often
> I say, Ah! Happened it so to another?
> For suddenly Love assaults me
> So that life almost leaves me
> A living spirit only remains
> (And this remains, because he speaks of you)
> Then I force myself to seek aid
> And thus dead-like & without strength
> I come to see you trusting to be healed
> And if I lift my eyes to look at you
> In the heart begins a quaking
> Which drives the soul from the pulses.

XVII

After I had said these three sonnets in which I addressed this lady, because they were, as it were, reporters of all my condition, believing that I should be silent & say no more, since I seemed to me to have expressed myself sufficiently. Since then I refrained from speaking to her. It behoved me to take new & nobler argument than the past, &, because the occasion of my new subject is delightful to hear, I will relate it as beiefly as I can.

XVIII

Whereas many persons by my countenance had become acquainted with my secret, certain ladies who were met for their mutual entertainment, knew well my heart, because each of them had been present at my many discomfitures, & I passing near them as led by my chance, was called by one of these gentlewomen and she who spoke to me was a lady of very graceful speech, so that when I joined them, & saw well that my most gentle lady was not there, recollecting myself, I saluted them, & inquired their pleasure. The ladies were many, among whom were some who laughed among themselves: others of them looked at me, awaiting what I should say: others of them spoke apart, of whom one turning her eyes towards me, & calling me by name, said these words; "To what end lovest thou this lady of thine, since thou canst not sustain her presence? Tell us what is the end of such a love, which should be a thing wholly new." And when she had spoken these words, not only she but all the others began to listen for my reply. Then I said these words; Ladies, the end of my love was truly the salute (saluto) of this lady, of whom perhaps you have heard, and therein abides the happiness of the end of all my desires; but since it pleases her to deny it to me, my lord Love (I thank him for it) has placed all my firmness in that which cannot be taken away. Then these ladies began to speak among themselves, & if sometimes we see fall water mixed with beautiful snow, so seemed it to me to hear their words come forth mingled with sighs; and after they had spoken awhile apart, again said to me that lady who had first spoken, these words; "We pray thee that thou wouldest tell us where is thy felicity?" And I, answering her, said thus much; "In those words which praise my lady." Then answered me this one who spoke before, "If thou toldest me truly, those words which thou saidest describing thy condition, thou wouldst have turned with another intention." Whereupon, I thinking on these words, as one ashamed, departed from them, & came away speaking to myself; 'Since there is so much felicity in those words which praise my lady, why have I used others,' and therefore I proposed to take for the argument of my speaking evermore this which should be the praise of this most gentle one, & thinking much on that point it seemed to me that I had undertaken too high argument for me. So that I dared not begin, & so waited several days, with desire to speak & with fear to commence.

XIX

It then chanced that passing through a road along which ran a very clear brook, I felt such willingness to speak that I began to think of the manner I used and I thought that to speak of her, was not fit; but that I ought to speak to ladies in the second person, and not to every lady, but only to those who are gentle, & who are not merely women. Then I say, that my tongue spoke as if moved by itself, & I said then "Ladies who apprehend love." These words I laid up in my mind with great joy thinking to take them for my beginning; therefore being afterwards returned to the abovenamed City, & thinking for some days, I began the regular ode in the usual manner, as follows.

> Ladies, who have heard of Love,
> I wish to speak with you of my Lady,
> Not because I think I can perfect her praise
> But to discourse that I may relieve my mind;
> I say, that thinking on her worth
> Love so gently taught me to feel
> That if I then did not lose my fire
> I would put all men in love by my speech.
> And I do not wish to speak so proudly
> That I might become vile through fear,
> But I will treat of her gentle estate
> For her sake lightly,
> Ladies & amorous maidens with you,

Since it is not fit to speak to others of her.
An Angel calls in the divine intellect,
   And says, Sire, in the world is seen
   A living wonder, which issues
   From a soul which even up hither shines.
   Heaven which has no other defect
   Than wanting her, asks her of the Lord.
   And each saint asks Mercy
   Only pity pleads on our part.
   That the Lord says who understands it of my lady;
   Dear children now suffer me in peace;
   Pleases me that your hope is so great,
   There is one who expects to lose her
   And who will say in Hell to the Ill-born,
   I have seen the hope of the Blessed.
My Lady is desired in highest heaven.
   Now I proceed to make you know her virtue:
   I say, that whoso would seem a gentle lady,
   Go with her; since when she goes in the road
   Love casts in evil hearts a frost
   So that every thought of theirs freezes,
   And whatever can stand there to see,
   Must become a noble thing, or die.
   And when any one finds that he is worthy
   To see her, he proves his virtue,
   For that happens to him that imparts health
   And so humbles him that he forgets all sin.
   Yet has God, through greater grace, given,
   That he cannot end ill, who has spoken to her.
Love said of her; A mortal thing—
   How can it be so adorned, & so pure?
   Then he beheld her & swore by himself
   That God did not mean to make a new thing.
   Color of pearl in her form, as
   It befits a lady to have, not out of measure,
   She has as much goodness as nature can;
   By her pattern beauty is tried;
   From her eyes, as she moves them,
   Proceed spirits of love inflamed,
   Which enkindle the eyes of whoso watches her,

And pass through, so that each finds the heart.
You see Love painted in the face
So that none can behold her steadily.
Canzone! I know that you will go speaking
To many dames, when I shall send you forth.
Now I warn you, since I have trained you up
For the daughter of Love, young & smooth,
That where you go, you say praying,
'Direct me to go, since I am sent
To her for whose praise I am adorned';
And if you will not go as a vain one,
Nor remain where are mean people,
Endeavour if you can to be made known
Alone to a lady, or to a courteous man,
Who shall swiftly deserve thee.
Thou wilt find Love; with him, her;
Commend me to him as you ought.

XX

After this sonnet had got abroad a little, because a friend
had heard it, his desire moved him to pray me that I would
tell him what is Love, having, perhaps, through the words he
had heard, a hope of me beyond what was due. Then I think-
ing that after such a piece, it would be fine to discourse some-
what, of love, & thinking that my friend should be served, I
proposed to speak words in which I should treat of love, &
then I said this sonnet.

Love & the gentle heart are one thing;
As the Sage in his precept has it;
And you may dare be one without the other,
As well as a rational soul without reason.
Nature, when it is amorous, makes
Love the Sire, the heart for his abode
Within which sleeping he reposes
As little and as long as he will.
Beauty then appears in wise woman,
Which pleases the eyes, so that within the heart
Is born desire of the pleasant object,

And so abides in it,
That it causes the spirit of Love to awake.
And the like does a valiant man, in a woman.

XXI

After I had treated of Love in the rhyme aforesaid, there came to me the wish to speak words also in praise of this most gentle one, by which I might show how, through her, this love awoke, & how not only it awoke where it had slept, but where it is not in energy & there working wonderfully, made it appear; and then I said;

In her eyes my Lady carries Love,
Because she makes that noble which she looks upon.
Where she passes, every man turns to see her,
And whom she salutes, his heart quakes,
So that looking down, his whole countenance is changed,
And on every fault of his sighs.
Flees before her, all anger, & pride.
Aid me, Ladies, to do her honour,
Every sweetness, every lowly thought
Is born in the heart of him who hears her speak,
Therefore is he blessed who first sees her.
How she looks when she smiles a little,
Cannot be told, nor held in the mind,
So new & so gentle a miracle is it.

XXII

Not many days after this, it pleased that glorious Lord who refused not himself to die, that he who was the father of so great a marvel as this most noble Beatrice, departing out of this life should ascend to the eternal glory. Therefore, because such departure is woeful to those who remain, and were his friends, and there is no friendship so close as that of a good father with a good child, and this lady was at the summit of goodness, and her father, as many believed, and as was true, was good in a high degree, it is manifest that this lady was bitterly full of grief, & when, according to the custom of the city, ladies with ladies & men with men assembled there, where this Beatrice piteously lamented,—I seeing so many ladies return from her, heard them speak their words of this most gentle one, how she lamented, among which words I heard them say, "Indeed she wept so that whoever saw her might die with pity." Then these ladies passed by, & I remained in so great sadness that some tears then bathed my face; which I concealed, covering my eyes often with my hands; and if I had not expected to hear again of her, since I was in place where most of those ladies passed who came from her, I should have concealed myself immediately when my tears came, & yet tarrying longer in the same place, ladies also passed near me conversing together in these words, "Which of us can ever be glad, who have heard this lady speak so piteously?" After these came others, saying, "This one weeps neither more nor less than if he had seen her as we saw her." Others then said of me, "You shall see this one so changed that he does not appear to be himself." And thus these ladies passing, I heard their words of her & of me (in this manner I have set down), thinking whereupon, I proposed to say such words as I might worthily find occasion, in which words I comprised all which I had heard from these ladies, and, since I should willingly have questioned them, if it had not been blameable, I took occasion to speak as if I had, & as if they had answered me, and I made two sonnets; and in the first I ask whatever I had to ask, & in the other I report their answer, taking that which I heard from them as they would have said to me in reply; & I began the first;

> Ye who wear a lowly semblance
> With downcast eyes showing grief,
> Whence come you that your colour
> Appears like that of stone?
> Saw ye our gentle Lady,
> Her face bathed in the pity of Love?
> Tell me, ladies, what the heart says
> Since I see you go with honest action,
> And if ye come from so great piety,
> Please you to stay here with me a little,
> And hide nothing of her from me.

> I see tears in your eyes,
> And I see you come so disfigured
> That my heart quakes to see you so.

The second;

> Art thou he who has discoursed with us often
> Of our lady, alone speaking to us?
> Thy voice resembles him well
> But thy sad form appears of quite another.
> Ah! why weepest thou so cordially,
> That you compel others to pity thee?
> Hast thou seen her weep, that thou canst not
> Conceal at all thy woful mind?
> Leave us to weep, & to go disconsolate,
> (And it were sin, if we should not,)
> Who in her sorrow have heard her speak.
> She has in her face sorrow so wise
> That who would have beheld her
> Would fall dead before her.

XXIII

After this, in a few days, it chanced that in (some) part of my body there fell on me a grievous infirmity, from which I suffered for many days the bitterest pain, which brought me to such debility, that I was forced to remain like those who cannot move themselves. In the ninth day, feeling my pain as it were intolerable, there came to me a thought of my lady. And when I had thought a little of her, & I returned to think of my debilitated life, and seeing how frail was its duration, even if I were well, I began to bewail myself of so much misery, and, deeply sighing, I said to myself, Of necessity, it must be that the most gentle Beatrice will some time die; and then I felt such an amazement of fear that I closed my eyes, and began to work like a raving person, & to imagine in this manner. In the commencement of the wandering which my fancy made, appeared to me certain faces of ladies dishevelled, who said to me, "Thou too shalt die;" and after these ladies appeared certain different faces horrible to see, who said to me,

"Thou art dead." Thus my fancy beginning to wander, I came
to that pass, that I knew not where I was, & I seemed to see
ladies go dishevelled, weeping in a manner wonderfully sad,
& it appeared to me that I saw the sun darkened, so that the
stars showed themselves in such a colour that I thought they
also wept, & very great earthquakes, & I, admiring in such a
fancy, & greatly afraid, imagined that some friend came &
said to me, "Now knowest thou not thy wonderful lady is
departed from this world?" Then began I to weep very pite-
ously, & not only wept in fancy, but I wept with my eyes,
bathing them with real tears. I imagined that I looked to-
wards the heaven & I seemed to see a multitude of angels
who returned upward, & had before them a very white little
cloud, & I thought these angels sang gloriously, and the
words of their song I seemed to hear were these, Osanna in
excelsis. And others heard I none. Then it seemed to me that
the heart, where so much love was, said to me, True it is that
our lady lies dead; and through this I seemed to go to see the
body in which that most noble soul had been, & so strong
was the erroneous fancy that it showed me this lady lying
dead, & I thought that ladies dressed her, her head, namely,
with a white veil; And I thought her face had such an aspect
of humility, that it seemed to me that it said, "I am to see the
beginning of peace." In this imagination I felt such humility
from beholding her, that I called Death, & said, "Sweetest
Death, come to me, and be not rough with me, since thou
oughtest to be gentle, seeing where thou hast been. Now
come to me who desire thee much. Thou seest that I already
wear thy complexion. And when I had seen fulfilled all the
doleful mysteries which are used towards the bodies of the
dead, I thought I returned to my chamber, & here I looked
towards Heaven, & so strong was my fancy, that weeping I
began to say with true voice, "Oh beautiful soul, how happy
is he who sees thee!" And I saying these words with dolorous
sobs, and calling death that he should come to me, a young &
gentle lady who was by my bedside believing that my weep-
ing & my words were only for the pain of my infirmity, began
to lament with fear, and other ladies who were near the cham-
ber, having compassion of me who wept, & of the lamenta-
tion which they saw this lady make, causing her to depart

from me, (she who was my nearest blood-relation,) they came towards me to wake me, believing that I was dreaming, & they bade me sleep no more, & not to disorder myself, & on their thus speaking to me the strong fantasy ceased at the moment when I would say, "O Beatrice! blessed mayest thou be!", and I had already said, "O Beatrice!" And recovering myself, I opened my eyes & saw that I was deceived, and as soon as I had called this name, my voice was so broken with the sob of grief, that these ladies could not understand me, (as I believe.) Add, that I waked, and was much ashamed, although through some admonition of love I turned myself from them, and when they saw me, they began to say, He appears as dead, & to say apart, Let us devise how to comfort him. Then they said many things to comfort me, & sometimes they inquired whereof I had had fear; Then I being somewhat reassured, and the imaginary disaster understood by me, I answered them, I will tell you what I have suffered. Then I began from the beginning, & told them unto the end what I had seen, suppressing the name of this most gentle one. Then afterwards, being healed of this infirmity, I proposed to speak words of this which had befallen me, since it seemed to me an amorous thing to hear, & so I said it in this canzone.

> A gentle dame & young
> Well adorned with human gentleness
> Who was there where I often invoked death
> Seeing my eyes full of sorrow
> And hearing my vain words
> Was moved with fear to tears.
> And other ladies who were apprised by me
> For what she lamented with me
> Made her depart
> And approached to make me hear
> One said Do not sleep
> And one said Why do you grieve
> Then I left my new fancy
> Invoking the name of my lady
> My voice was so mournful
> So broken with anguish & tears

That I alone heard the name in my heart
And with looks of shame
That overspread my face
Love made me turn towards them
And such was my colour
As the speaking of the death of others brings.
Ah let us comfort this one
Said one to the other softly
And they said often
What seest thou that thou faintest
And when I was a little recovered
I said, Ladies I will tell it you.
While I thought on my frail life
And saw how short its term is,
Love pitied me in the heart where he dwells,
Because my soul was so sad
That sighing I said in my thought
It will befall that my lady will die.
Thence I took such dismay
That my eyes closed, being weighed down
And my spirits were so discouraged
That they went wandering each his way
Then given up to imagination
Out of knowledge, out of truth,
Faces of afflicted ladies appeared to me
Who said to me, Thou wilt die, thou wilt die,
Then I saw many vague forms
In the vain imagination in which I was
And I seemed to be I know not where
And to see ladies go dishevelled
Weeping & lamenting
Who shot up flames of sadness
Then methought gradually
The sun was darkened & the moon appeared
And they wept, he and she.
The birds fell flying thro the air
And the earth quaked
And a man appeared to me pale & faint
Saying What dost thou knowest thou not

Thy lady is dead who was so fair?
I lifted my eyes bathed in tears
And saw what seemed a shower of manna
Angels who returned up into heaven
And they bore a little cloud before them
After which they cried Hosanna
And if they had said more I would tell you
Then said Love I hide it from you no more
Come & see thy lady who lies dead.
The fallacious imagination
Led me to see my dead lady
And when I had seen her
Methought ladies covered her with a veil
And she bore in her looks true lowliness
Which seemed to say I am in peace.
I became in grief so humble
Seeing in her such finished humility
That I said Death I hold thee very gentle
Thou shouldst ever be a delicate thing
Since thou dwellest in my lady
And thou oughtest to have pity & not disdain.
See I come to thee with such desire
To be of thine that I resemble thee in faith
Come since the heart seeks thee
Then I departed every grief being fulfilled
And when I was alone
I said looking towards the other kingdom
Blessed, o beautiful soul, is whoever sees thee.
Ladies, you called me then, I thank you.

XXIV

After this vain imagination, it happened one day that I sitting thoughtful in some place, felt a quaking commence in my heart as if I had been in the presence of this lady, then I say that there came to me an imagination of Love, who appeared to come from that place where my lady stood, & I thought that he said in my heart, "See thou bless the day when I took thee, since thou oughtest to do it," and certainly my heart seemed so glad that it did not appear to me to be my heart, through its new condition; and a little after, these words which my heart said to me with the tongue of love, I saw come towards me a gentle lady who was of famous beauty, and was long since the wife of my first friend (Guido Cavalcanti). The name of this lady was Giovanna, save that through her beauty, as some believe, the name of Primavera (The Spring) was bestowed on her, & so was she called. And looking near her, I saw come the wonderful Beatrice. These ladies came near me, one after the other, and I thought that Love spoke in my heart & said, "This first one is named Primavera, only for this coming of today, since I moved the bestower of her name to call her also Primavera, because *prima verra* (she shall first see) the day when Beatrice shall show herself according to the imagination of her faithful servant; and if I also wish to consider her name to signify that she is what (the Spring) Primavera is." And then I thought that I said other words to myself, that "whoever wishes to consider subtilly this Beatrice, would call her Love, through the strong resemblance which she has to me," whereupon I afterwards musing, proposed to write in rhyme to my first friend, suppressing certain words which it seemed fit to omit, I thinking that also his heart would admire the beauty of that gentle primavera (spring), and I said this sonnet;

> I felt awaken within my heart
> An amorous spirit which slept,
> Then saw I Love come from far
> So cheerful that hardly I knew him
> Saying, Bethink thee to do me honour;
> And at each word, he smiled;
> And my lord remaining with me a little while,
> I looking in that quarter whence he came,
> Saw Mona Vanna and Mona Bice
> Come towards that place where I was,
> The one marvel after the other;
> It is as if my mind said to me again,
> Love said to me, This is Primavera,
> And this is called Love, who so resembles me.

XXV

Could any person capable of clearing up these things, here doubt of that which I say of Love, as if it were a thing by itself, & not only an intelligent substance, but as if it were a corporeal substance, which in reality is false, since Love is not by itself as a substance but is an accident in a substance, and as I may say of it, as if he were a body, nay, as if he were a man, appears from three things which I say of him. I say that I saw him come; and to come imports locomotion, and, according to the philosopher, body alone can be locomotive. If it appear that I rank Love as a body, I say also of it, that he laughs, & that he speaks, which things seem to be proper to man, especially laughter, & therefore it seems I make him a man. To clear this matter, as far as the present necessity requires, we must first understand, that anciently there were no speakers of Love in the vernacular tongue, on the contrary, the speakers of love were certain poets in the Latin tongue, (among us, I say) that happened which happened in other nations, and still happens, that as in Greece not vernacular but lettered poets handled these things, and not many years have passed since those vernacular poets appeared who speak rhyme in the vernacular; so much is to be said of verses in Latin (if with any adequateness & mark) that there is too little time; and if we wish to regard the Occitan dialect (Langue d'Oc) or the Northern French (Langue d'Oui) we do not find these things before the present time, for five hundred years. And the reason why some conspicuous persons had the fame of knowledge & poetry is that they were the first (writers) in the Northern French (Langue d'Oui). And the first who began to speak as a vernacular poet, did so, because he wished to make his mistress understand his words, to whom latin verses were not intelligible. And this is against those who rhyme on other than amatory subjects, because that mode of speaking was first used to speak of Love. Therefore, since to poets may be conceded a greater license of speech than to prose speakers, and these speakers in rhyme are nothing else than vernacular poets, it is fit & reasonable that they should be indulged in a greater liberty of speech than other vernacular speakers. Therefore if any figure or rhetorical trope is conceded to poets, it is conceded to the rhymers. If then we find that the poets have addressed inanimate things as if they had sense or reason, & have made them speak together & not only things true, but things not true, that is, have spoken of things which cannot speak, & have said that many accidents speak, as if they were substances & men, it is fit that the speaker in rhyme should do the like, not indeed without reason, but with reason, which might be expressed in prose. That the poets have spoken in this manner appears by Virgil, who says that Juno, that is, a goddess unfriendly to the Trojans, spoke to Æolus, lord of the winds, as in the first of the Æneid;

> Æole namque tibi, &c

and that this lord replied;

> Tuus, o regina, quid optes
> Explorare labor; mihi jussa capessere fas est

In the same poet, an inanimate thing speaks to animated things, in the Second of the Æneid;

> Dardanidae duri

In Lucan, an animated thing speaks to an inanimate;

> Multum Roma tamen debes civilibus armis.

In Horace, a man speaks to his own knowledge as to another person, and not only are the words those of Horace, but he speaks them as out of the midst of Homer in his *Ars Poetica*;

> Dic mihi Musa virum.

In Ovid, Love speaks as if it were a human person, in the beginning of the book called The Remedy of Love;

> Bella mihi video, bella parantur, ait.

And hence it is manifest to whosoever hesitates at any part of this my little book, & provided that some coarse person do not take a license from it, I say that neither the poets speak thus without reason, nor ought the rhymers to speak thus not having some reason in them of that which they say. Since great shame would accrue to him who should rhyme things under the guise of a trope or rhetorical figure, &, being interrogated, should not know how to strip his words of such a garment in a guise that they should have a true meaning. And this my first friend & I knew very well those persons who rhymed so absurdly.

XXVI

That most gentle lady of whom we have discoursed in the preceding words, came into so great grace of the people, that when she passed through the street persons ran to see her, whence a miserable joy came to me, and when she was near any one, so much honour came into that person's heart, that he dared not lift up his eyes nor reply to her salute. And of this, many as witnesses could testify to what was incredible. She, crowned & clothed in humility, went showing no glorying in that which she saw or heard. Many said, when she had passed, "This is not a woman, but is like one of the most beautiful angels of heaven." Others said; "This is a wonder, & blessed be the Lord who knows how to work so wonderfully." I say that she showed herself so gentle & so full of charms, that those who saw her felt in themselves an excellent beauty and so sweet that they did not know how to express nor was there any one who could look at her who at first without sighs. These & more wonderful things proceeded from her well & virtuously. Wherefore I thinking thus wishing to take up again the pen in her praise, proposed to speak words in which I should give to understand her wonderful & excellent works to the end that not only such as could see her with eyes, but also others might know of her what I could make known by words & then I said this sonnet.

So gentle & so gracious appears
My Lady when she salutes others,
That every tongue trembling becomes mute,
And the eyes dare not behold her.
She goes on hearing herself praised
Benignly clothed with humility
And it seems that she is something descended
From heaven to show a miracle in earth.
She shows herself pleasing to whoso beholds her
That she sends through his eyes a sweetness to the heart

Which none can apprehend who does not taste it;
And it seems that from her lips proceeds
A soft spirit, full of Love,
Which goes to the soul, saying, Sigh.

I say that this my lady came into such grace that not only
was she honoured & praised, but through her were many ho-
noured & praised. And I seeing that, & wishing to make it
known to such as saw it not, proposed also to speak words in
which this should be signified, & then I said this sonnet.

He sees perfectly all wellbeing
Who sees my lady among ladies
Those who go with her are holden
To render thanks to God for her beautiful grace.
And her beauty is of such virtue
That no envy proceeds from it to others
Rather it makes them go with her clothed
With the gentleness of love & of faith
The sight of her makes everything humble
And does not make her alone pleasing
But each through her receives honour
And in her acts she is so gentle
That no one can recall her to mind
Without sighing in the sweetness of Love.

XXVII

After this I begun to think one day on what I had said of
my lady in the two preceding sonnets, & considering that I
had not spoken of that which in the present time wrought in
me it seemed to me that I had spoken the truth defectively, &
therefore I proposed to add words in which I should say how
her virtue wrought in me & not thinking that this could be
told in the shortness of a sonnet I begun this canzone.

So long has Love held me
And trained me to his lordship
That as it was strong in me at first
So now it remains sweet at my heart,
Therefore when his courage so seizes me,
That it seems the spirits flee away,

Then my frail soul feels
Such sweetness that my face grows pale.
Then Love in me takes so much virtue
That he makes my spirits go speaking
And they issue forth calling
My lady to give me more favor;
This happens wherever she sees me,
And so humble is she that you would not believe it.

XXVIII

How is the populous city become solitary and she is a widow who was queen of nations. I was still in the preparation of this canzone & had completed this stanza abovewritten when the Lord of justice called this most gentle one to glorify, under the sign of the Queen, the Blessed Mary, Himself, whose name was always in the utmost reverence in the words of this Beatrice. And although it might be grateful here to say somewhat of her departure from us, it is not my design to treat it here for three reasons; first, that such is not the present argument if we will respect the proem which precedes this book. Secondly that even if it were within our present design yet my tongue would not be sufficient to treat that as it ought to be treated; Thirdly, that supposing both the first & the second, it is not fit that I should treat of that which being treated would require that I should be a praiser of myself, which thing is entirely blameable in whatsoever person. And therefore I leave such a discourse to another commentator. Nevertheless since several times the number nine has occurred in the foregoing words, whence it seems that it was not without reason & in her departure that number seems to have had much reason, it may behove us here to say something as far as belongs to the subject. Wherefore I will say first how it had place in her departure & then will assign some reason why this number was so friendly to her.

XXIX

I say that her soul departed, (according to the time-measure of Italy) in the first hour of the ninth day of the month: and according to the measure of Syria she departed in the ninth month of the year since the first month there is Tismin which with us is October, & according to our measure, she departed in that year of our era (that is, in that year of the Lord,) in which the perfect number was completed nine times in that century of the world in which she was placed, and she was of the thirteenth century of Christians. And this may be one reason of it. Since according to Ptolemy, & according to the Christian truth there be nine heavens which revolve, and according to the faith of Astrology these heavens are operative here below according to their united habitude, this number was friendly to her, to give to understand that in her nativity all the nine moveable heavens went perfectly together; this is one reason of that. But more subtilly thinking, according to the ineffable truth, this number was herself, I speak by similitude, & that I mean thus.

The number three is the root of nine since, without any number, multiplied by itself it makes nine as we see plainly that three times three make nine. Then if three by itself is the factor of nine, and the (factor or) maker of miracles is three, that is, Father, Son, & Holy Spirit which are three & one. This lady was accompanied by this number of nine, to give to understand, that she was a nine, that is a miracle, whose root that is of the miracle, is only that wonderful Trinity. Perhaps also by a more subtle person this would appear in more subtle reason; but this is what I see, & what pleases me more.

XXX

After this most gentle lady had departed from this world this city remained as it were a widow & despoiled of all dignity. Wherefor I also lamenting in this desolate city wrote to the princes of the land somewhat of her estate. And if any one should blame me that I do not here set down the words which follow what I here quote, I excuse myself because my design was not from the beginning to write otherwise than for the people. Therefore since the words which follow those which are quoted, are all latin, it would be out of my design, if I wrote them and the like intention I know that this my first

friend had, to whom I write, this is, since I wrote to him only
in the vernacular.

XXXI

After my eyes had for some time wept & were so wearied
that I could not relieve my sadness I thought of relieving it by
some sad words & then I proposed to make a canzone in
which lamenting I conversed of her, my grief for whom was
made the destroyer of my life, & I begun

Eyes grieving for pity at heart
Have suffered the pain of tears
So that they remain vanquished
Now if I wish to relieve the woe
Which little by little leads me to death
It behoves me to speak
And because I remember that I spoke
Of my lady whilst she lived
Gentle ladies willingly with you
I will not speak to others
Than to a gentle heart which is a lady
And I will then say of her weeping
That suddenly she has gone to heaven
And has left Love grieving with me.
Beatrice is gone into high heaven
Into realms where the angels have peace
And stands with them & you ladies has she left
Not there has the quality of cold rapt her
Nor that of heat, as it has rapt others,
But it was her great benignity
Which shining from her humility
Passed the heavens with so much virtue
That it made the Eternal Sire wonder
So that sweet desire
Came to him to summon so much health
And made her come to him from here below,
Because he saw that this troublesome life
Was not worthy of so gentle a being.
Parted from her beautiful person
Full of grace the gentle soul

And mounted glorious into worthy place.
Who weeps her not when he speaks of her
Has heart of stone, so wicked & base
That a benign spirit could not enter there.
There is not in a bad heart so high genius
That can imagine anything of her,
And therefore such will not weep for her.
But sadness & sobs of grief
And a death of sorrow
And a life despoiled of all solace
Comes to such as at any time saw in thought
What she was, and how she is taken.
My sighs give me deep anguish
When thought in the deep mind
Brings to me that which has cut my heart.
And often thinking on death
Comes to me a desire of it so sweet
That it changes the color of my face
When the thought of her becomes fixed
Pain attacks me from every side
That I recover myself through the pain I feel
And I become such
That shame drives me from the company.
Then weeping alone in my sorrow
I call Beatrice & I say Art thou too dead
And whilst I call her I am consoled
With weeping & with sighing
My heart pines away wherever I am,
So that it wearies whoever sees it
And what has been my life since
My lady went into the new world
No tongue can tell
And yet, o my Ladies, though I should desire it,
I should not know how to tell you what I am
Bitter life has so afflicted me
And it is so injured
That every man seems to say to me, I abandon you
Seeing my fainting
But be it as it may, my lady sees it,

And I hope yet a reward from her
My pious canzone now go lamenting
   And find the dames & the damsels
   Unto whom thy sisters
   Were wont to carry joy
   And thou who art a daughter of sorrow
   Go disconsolate & stand with them
   Sad that Beatrice more beautiful than all
   Is gone to the feet of the Lord
   And has left Love with me lamenting.

XXXII

After this canzone was said, one came to me who in the degrees of friendship is friendly to me, next to the first, and this one was so near in blood to that beautiful person that none was more near than he. And when he conversed with me he prayed me that I would say to him some thing for a lady who was dead and he feigned his words so that it appeared that he spoke of another who was certainly dead, therefore I becoming sensible that this one spoke only of that blessed soul, said that I would do that which he had entreated of me. Therefore then thinking I proposed to make a sonnet in which I bewailed myself, & to give it to this friend so that it appeared that I had made it for him, and thus it was;

   O gentle hearts, whom pity desires,
   Come to hear my sighs,
   Which disconsolate go their way;
   And but for them I should die with grief,
   Because my eyes would be worse than I could bear,
   Weary of weeping so much for my lady,
   That they would choak the heart by lamenting.
   You shall hear them often call
   My gentle lady who is gone away
   To the world worthy of her virtue,
   And despise now this life
   In the person of the mourning soul
   Abandoned by her welfare.

XXXIII

After I had spoken this sonnet thinking that this was for him who designed to ask it, as if it were made by him I saw that this service appeared to me poor & naked for a person so near to this beloved one. And therefore before I gave him the abovewritten sonnet, I said two stanzas of a canzone, the one indeed for him, & the other for me. And though to one who should not read attentively it might seem that both of them were spoken by one person, yet whoever looks at them attentively will see that different persons, that one does not call his lady   and the other does as plainly appears. This canzone & the abovewritten sonnet I gave to him, saying to him that I had made it for him alone. The canzone begins

> *How often alas, I remember.*

In the first stanza, this my friend and near kinsman of hers, laments himself. In the second, I lament; that is, in the other stanza, which begins,

> *There is heard in my sighs,*

And thus it appears that in this canzone two persons deplore, one complaining as a brother the other as a lover.

> How often alas I remember
> That I may never more
> Behold the Lady, therefore I go sorrowing thus;
> My woeworn mind
> Concentrates so much grief within the heart
> That I say, My Soul, why dost thou not depart
> Since the torments which thou shalt carry
> In the world which is already so troublesome to you
> Make me pensive with much fear
> Wherefore, I call on Death
> As gentle, & my sweet repose
> And I say, Come to me, with such love,
> That I am envious of such as die.
>
> ———
>
> There is heard in my sighs
> An undertone of pity

Which calls on Death continually
To it turn all my desires
Since my Lady
Was reached by his cruelty.
Because the pleasure of her beauty
Withdrawing itself from our view
Becomes spiritual beauty & grand
Which through the heaven expands,
The light of Love, which greets the Angels;
And makes their high & subtle intellect
Wonder, so gentle it is.

XXXIV

On that day on which the year was completed in which this lady was made one of the citizens of the Eternal Life I sat in a place, where, recollecting myself, I drew an angel on certain tablets, and while I was drawing, I turned my eyes and saw beside me men to whom it behoved that I should do reverence and they saw what I did and according to what was then told me, they had been there for some while, before I had been aware of them. When I saw them, I rose, & saluting them I said, "I was just now in another place, & I was thinking of that." Then these departing and I returning to my work, that is, of drawing, whilst I wrought, the thought came to me of saying words in rhyme as for an Anniversary piece to her, and to write it to them who came to me; & I said then this sonnet which has two beginnings; one is;

Into my thought had come
The gentle Lady who for virtue
Was by the most high Lord
Placed in the heaven of humility, where is Mary,
&c &c

The second is;

Into my thought had come
That gentle lady whom Love mourns
To that degree that her virtue
Would draw you to see what I do.

> Love who in the mind feels her,
> Was waked in the dissolved heart,
> And said to my sighs, Go forth
> For each may go lamenting.
> Forth issued they from my breast
> With a voice which often leads
> Sad tears to my sad eyes
> But those which go not forth, with greater pain
> Come saying, O noble mind!
> Today the year is complete, since thou didst
>   mount to heaven.

XXXV

Then for some time although I was in a place in which I remembered the time past, I remained very thoughtful, & with painful thoughts so that they made me appear abroad a spectacle of fright. Therefore I becoming sensible of my state, lifted my eyes to see if others saw me. Then I saw that a gentle lady from a window looked at me so piteously that all pity appeared collected in her. Therefore because when the wretched see in others pity for them so much the more they lament as having pity of themselves, I then perceived my eyes begin to wish to weep & yet fearing to exhibit my vile life I withdrew myself from the eyes of that gentle person & said to myself "It cannot be that with this pious lady there should not be very noble love" then I proposed to say a sonnet in which I should speak to her, & I comprised in it all which is narrated in this account, and I began.

> My eyes beheld how much compassion
> Appeared in your figure
> When you saw the deeds & the form
> Which from grief I many times showed
> Then was I aware that you contemplated
> The quality of my dark life
> So that the fear entered my heart
> Of showing my vileness in your eyes
> And I took myself from before you, feeling
> That the tears started from my heart

Which were moved by sight of you
Then I said in my sad soul
Blessed is in that lady the love
Which makes me weep thus.

XXXVI

It afterwards happened that whenever this lady saw me she made a piteous face & of a pale colour, as it were, like that of love. Therefore I often was reminded of my most noble lady who always showed a similar colour, & truly many times not being able to weep nor to relieve my sadness I went to see this compassionate lady, who seemed to have drawn tears out of my eyes by the sight of her, & then there came to me the will to say words also, speaking to her, & I said this sonnet.

Colour of Love and semblances of pity
Have never taken so wonderfully
The face of the lady

XXXVII

I came so far through the sight of this lady that my eyes begun to delight too much to see her, wherefore often I tormented myself in my heart & held myself for very vile, & many times I blasphemed the vanity of my eyes & said to them in my thought; Now I have accustomed you to cause to weep whosoever saw your sad condition, & now it appears that you wish to belie it for this lady who looked at you but who would not have looked at you, had not the thought so much weighed on her of the glorious lady whom you were wont to lament. But inasmuch as you can, cause that I remind you of her, O evil eyes! that never until after death your tears shall be restrained. And when I had thus spoken, myself to my eyes, & the largest sighs assailed me, and painfullest,—to the end that this battle which I had with myself should not remain only by the wretch who felt it I proposed to make a sonnet, & to comprise in it this horrible condition, & I said thus;

> The bitter tears which ye shed
> O mine eyes for so long time
> Made others wonder
> With pity as ye see
> Now methinks ye would forget it
> If I, on my part, were such a felon
> That I did not disturb you with every reason
> Reminding you of her whom ye lamented
> Your vanity makes me think
> And alarms me so that I vehemently fear
> The sight of the lady who beholds you;
> Ye should never until death
> Forget our lady who is dead;
> So says my heart, & then sigheth.

XXXVIII

I recovered then the sight of this lady in so new condition that many times I thought of her as of a person who pleased me too much & I thought of her thus; This is a gentle fair young & wise lady, who has appeared perhaps through the will of love in order that my life might repose & many times I thought more amorously, so that the heart consented in it that is, in its reasoning & when I had consented so, I reconsidered it as moved by reason, & I said to myself; Ah! what thought is this, that in so vile mode would console me, & not let me think otherwise? Then arose another thought & I said to myself—Now thou hast been in so much tribulation, why wilt thou not withdraw thyself from so much bitterness? Thou seest that this is one breathing which may bring the desires of love forward & is moved by so gentle a party as that of the eyes of this lady who has shown herself so pitying. Wherefore I having often thus contended with my self yet would not say any words, & because the battle of thoughts conquered those who spoke for her, methought it behoved me to speak to her & I said this sonnet, which begins;

> Gentle thought which speaks of you
> Comes often to stay with me
> And talks of love so softly
> That it makes the heart consent to him
> The soul says to the Heart, Who is this
> Who comes to console our mind?
> And is its virtue so strong
> That it will suffer no other thought to abide?
> He answered her; O thoughtful soul
> This is a new little-spirit of love
> Which brings its desires forth to me
> And its life & all its strength
> Is moved by the eyes of this pitying one
> Who so concerned herself in our sufferings.

And I call that gentle, inasmuch as it speaks of a gentle lady, which, on other grounds, was most vile. I make in this sonnet parties of myself, according as my thoughts were divided in two; the one party I call Heart, that is, appetite; the other I call Soul, that is, reason; and I speak as one speaks to the other. And that it is fit to call the appetite Heart, & the reason, Soul, is very manifest to those to whom I am pleased that this should appear. It is true that in the preceding sonnet I make the party of the Heart counter to that of the Eyes and this appears contrary to that which I say in the present and therefore I say that there also I design the Heart for the appetite since I had a greater desire to remember that most gentle Lady of mine than to behold this one. Though I had some appetite for this yet it appeared to me slight. Thus it appears that one saying is not contrary to the other.

XXXIX

Against this adversary of the reason arose, one day, as it were in the ninth hour a strong imagination in me that I thought I saw this only Beatrice in those bloodred garments in which she first appeared to my eyes and she seemed youthful, of the same age as when I first beheld her. Then I began to think of her & recollecting her in the order of the past time my heart began to repent itself bitterly of the desire to which it had been so basely abandoned for some days, contrary to the constancy of reason. And this mischievous desire being driven out my thoughts turned themselves all to their most gentle Beatrice & I say, that, from that hour forward I began to think so, with all my heart ashamed, that the spirits manifested this many times because as it were all said in their outgoing that which was thought in the heart, namely, the honour of this most gentle one & how she had parted from us. And it often happened that some thought had in it so much grief that I forgot it and there where I was by this rekindling of sighs my intermitted weeping was renewed in a manner that my eyes appeared to be two things which desired only to weep & it often happened that through the long continuing of the weeping a purple colour came out around them which was wont to appear for some witness to others, whence it seemed that they were fitly punished for their vanity. So that thenceforward they could not look at any person who looked at them in a manner to draw them to an understanding. Wherefore I willing that such wicked desire & vain temptation should appear destroyed, so that the rhymed words which I had before said could not breed any doubt proposed to make a sonnet, in which I should comprise the sense of this state of mind & I said

Alas, through the force of many sighs
Which proceed from the thoughts which are in the heart
The eyes are conquered & have no strength
To look at the person who looks at them.
And they are come to that, that they seem two desires
Of weeping & of showing grief.
And often they so lament, that Love
Encircles them with a crown of martyrs.
These thoughts & the sighs which I cast out
Become within the heart so bitter
That Love there faints and so suffers
Because they have in these dolorous (eyes)

Written the sweet name of My Lady,
And many words, of her death.

I said, Alas! so much was I ashamed that my eyes had been thus frivolous.

XL

After this tribulation it happened at that time that many people came to see that Blessed image which Jesus Christ left to us, for the example of his most beautiful figure, my Lady gloriously beholds, that some pilgrims passed by a road which is as it were the midst of the city where was born, lived, & died the most gentle Lady, and they went (as it appeared to me) very thoughtful. Then I, thinking on them, said to myself, These pilgrims appear to me to come from distant parts, & I do not believe that they have even heard speak of this lady, & they know nothing of her; rather their thoughts are of other things, than of those here; they perhaps are thinking of their distant friends, whom we do not know. Then I said to myself I know that if they were of the neighboring country, they would appear in some sort disturbed passing through the midst of this painful city. Then I said to myself, If I could detain them a little I would make them weep before they go forth of this city, because I would speak words which should cause to weep whoever heard them. Then these having passed out of my sight, I proposed to make a sonnet in which I should signify that which I had said to myself & to the end that it should appear more piteous I proposed to speak as if I had addressed them, & I said this sonnet;

Ah Pilgrims who go thoughtful
On things perhaps which are not here present,
Come ye from so distant a tribe
As ye show in your aspect
That ye do not weep as ye pass
Through the midst of the mourning city,
As those persons who seem
To know nothing of its woe.
If you will stay & hear it

> Verily my heart with sighs tells me
> That ye shall go forth of it with tears
> It has lost its Beatrice;
> And the words which man can say of her
> Have power to make others weep.

I said Pilgrims, in the large sense of the word as pilgrims may be understood in two senses in a liberal & a strict one, in the one, inasmuch as whosoever goes out of his country is a pilgrim; in the other, one is not a pilgrim unless he goes towards the house of St James, or returns. There are moreover three modes in which those people are properly distinguished who travel in the service of the Most High. They are called Palmers who go beyond sea, whence they often fetch home palms. They are called Pilgrims as many as go to the house of Galizia because the sepulchre of St James was farther from his country than of any other apostle. They are called Romans (Romei) as many as go to Rome, thither, where these whom I call Pilgrims were going.

XLI

Then two gentle ladies sent to me praying me that I would send them some of these my rhymed words; and I considering their nobility, proposed to send them these, and to make something new which I might send them with these, so that I might more honorably fulfil their requests; and I then said a sonnet which tells of my state, & sent it to them in company with the preceding, & with another which begins, *Come to hear* &c. The sonnet which I then made, is;

> Beyond the hope which goes largest
> Passes the sigh which comes from my heart,
> New tidings, that Love weeping placed in it, then
>   draws up again;
> When he is come there where he would be,
> He sees a lady who receives honour,
> And shines so that by her splendour
> The pilgrim soul beholds her;
> Sees her such that when he tells me,
> I understand him not; so subtilly he speaks

To the mourning heart that he makes it speak.
I know that he speaks of that gentle one,
Because often he mentions Beatrice,
So that I understand him well, o Ladies dear!

XLII

After this sonnet, appeared to me a wonderful vision, in which I saw things which made me determine to say no more of this Blessed one, until I could more worthily discourse of her; and to come at that, I study to the utmost, as she verily knows. So that, if it shall be the pleasure of Him to whom all things live, that my life should continue for some years, I hope to say of her that which was never said of any one; and then may it please him who is the Lord of courtesy, that my soul, if it be possible, may go to see the glory of Him who is blessed through all ages.

———

End of the New Life.

———

CHRONOLOGY

NOTE ON THE TEXTS

NOTES

INDEX OF TITLES AND FIRST LINES

Chronology

1803   Born Ralph Waldo Emerson May 25, Election Day, in Boston, the fourth child of William Emerson (pastor of Boston's First Church since 1799, and editor of the *Monthly Anthology*, precursor of the *North American Review*) and Ruth Haskins Emerson (daughter of John Haskins, prosperous Boston distiller); brother of John Clarke, b. 1799, and William, b. 1801 (a sister, Phebe, b. 1798, had died in 1800); descendant of a long line of ministers on both sides of the family, among them Peter Bulkeley (1583–1659), one of the founders of Concord, Massachusetts, and paternal grandfather William Emerson (1743–76), known as the "patriot minister of the Revolution."

1805   Brother Edward Bliss born.

1806   Begins schooling at Mrs. Whitwell's school near the parsonage.

1807   Older brother John dies of tuberculosis in April. Brother Robert Bulkeley, mentally retarded from birth, born.

1808   Brother Charles Chauncy born.

1811   Sister Mary Caroline born in February. Father dies in Portland, Maine, on May 12. Aunt Mary Moody Emerson, who is visiting the parsonage at the time of father's death, stays for several months to help care for the children.

1812   Enters Boston Latin School to study Latin and Greek, and takes courses in mathematics and writing at Rufus Webb's grammar school, where he begins lifelong friendship with William H. Furness (later a Unitarian minister and opponent of slavery). Begins writing poetry.

1814   Early in year, aunt Mary returns to Boston to assist in managing the household; her strong character and Calvinist temperament will have a marked influence on Emerson. Sister Mary Caroline dies. Makes trip with schoolmates to Noddle's Island in Boston Harbor to help build fortifications against rumored British attack. Family moves in November to house in Concord built by Emerson's grandfather and now lived in by grandmother Phebe and her second husband, Ezra Ripley (house is later named the "Old Manse" by Nathaniel Hawthorne). Continues writing poetry, mainly about historical persons and events.

1815 Family returns to Boston and lives in the house of merchant Daniel Parker, who is traveling; mother lets rooms to paying guests, including Lemuel Shaw (later chief justice of the Massachusetts supreme court and father-in-law of Herman Melville). Borrows books from the Athenaeum and from friends. Reenters the Latin School with brother Edward and studies French at a private school; in addition to classical authors, reads Johnson's *Lives of the Poets* and poetry of Thomas Campbell. Brothers taunted by classmates for having only one coat to share between them.

1816 Chooses to be known by his middle name, Waldo.

1817 Hears President James Monroe speak on Boston Common. Enters Harvard College, the youngest member of the class of 1821. Receives aid in meeting expenses by award of "Penn legacy" from First Church (an award previously granted to older brother William); also helped financially by position as Harvard president John Kirkland's "freshman" (orderly) and by tutoring.

1818–19 Studies standard curriculum of Latin, Greek, English, history, and rhetoric; on his own, reads Shakespeare, Montaigne, Hume, Swift, Addison, Boswell, and Byron. Though passed over for a number of student societies, feels honored by election to Pythologian Club.

1820 Begins keeping a journal on January 25, titling it "The Wide World." Second entry reads: "I do hereby nominate and appoint 'Imagination' the generalissimo and chief marshall of all the luckless ragamuffin Ideas which may be collected & imprisoned hereafter in these pages." Delivers poem "Improvement" to the Pythologian Club and wins second prize in the Bowdoin essay contest for "The Character of Socrates."

1821 Wins another Bowdoin second prize for "The Present State of Ethical Philosophy." Chosen "Class Poet" after seven others refuse the honor. Graduates from Harvard on August 29, ranked 30th in a class of 59; is captivated by the commencement oration given by Sampson Reed, a Swedenborgian who believes that true eloquence reveals the link between language and nature. Takes a position teaching at brother William's school for young women in Boston.

1822   Dedicates seventh "Wide World" journal to "the Spirit of America." Publishes essay on "The Religion of the Middle Ages" in *The Christian Disciple*, a leading Unitarian review.

1823   Moves to Roxbury, outside Boston, in May and joins First Church, where father had preached. In August makes a walking trip through the Connecticut Valley. Takes over brother's school when William leaves to study theology at Göttingen in Germany. Reads widely in philosophy, including Jonathan Edwards, Dugald Stewart, and Thomas Reid; writes to William that "I am an idolater of Hume except when he meddles with law & prophets." Complains in journal that childhood dreams "are all fading away & giving place to some very sober & very disgusting views of a quiet mediocrity of talents and condition."

1824   In April, writes in journal: "In a month I shall be *legally* a man. And I deliberately dedicate my time, my talents, & my hopes to the Church"; though self-critical about social abilities and reasoning power, hopes to thrive as a minister by putting "on eloquence as a robe." Closes school in December and prepares for entry into Harvard Divinity School.

1825   Moves into Divinity Hall at Harvard in February. Studies are interrupted by eye trouble and rheumatism. Goes to uncle William Ladd's farm in Newton, Massachusetts, to recover. Undergoes eye surgery twice in Boston. Begins teaching school in Chelmsford, Massachusetts, in fall. William returns from Germany in October and decides against a career in the ministry because of religious doubts. Edward, failing in health, closes his Roxbury school for boys and sails to Europe to recover.

1826   Emerson's eyes improve. Reopens Edward's school in Roxbury, but closes it after three months because of continuing problems with rheumatic hip. Begins teaching in mother's home in Cambridge (where she had moved in April). Described by one student as "not inclined to win boys by a surface amiability, but kindly in explanation or advice." Praises Sampson Reed's newly published *Observations on the Growth of the Mind* as "the best thing since Plato." William and Edward (returned from Europe) study law, William on Wall Street in New York, Edward with Daniel Webster's firm in Boston. Emerson is licensed to preach as a Unitarian in October, and delivers his first sermon in the church of his uncle, the Rev. Samuel Ripley, in Waltham, Massachusetts, using as his text "Pray without ceasing" (1 Thessalonians 5:17). Suffering from lung trouble, borrows money from uncle Ripley and sails to Charleston, South Carolina, to improve health.

1827   Feeling that "I am not sick; I am not well, but luke-sick," sails to St. Augustine, Florida, in January for a warmer climate. Meets and is fascinated by Achille Murat, nephew of Napoleon and a "consistent Atheist." Continues writing poetry and working on sermons, finding "pleasure in the thought that the particular tone of my mind at this moment may be new in the Universe." Returns to Boston in late spring and preaches from several pulpits in New England, including Boston's First Church. Meets 16-year-old Ellen Louisa Tucker in December while preaching in Concord, New Hampshire.

1828   Edward returns to Concord suffering from fainting spells and delirium and is placed in the McLean Asylum in Charlestown, Massachusetts. Emerson preaches in the Second Church, Boston, while Henry Ware Jr., the regular minister, recovers his health. Made honorary member of Phi Beta Kappa Society. Becomes engaged to Ellen Tucker in December.

1829   Ordained Unitarian minister of the Second Church on March 11 at salary of $1,200 (later, after Ware's resignation, at salary of $1,800). Marries Ellen September 30 in Concord, Massachusetts, though they both know she has tuberculosis. Writes admiringly of Samuel Taylor Coleridge to aunt Mary, calling him one of the "citizens of the Universe" who can cast "sovereign glances to the circumference of things." Elected to Boston School Committee.

1830   Accompanies Ellen when she goes to Philadelphia in March for a healthier climate. Returns alone to Boston as her condition improves and resumes duties at the Second Church. Moves with Ellen and mother to Brookline, Massachusetts, in late May, then to house on Chardon Street, Boston, in November. Edward sails to St. Croix in December hoping to recover from lung trouble.

1831   Ellen dies of tuberculosis on February 8. Emerson writes to aunt Mary, "My angel is gone to heaven this morning & I am alone in the world." Walks to her tomb each morning and begins a series of elegiac poems on her death. Brother Charles, whose health has begun to fail, sails to Puerto Rico, where Edward is now employed as clerk to the American consul. Emerson is defeated for re-election to Boston School Committee.

1832   Writes in journal that the profession of the ministry is "antiquated" and worships "the dead forms of our forefathers." Visits Ellen's tomb in March and opens her coffin. Requests of the governing board of the Second Church in June that he not be required to offer the communion service; delivers his views to congregation on September 9 in sermon "The Lord's Supper." Offers his resignation on September 11; it is accepted in divided vote (receives salary until the end of the year). In poor health much of the year, sails for Europe on December 25.

1833   Lands in Malta in February much improved in health. Travels north through Italy and spends Easter in Rome. Finds the ceremony at the Sistine Chapel full of "millinery & imbecility" but appreciates the "sublime spectacle" of the Pope's Easter service at St. Peter's. Meets Walter Savage Landor and American sculptor Horatio Greenough in Florence and travels to Paris, arriving there in June and finding it "a loud modern New York of a place." Visits the Jardin des Plantes and becomes interested in natural history. In July travels to England, where he meets Coleridge, William Wordsworth, and John Stuart Mill. Meets Thomas Carlyle in Scotland, beginning a lifelong friendship. Sails home in September. Preaches at the Second Church and in other New England pulpits; in November lectures on "The Uses of Natural History." Writes hymn sung for ordination of successor at Second Church, the Rev. Chandler Robbins.

1834   Lectures in Boston on natural history and continues to preach nearly every Sunday. Begins correspondence with Carlyle. Meets Lydia ("Lidian") Jackson, a 33-year-old woman from Plymouth, Massachusetts, who had heard him preach in Boston and Plymouth. Receives first half of Ellen's estate in the spring (about $11,600, mostly in stocks and bonds). Reads a poem before Harvard Phi Beta Kappa Society in August. After spending summer in Newton moves with mother to Ezra Ripley's home in Concord in October. Learns of Edward's death from tuberculosis in Puerto Rico on October 1; writes in journal: "I am bereaved of a part of myself." Appalled by American politics, especially the supporters of President Andrew Jackson. Vows in journal "not to utter any speech, poem, or book that is not entirely & peculiarly my work."

1835   Writes to Lidian Jackson on January 24, proposing marriage; she accepts. Lectures in Boston on "great men" — Michelangelo, Luther, Milton, Fox, Burke — and, later, on English literature, including Chaucer, Shakespeare, Bacon, Jonson, and Herrick. Declines pastorate in East Lexington, Massachusetts, but agrees to preach there each Sunday or to find a substitute. Buys house in Concord for $3,500 in July. Marries Lidian Jackson on September 14 in Plymouth. Begins friendship with Bronson Alcott. Delivers address on Concord history for the town's bicentennial.

1836   Gives a course of lectures in Salem in the spring on English biography and history. Brother Charles dies May 9 of tuberculosis; in journal, laments loss of "[m]y brother, my friend, my ornament, my joy & pride." Forms friendship with Margaret Fuller in July when she visits for three weeks. Purchases 15-volume set of Goethe's works and writes to William: "I read little else than his books lately." *Nature* is published in September. Becomes founding member of the Symposium, or Hedge's Club (named after Frederic Henry Hedge), later known as the Transcendental Club; other members include George Ripley, Bronson Alcott, James Freeman Clarke, and Orestes Brownson. Son Waldo born October 30; Emerson wonders at his "graces & instincts" and writes, "I see nothing in it of mine. . . . I seem to be merely the brute occasion of its being." Gives series of 12 lectures on "The Philosophy of History" in Boston.

1837   Writes "Hymn" to be sung at the unveiling of the Concord Monument on July 4. In June gives "Address on Education" in Providence; in August delivers "The American Scholar" as Harvard Phi Beta Kappa oration. Receives second half of Ellen's estate, inheriting a total of $23,000; freed by its income to devote time to writing. Becomes friends with Henry David Thoreau, who has recently returned to Concord after graduating from Harvard. Arranges for American publication of Carlyle's *The French Revolution*, ensuring that Carlyle will receive royalties. Begins to feel obligations to the pulpit a burden, preferring to lecture; begins winter series of ten talks on "Human Culture" in Lowell, Massachusetts.

1838   Gives successful lecture series in Boston. Asks in February to be relieved of his duties at the East Lexington Church, where he had been preaching regularly since settling in Concord. Shares walks with Thoreau, of whom he writes: "I delight much in my young friend, who seems to have as free and erect a mind as any I have ever met." Writes public letter in April to President Martin Van Buren protesting the forced removal of the Cherokees from their lands in Georgia. Meets poet and lecturer Jones Very; writes to Margaret Fuller regarding mental condition of Very, who had been confined for a month in a Boston asylum following an intense religious experience, "Monomania or mono *Sania* he is a very remarkable person." On July 15 delivers controversial address at the Harvard Divinity School (will not be invited back to Harvard for almost 30 years). Address is praised by Theodore Parker and others, and attacked in press as "the latest form of infidelity." Delivers oration on "Literary Ethics" at Dartmouth College. Speaks on "Human Life" in Boston.

1839   Preaches last sermon in January. Daughter born February 24, with Thoreau's mother serving as midwife; at Lidian's suggestion, they name her Ellen Tucker after his first wife. Despite constant hospitality to visitors like Very, Fuller, Alcott, and Caroline Sturgis, writes in journal of a

"porcupine impossibility of contact" with others. Edits
Very's poems and essays (when Very objects to Emerson's
emendations, on the grounds that the poems were di-
vinely inspired, Emerson replies: "We cannot permit the
Holy Ghost . . . to talk bad grammar"); arranges for
their publication by Little, Brown as *Essays and Poems*. In
December begins lecture series on "The Present Age" at
Boston's Masonic Hall (later repeats series). Visited in
Concord by young poet and Unitarian minister Christo-
pher Pearse Cranch.

1840   With Margaret Fuller, brings out first issue of *The Dial* in
July, hoping it will be a "cheerful and rational voice amidst
the din of mourners and polemics," and regularly contrib-
utes essays, poems, and reviews; contributors to first issue
include Emerson, Fuller, Thoreau, Alcott, Cranch, Chan-
ning, Theodore Parker, and George Ripley. Works on a
book of essays "on various matters as a sort of apology to
my country for my apparent idleness." Attends reformers'
Chardon Street Convention, but declines invitation to
join Brook Farm community and thus "remove from my
present prison to a prison a little larger." Lecturing in-
creases; three talks at the New York Mercantile Library
outsell all other lectures there.

1841   *Essays*, initially titled *Forest Essays*, published in March.
Foreign admirers include Carlyle and Harriet Martineau;
aunt Mary pronounces it "a strange medly of atheism &
false independence." Thoreau joins household in spring,
receiving room and board in exchange for "what labor he
chooses to do." Emerson delivers "The Method of Na-
ture" at Waterville College in Maine in summer. Daughter
Edith born November 22.

1842   Devastated by death of son Waldo from scarlet fever on
January 27. Lectures on "The Times" in New York (re-
viewed by young *Aurora* editor Walt Whitman) and visits
Horace Greeley, Albert Brisbane (a leading advocate of
Fourierism), and the elder Henry James; sees James' new-
born son, William. Succeeds Fuller as editor of *The Dial*
in July after she resigns. Raises money to send Bronson
Alcott to England. Along with Thoreau, William Ellery
Channing (nephew of the Unitarian clergyman of the

same name and known as Ellery) is temporary member of Emerson household; in August, Margaret Fuller arrives for about a month's stay. Takes walking trip in September with Nathaniel Hawthorne (who now lives at the "Old Manse") to visit the Shaker community at Harvard, Massachusetts.

1843   Lectures on "New England" and other topics. Finds Thoreau employment in spring as tutor to children of brother William (now a New York State district judge). Completes a translation of Dante's *La Vita Nuova*. Sees Daniel Webster in the summer and pronounces him "no saint . . . but according to his lights a very true & admirable man." In October, publishes essay on Ellery Channing's poetry in *United States Magazine and Democratic Review*.

1844   Last issue of the financially troubled *Dial* appears in April. Son Edward Waldo born July 10. Purchases land at Walden Pond in Concord. Opposes "tooth & nail" the annexation of Texas. Delivers address on the anniversary of Britain's emancipation of West Indian slaves. *Essays: Second Series* published in October.

1845   Contributes $500 toward purchase of a house for the Alcotts in Concord, and deeds eight acres of land in trust to Abba May Alcott. Makes a will in which he leaves his land at Walden Pond to Thoreau. Begins friendship with James Elliot Cabot, who had contributed to *The Dial*. Reads with enthusiasm English translation of the *Bhagavadgita*. On July 4 Thoreau moves into cabin he is building on Emerson's Walden Pond property. Emerson lectures at Waltham against slavery; refuses to speak at New Bedford lyceum because they exclude "a colored person" and so "ought to exclude me." Helps sponsor visit to Concord of Robert Owen, Welsh social reformer and organizer of communal society at New Harmony, Indiana. Begins lecture series "Representative Men" in winter.

1846   Hears Edward Everett's inaugural address as president of Harvard on April 30; in journal decries "the corpse-cold Unitarianism & Immortality of Brattle street & Boston." Acquires Joseph von Hammer-Purgstall's German translation of the Persian poet Hafiz. In July, feels limited sympathy when Thoreau is jailed for a night for refusing to pay his poll tax on anti-slavery grounds: "this prison is one step to suicide." Publishes letter protesting return of fugitive slave to Louisiana by a Boston merchant, and speaks at Dedham against slavery. *Poems* published in December; the book goes through four printings within a year.

1847–48   With Theodore Parker, James Elliot Cabot, and Charles Sumner, plans *Massachusetts Quarterly Review* as a successor to *The Dial* (first issue published in December 1847). Revised edition of *Essays* (now titled *Essays: First Series*) published in September 1847. Success as writer and as lecturer for lyceums and mechanics' associations brings invitation to speak in various English industrial cities; sails in October (Thoreau moves from Walden Pond to stay with the Emerson household). Lectures extensively from November 1847 to February 1848 on various topics, including "Natural Aristocracy," amid political unrest in England and Scotland. Sees Carlyle, Wordsworth, Harriet Martineau, Thomas De Quincey, Charles Dickens, Alfred Tennyson, and Arthur Hugh Clough. Visits Paris in May during revolutionary upheavals and meets Alexis de Tocqueville. Returns to England in June 1848 and lectures in London on "Mind and Manners in the Nineteenth Century" and other topics. Dines with Frederic Chopin; visits Stonehenge with Carlyle; meets Mary Ann Evans (who later writes as George Eliot) and Leigh Hunt. Returns to Boston in July 1848.

1849   Repeats "Mind and Manners" series of lectures in winter and spring. In August gives anti-slavery lecture in Worcester. *Nature; Addresses and Lectures* published in September. Essay "War" published by Elizabeth Peabody in her volume *Aesthetic Papers*.

1850   *Representative Men* published in January. Lectures extensively in New England, New York, Philadelphia, Cleveland, and Cincinnati, including series on "The Natural History of the Intellect." Mourns Margaret Fuller Ossoli, who drowns July 19 with her Italian husband and infant son in a shipwreck off Fire Island, New York, while returning from Italy ("I have lost in her my audience"). Sends Thoreau to Fire Island beach to search, with little success, for her effects. Expresses support for Woman's

Rights Convention at Worcester, Massachusetts, but admits that "a public convention called by women is not very agreeable to me."

1851   Outraged by Daniel Webster's support of the 1850 fugitive slave law, condemns his former hero in journal entries ("The word *liberty* in the mouth of Mr. Webster sounds like the word *love* in the mouth of a courtezan"); in May addresses citizens of Concord in opposition to the new law and Webster's support of it. In summer, expresses temporary disenchantment with Thoreau in journal: "instead of being the head of American Engineers, he is captain of a huckleberry party."

1852   Contributes to and edits, with William Henry Channing and James Freeman Clarke, *Memoirs of Margaret Fuller Ossoli*. Welcomes Hungarian patriot Louis Kossuth to Concord in public ceremony; also visited by sculptor Horatio Greenough and English poet Arthur Hugh Clough. Lectures in winter of 1852–53 to enthusiastic audiences in various cities, including St. Louis, Philadelphia, and Montreal.

1853   Mother dies November 16 at age 85.

1854   Contributes money for Philadelphia memorial to Wordsworth, whom he calls "the solitariest and wisest of poets." Continues demanding lecture schedule; speaks against fugitive slave law on March 7 in New York City. On July 4 the Emersons, at Lidian's suggestion, drape the gates of their home in black to protest the Kansas-Nebraska Act, which repeals the anti-slavery restriction in the Missouri Compromise.

1855   Continues anti-slavery and other lectures. Helps F. B. Sanborn establish a school at Concord, whose pupils will include children of Emerson, Hawthorne, and the elder Henry James. Joins Louis Agassiz, Richard Henry Dana, James Russell Lowell, and E. P. Whipple in founding Saturday Club in Boston (Longfellow, Holmes, Hawthorne, and Whittier also become members). In July, reads and admires *Leaves of Grass*, sent to him by Walt Whitman. Writes to Whitman: "I give you joy of your free & brave thought. . . . I greet you at the beginning of a great career." Raises money to create an annuity for Alcott. Addresses Woman's Rights Convention in Boston in September.

1856   Speaks at meeting in May protesting brutal beating of Massachusetts senator Charles Sumner by South Carolina congressman Preston Brooks. Attends meetings and helps raise money for relief of free-soil Kansas settlers threatened by pro-slavery militia from Missouri. Reads the *Upanishads*. In August publishes *English Traits*; over half the printing of 3,000 is sold in four days, the rest within a month. Lectures take him through New England and as far west as Illinois.

1857   Listens approvingly to anti-slavery speech by John Brown in Concord. Writes sketch of Bronson Alcott for first volume of *New American Cyclopaedia*, edited by George Ripley and Charles A. Dana (published 1858). Moves remains of mother and Waldo to Sleepy Hollow Cemetery in Concord, and looks into son's coffin. Continues to lecture widely, especially from "Conduct of Life" series and on "Works and Days" and "Country Life." In November, poems "Days," "Brahma," and "Illusions" appear in first number of James Russell Lowell's *Atlantic Monthly*.

1858   Writes in journal about the "cowardly" politics of Massachusetts: "Why do we not say, We are abolitionists of the most absolute abolition, as every man that is a man must be?" Publishes five poems and essays in *Atlantic Monthly*, among them the essay "Persian Poetry," which includes translations (from German versions) of Hafiz and others. Spends two weeks in August in Adirondack Mountains with Agassiz, Lowell, and others.

1859   Brother Robert Bulkeley dies May 27. After John Brown's unsuccessful raid on the federal arsenal at Harpers Ferry, Virginia, Emerson predicts that Brown's execution will make the gallows "glorious as the cross." Speaks at meetings for the relief of Brown's family and continues other lecturing.

1860   Lectures in Buffalo, Detroit, Chicago, Milwaukee, and other cities. Meets Whitman in March; walks with him for two hours on Boston Common, advising him to tone down the "sex element" in "Enfans d'Adam" (later "Children of Adam"), poems written for 1860 edition of *Leaves of Grass*. Meets William Dean Howells in Concord in August. Considers Abraham Lincoln's election "sublime . . . the pronunciation of the masses of America against slavery." Publishes 13 short poems in James Freeman Clarke's *The Dial* (Cincinnati). *The Conduct of Life* published in December and is reprinted four times within six weeks.

1861   Speaks at public meeting held by Massachusetts Anti-Slavery Society; told to "dry up" by unruly crowd. Impressed by unity and patriotism of New England following attack on Fort Sumter in April. Visits nearby Charlestown Navy Yard; decides that "sometimes gunpowder smells good." Lectures on "Life and Literature" in spring and "American Nationality" and "Immortality" in fall and winter.

1862   In Washington lectures on "American Civilization"; introduced by Senator Charles Sumner to Secretary of State William H. Seward and President Lincoln. Thoreau dies on May 6 of tuberculosis; in address at funeral Emerson declares that "the country knows not yet, or in the least part, how great a son it has lost." Expresses renewed faith in Lincoln and the Union in the *Atlantic Monthly* after the Emancipation Proclamation is issued in September.

1863   Lectures during winter in Canada, the Midwest, and Northeast. Aunt Mary dies on May 1 at age 89. In May, accepts invitation to serve on Board of Visitors to the U.S. Military Academy, whose task is to review standards for the academy. Speaks on "The Fortune of the Republic" in winter 1863–64.

1864   Elected in January to American Academy of Arts and Sciences. Writes preface to American edition of Persian poet Saadi's *The Gulistan, or Rose Garden* (published 1865). Hawthorne dies May 19; attends funeral and writes in journal of "the painful solitude of the man—which, I suppose, could not longer be endured, & he died of it." Gives winter lecture series on "American Life."

1865   Eulogizes Lincoln to citizens of Concord as "the true representative of this continent." Daughter Edith marries

Colonel William H. Forbes (future president of Bell Telephone Company and son of railroad magnate John Murray Forbes). Lectures 77 times, including a talk on William Cullen Bryant; writes that his lectures "are the correctors" of his manuscripts.

1866   Lectures in Midwest and Northeast in January and February, including series on "Philosophy for the People." First grandchild, Ralph Emerson Forbes, born July 10. Receives honorary Doctor of Laws degree from Harvard. Reads his poem "Terminus" to son Edward Waldo.

1867   Lectures 80 times, the peak of his platform career, twice traveling as far west as Minnesota and Iowa to address topics that include "Eloquence" and "Success"; entertained in St. Louis by William Torrey Harris, a leading American Hegelian. *May-Day and Other Pieces*, second book of verse, published in April; Emerson amused by newspaper parodies of "Brahma." Speaks on religion at meetings of the Radical Club and the Free Religious Association in Boston. Delivers Phi Beta Kappa address at Harvard, his first speech there since 1838 "Divinity School Address"; named overseer of Harvard College (serves until 1879). In November attends dinner for Charles Dickens in Boston at home of James T. and Annie Fields.

1868   Begins correspondence with 19-year-old Emma Lazarus, who had sent him her first book of poems. Brother William dies in New York September 13. Publishes essay "Quotation and Originality" in *Atlantic Monthly*. Continues heavy lecture schedule, including six-day series in Boston managed by publisher James T. Fields that earns him $1,655.75, "much the largest sum I ever received for work of this kind."

1869   Gives almost 50 lectures and an informal spring class at Harvard on Chaucer, Shakespeare, Jonson, Bacon, and other English writers. Endorses woman suffrage as "an important step in civilization." Writes New York friend Anne Botta that "today & tomorrow & the year through I find myself the drudge of tasks I cannot praise."

1870   *Society and Solitude* published in March. Offers course in Harvard philosophy department on "Natural History of

Intellect" and is much occupied with university affairs and other projects, including a new book required to preempt an unauthorized edition of essays planned by English publisher John Camden Hotten. Writes preface for an edition of *Plutarch's Morals*, one of his favorite books.

1871   In February, speaks at opening of Boston Museum of Fine Arts. Feeling fatigued, cuts short repeat of Harvard course; takes trip with family and friends to West Coast and back, April–May, in a private Pullman car leased by John Murray Forbes (Edward Emerson later says the trip "very probably prolonged his life"). Meets naturalist John Muir and notes that California "has better days, & more of them" than any other place. Visited by Bret Harte in October. Publishes preface to Ellery Channing's *The Wanderer*.

1872   Lectures in Baltimore; sees Whitman and Sumner. Reads "Amita," his memoir of aunt Mary, to a gathering at the home of James T. and Annie Fields in March. Health and memory decline, especially after family house in Concord burns July 24. Travels to Maine with daughter Ellen to recuperate, and expresses fears that his life is nearing its end; they discuss future disposition of his manuscripts and possibility of asking James Elliot Cabot to oversee his literary estate and help with the current book of essays. Friends raise money to repair house and send Emerson and Ellen (who has become indispensable in the management of his affairs) on a trip to Europe and Egypt in October. In England, sees Carlyle and son Edward, who is studying medicine in London. Arrives in Paris November 15; spends time with James Russell Lowell and is conducted through the Louvre by the young Henry James. After travels in Italy, arrives in Alexandria, Egypt, on Christmas Day; visits Cairo.

1873   Enjoying improved health, travels on the Nile for sightseeing. Sails from Alexandria in February. Visits Florence; in Paris, meets Hippolyte Taine, Ivan Turgenev, and Ernest Renan. Returns to England and sees Carlyle (for the last time), philologist and religious scholar Max Müller, John Stuart Mill, Robert Browning, T. H. Huxley, John Ruskin, Charles Dodgson (Lewis Carroll), and classical scholar Benjamin Jowett. Confers with Moncure Conway, his friend and liaison with publisher John Camden Hotten, about promised book of essays. Returns with Ellen to Concord May 27 and is met by a cheering crowd and brass band; moves into fully restored home. In October gives speech at opening of new Concord library building.

1874 In December, publishes *Parnassus*, an anthology of his favorite poetry, which he and daughter Edith had worked on for years (Whitman is hurt that none of his poems are included).

1875 Gradually stops writing in journal. Reads speech on April 19, the centenary of the battle of Concord, at the dedication of Daniel Chester French's "Minute-Man" monument. With Ellen, continues to work on volume of uncollected essays. Persuaded by Ellen, accepts James Elliot Cabot's editorial help in shaping existing materials for the book *Letters and Social Aims*, published in December. Begins work on final selection and revision of his poetry, assisted by family and friends.

1876 Draws up a new will naming Cabot as his literary executor and giving son Edward ownership of all copyrights, plates, and publishing contracts. In June, travels with Ellen to University of Virginia for only lecture he will ever give in the South (it is received inhospitably). Emma Lazarus visits in August. *Selected Poems* published by James R. Osgood in the fall. Addresses Boston Public Latin School at a centennial anniversary in November.

1877–81 Memory and concentration fade; Bronson Alcott terms it "a happy euthanasia, and a painless." Ellen and Cabot continue to collaborate with him in arranging previously written material for lectures and essays, including "Perpetual Forces," "The Sovereignty of Ethics," "The Preacher," and "Fortune of the Republic"; Ellen helps him through public appearances. Of the address "Education," delivered at the Concord Lyceum in 1878, he remarks good-humoredly, "A funny occasion it will be—a lecturer who has no idea what he is lecturing about." Sits for bust by Daniel Chester French in 1879. Appears at Massachusetts Historical Society in 1881 to speak on Carlyle, who had recently died. Whitman visits him at home in 1881 and terms it "a long and blessed evening."

1882   Attends funeral of Henry Wadsworth Longfellow in March; after viewing the body asks, "Where are we? What house? And who is the sleeper?" Dies at home of pneumonia on April 27, and is buried April 30 in Sleepy Hollow Cemetery, Concord.

This volume contains all of the 233 poems and translations of poems published by Ralph Waldo Emerson during his lifetime, as well as a selection of 450 poems, fragments of poems, and translations of poems that were left in manuscript at his death in 1882. It prints the complete texts of *Poems* (1847) and *May-Day and Other Pieces* (1867); eight poems published in *Selected Poems* (1876) that had not been previously collected by Emerson; 28 poems and 49 translations of poems that appeared between 1829 and 1880 in gift-book anthologies, magazines, and collections of Emerson's essays and as contributions to books by others; and 358 poems and 92 translations of poems left in manuscript, including his English version of Dante's *Vita Nuova*.

More than half of the 60 poems and translations included by Emerson in his first collection of poetry had previously appeared in periodicals and gift-book anthologies. Emerson completed work on the manuscript for *Poems* in October 1846 and gave it to the Boston firm of James Munroe and Company, who had agreed to publish the volume under an arrangement in which Emerson would pay the publishing costs in return for ownership of the printing plates. At the same time, Emerson sent the manuscript to Chapman Brothers in London, who published an English edition of *Poems* on December 12, 1846. Emerson read proof for the Munroe edition and made corrections and a few revisions. He received his first printed copy of the Munroe edition, which was dated 1847, on December 25, 1846. On December 29 he sent a copy to Chapman Brothers with a letter acknowledging the difficulty they had faced in setting their edition from manuscript without his assistance and requesting that they use the Munroe edition to correct future English printings. Emerson made minor revisions in subsequent American printings of *Poems* (some of the more significant revisions are shown in the notes to this volume). The text of *Poems* printed here is that of the first printing of the 1847 James Munroe edition.

May-Day and Other Pieces, a volume collecting 90 of Emerson's poems and translations, was published by Ticknor and Fields in Boston on April 29, 1867. As in the case of *Poems*, Emerson paid the publication costs and owned the resulting printing plates. He included in the volume one poem by his brother Edward Bliss Emerson, "The Last Farewell," which he paired with his own "In Memoriam / E.B.E." The first printing of *May-Day* contained two significant errors. In the quatrain "Botanist," the word "hours" appeared incorrectly as "flowers"; this error was corrected by Emerson in subsequent printings, and is corrected here at 207.18 (all page and line number references are to the present volume). In the poem "Days," the word "Daughters" (178.14) was incorrectly printed as "Damsels" in the first printing, and as "Daughter" in subsequent printings. This volume restores "Daughters," following the text of "Days" that appeared in the November 1857 *Atlantic Monthly*. The text of *May-Day and Other Pieces* included here is otherwise that of the first printing of the 1867 Ticknor and Fields edition.

Selected Poems was published by James R. Osgood and Company in Boston in the autumn of 1876 as the ninth and final volume in its small-format "Little Classics" edition of Emerson's works. The volume collected 38 poems from *Poems*, 21 poems from *May-Day*, and eight poems not previously collected by Emerson, which are printed here. One of them, "The Harp" (223.1–226.19), consists of 123 lines from the 1867 text of the poem "May-Day" (143.29–146.36), with the addition of four new lines (225.30–33).

Many poems appeared in *Selected Poems* in versions significantly revised from their earlier publication, but it is uncertain what role Emerson played in making these changes. (Some significant revisions are indicated in the notes to this volume.) Emerson's memory and concentration declined during the 1870s, and as a consequence many people became involved in the selection and revision of the poetry collected in *Selected Poems*, including his daughters Edith Emerson Forbes and Ellen Emerson, his son Edward Emerson, his literary executor James Elliot Cabot, family friends Elizabeth Hoar and F. B. Sanborn, and the poet James Russell Lowell.

In 1884, two years after Emerson's death, the ninth volume of the posthumous "Riverside" edition of the collected works, edited by James Elliot Cabot and published by Houghton, Mifflin, became the standard edition of the poetry. Cabot printed *Poems* and *May-Day* as separate sections, deleted seven poems from *Poems* and five poems from *May-Day*, and added an appendix, assembled with the aid of the Emerson family, of unpublished poems and fragments.

The Riverside edition was superseded by the "Centenary" edition, prepared by Edward Emerson and published by Houghton, Mifflin, in 1903–4, with the collected poetry again appearing as the ninth volume of the edition. In the Centenary edition, Edward Emerson deleted five poems from *Poems* and one poem from *May-Day*, while restoring other poems that Cabot had omitted from the Riverside edition. The Centenary edition significantly changed the order in which the poems appeared within the sections titled *Poems* and *May-*

Day, included further selections from Emerson's unpublished poetry in its appendix, and presented, in a separate section titled "Poems of Youth and Early Manhood," 17 early poems that had not been published during Emerson's lifetime.

Both Cabot and Edward Emerson chose to incorporate some, but not all, of the late changes Emerson made in his published poetry, at times preferring, in Cabot's words, "corrections made by him when he was in fuller strength than at the time of the last revision." They also frequently altered Emerson's punctuation and occasionally altered titles and rearranged lines. In the previously unpublished poems, they sometimes made substantive alterations in the texts, changed titles or supplied new titles, and joined together separate versions of poems or separate poems; for example, the text of "The Poet" that appears in the Riverside and Centenary editions was made by taking hundreds of lines from disparate unpublished poems and fragments. Some of the more significant alterations made by Cabot and Edward Emerson in the manuscript poems are shown in the notes to this volume.

This volume prints wherever possible texts of the published poetry supervised by Emerson himself and, by printing the complete texts of *Poems* and *May-Day and Other Pieces*, includes published poems that were deleted from the posthumous Riverside and Centenary editions.

In this volume, the texts of poems published but not collected by Emerson during his lifetime are taken from the sources in which they originally appeared. (Poems that appeared in Emerson's essays are printed here from the Library of America volume, *Ralph Waldo Emerson, Essays and Lectures*.) Two of the poems were published in *The Offering for 1829*, a literary miscellany intended to be given as a gift, edited by Andrews Norton and published in Cambridge, Massachusetts. Three poems first appeared in *The Dial*; one poem was published in *Our Pastors' Offering*, a compilation of writings by pastors of the Second Church of Boston, published in 1845; and 15 poems first appeared as mottoes in the two series of his *Essays* and in *Nature; Addresses, and Lectures* and *The Conduct of Life*. One poem is printed from *Thoreau: The Poet-Naturalist*, published in 1873 by William Ellery Channing, because no other text of this version is available; four other poems that appeared in *Thoreau* are printed here from the manuscript texts published in *The Poetry Notebooks of Ralph Waldo Emerson*, since Channing did not follow Emerson's texts exactly. Of the 49 translations of poetry that Emerson published but did not collect, 43 first appeared in the article "Persian Poetry," published in the *Atlantic Monthly* in April 1858 (the translations were made from German texts of the poems). A version of this article appeared in *Letters and Social Aims*, a collection of Emerson's writings prepared by Cabot and published in 1876; the present volume prints the 1858 text. Five translations attributed to Emerson appeared in *Nature; Addresses, and Lectures*, *Representative Men*, and *The Conduct of Life*, and one of his translations first appeared in *Sketches and Reminiscences of the Radical Club of Chestnut Street, Boston*, a volume edited by Mary E. Sargent and published in 1880.

Of the 450 poems, fragments of poems, and poetic translations selected for inclusion here from those left by Emerson in manuscript, the texts of 334 are taken from *The Poetry Notebooks of Ralph Waldo Emerson*, edited by Ralph H. Orth, Albert J. von Frank, Linda Allardt, and David W. Hill (1986). The texts of 88 poems and translations are taken from *The Journals and Miscellaneous Notebooks of Ralph Waldo Emerson* (16 vols., 1960–82). Eight poetic translations are printed from *The Topical Notebooks of Ralph Waldo Emerson* (2 vols. to date, 1990–93), and the texts of seven poems are taken from Albert J. von Frank, "Emerson's Boyhood and Collegiate Verse: Unpublished and New Texts Edited from Manuscript," in *Studies in the American Renaissance 1983*, edited by Joel Myerson. Two poems are taken from *The Letters of Ralph Waldo Emerson*, edited by Ralph L. Rusk (vols. 1–6, 1939) and Eleanor M. Tilton (vols. 7–8, 1990–91). Another two poems are taken from *One First Love: The Letters of Ellen Louisa Tucker to Ralph Waldo Emerson*, edited by Edith W. Gregg (1962). The text of Emerson's English version of the *Vita Nuova* is printed from J. Chesley Mathews, "Emerson's Translation of Dante's *Vita Nuova*," in the *Harvard Library Bulletin* (1957). Eight poems are printed from manuscripts, or facsimiles of manuscripts, in the Houghton Library, Harvard University; the Carl F. Strauch Papers, Lehigh University; and the Berg Collection of the New York Public Library.

The Poetry Notebooks of Ralph Waldo Emerson, *The Journals and Miscellaneous Notebooks of Ralph Waldo Emerson*, *The Topical Notebooks of Ralph Waldo Emerson*, and "Emerson's Boyhood and Collegiate Verse: Unpublished and New Texts Edited from Manuscript" present genetic texts of Emerson's manuscript poetry, using various typographical symbols to indicate cancellations, revisions, interlinear and marginal interpolations, and other changes. The present volume prints clear texts, derived from these genetic texts, in which cancellations and their related editorial symbols have been omitted; Emerson's revisions are printed without the editorial symbols indicating various forms of interpolations. (In a few cases where Emerson inserted a new word at the beginning of a line but did not adjust the

capitalization of the original first word on the line, that word is
printed lowercase in this volume.) Manuscript material that the edi-
tors of the genetic texts were unable to recover is indicated in this
volume by a bracketed space, i.e., [   ]. In places where there are
unresolved authorial choices in the manuscript, the first alternative
presented in the genetic text is printed in the main text of this vol-
ume and the other alternatives are presented in the notes. A blank
two-em space is used in this volume to indicate places where Emer-
son left a blank space in the manuscript, probably with the intention
of returning to the poem at a future time and completing the line. In
"Emerson's Translation of Dante's *Vita Nuova*," J. Chesley Mathews
presented an Emerson manuscript in a text in which cancelled mate-
rial was not printed and unresolved authorial choices were editorially
decided in favor of the alternative believed to represent Emerson's
later choice. Mathews deleted words unintentionally repeated by
Emerson and, in a few places, supplied within square brackets punc-
tuation, letters, or words inadvertently omitted by Emerson; the
present volume accepts these conjectural readings and prints them
without brackets.

   The following is a list of the poems and translations included in
this volume in the sections titled "Other Published Poems and Trans-
lations" and "Manuscript Poems and Translations," giving the source
of each text. The most common sources are indicated by these abbre-
viations:

Channing   William Ellery Channing, *Thoreau: The Poet-Naturalist*
              (Boston: Roberts Brothers, 1873).

Houghton   The Houghton Library, Harvard University. Reprinted
              by permission of the Ralph Waldo Emerson Memorial
              Association and of Houghton Library, Harvard Uni-
              versity.

JMN   *The Journals and Miscellaneous Notebooks of Ralph Waldo
              Emerson*, William H. Gilman, chief editor, vols. 7–13,
              Ralph H. Orth, vols. 14–16 (16 vols., Cambridge: The
              Belknap Press of Harvard University Press, 1960–82).
              Volume I, edited by William H. Gilman, Alfred R. Fer-
              guson, George P. Clark, and Merrell R. Davis (1960);
              volume II, edited by William H. Gilman, Alfred R. Fer-
              guson, and Merrell R. Davis (1961); volume III, edited by
              William H. Gilman and Alfred R. Ferguson (1963); vol-
              ume IV, edited by Alfred R. Ferguson (1964); volume VI,
              edited by Ralph H. Orth (1966); volume VII, edited by
              A. W. Plumstead and Harrison Hayford (1969); volume

VIII, edited by William H. Gilman and J. E. Parsons (1970); volume IX, edited by Ralph H. Orth and Alfred R. Ferguson (1971); volume X, edited by Merton M. Sealts, Jr. (1973); volume XIV, edited by Susan Sutton Smith and Harrison Hayford (1978); volume XV, edited by Linda Allardt and David W. Hill, Ruth H. Bennett, associate editor (1982); volume XVI, edited by Ronald A. Bosco and Glen M. Johnson (1982). Copyright © 1960, 1961, 1963, 1964, 1966, 1969, 1970, 1971, 1973, 1978, 1982, by the President and Fellows of Harvard College. Reprinted by permission of the publishers.

LOA   *Ralph Waldo Emerson, Essays and Lectures*, edited by Joel Porte (New York: The Library of America, 1983).

PN   *The Poetry Notebooks of Ralph Waldo Emerson*, edited by Ralph H. Orth, Albert J. von Frank, Linda Allardt, and David W. Hill (Columbia: University of Missouri Press, 1986). Copyright © 1986 by the Ralph Waldo Emerson Memorial Association and the Curators of the University of Missouri. Notebook material reprinted by permission of the Ralph Waldo Emerson Memorial Association.

TN   *The Topical Notebooks of Ralph Waldo Emerson*, Ralph H. Orth, chief editor (2 vols. to date, Columbia and London: University of Missouri Press, 1990–93), volume II, edited by Ronald A. Bosco (1993). Copyright © 1993 by the Ralph Waldo Emerson Memorial Association and the Curators of the University of Missouri. Notebook material reprinted by permission of the Ralph Waldo Emerson Memorial Association.

von Frank   Albert J. von Frank, "Emerson's Boyhood and Collegiate Verse: Unpublished and New Texts Edited from Manuscript," in *Studies in the American Renaissance 1983*, edited by Joel Myerson (Charlottesville: University Press of Virginia, 1983), pp. 1–56. Copyright © 1983 by Joel Myerson. Reprinted by permission.

OTHER PUBLISHED POEMS AND TRANSLATIONS

William Rufus and the Jew. *The Offering for 1829* (Boston: Hilliard and Brown, 1829), 17–18.

Fame. *The Offering for 1829* (Boston: Hilliard and Brown, 1829), 52–53.

Silence. *The Dial*, October 1840.

Mottoes to "History." *Essays: First Series* (Boston: James Munroe, 1847), in *LOA*, 235–36.

Grace. *The Dial*, January 1842.

The Three Dimensions. *The Dial*, October 1843.

Motto to "The Poet." *Essays: Second Series* (Boston: James Munroe, 1844), in *LOA*, 445.

Motto to "Gifts." *Essays: Second Series* (Boston: James Munroe, 1844), in *LOA*, 533.

Motto to "Nature." *Essays: Second Series* (Boston: James Munroe, 1844), in *LOA*, 539.

Motto to "Nominalist and Realist." *Essays: Second Series* (Boston: James Munroe, 1844), in *LOA*, 573.

My Thoughts. *Our Pastors' Offering* (Boston: printed by George Coolidge, 1845), 107–8.

Motto to "Prudence." *Essays: First Series* (Boston: James Munroe, 1847), in *LOA*, 355.

Motto to "Circles." *Essays: First Series* (Boston: James Munroe, 1847), in *LOA*, 401.

Motto to "Intellect." *Essays: First Series* (Boston: James Munroe, 1847), in *LOA*, 415.

Motto to *Nature. Nature; Addresses, and Lectures* (Boston: James Munroe, 1849), in *LOA*, 5.

Motto to "New England Reformers." *Essays: Second Series* (Boston: James Munroe, 1850), 240.

Motto to "Fate." *The Conduct of Life* (Boston: Ticknor and Fields, 1860), in *LOA*, 941.

Motto to "Power." *The Conduct of Life* (Boston: Ticknor and Fields, 1860), in *LOA*, 969.

Motto to "Considerations by the Way." *The Conduct of Life* (Boston: Ticknor and Fields, 1860), in *LOA*, 1077–78.

Motto to "Illusions." *The Conduct of Life* (Boston: Ticknor and Fields, 1860), in *LOA*, 1113–14.

The cup of life is not so shallow. *PN*, 436; first printed in *Channing*.

Where is Skrymir? Giant Skrymir? *PN*, 49–50; first printed in *Channing*.

There are beggars in Iran and Araby. *Channing*, 161.

Quoth Saadi, when I stood before. *PN*, 587; first printed in *Channing*.

South Wind. *PN*, 442–43; first printed in *Channing*.

TRANSLATIONS

Sunshine was he. "Man the Reformer," *Nature; Addresses, and Lectures* (Boston: James Munroe, 1849), in *LOA*, 149.

Go boldly forth, and feast on being's banquet. "Swedenborg; or, the Mystic," *Representative Men* (Boston: Phillips, Sampson and Company, 1850), in *LOA*, 662.

The principle of all thing; entrails made. "Persian Poetry," *Atlantic Monthly*, April 1858.

The secret that should not be blown. "Persian Poetry," *Atlantic Monthly*, April 1858.

On earth's wide thoroughfares below. "Persian Poetry," *Atlantic Monthly*, April 1858.

Color, taste, and smell, smaragdus, sugar, and musk. "Persian Poetry," *Atlantic Monthly*, April 1858.

I batter the wheel of heaven. "Persian Poetry," *Atlantic Monthly*, April 1858.

See how the roses burn. "Persian Poetry," *Atlantic Monthly*, April 1858.

Alas! till now I had not known. "Persian Poetry," *Atlantic Monthly*, April 1858.

The understanding's copper coin. "Persian Poetry," *Atlantic Monthly*, April 1858.

'Tis writ on Paradise's gate. "Persian Poetry," *Atlantic Monthly*, April 1858.

The world is a bride superbly dressed. "Persian Poetry," *Atlantic Monthly*, April 1858.

Loose the knots of the heart; never think on thy fate. "Persian Poetry," *Atlantic Monthly*, April 1858.

There resides in the grieving. "Persian Poetry," *Atlantic Monthly*, April 1858.

I will be drunk and down with wine. "Persian Poetry," *Atlantic Monthly*, April 1858.

To be wise the dull brain so earnestly throbs. "Persian Poetry," *Atlantic Monthly*, April 1858.

The Builder of heaven. "Persian Poetry," *Atlantic Monthly*, April 1858.

I am: what I am. "Persian Poetry," *Atlantic Monthly*, April 1858.

What lovelier forms things wear. "Persian Poetry," *Atlantic Monthly*, April 1858.

Take my heart in thy hand, O beautiful boy of Schiraz. "Persian Poetry," *Atlantic Monthly*, April 1858.

Out of the East, and out of the West, no man understands me. "Persian Poetry," *Atlantic Monthly*, April 1858.

Fit for the Pleiads' azure chord. "Persian Poetry," *Atlantic Monthly*, April 1858.

I have no hoarded treasure. "Persian Poetry," *Atlantic Monthly*, April 1858.

High heart, O Hafiz! though not thine. "Persian Poetry," *Atlantic Monthly*, April 1858.

O Hafiz! speak not of thy need. "Persian Poetry," *Atlantic Monthly*, April 1858.

Oft have I said, I say it once more. "Persian Poetry," *Atlantic Monthly*, April 1858.

The Phoenix. "Persian Poetry," *Atlantic Monthly*, April 1858.

Come!—the palace of heaven rests on aëry pillars. "Persian Poetry," *Atlantic Monthly*, April 1858.

By breath of beds of roses drawn. "Persian Poetry," *Atlantic Monthly*, April 1858.

All day the rain. "Persian Poetry," *Atlantic Monthly*, April 1858.

O'er the garden water goes the wind alone. "Persian Poetry," *Atlantic Monthly*, April 1858.

Whilst I disdain the populace. "Persian Poetry," *Atlantic Monthly*, April 1858.

A friend is he, who, hunted as a foe. "Persian Poetry," *Atlantic Monthly*, April 1858.

The chemist of love. "Persian Poetry," *Atlantic Monthly*, April 1858.

And since the round lines are drawn. "Persian Poetry," *Atlantic Monthly*, April 1858.

Ah, could I hide me in my song. "Persian Poetry," *Atlantic Monthly*, April 1858.

Fair fall thy soft heart. "Persian Poetry," *Atlantic Monthly*, April 1858.

They strew in the path of kings and czars. "Persian Poetry," *Atlantic Monthly*, April 1858.

I know this perilous love-lane. "Persian Poetry," *Atlantic Monthly*, April 1858.

Plunge in yon angry waves. "Persian Poetry," *Atlantic Monthly*, April 1858.

While roses bloomed along the plain. "Persian Poetry," *Atlantic Monthly*, April 1858.

Body and Soul. "Persian Poetry," *Atlantic Monthly*, April 1858.

I read on the porch of a palace bold. "Persian Poetry," *Atlantic Monthly*, April 1858.

The eternal Watcher, who doth wake. "Persian Poetry," *Atlantic Monthly*, April 1858.

from Bird Conversations. "Persian Poetry," *Atlantic Monthly*, April 1858.

'Tis heavy odds. "Culture," *The Conduct of Life* (Boston: Ticknor and Fields, 1860), in *LOA*, 1027.

At the last day, men shall wear. "Worship," *The Conduct of Life* (Boston: Ticknor and Fields, 1860), in *LOA*, 1072.

Fooled thou must be, though wisest of the wise. "Illusions," *The Conduct of Life* (Boston: Ticknor and Fields, 1860), in *LOA*, 1123.

Alms. Mary E. Sargent, *Sketches and Reminiscences of the Radical Club of Chestnut Street, Boston*, (Boston: James R. Osgood and Company, 1880), 398.

MANUSCRIPT POEMS AND TRANSLATIONS

No. 13 Hymn Written in Concord Sept. 1814. *von Frank*, 26.

On the Death of Mr. John Haskins. *von Frank*, 27.

Lines on the Death of Miss. M. B. Farnham. *von Frank*, 32–33.

Poem on Eloquence by R. W. Emerson. *von Frank*, 34–35.

Original—"Apropos." *von Frank*, 36–37.

William does thy frigid soul. *The Letters of Ralph Waldo Emerson*, I, edited by Ralph L. Rusk (New York: Columbia University Press, 1939), 41–42. Copyright © 1939 Columbia University Press, New York. Reprinted with permission of the publisher.

Song. *von Frank*, 42–43.

Perhaps thy lot in life is higher. *JMN*, I, 40.

Valedictory Poem. *von Frank*, 48–55.

From Frodmer's Drama "The Friends." *JMN*, I, 292.

By the unacknowledged tie. *JMN*, I, 321–22.

Idealism. *JMN*, I, 81.

I spread my gorgeous sail. *PN*, 11–12

A Shout to the Shepherds. *JMN*, II, 114.

I wear no badge; no tinsel star. *PN*, 38.

I love thy music, mellow bell. *PN*, 427–28.

I rake no coffined clay, nor publish wide. *JMN*, II, 244.

O What have I to do. *JMN*, II, 404–5.

Have ye seen the caterpillar. *PN*, 556–57.

The panoply of Paradise is mine. *JMN*, II, 406–7.

No fate, save by the victim's fault, is low. *PN*, 458.

When success exalts thy lot. *JMN*, II, 387–88.

The spirits of the wise, sit on the clouds. *JMN*, II, 408–9.

Let not conceited sages laugh aloud. *JMN*, III, 35–36.

My days roll by me like a train of dreams. *JMN*, III, 36.

One hand washes the other. *JMN*, VI, 15.

Whoso alas is young. *PN*, 715.

When thy soul. *JMN*, III, 85–86.

The blackbird's song the blackbird's song. *JMN*, III, 86–87.

I am an exile from my home; heavily. *JMN*, III, 88.

He must have. *PN*, 4–6.

St. Augustine. *PN*, 6–8.

Awed I behold once more. *PN*, 8–9.

An ancient lady who dwelt in Rome. *PN*, 14.

Be of good cheer, brave spirit; steadfastly. *PN*, 83–84.

The winds are cold, the days are dark. *PN*, 15.

Written in Sickness. *PN*, 31.

Oil & Wine. *PN*, 12

All that thy virgin soul can ask be thine. *JMN*, II, 410–11.

That wandering fire to me appears. *PN*, 37.

Though her eye seek other forms. *PN*, 69.

Dear Ellen, many a golden year. *PN*, 10.

I call her beautiful;—she says. *PN*, 10–11.

I've found the dainty malice out. *JMN*, III, 151.

And do I waste my time. *One First Love: The Letters of Ellen Louisa Tucker to Ralph Waldo Emerson*, edited by Edith W. Gregg (Cambridge: The Belknap Press of Harvard University Press, 1962), 25. Copyright © 1962 by the President and Fellows of Harvard College. Reprinted by permission of the publishers.

And though he dearly prized the bards of fame. *PN*, 61.

And Ellen, when the greybeard years. *JMN*, III, 181–82.

The brave Empedocles defying fools. *PN*, 36.

Dear brother, would you know the life. *PN*, 121–22.

Dost thou not hear me Ellen. *JMN*, III, 228.

Teach me I am forgotten by the dead. *JMN*, III, 228–29.

Why should I live. *JMN*, III, 230–31.

Shall the Muse sing for thousands & not sing. *JMN*, III, 231–34.

What from this barren being do we reap. *JMN*, III, 232.

Dust unto dust! and shall no more be said. *JMN*, III, 235.

The days pass over me. *PN*, 47.

Why fear to die. *PN*, 36–37.

I am alone. Sad is my solitude. *One First Love: The Letters of Ellen Louisa*

Tucker to Ralph Waldo Emerson, edited by Edith W. Gregg (Cambridge: The Belknap Press of Harvard University Press, 1962), 127. Copyright © 1962 by the President and Fellows of Harvard College. Reprinted by permission of the publishers.

On thee has God conferred. *PN*, 669.

All the great & good. *PN*, 14–15.

Seemed to me—never maid. *Houghton*. MS Am 1280.235 (39).

Where art thou. *Houghton*. MS Am 1280.235 (39).

I live among ideal men. *Houghton*. MS Am 1280.235 (43).

What avails it me. *Houghton*. MS Am 1280.235 (91).

She never comes to me. *JMN*, III, 285–86.

Leave me, Fear! thy throbs are base. *PN*, 342.

Γνωθι Σεαυτον. *JMN*, III, 290–94.

A dull uncertain brain. *JMN*, III, 294–95.

There is in all the sons of men. *JMN*, III, 370–72.

I will not live out of me. *JMN*, IV, 47–48.

Hard is it to persuade the public mind of its plain duty & true interest. *JMN*, IV, 56.

Always day & night. *JMN*, IV, 227.

Hearst thou, sweet spirit, thou hast heard before. *Houghton*. MS Am 1280.235 (39).

None spares another yet it pleases me. *JMN*, IV, 65.

Written in Naples, March, 1833. *PN*, 18.

What is it to sail. *JMN*, IV, 70.

Alone in Rome! Why Rome is lonely too. *PN*, 383.

At Sea, September 1833. *PN*, 621–22.

I will not hesitate to speak the word. *JMN*, IV, 89–90.

The Sun is the sole inconsumable fire. *JMN*, IV, 370.

Poem, Spoken Before the ΦBK Society. *Houghton*. MS Am 1280.233.

O what is Heaven but the fellowship. *JMN*, XVI, 507.

Ah strange strange strange. *PN*, 21.

See yonder leafless trees against the sky. *PN*, 23.

Do that which you can do. *PN*, 25.

Few are free. *PN*, 25.

Van Buren. *PN*, 28.

The Future. *PN*, 28.

Rex. *PN*, 37–38.

Written in a Volume of Goethe. *PN*, 441.

I left my dreamy page & sallied forth. *PN*, 39.

S.R. *PN*, 452–53.

Philosophers are lined with eyes within. *PN*, 42.

The simple people each with basket or tool. *PN*, 44–45.

On bravely through the sunshine & the showers. *PN*, 45.

Let me go where e'er I will. *PN*, 46.

And when I am entombed in my place. *PN*, 46.

Bard or dunce is blest, but hard. *PN*, 46.

It takes philosopher or fool. *PN*, 46.
Tell men what they knew before. *PN*, 46–47.
I use the knife. *PN*, 47.
There is no evil but can speak. *PN*, 47.
The sea reflects the rosy sky. *PN*, 51
In this sour world, o summerwind. *PN*, 54.
Look danger in the eye it vanishes. *PN*, 56.
As I walked in the wood. *PN*, 56.
I sat upon the ground. *PN*, 56.
Good Charles the springs adorer. *PN*, 57.
Around the man who seeks a noble end. *PN*, 595.
In the deep heart of man a poet dwells. *PN*, 57.
O what are heroes prophets men. *PN*, 59.
Yet sometime to the sorrow stricken. *PN*, 59.
When thou sittest moping. *PN*, 103–4.
Woods. *JMN*, VII, 248.
I have supped with the gods tonight. *JMN*, VII, 492.
Once the priest. *JMN*, VIII, 449.
Natures web star broidered. *PN*, 403.
For that a man is a mark. *JMN*, VIII, 470.
The Bohemian Hymn. Photofacsimile of manuscript, Carl F. Strauch Papers, Special Collections, Lehigh University Libraries. Reprinted by permission of the Lehigh University Libraries.
Kind & holy were the words. *The Letters of Ralph Waldo Emerson*, VII, edited by Eleanor M. Tilton (New York: Columbia University Press, 1990), 430–31. Copyright © 1990 Columbia University Press, New York. Reprinted with permission of the publisher.
Bluebeard. Let the gentle wife prepare. *JMN*, VII, 411.
Divine Inviters! I accept. *PN*, 659.
Go if thou wilt ambrosial Flower. *PN*, 59.
In Walden wood the chickadee. *PN*, 60.
Star seer Copernicus. *PN*, 60.
At last the poet spoke. *PN*, 62.
The Discontented Poet: a Masque. *PN*, 63–65.
— — Love. *PN*, 65.
Hold of the Maker, not the made. *PN*, 384.
He walked the streets of great New York. *PN*, 65–66.
The Archangel Hope. *PN*, 66–67.
Atom from atom yawns as far. *PN*, 443.
I grieve that better souls than mine. *PN*, 255.
Nantasket. *PN*, 242–43.
Water. *PN*, 586.
Where the fungus broad & red. *PN*, 67–69.
The Skeptic. *PN*, 40–41.
When Jane was absent Edgar's eye. *PN*, 69.
I have found a nobler love. *PN*, 69–70.

Fine presentiments controlled him. *PN*, 73.
We sauntered amidst miracles. *PN*, 76.
This world is tedious. *PN*, 77.
What are all the flowers. *PN*, 77–78.
A pair of crystal eyes will lead me. *PN*, 78.
Knows he who tills this lonely field. *PN*, 80–81.
Far seen the river glides below. *PN*, 81.
From the stores of eldest Matter. *PN*, 81.
And the best gift of God. *PN*, 82.
Stout Sparta shrined the god of Laughter. *PN*, 82–83.
Brother, no decrepitude. *PN*, 277.
Who knows this or that. *PN*, 86.
Saadi loved the new & old. *PN*, 88.
But if thou do thy best. *PN*, 89–90.
An ancient drop of feudal blood. *PN*, 94–95.
These trees like tho'ts that to visions congeal. *PN*, 95.
Vain against him were hostile blows. *PN*, 146.
Like vaulters in the circus round. *PN*, 426.
If he go apart. *PN*, 155.
Nature will not lose. *PN*, 155.
The crowning hour when bodies vie with souls. *PN*, 155.
And as the light divided the dark. *PN*, 157–58.
When devils bite. *PN*, 165.
Comfort with a purring cat. *PN*, 171.
I cannot find a place so lonely. *PN*, 172.
He whom God had thus preferred. *JMN*, VIII, 226.
Bended to fops who bent to him. *JMN*, VIII, 226.
On that night the poet went. *JMN*, VIII, 226–27.
Ye have Grace. *JMN*, VIII, 227.
The Dervish whined to *Said*. *PN*, 655.
Life is great. *JMN*, VIII, 328–29.
The husband has the nearest acres. *JMN*, VIII, 333.
From a far mountain creeping down. *JMN*, VIII, 344.
In dreamy woods, what forms abound. *JMN*, VIII, 418.
But O to see his solar eyes. *JMN*, VIII, 427–28.
Who saw the hid beginnings. *PN*, 551.
What never was not, & still will be. *PN*, 175
Enough is done highminded friend go sleep. *PN*, 179–80.
Thou shalt make thy house. *PN*, 180.
The gods walk in the breath of the woods. *PN*, 437.
Would you know what joy is hid. *PN*, 84.
Tell me maiden dost thou use. *PN*, 84–85.
I have no brothers & no peers. *PN*, 127–28.
Solar insect on the wing. *PN*, 136.
And man of wit & mark. *PN*, 136.
I know the appointed hour. *PN*, 428.

You shall not love me for what daily spends. *PN*, 436.
Elizabeth Hoar. *PN*, 660.
Proteus. *PN*, 185–90.
To every creature. *PN*, 48–49.
Cloud upon cloud. *PN*, 201–2.
Since the devil hopping on. *PN*, 228.
Samson stark at Dagon's knee. *PN*, 252.
Pour the wine! pour the wine. *PN*, 557.
Heartily heartily. *PN*, 256.
Poets are colorpots. *PN*, 256.
Thanks to those who go & come. *PN*, 393.
Is Jove immortal. *PN*, 257.
Heartily heartily sing. *PN*, 258.
Thank the gods thy governors. *PN*, 258.
If thy body pine. *PN*, 260.
Scholar is a ball thats spent. *PN*, 262.
Ask not treasures from his store. *PN*, 262.
King.   If farmers make my land secure. *PN*, 275.
Intellect. *PN*, 276–77.
Chladni strewed on glass the sand. *PN*, 413–14.
I must not borrow light. *PN*, 277.
Go into the garden. *PN*, 314.
But as this fugitive sunlight. *JMN*, VIII, 459.
Comrade of the snow & wind. *PN*, 706–7.
God only knew how Saadi dined. *JMN*, IX, 110.
Friends to me are frozen wine. *JMN*, IX, 165.
That each should in his house abide. *PN*, 606.
New England Capitalist. *PN*, 692–93.
On a raisin stone. *PN*, 695.
Go out into Nature and plant trees. *JMN*, X, 65.
But God will keep his promise yet. *JMN*, X, 97–98.
Poet of poets. *PN*, 325–28.
The patient Pan. *PN*, 329, 196–97, 330–31.
To transmute crime to wisdom, & to stem. *PN*, 333.
Pale Genius roves alone. *PN*, 336.
Burn your literary verses. *PN*, 362.
Intellect / Gravely broods apart on joy. *PN*, 340.
What all the books of ages paint, I have. *PN*, 341.
The civil world will much forgive. *PN*, 650.
Mask thy wisdom with delight. *PN*, 680–81.
Roomy Eternity. *PN*, 590.
Dark Flower of Cheshire garden. *PN*, 514–15.
Terminus. *PN*, 539.
I to my garden went. *PN*, 342.
More sweet than my refrain. *PN*, 342.
Wisp & meteor nightly falling. *PN*, 343.

God The Lord save Massachusetts. *PN*, 344.
A poet is at home. *PN*, 276.
O Boston city lecture-hearing. *PN*, 349–50.
A patch of meadow & upland. *PN*, 351–52.
And he like me is not too proud. *PN*, 353.
Parks & ponds are good by day. *PN*, 354.
Cloud upon cloud. *PN*, 362.
For Lyra yet shall be the pole. *PN*, 362.
A score of airy miles will smooth. *PN*, 435.
All things rehearse. *PN*, 436.
Webster. *PN*, 436.
The atom displaces all atoms beside. *PN*, 437.
I have an arrow that can find its mark. *PN*, 587.
From high to higher forces. *PN*, 588.
All day the waves assailed the rock. *PN*, 591.
Honor bright o muse. *PN*, 363.
Such another peerless queen. *PN*, 364.
See how Romance adheres. *PN*, 367.
With the key of the secret he marches faster. *PN*, 597.
For what need I of book or priest. *PN*, 368.
And rival Coxcombs with enamored stare. *PN*, 369.
For joy & beauty planted it. *PN*, 377.
Papas Blondine. *PN*, 378–80.
The Asmodaean feat be mine. *PN*, 382.
A puff of air or dry or damp. *PN*, 388–89.
Coin the daydawn into lines. *PN*, 393.
He loved to watch & wake. *PN*, 173.
She walked in flowers around my field. *PN*, 400.
The bird was gone   the ghastly trees. *PN*, 400.
Pedants all. *PN*, 477.
If bright the sun, he tarries. *PN*, 591–92.
Teach me your mood, O patient stars. *PN*, 593.
O sun! take off thy hood of clouds. *PN*, 596.
As the drop feeds its fated flower. *PN*, 403–4.
I leave the book, I leave the wine. *PN*, 404.
Gentle Spring has charmed the earth. *PN*, 404.
The coral worm beneath the sea. *PN*, 407.
Easy to match what others do. *PN*, 415.
If wishes would carry me over the land. *PN*, 422.
Maia. *PN*, 422.
Seyd planted where the deluge ploughed. *PN*, 426
For every god. *PN*, 427.
For Genius made his cabin wide. *PN*, 427.
He lives not who can refuse me. *PN*, 414–15.
Forbore the ant hill, shunned to tread. *PN*, 437.
By art, by music, overthrilled. *PN*, 438.

Borrow Urania's subtile wings. *PN*, 440.
The comrade or the book is good. *PN*, 453.
Is the pace of nature slow. *PN*, 414.
Why honor the new men. *JMN*, XIV, 6.
I never knew but one. *JMN*, XIV, 70.
Think not the gods receive thy prayer. *JMN*, XIV, 127.
Turtle in swamp. *JMN*, XIV, 151.
Inspired we must forget our books. *JMN*, XIV, 161.
She had wealth of mornings in her year. *JMN*, XIV, 183.
When wrath & terror changed Jove's regal port. *PN*, 473.
Softens the air so cold & rude. *PN*, 473.
Spices in the plants that run. *PN*, 479.
She paints with white & red the moors. *PN*, 481.
The Earth. *PN*, 515.
The sun athwart the cloud thought it no sin. *PN*, 584.
October woods, wherein. *PN*, 520.
How drearily in College hall. *PN*, 531, 454–55.
If curses be the wage of love. *PN*, 532.
The land was all electric. *PN*, 538.
For Nature true & like in every place. *PN*, 398–99.
History & prophecy are alike. *PN*, 399.
The coil of space the cones of light. *PN*, 556.
The heavy blue chain. *PN*, 605.
This shining hour is an edifice. *JMN*, XIV, 211.
He could condense cerulean ether. *JMN*, XIV, 325.
The sparrow is rich in her nest. *JMN*, XIV, 326.
James Russell Lowell. Manuscript, Henry W. and Albert A. Berg Collection, The New York Public Library, Astor, Lenox and Tilden Foundations. Reprinted by permission.
Ever the Rock of Ages melt. *PN*, 512.
But never yet the man was found. *PN*, 483–84.
From Nature's beginning. *PN*, 491.
A queen rejoices in her peers. *PN*, 494–95.
By kinds I keep my kinds in check. *PN*, 495.
But Nature whistled with all her winds. *PN*, 495.
Dear are the pleasant memories. *PN*, 497.
The genial spark the poet felt. *PN*, 498.
One night he dreamed of a palace fair. *PN*, 498–99.
The low December vault in June be up-lifted high. *PN*, 499.
At Plymouth in the friendly crowd. *PN*, 504.
Old Age. *PN*, 545.
To the Clock. *PN*, 545.
Nature says. *PN*, 559.
Shun passion, fold the hands of thrift. *PN*, 386.
To the mizen, the main, & the fore. *PN*, 388.
The rules to men made evident. *PN*, 559.

Thy poems Hafiz shame the rose leaves. *PN*, 320.

In the kingdom of Poesy Hafiz waves like a banner. *PN*, 320.

Where o where is the message which today. *PN*, 320–21.

Come let us strew roses. *JMN*, IX, 398.

Who gave thy cheek the mixed tint. *JMN*, X, 67–68.

Drink, hear my counsel, my son, that the world fret thee not. *JMN*, XIII, 304–5.

Ruler after word & thought. *JMN*, XIII, 305.

O follow the sonnet's flight. *JMN*, XIII, 423.

O Hafiz, give me thought. *JMN*, XIV, 140.

In thy holiday of life. *PN*, 461.

The roguish wind and I. *PN*, 464.

The treacherous wind pipes a lewd song. *PN*, 464.

We would do nought but good. *PN*, 465.

Lo! where from Heaven's high roof. *PN*, 466.

Drink wine, and the heaven. *PN*, 466.

A stately bride is the shining world. *TN*, II, 64.

Who ever suffered as I from separation. *TN*, II, 110.

I shall go from my sickbed to heaven. *TN*, II, 113.

See & hear the fraud, the malice of the change of fortune. *TN*, II, 129.

Who loves his friend with his heart of hearts. *JMN*, XV, 383.

Had I the world for my enemy. *JMN*, XV, 383.

Salve senescentem. *JMN*, XV, 384.

The pain of love's a better fate. *PN*, 606.

In Senahar, my first born sleeps. *TN*, II, 96–97.

Unbar the door, since thou the Opener art. *PN*, 460–61.

For two rewards, & nought beside. *PN*, 464–65.

Shah Sandschar, whose lowest slave. *TN*, II, 54–55.

Wilt thou life's best elixir drain. *TN*, II, 90.

The Soul. *TN*, II, 48.

Teach your child to earn his meal. *PN*, 391.

Only three things lengthen life. *PN*, 391.

For pearls, plunge in the sea. *PN*, 391.

Arabian Ballad. *PN*, 415–18.

Fortune and Hope! I've made my port. *PN*, 591.

Alas, Alas, that I am betrayed. *JMN*, XIV, 219.

Wo is me woe's me when I think. *JMN*, XIV, 219–20.

Sweet, sweet, is sleep,—Ah! sweeter, to be stone. *JMN*, XIV, 224.

The power of a beautiful face lifts me to heaven. *JMN*, XV, 57.

Dante's Vita Nuova. J. Chesley Mathews, "Emerson's Translation of Dante's *Vita Nuova*," in *Harvard Library Bulletin*, XI: 2, 3 (Spring, Autumn 1957), 208–44, 346–62. Reprinted by permission of the Ralph Waldo Emerson Memorial Association and of Houghton Library, Harvard University.

The following is a list of pages where a stanza break coincides with the foot of the page (except where such breaks are apparent from the regular stanzaic structure of the poem): 32, 61, 66, 72, 76, 79, 89, 92, 95, 105, 153, 157, 159, 173, 184, 233, 234, 292, 295, 296, 314, 325, 348, 351, 354, 358, 395, 457, 458, 459.

This volume presents the texts of the printings chosen for inclusion here but does not attempt to reproduce features of their typographic design. The texts are printed without alteration except for the changes previously discussed and for the correction of typographical errors. Spelling, punctuation, and capitalization are often expressive features, and they are not altered, even when inconsistent or irregular. Untitled poems are listed using first lines as titles. The following is a list of typographical errors corrected, cited by page and line number: 16.13–14, (missing stanza break); 17.15, steam; 23.22, say; 25.21, favor; 36.22, fox; 43.25, part; 61.4, Prig.; 77.1, If; 77.9, I; 77.19, Higher; 77.24, I; 77.33, Once; 78.4, Now; 78.18, River; 84.34, [its counterpart,]; 92.12, In; 92.15, surprise.; 93.18, doors; 230.1, happy; 298.16, five'; 438.19, be be.

Notes

In the notes below, the reference numbers denote page and line of this volume (the line count includes titles). No note is made for material included in standard desk-reference books such as Webster's *Ninth New Collegiate*, *Biographical*, and *Geographical* dictionaries. For more detailed notes and references to other studies, see *The Journals and Miscellaneous Notebooks of Ralph Waldo Emerson, 1819–1882*, 16 vols. (Cambridge: The Belknap Press of Harvard University Press, 1960–82), ed. William H. Gilman, Ralph H. Orth, et. al.; *The Poetry Notebooks of Ralph Waldo Emerson* (Columbia: University of Missouri Press, 1986), ed. Ralph H. Orth, Albert J. von Frank, Linda Allardt, and David W. Hill; *The Topical Notebooks of Ralph Waldo Emerson*, 2 vols. to date (Columbia: University of Missouri Press, 1990–93), ed. Ralph H. Orth, Susan Sutton Smith, and Ronald A. Bosco; *The Letters of Ralph Waldo Emerson*, 8 vols. (New York: Columbia University Press, 1939, 1990–91), vols. 1–6, ed. Ralph L. Rusk, vols. 7–8, ed. Eleanor M. Tilton; *Ralph Waldo Emerson: A Descriptive Bibliography* (Pittsburgh: University of Pittsburgh Press, 1982), by Joel Myerson. The following abbreviations are used to refer in the notes that follow to other editions of Emerson's poetry:

SP   Ralph Waldo Emerson, *Selected Poems* (Boston: James R. Osgood, 1876).

RE   *The Complete Works of Ralph Waldo Emerson*, Riverside edition (Boston and New York: Houghton-Mifflin, 1883–92), ed. James Elliot Cabot, vol. 9, *Poems* (1884).

CE   *The Complete Works of Ralph Waldo Emerson*, Centenary edition (Boston and New York: Houghton-Mifflin, 1903–4), ed. Edward Emerson, vol. 9, *Poems* (1904).

POEMS (1847)

7.17   Profounder, profounder]   In SP, "To insight profounder"; in RE and CE, "To vision profounder".

15.14   *Uriel*]   An archangel in Islamic and Jewish tradition; the name means "fire of God."

15.22   SAID]   Mosharref od-Dīn ibn Mosleh od-Dīn Saʿdī (c. 1213–92) of Shiraz, traveler and poet best known for the Persian classics *Gulistān* (*The Rose Garden*) and *Būstān* (*The Orchard*); Emerson elsewhere spells the name Saadi, Seyd, and Seid.

18.15   help]   In SP, RE, and CE, changed to "taunt".

19.5   does not like]   In SP, RE, and CE, changed to "never swerves".

22.19   *Mithridates*]   Mithradates VI Eupator, king of Pontus in Asia Minor, 120–63 B.C., was said to have taken daily doses of poisons in order to develop immunity to them.

23.18–19   God! . . . Capitol.]   These lines are omitted from the poem in SP, RE, and CE.

23.20   *J. W.*]   John Weiss (1818–79) of Massachusetts, Unitarian pastor, writer, and German translator.

24.11   *Fate*]   Retitled "Destiny" in RE and CE.

26.9   Nor not receive . . . dues.]   After this line, six additional lines are inserted in RE and CE: "Fearless Guy had never foes, / He did their weapons decompose. / Aimed at him, the blushing blade / Healed as fast the wounds it made. / If on the foeman fell his gaze, / Him it would straightway blind or craze,".

27.1   *Tact*]   This poem was omitted in RE and CE.

28.1   *Hamatreya*]   Conjectured by Emerson's son Edward to be a variant of Maitreya, a *rishi* (an inspired poet or sage) and one of the interlocutors in the *Vishnu Purana*.

28.2   Minott . . . Flint]   Founders and early settlers of Concord, Massachusetts. In SP, "Minott, Lee," was changed to "Bulkeley, Hunt," (the names of two other founders) and this change was retained in RE and CE.

35.1   *Woodnotes*]   In "Woodnotes I" and "Woodnotes II," in SP, RE, and CE, some words are changed and a number of lines are omitted; examples of omissions in RE and CE are noted below.

35.3–8   For this present . . . him.]   Omitted in RE and CE.

35.19–22   With none . . . dim.]   Omitted in RE and CE.

35.28–30   Planter . . . vaunts.]   Omitted in RE and CE.

37.14–15   Linnæa . . . flowers]   Slender flowering plant named for Swedish naturalist Carl von Linné (1707–78; also known as Carolus Linnaeus).

39.33–40.34   Ancient . . . giver of honor]   Omitted in RE and CE.

41.5–6   Genius . . . nourish.]   Omitted in RE and CE.

41.34–39   Westward . . . art.]   Omitted in RE and CE.

42.17–18   Love . . . Fate;]   Omitted in RE and CE.

42.33–34   He shall never . . . foretold;]   Omitted in RE and CE.

43.5–11   The robe . . . shame.]   Omitted in RE and CE.

45.3–4   Whereto . . . fancies.]   Omitted in RE and CE.

46.28–31   I will teach . . . sublime.]   Omitted in RE and CE.

48.22–23   He giveth . . . or such.]   Omitted in RE and CE.

48.30–31   Pleaseth . . . wild;]   Omitted in RE and CE.

49.17   *Monadnoc*]   A number of changes in the poem were made in later printings and editions, and others in the posthumous editions; some are noted below.

50.7   Accept]   Changed in SP, RE, and CE to "Take".

50.28   The country's]   Beginning in the 1856 printing of *Poems*, this reads: "The people's pride, the country's"; in RE and CE changed to "An eyemark and the country's".

50.34   Their calendar]   Beginning in the 1856 printing, "This their calendar"; changed in SP, RE, and CE to "Gauge and calendar".

50.35   Barometer]   Beginning in the 1856 printing, this reads "Weatherglass", a revision retained in RE and CE.

51.4   own affairs]   Beginning in the 1856 printing, "sky-affairs", a revision retained in RE and CE.

51.5   Wide . . . high]   Beginning in the 1856 printing, "Rich rents and wide", a revision retained in RE and CE.

51.7   By the great sun]   Beginning in the 1856 printing, revised to read "By the sun"; in SP, RE, and CE, changed to "By morn and eve".

51.13   science done]   In SP, RE, and CE, changed to "science wrought".

51.19   my monarch]   In SP, RE, and CE, changed to "the dweller".

51.20–23   He was no . . . mug.]   Omitted beginning in the 1856 printing, a revision retained in RE and CE.

51.25   Lord! is yon]   Beginning in the 1856 printing, "Is yonder", a revision retained in RE and CE.

52.2   creature,]   In SP, RE, and CE, changed to "plant and creature".

52.3   And]   Beginning in the 1856 printing, revised to read "Yet"; in SP, RE, and CE, changed to "But".

52.10–11   Here Nature . . . meteors]   In RE and CE, changed to "And think how Nature in these towers / Uplifted shall condense her powers".

53.2–3   Found I . . . need.]   Omitted in SP, RE, and CE.

53.8–11   Smoking . . . they work.]   Omitted in SP, RE, and CE.

53.16   sweet hay . . . swamp]   In SP, RE, and CE, changed to "cloverheads the swamp".

53.18   wolves . . . lowing]   In SP, RE, and CE, changed to "wolf and fox, bring lowing".

53.26   And . . . iron]   In SP, RE, and CE, "And" is changed to "Whilst" and "iron" to "flinty".

53.31   For gardens . . . race.]   In SP, RE, and CE, changed to "For homes of virtue, sense and taste."

54.2   These exercises]   In SP, RE, and CE, changed to "Toil and tempest".

54.3   with which . . . boys]   Beginning in the 1856 printing, this reads "to breathe his stalwart boys", a revision retained in RE and CE.

54.11   Their secret . . . dulness]   Beginning in the 1856 printing, "In dulness now their secret", a revision retained in RE and CE.

54.16–17   These they turn . . . parson.]   Beginning in the 1856 printing, "But they turn them in a fashion / Past clerks' or statesmen's art or passion." The revision is retained in RE and CE.

54.28   Tough . . . birch-bark]   Beginning in the 1856 printing, "Scoff of yeoman, strong and stark", a revision retained in RE and CE.

54.32–35   To student . . . tough.]   Omitted in SP, RE, and CE.

54.37   the wide floor]   Beginning in the 1856 edition, "the floor", a revision retained in RE and CE.

55.16–17   Where I . . . shall gaze]   In the 1856 printing this reads "Where I gaze, and still shall gaze", followed by an added line, "Thro' tempering nights and flashing days", a change further altered to "Through hoarding nights and spending days" in SP (RE and CE have the 1856 reading).

55.24–27   'Ah! welcome, . . . strain.]   Omitted in RE and CE.

55.33–34   'Tis the law . . . own.]   Omitted in SP, RE, and CE.

56.22   Cannot forget the sun]   In SP, RE, and CE changed to "The sun obeys them and".

56.33   Measure . . . man.]   In SP, RE, and CE, changed to "Zion or Meru, measure with man."

56.34   temples]   Beginning in the 1847 corrected fourth printing, this reads "zodiacs", a revision retained in RE and CE.

57.3–4   all time, . . . heard]   Beginning in the 1856 printing, this reads "all time, in light, in gloom / Well I hear", a revision retained in RE and CE.

57.5   Along]   Beginning in the 1856 printing, and in RE and CE, this reads "On the".

57.9   now the]   Beginning in the 1856 printing, and in RE and CE, this reads "doth this".

57.17 Gaze o'er] In SP, RE, and CE, changed to "See".

58.5 drink] In SP, RE, and CE, changed to "drain".

58.6 thoughts . . . shall think] In SP, RE, and CE, changed to "coinage of his brain".

59.25–26 the rocks . . . pestering] In SP, RE, and CE, changed to "thy rocks . . . folded".

59.32 Yet flowers] In RE and CE, changed to "Where flowers".

59.36 Having] In SP, RE, and CE, changed to "Holding".

60.29 Thou dost supply] In SP, RE, and CE, changed to "Thou dost succor and remede".

61.22 *W. H. Channing*] Social reformer and clergyman William Henry Channing (1810–84).

62.10–11 Contoocook! . . . Agiochook!] A river and a mountain in New Hampshire.

63.25 I invite] Beginning in the 1847 corrected fourth printing, and in RE and CE, this reads "I implore".

64.16 *Astræa*] Greek goddess of justice.

64.17 Himself it was] From the 1856 to the 1860 printing this reads, "Each the herald is"; in 1863 and subsequent printings, "Thou the herald art". SP, RE, and CE use the 1856 reading.

64.27 With this prayer upon] Beginning in the 1856 printing, and in RE and CE: "With this tablet on".

65.31 *Étienne de la Boéce*] Étienne de La Boétie (1530–63), French poet and friend of Montaigne.

66.21 *Suum Cuique*] Not included in SP, RE, or CE.

70.32 Salvator] Salvator Rosa (1615–73), leading painter of the Neapolitan school.

70.38–71.2 Olympian bards . . . us so.] These lines are the second motto to "The Poet" in *Essays: Second Series* (1844).

73.17–18 *To Ellen, at the South*] Published in *The Dial* (Jan. 3, 1843) as "To Eva at the South."

75.1 *Eva*] In this poem and others, "Eva" refers to Emerson's first wife Ellen Tucker Emerson.

79.1 *Initial, . . . Celestial Love*] Printed in SP, RE, and CE with extensive revisions; a few are noted below.

82.9–12 Godlike . . . wit!] Omitted in SP, RE, and CE.

82.29–30 Arguments . . . badinage;] Omitted in SP, RE, and CE.

83.11 *The Dæmonic . . . Celestial Love*] In SP, RE, and CE, section II is titled "The Dæmonic Love" and III is titled "The Celestial Love."

83.18 These, like . . . preferred,] Beginning in a later 1847 printing, "Names from awful childhood heard", a revision retained in RE and CE.

83.34–84.24 But God . . . same again.'] In SP, RE, and CE, these lines are printed at the beginning of section III.

86.22–25 He is . . . drones;] Omitted in SP, RE, and CE.

91.9 *Merlin*] Myrrdhin, 6th century A.D. Welsh or British bard to whom a number of poems have been doubtfully attributed, considered to be the prototype of Merlin in the Arthurian romances.

93.34 Coeval] Beginning in the 1847 corrected fourth printing, "In one body", a revision retained in RE and CE.

97.1 *Loss and Gain*] This poem was not included in SP, RE, or CE.

97.18 *Merops*] A soothsayer in Homer's *Iliad*; the name means "articulate speech."

101.6 Dschami's] Mowlanā Nūr od-Dīn 'Abd or-Rahmān Jāmī (1414–92) of Herat, Persian poet and mystic.

102.34 Ali's sunbright sayings] 'Alī ibn Abī Tālib (c. 598–661), fourth Arabian caliph and son-in-law of the Prophet Muhammad, who is revered by Shia Muslims. His sayings are collected in the *Nahj al-Balāgah* (*The Way of Eloquence*).

104.9 *Painting and Sculpture*] This poem was not included in SP, RE, or CE.

104.14 *From the Persian of Hafiz*] Shams od-Dīn Muhammad Hāfiz (1326?–?1390) of Shiraz, lyric poet. The poem is not included in SP, RE, or CE.

104.16 *Von Hammer*] Joseph von Hammer-Purgstall (1774–1856), Austrian translator of Persian poets; Emerson used his *Der Diwan von Mohammed Schemsed-din Hafiz* (2 vols., 1812–13), and *Geschichte der schönen Redekünste Persiens* (1818).

104.26 Karun's treasure] Karun, like Midas, turned all things to gold.

105.2 Jamschid's glass,] The magic cup of the mythical early Persian king reflected the whole world in its depths. The legends of Jamschid and other kings and heroes in the poem are collected in Firdawsī's *Shāh-nāmeh* (1010; *Book*, or *Epic*, *of Kings*).

108.20 Nisami] Elyās Yūsof Nezāmī Ganjavi (c. 1141–1202 or 1217), Persian mystic and author of romantic epic poems.

108.28−29 *Ghaselle: . . . Hafiz*] A ghazal is a Persian poetic form consisting of couplets on the surface independent in theme but linked by rhyme-scheme and meter; the poet's name appears in the last couplet. Hāfiz is considered a master of the form. The poem is not included in SP, RE, or CE.

110.4 they differ] Beginning in the 1847 corrected fourth printing, this reads "they part", a revision retained in RE and CE.

112.35 With most . . . taught,] Deleted beginning in the 1856 printing, a revision retained in RE and CE.

113.1 *Musketaquid*] The Concord River (Musketaquid was an Indian name for the area where Concord was settled).

117.1 *Threnody*] This poem was written after the death of Emerson's son Waldo (1836−42).

125.1 *Hymn*] "Concord Fight" in SP; the editors of RE and CE use "Concord Hymn".

125.3 *April 19, 1836*] In CE, changed to "July 4, 1837", when, according to Edward Emerson, the monument was dedicated and the hymn sung. The dedication was originally planned for the April 19, 1836, the anniversary of the battle, but had been postponed.

MAY-DAY AND OTHER PIECES (1867)

131.1 *May-Day*] In SP, RE, and CE, some words are changed, a few lines added, more than 140 omitted, and the piece is completely rearranged. Examples of the omissions are noted below.

131.8−12 Girls . . . times three.] Omitted in SP, RE, and CE.

131.17 Or clapping . . . hands,] Omitted in SP, RE, and CE.

134.4 With wicked ingenuity,] Omitted in SP, RE, and CE.

134.16−20 The cowslips . . . roam.] Omitted in SP, RE, and CE.

136.7−10 Boils . . . globe,] Omitted in SP, RE, and CE.

136.23 All figures, . . . graces?] Omitted in SP, RE, and CE.

137.10−11 We will hear . . . evermore,] Omitted in SP, RE, and CE.

138.6−7 Lo Love's . . . abroad!] Omitted in SP, RE, and CE.

143.29−146.36 One musician . . . spoil.] In SP, RE, and CE, these lines are omitted from "May-Day" and printed (with four additional lines) as "The Harp" (page 223 in this volume).

145.8−9 Merlin . . . air,—] In an Arthurian legend, when Merlin becomes infatuated with the enchantress Nimue she imprisons him forever in a forest of air in Broceliande (conjectured to be Brecheliant in Brittany, where travelers sought his tomb).

149.3   *Fellow-Travellers*]   Louis Agassiz, Dr. Jeffries Wyman (a professor of anatomy), Dr. Estes Howe, John Holmes (Oliver Wendell Holmes's brother), Dr. Amos Benney, Judge Ebenezer Rockwood Hoar, James Russell Lowell, William J. Stillman (artist and journalist), and Horatio Woodman.

153.6   Hypnum and hydnum]   Feather-moss and a type of fungus.

160.22–25   For the prevision . . . creates.]   These lines are also in the motto to the essay "Fate" (page 248.21–24 in this volume).

166.1   *Voluntaries*]   In September 1863, Emerson sent a copy of this poem to the father of Colonel Robert Gould Shaw (1837–63), who had commanded the 54th Massachusetts Infantry, the first African-American regiment raised by a Northern state. Shaw had been killed along with many of his troops in an attack on the Confederate stronghold at Fort Wagner, near Charleston, South Carolina, in July 1863.

168.23   And the sweet . . . secures.]   Following this line in SP, RE, and CE, four lines are inserted: "Peril around all else appalling, / Cannon in front and leaden rain, / Him Duty through the clarion calling / To the van called not in vain."

168.33–169.4   Forever: . . . speechless fate.]   Omitted in RE and CE.

170.1   *Lover's Petition*]   This poem was not included in SP, RE, or CE.

172.14   *Merlin's Song*]   Not included in SP or RE. In CE, the first 27 lines of the motto to "Considerations by the Way" (page 249.2–28 in this volume) were added as the second numbered section of "Merlin's Song."

173.2   *(Musa loquitur.)*]   Latin: "The Muse speaks."

174.18   Plinlimmon's]   Mountain in Wales.

174.30   EMANUEL]   Emanuel Swedenborg (1688–1772).

178.14   Daughters]   Erroneously printed "Damsels" in the first printing of *May-Day and Other Pieces*, and incorrectly printed "Daughter" in subsequent printings; corrected to "Daughters" in SP.

188.22   Musketaquit]   See note 113.1

189.10   Who drink . . . again.]   Cf. John 4:14.

189.13   *Waldeinsamkeit*]   German: "forest solitude."

190.29–32   And if, amid . . . found.]   Omitted in SP, RE, and CE.

191.33   Baresark]   In old Norse legend, a fierce Scandinavian warrior.

194.17   *E. B. E.*]   Emerson's brother Edward (1805–34).

194.18   battle-field]   The first battle of the Revolutionary War was fought at Concord, April 19, 1775.

196.38–197.4   Work . . . every act.]   These lines comprise the second motto to "Character" in *Essays: Second Series* (1844), where "He nor repents" reads "He nor commends".

198.1   ELEMENTS]   The poems in this section are mottoes for essays bearing these titles in the two series of *Essays* and in *The Conduct of Life* (1860); exceptions are "Manners," the motto to "Behavior," and "Unity," motto to "The Over-Soul."

200.29–201.2   The sun . . . time.]   These lines are incorporated by the editors of RE and CE into "The Poet," an editorially constructed poem in their editions.

202.8   *Beauty*]   Emerson originally drafted the lines as part of "There are beggars in Iran and Araby" (see page 251.19 and note in this volume). They serve as the motto to the essay "Beauty" in *The Conduct of Life*.

202.10   SEYD]   See note 15.22.

206.2   *S. H.*]   Samuel Hoar (1778–1856), Massachusetts judge and congressman, and father of Elizabeth Hoar, to whom Emerson's brother Charles had been engaged before his death.

206.7   *A. H.*]   Anne Sturgis Hooper, sister of Emerson's close friend Caroline Sturgis Tappan.

207.20   What me the hours]   In the first printing, "What me the flowers"; the error was corrected in subsequent printings.

207.25   beurré]   A variety of pear.

209.17   *Power*]   Motto to the essay "Self-Reliance."

210.1   *Heri, Cras, Hodie*]   Latin: "Yesterday, tomorrow, today."

210.19–20   ' 'Tis man's . . . die.']   Quoted from a 1642 sermon by the English Puritan Caleb Vines.

211.1   *Casella*]   Musician and friend of Dante, who sings a love song to the poet in *Purgatorio* II.76–133.

211.21   'ΑΔΑΚΡΥΝ NEMONTAI ΑΙΩΝΑ]   Greek: "They enjoy a tearless age."

212.18   *Kermani*]   Khvājū of Kirman (d. ?1352), Persian poet and traveler of an aristocratic Kirman line; he composed the *Humāy u Humāyūn*, the source of these verses, during his stay in Baghdad.

212.19   Farsistan]   Variant of Fars, a southern province of the Persian empire (literally "land of the Farsis"); its capital was Shiraz.

215.7   *Ibn Jemin*]   Ibn-i-Yamīn (Amīr Mahmūd ibn Amīr Yamīnu'd-Dīn Tughrā'ī; d. ?1368), Persian poet.

215.15   *Hilali*]   The translation is actually of a poem by Jalāl ad-Dīn ar-Rūmī (c. 1207–73), Persian mystic, founder of the Mevlevi Sufi order (whose members are known in the West as "whirling dervishes"), and poet whom Helālī (1470–1529) sometimes imitated. Emerson may have misattributed the poem while copying an earlier draft of the translation onto another page in one of his notebooks.

216.6   *Enweri*] Or Anvarī, pseudonym of Awhad ad-Dīn ʿAli ibn Vāhid ad-Dīn Muhammad Khāvarānī (c. 1126–c. 1189), Persian court poet to Muʿizz ad-Dīn Sanjar (1086?–1157), prince of Khorāsān.

216.19   *Seid Nimetollah*] Sayyid (or Shah) Niʿmatuʾllāh of Kirman (Amīr Nūruʾd-Dīn Niʿmatuʾllāh; d. 1431), Persian mystic and poet; he was called the king of the dervishes.

from SELECTED POEMS (1876)

223.1   *The Harp*] See note 143.29–146.36.

224.23–24   Merlin paying . . . air] See note 145.8–9.

225.30–33   Therein I hear . . . strain.] These lines do not appear in the poem "May-Day."

226.27   clews . . . Rosamonds] In RE and CE, "cobweb clues of Rosamond".

227.6   *Wealth*] Motto to the essay "Wealth."

231.3   *Rev. Chandler Robbins*] The successor of Emerson, who had resigned in 1832.

232.1   *Boston*] Earlier versions, titled "Trimountain," contain a number of stanzas inspired by the Civil War; for an 1864 manuscript version, see page 456.13 in this volume.

232.2   *Sicut . . . nobis.*] Latin: "God with the fathers, so with us"; it is Boston's motto.

232.5   hill-tops three] Boston was originally dominated by the "Trimountain," consisting of the three peaks of Beacon Hill: Mt. Vernon, Cotton (Pemberton) Hill, and Beacon Hill.

OTHER PUBLISHED POEMS AND TRANSLATIONS

241.1, 242.1   *William Rufus, Fame*] Emerson's first published poems (1829). William II of England (reigned 1087–1100) was called William Rufus.

241.20   Magog] In Ezekial, Magog refers to the ruler of a northern country of armed bands, and in Revelation, to the future enemies of the Kingdom of God.

242.4   from Beersheba to Dan] An expression meaning "from the extreme northern to southern limits."

243.7   *Mottoes to "History"*]   In CE, the two mottoes are combined under the title "The Informing Spirit."

244.1   *The Three Dimensions*]   Not included in RE or CE.

245.1   *Motto to "Nature"*]   In CE, these lines are published as the second section of an editorially constructed poem the editors title "Nature" (see also note 247.20).

245.12   *Motto . . . Realist"*]   Titled "Promise" in CE.

245.23   *My Thoughts*]   Not included in RE or CE.

247.20   *Motto to "Nature"*]   Motto to the 1849 revised edition of the book *Nature*; in CE, printed as part of "Nature" (see note 245.1).

248.1   *Motto . . . Reformers"*]   Titled "Caritas" in CE.

248.11–20   Delicate omens . . . lay.]   In RE and CE, a version of these lines appears in the editorially constructed "Fragments on the Poet and the Poetic Gift."

248.21–24   For the prevision . . . creates.]   These lines also appear in the poem "Fate" (page 160.22–25 in this volume).

249.1   *Motto . . . Way"*]   See note 172.14.

249.2   British Merlin]   See note 91.9.

249.13   Cyndyllan's]   Legendary Welsh chieftain.

251.1   The cup . . . shallow]   Titled "Good Hope" in CE.

251.9   Where . . . Skrymir?]   This poem is not included in RE or CE. Skrymir was a mighty giant of Norse mythology who created magical illusions.

251.19   There are beggars . . . Araby]   Emerson drafted a number of versions of this poem in his notebooks and journals, but the version printed in this volume is taken from *Thoreau: The Poet-Naturalist* (1873) by William Ellery Channing. In RE and CE, a version is printed in "Fragments on the Poet and the Poetic Gift."

252.18   Quoth Saadi, . . . before]   In RE and CE, a version of these lines appears in "Fragments on the Poet and the Poetic Gift." For Saadi, see note 15.22.

253.1   *South Wind*]   In CE, titled "September."

253.10–17   Sudden gusts . . . maid.]   RE prints these lines under the title "The South Wind."

256.10   *Adsched of Meru*]   'Asjadi (Abū Nadhar 'Abdu'l-'Azīz; fl. 11th cent. A.D.), Persian poet born in Mansur and described variously as being of Merv or Herat.

257.10–11   Loose the knots . . . snarl.]   This, and the couplet "I will be drunk . . ." (page 258.1), was revised from an earlier translation; see "Secretly to love & drink . . ." page 473.11 in this volume.

258.7   The Builder of heaven]   For fuller translations of Hafiz's poem, see
"Drink the wine . . . ", page 489.1, and note.

259.17   I have no hoarded treasure]   First published in the anti-slavery
gift-book *The Liberty Bell* (Boston, 1851), where this line reads "I truly have no
treasure," and where the quatrain was mistakenly printed as the conclusion of
"The Poet" (see following note).

260.1−4   High heart . . . more.]   A version of these lines was first pub-
lished as part of a fuller translation titled "The Poet" in *The Liberty Bell* (1851).
"The Poet" reads:

> Hoard knowledge in thy coffers,
> The lightest load to bear;
> Ingots of gold, and diamonds,
> Let others drag with care.
>
> The devil's snares are strong,
> Yet have I God in need;
> And if I had not God to friend,
> What can the devil speed?
>
> Courage! Hafiz, though not thine
> Gold wedge and silver ore,
> More worth to thee the gift of song,
> And the clear insight more.

260.6   O Hafiz! speak not of thy need;]   Titled "To Himself" in *The
Liberty Bell* (1851), where the first line reads "Hafiz, speak not of thy need",
and the last line, "Thou canst at nought repine."

261.1   *The Phoenix*]   First published in *The Liberty Bell* (1851), where a
footnote to the title reads "The Soul."

261.11   Tuba's]   "The Tree of Life"—Emerson's manuscript note.

264.5   *Enweri*]   See note 216.6.

264.14   *Ibn Jemin*]   See note 215.7.

264.19   *Dschami*]   See note 101.6.

265.11   Fair falls . . . heart!]   For the translation from which Emerson
revised these lines, see "Thou who with thy long hair", page 468.16 in this
volume.

266.10−17   Plunge in . . . turnest thine.]   Titled "Faith" and with a third
stanza, these lines were first published in the *The Liberty Bell* (1851). Emerson
revised the lines from a fuller translation (see "Novice, hear me . . . ", page
470.20, and note 471.24).

267.1   While roses . . . plain,]   A slightly different version was published
under the title "Word and Deed" in *The Liberty Bell* (1851).

267.21   *Nisami*]   See note 108.20.

268.12   *Feisi*]   Also transliterated Faydi, Fayzi, Feizi (1547–95); Persian poet of Agra, India; court poet to Emperor Akbar in 1572.

268.13   *"Bird Conversations"*]   *Conference of the Birds* by Farīd od-Dīn Abū Mohammad ebn Ebrāhīm 'Attār (c. 1142–c. 1220), poem described by Emerson as a "mystical tale, in which the birds, coming together to choose their king, resolve on a pilgrimage to Mount Kaf, to pay their homage to the Simorg."

268.22   Simorg]   Or Simurgh, the King of the Birds, in 'Attār's poem, a symbol of the Divine.

MANUSCRIPT POEMS AND TRANSLATIONS

Emerson's manuscripts sometimes show uncanceled alternate words, phrases, or lines; this volume uses the first reading and supplies the alternatives in the notes. In this volume, brackets denote illegible material in the manuscripts; blank spaces within lines of a poem are spaces that Emerson left in his manuscripts.

285.22   *John Haskins*]   Emerson's maternal grandfather, died October 27, 1814.

286.1   *M. B. Farnham*]   Mary Bliss Farnham, died February 10, 1816, at age 23; she was the daughter of Emerson's aunt, Hannah Bliss (Emerson) Farnham.

287.1   *Poem on Eloquence*]   Emerson recited a long version of this poem during exercises at the Boston Latin School in 1816.

288.4   Phillip]   Philip II of Macedon (382–336 B.C.), whose control of rich gold mines enabled him use bribery as a means of diplomacy.

288.21   long-fought field]   No other lines are known to be extant.

289.13   William . . . soul]   Emerson sent this poem to his brother, William, in a letter dated September 13, 1817.

290.13–14   *Song . . . bled"*]   "For the Fourth of July 1820."—Emerson's footnote. The traditional Scottish tune is known by the title of a poem by Robert Burns that was set to it.

291.9   *Valedictory Poem*]   Emerson appended the notation "Cambridge July 1821"; as Class Poet, he delivered the poem on July 17, 1821, at Harvard College Class Day exercises.

292.21   rare bird]   "Phoenix"—Emerson's note.

297.36   Enthroned . . . Chair]   "These lines were a salutation to the President."—Emerson's note, referring to John Kirkland, president of Harvard College.

298.4   *rebel*] Emerson's sophomore class withdrew from the college in protest for several weeks after some of its members were sent home for participating in a fight between freshmen and sophomores at dinner on November 1, 1818.

298.10   *parts*] Assignments of duties to be performed at college ceremonies; Emerson distributed them when he served as the "President's freshman."

298.14   "the Company."] "Every one acquainted with College knows that admission to the 'Harvard Washington Corps' is a matter of no slight interest." — Emerson's note.

299.2−4   Quem . . . Virgilian lot.] Virgil, *Aeneid*, V, 742−43: "Whom fleest thou? Or who bars you from our embraces? So speaking, he rouses the embers of the slumbering fires." A Virgilian lot (*sortes Virgilianae*) is a means of divination performed by opening *Aeneid* at random and haphazardly placing a finger on a page; the passage touched is considered oracular.

300.11   I spread . . . sail] Dated "1822" by Emerson.

300.28   Apollo's . . . isle] The Greek island of Aegina, opposite Athens, where festivals in honor of Apollo, god of music, were held.

300.29−30   Castalie . . . Nine] Castalia, a spring on Mt. Parnassus sacred to the nine muses.

301.1   *A Shout . . . Shepherds*] Dated "March 28" [1823] by Emerson.

301.21   I wear . . . star] Titled "Thought" in CE, where the first stanza is omitted. Dated by Emerson "1823. Boston", when the earliest version was written.

302.1   I love . . . bell] Titled "The Bell" in CE. Emerson dated the poem "1823."

302.17   I rake . . . clay] Titled "To-Day" in CE.

303.5   Cynic tubs] Diogenes (c. 320 B.C.), philosopher of the Cynic school, was said to have lived in an earthenware tub.

303.7   O What . . . do] Emerson wrote the date "Dec. 22d." [1824] on the right margin over this poem in his notebook.

304.4−27   A sterner . . . I go.] In CE, these lines are printed under the title "The Summons."

304.12   smooth passage] The alternative reading in the manuscript is "glad heyday".

304.21   burthen . . . sad history] Alternative readings for "burthen" are "sum" and "purport"; for "sad", the alternative is "heavy".

305.1   Have ye . . . caterpillar] Titled "Riches" in CE.

305.3   siller]   Silver; money.

305.13   The panoply . . . mine]   Emerson's headnote to the poem reads "[Prose run mad.]", a reference to Alexander Pope's "Epistle to Dr. Arbuthnot" (1735), lines 187–88: "And whose fustian's so sublimely bad / It is not poetry, but prose run mad."

305.14   Eteian forge]   Mt. Etna, a volcano in Sicily, was said to be the forge of the fire-god Vulcan, who made Achilles' armor.

305.27   deceived mankind]   Alternative reading: "betrayed the cause of mankind."

305.29   Capitoline god]   The temple of Jupiter was on the Capitoline Hill in Rome.

306.26   No fate, . . . low]   Emerson drew these lines from a poem that he notes was drafted in 1825; it reads:

> Forth to encounter thy affianced doom
> And art affianced to a noble doom
> Shalt be affianced to a heavenlier bride
> For I see Glory hasting to thy side;
> Not frolic Beauty weaving wanton nets
> From her soft ambush peeps with radiant eye
> Tis safer when the curled Syren frowns
> No fate, save by the victim's fault, is low
> For God hath writ all dooms magnificent
> So guilt not traverses his tender will.
> I make ye witness prophesying Stars
> And by the light of prophesying Stars
> And men whose faces were a history
> Be of thine Age the priceless ornament.
> Outface the brass browed slanders of the time
> Trust not the words of ruby lips suspect those rolling eyes
> Those rosy wreaths hide scorpion whips
>
>   Are these bare trees
> The orchestra whence all that music rang
> Nor all the rich elixirs of the world
> Can bring the life that's sped.

307.1   When success . . . lot]   Titled "Prayer" in RE and CE.

307.9   The spirits . . . clouds]   Emerson dated this poem "1826".

308.20   Let not conceited . . . aloud]   Two spaces above this line and toward the right margin, Emerson inserted a line in his journal: "It was as if a standardbearer fainted."

316.10–13   x . . . x]   The rows of x's and the parenthetical remark are Emerson's.

316.28 Awed I . . . more] Dated by Emerson in the right margin, "Concord, Mass—June 1827". The poem is titled "The River" in CE, where the first word is printed "And".

317.22 admonishment] The manuscript reads "(ad)monishment"; parentheses usually enclose something Emerson had not decided whether to include.

318.19 Be of good . . . steadfastly] The poem was revised by Emerson from lines 12–27 of an earlier draft (in which he canceled line 25: "To seal the marriage of these minds with thine"). The earlier draft, written in Emerson's hand in the 1821–29 period, reads:

> You fast at feasts and oft invited shun
> The pleasant morsel & oft provoked
> Amid the wiles of talk to egotism
> You turn the bait aside & speak of others
> Or smarting under unjust blame, make gentle answer.
> To what good end? Were it not better done
> As oft you think & do, to let things go
> Even as they will down the swallowing stream
> Of universal custom than to resist
> And make those sharp encounters which perhaps
> Shall presently be as they had never been
> Be of good cheer, brave spirit! Steadfastly
> Serve that low whisper thou hast served, for know
> God hath a select family of sons
> Now scattered wide thro' earth, & each one alone,
> Who are thy spiritual kindred, & each one
> By constant service to that inward law
> Is rearing up the bright proportions
> Of his majestic mind. Beauty; & Strength;
> The riches of a spotless Memory;
> The eloquence of truth; the Wisdom got
> By a purged & benevolent eye
> That seeth as God seeth. These are their gifts
> And time who keeps Gods word brings in the day
> Thine everlasting friends   Ye shall be
> The salt of things   The church of the first born
> A constellation of sweet influence
> To all that live.
>   They and you
> Shall have delight each in the other's worth
> And breathe your virtues in an emulous love
> Tasking the monumental strength of truth
> And love in ages grown to act for aye.

319.13   *Written in Sickness*]   Emerson dated the poem "Cambridge 1827",
when the earliest-known version was written.

322.1   Though her eye . . . forms]   Titled "Security" by the editor of CE,
who dates the poem "1829," during Emerson's courtship of Ellen Tucker.

322.7   like mine is unconfined]   Alternative reading: "is frank as the
Ocean wind".

322.13   Dear Ellen, . . . year]   Emerson appends the notation "Pepperell
Sept. 1829—"; at that time he was traveling with his fiancée, her mother, and
her sister, and had stopped with them at Pepperell, Massachusetts.

323.1   I call her . . . says]   Dated "Pepperell, Sept. 1829—".

324.3   And Ellen, . . . years]   Titled "To Ellen" in CE.

324.15   The brave Empedocles . . . fools]   A versification of a passage
from Marie Joseph de Gérando, *Histoire Comparée des Systèmes de Philosophie*
(4 vols., Paris, 1822–23), Vol. 2, p. 36.

325.1   Dear brother, . . . life]   Titled "A Letter" in CE. Emerson mistak-
enly dated this revised version of the poem "Chardon Street 1830"; the earlier
version was headed: "Lines written in 1831. Boston." Ellen Tucker Emerson,
Emerson's first wife, died February 8, 1831, in Boston at the Chardon Street
home of Abel Adams.

325.6–22   Each street . . . Sun.]   In an earlier version, this reads:

> Each street & spire & suburb, known from birth
> Then following where the impatient Genius leads
> Deep in a woodland seek a sunny farm
> Amid the mountain counties, Franklin, Berks,
> Where down the steep ravine a river roars
> Even from a brook, & where old woods,
> Spared by the ax, cumber the ample ground
> With their centennial wrecks.
> Find me a slope where I can feel the sun,
> And mark the rising of the early stars
> There will I bring my books & make my home
> With pious care my household gods will bring
> The dear remembrance of now ruined days
> The relics of my dead & dwell again
> In the sweet odor of her memory.
> There, in the uncouth solitude, unlock
> My slender stock of art,
> Adjust my dial on a grassy mound,
> Hang in the air a bright thermometer,
> And aim a telescope at Uranus

325.9   Hants . . . Berks]   Massachusetts counties; "Hants" is Hampshire,
"Berks," Berkshire.

330.22   Why fear to die] Titled "A Mountain Grave" in CE. Emerson dated the poem "Williamstown, Vermont: 1 June, 1831", when the earliest version was written.

331.26   On thee . . . conferred] Emerson dated the poem "1831".

331.26–332.7   On thee . . . unbefriended] RE prints a version of these lines in the editorially constructed "Fragments on Nature and Life."

332.9–12   Let Webster's . . . sign.] In CE, these lines appear under the date "1831" in a group titled "Webster" (see also pages 355.1–22 and 424.2–3 and notes).

332.13   All the great & good,] Dated "6 July 1831" by Emerson.

335.19   She never . . . me] Dated "19 September" [1831] by Emerson.

336.17   Leave me, . . . base,] Included in RE but not CE.

337.1   Γνωθι Σεαυτον] "Know thyself," the inscription over the entrance to the temple of Apollo at Delphi.

340.2   And the souls . . . sad] After this line, Emerson began another but wrote only the word "See".

340.6   Light . . . dim.] After this, Emerson began another stanza but entered only the aborted line "It would not become" before proceeding to the next stanza.

341.1   There is in all . . . men] Titled "Hymn" in CE.

342.10–14   Henceforth, . . . Voice therein] In CE, these lines and, after a dotted line, lines 342.22–26 ("The little needle . . . act aright."), are printed under the title "Self Reliance."

343.29   sister] Margaret Tucker; she died of tuberculosis in November 1832, the year after Ellen Tucker Emerson.

346.8   Alone in Rome! . . . too,] This revised version is dated by Emerson "Rome March 22   1833" (he actually arrived in Rome on March 26, 1833). Titled "Written at Rome, 1833" in RE and "Written at Rome" in CE, which take their texts from an earlier draft that reads:

> Alone in Rome! Why Rome is lonely too
> Besides, you need not be alone; the soul
> Shall have society of its own rank.
> Be great, be true, & all the Scipios,
> The Catos, the wise patriots of Rome
> Shall flock to you, & tarry by your side,
> And comfort you with their high company.
> Virtue alone is sweet society
> It keeps the key to all heroic hearts,

And opens you a welcome in them all.
You must be like them if you desire them
Scorn trifles & embrace a better aim
Than wine or sleep or praise
Hunt knowledge as the lover woos a maid
And ever in the strife of your own thoughts
Obey the nobler impulse; that is Rome
That shall command a senate to your side
For there is no might in the Universe
That can contend with love. It reigns forever
Wait then, sad friend, wait in majestic peace
The hour of heaven. Generously trust
Thy fortune's web to the beneficent hand
That until now has put his world in fee
To thee. He watches for thee still. His love
Broods over thee & as God lives in heaven
However long thou walkest solitary
The hour of heaven shall come, the man appear.

353.22   Auburn]   Town in central Massachusetts.

354.28   Runnimede to Faneuil Hall]   At Runnymede, a meadow by the
Thames in Surrey, King John signed the Magna Charta in 1215. Boston's
Faneuil Hall, site of Revolutionary speeches and meetings, is known as "the
cradle of American liberty."

355.1–22   Ill fits . . . prophecy.]   In CE, these lines (titled "From the Phi
Beta Kappa Poem, 1834") appear in a group titled "Webster" (see also pages
332.9–12 and 424.2–3 and notes).

355.29–30   The towers . . . undermine.]   See note 357.7.

356.13   O what is Heaven . . . fellowship]   Emerson usually inscribed
these lines when he was asked to write a sample of his verse in an album.

356.19   But half . . . his act]   Following this, Emerson began a fifth line
but wrote only the letter "S".

356.20   See yonder . . . sky,]   Titled "Transition" in CE.

357.7   *Van Buren*]   This couplet was originally part of Emerson's Phi Beta
Kappa poem (page 355.29–30 in this volume).

357.13   *Rex*]   "Rex." is written in the left margin, beside line 2; its place-
ment in the manuscript makes it uncertain whether it is meant as the poem's
title. Published without title in RE; titled "Rex" in CE.

358.10   I left my dreamy page]   Given the title "Night in June" in CE,
where "dreamy" is printed "dreary".

358.21   *S. R.*]   Sampson Reed (1800–80) of Massachusetts, disciple of Swedish mystic philosopher Emanuel Swedenborg.

359.5   New Jerusalem]   The Church of the New Jerusalem, based upon Swedenborg's ideas; Reed was among its leaders in America.

360.4   Philosophers . . . within]   Published under the title "Philosopher" in RE and CE.

360.16   basket]   Alternative reading: "sack".

361.10–11   On bravely . . . Ours.]   Emerson included in his manuscript the line from Allesandro Manzoni's novel *I promessi sposi* (1825–27) on which this couplet is based: "Il tempo il suo mestiere, ed io il mio."

361.12   Let me go . . . will]   Titled "Music" in CE.

364.15   Charles]   Emerson's brother.

365.1   In the deep . . . dwells]   Titled "The Enchanter" in RE and CE.

365.16   O what are heroes . . . men]   Titled "Pan" in RE and CE.

367.1   I have supped . . . tonight]   A version is printed in "The Poet" in RE and CE.

370.1   Divine . . . accept]   Included in "The Poet" in RE and CE.

371.12   A devil . . . deeps]   In another draft, this reads: "A devil hides in heavenly deeps".

371.13   *The Discontented . . . Masque*]   The editors of RE and CE print much of this poem, combined with more than 200 lines from other sources, in "The Poet."

374.16–17   Hold . . . glad.]   Emerson wrote "Poet" over the couplet in the left margin. In RE and CE, the lines are printed among the "Fragments on the Poet and the Poetic Gift." Another version reads: "We are of the makers / As of the made / By us also the game is played."

376.3   I grieve . . . mine]   In RE and CE, these lines are combined with another poem that Emerson originally drafted around 1837; it reads:

> Ever find me dim regards,
> Love of ladies, love of bards
> Marked forbearance, compliments,
> Tokens of benevolence
> What then   can I love myself
> Fame is profitless as pelf
> A good in nature not allowed,
> They love me as I love a cloud
> Sailing falsely in the sphere
> Hated mist if it come near

376.11   *Nantasket*]   Dated 1841 by Emerson.

377.14   Where the fungus . . . red]   CE prints various lines from this poem in "Fragments on Nature and Life."

377.30   damp ray]   Alternative reading: "smoky ray".

380.6–8   Ur . . . Mahmoud]   Ur, a city of ancient Sumer, is considered the birthplace of Abraham; Alcides is a name for Hercules; Mahmoud is Muhammad.

381.21   We sauntered . . . miracles]   Published in the notes of CE, page 512, where "of the bells" is printed "of the fells".

381.26   In Natures . . . tides]   Below this, Emerson began another line but wrote only "The", followed by line 381.27 as it appears in this volume.

383.1   Knows he who . . . field]   Titled "Peter's Field" in RE and CE, with the changes noted below. The first and third stanzas of the present poem are also part of "Dirge" (page 115.10–17 in this volume).

384.1–4   There is no mystery . . . bowers]   Omitted in RE and CE. A version of these lines is in "The Apology" (page 91.5–8 in this volume).

384.9   Far seen . . . below]   The editors of RE and CE print these lines as the conclusion of "Peter's Field" in their editions (see note 383.1).

385.1–4   Brother, . . . sublime.]   These lines were first written in the 1830s as part of a 20-line fragment. In RE and CE, the first and third stanzas of the fragment are printed as an untitled poem and a version of the second concludes "The Poet". The fragment reads:

> Day by day returns
> The everlasting sun
> Replenishing material urns
> With God's unspared donation
> But the day of day
> The orb within the mind
> Creating fair & good alway
> Shines not as once it shined.
>
> Brothers, no decrepitude
> Cramps the limbs of Time
> As fleet his feet, his hands as good,
> His vision as sublime;
> On nature's wheels there is no rust
> Nor less on man's enchanted dust
> Beauty & Force alight

> Vast the realm of Being is
> In the waste one nook is his
> What soever hap befals
> In his visions narrow walls
> He is there to testify

385.7   Who knows . . . that] Titled "Limits" in RE and CE.

385.19   Saadi] See note 15.22.

385.21–22   Him when Genius . . . home] A version of these two lines that appears separately in the poetry notebooks is published in RE and CE: "Him strong Genius urged to roam / Stronger Custom brought him home."

386.13   Bulkeley-Mere] Emerson was descended, on his father's side, from the Rev. Peter Bulkeley (1582?–?1658), a founder of Concord whose mother, Olyff Irby Bulkeley, was of distinguished ancestry.

386.22   Vain . . . blows] For a version of these lines that appears in "Guy" in RE and CE, see note 26.9.

388.16   He whom God . . . preferred] In RE and CE, some lines are incorporated into "The Poet."

388.21   [   ]] The bracketed portion of the line was lost when the manuscript page was torn; in RE and CE the missing words read: "And bragged his virtues".

389.1   Bended to fops . . . him] In RE and CE, a version is included in "The Poet."

389.9   On that night . . . went] A version is included in "The Poet" in RE and CE.

390.7   Eblis] Iblis is a personal name of the devil in Islamic tradition.

391.20   But O . . . eyes] Included in "The Poet" in RE and CE.

392.16   Who saw . . . beginnings] Titled "May Morning" in RE and "Cosmos" in CE.

394.27   Cheered . . . plenty] After this line is an aborted start, "Hence-for".

395.12   The gods . . . woods] In RE and CE, an earlier version is incorporated in "The Poet"; the earlier version reads:

> The gods talk in the breath of the woods
> They talk in the shaken pine,
> And fill the long reach of the old seashore
> With dialogue divine
> And the poet who overhears
> Some random word they say

Is the fated man of men
Whom the ages must obey
One who having nectar drank
Into blissful orgies sank;
He takes no mark of night or day,
He cannot go, but cannot stay,
He would, yet would not, counsel keep,
But like a walker in his sleep
With staring eye that seeth none
Ridiculously up & down
Seeks how he may fitly tell
The heart o'erlading miracle.

395.20   Would you know . . . hid] Emerson composed this poem from
lines of an earlier version; for RE and CE, Emerson's editors drew on both
versions to form the 37-line "Sunrise." The earlier version reads:

Would you know what charm is hid
In our green Musketaquid
And for travelled eyes what charms
Draw us to these meadow farms
Come & I will show you all
Makes each day a festival
Stand upon this pasture hill
See the face of [   ] until
The slow eye of [   ] show
The world above the world below,
Out of quiet [   ] cloud
Behold the miracle
Thou sawst but now the twilight sad
And stood beneath the firmament
A watchman in a dark grey tent
Waiting till God create the earth
Behold the new majestic birth
The mottled clouds like scraps of wool
Steeped in the light are beautiful
What majestic Stillness broods
Over these colored solitudes
Sleeps the vast East in pleased peace
Up the far mountain walls the streams increase
Inundating the heaven
With spouting streams & waves of light
Which round the floating isles unite
See the world below
Baptized with the pure element
A clean & glorious firmament
Touched with life by every beam

I share the good with every flower
I drink the nectar of the hour
This is not the ancient earth
Whereof old chronicles relate
The tragic tales of crime & fate
But rather like its beads of dew
And dewbent violets fresh & new
An exhalation of the time
Oer earth heaven man is spread the morn
Tis Natures universal dawn

396.8   Tell me . . . use]   Though the editor of CE titles this poem "Lines
to Ellen" and dates it "1829", the earliest-known extant version is from 1844.

397.9   I know . . . hour,]   Emerson drew these lines from an earlier draft
(the editors of RE and CE incorporated it in "The Poet" in their editions); it
reads:

        Not yet, not yet
        Impatient friend,—
        A little while attend,—
        Not yet I sing: but I must wait
        My hand upon the silent string
        Fully until the end.

        I see the coming light
        I see the scattered gleams
        Aloft beneath on left & right
        The star-sown ether beams:
        These are but seeds of days
        Not yet a steadfast morn
        An intermittent blaze
        An embryo God unborn
        How all things sparkle
        The dust is alive
        To the birth they arrive
        I snuff the breath of my morning afar
        I see the pale lustres condense to a star
        The fading colours fix,
        The vanishing are seen,
        And the world that shall be
        Twins the world that has been.
        I know the appointed hour,
        I greet my office well,
        Never faster, never slower,
        Revolves the fatal wheel.
        The Fairest enchants me
        The Mighty commands me

Saying stand in thy place
Up & eastward turn thy face
As mountains for the morning wait
Coming early coming late
So thou attend the enriching Fate
Which none can stay, & none accelerate.
I am neither faint nor weary,
Fill thy will, o faultless heart!
Here from youth to age I tarry,—
Count it flight of bird or dart
My heart at the heart of things
Heeds no longer lapse of time
Rushing ages moult their wings
Bathing thy day sublime.

398.9   *Elizabeth Hoar*]   Known to the children as Aunt Lizzy, Elizabeth
Hoar was considered part of the Emerson family; see also note 206.2.

399.13   Brahma . . . sky]   Above this in his manuscript, Emerson made a
false start at a line, but crossed out only part of it; the remainder reads:
"scooped in dust with his hand".

401.15   To every creature]   An earlier version reads:

One by one to every creature.
Adam gave its name;
Let each to all unmask its feature
And cognizance proclaim;
No moth & bug worm & snail
Mite & fly & creeping atomy
Nor each nor any fail
Its lineage to proclaim

Let its function & its name
Be publicly enrolled:
Not a plant obscure
But on a day its flowers unfold
And tell the universe
Its family & fame;
No fly nor aphis bites the leaf
But comes a day
When egg or fretted path betray
The petty thief
And his small malfaisance.
Many things the garden shows
And, pleased, I stray
From tree to tree
Watching the pyrus flowers,

> Infested quince or plum.
> I could walk thus
> Till the slow ripening secular tree
> Had reached its fruiting time
> Nor think it long.
> The gardener's love
> Allows no more life in the garden
> Than he wots of
> Wastes no globule of sap,
> Waters his trees with wine.

401.32−402.5   Many things . . . long]   The editor of CE prints these lines under the title "The Garden" in his edition.

407.5   *Intellect*]   The editor of CE titles a version of this poem "Insight" in his edition.

407.12   Chladni]   Ernst Florens Friedrich Chladni (1756−1827), German physicist who founded the science of acoustics.

408.20   Comrade . . . wind]   Versions of this fragment are part of some of Emerson's drafts of "There are beggars in Iran and Araby" (see page 251.23 and note); a version is included in "There are beggars . . . " in RE and CE.

410.13   meditates]   Alternative reading: "ventures next".

410.15   On a raisin stone]   A version of this poem is printed in the notes to *Poems* in CE, combined with a version of "Pour the wine! pour the wine!" (page 403.5 in this volume).

410.18   spondyls]   The joints of a wheel.

411.5−412.36   Poet of poets . . . all men.]   Emerson revised these 61 lines from an earlier 79-line draft and combined them with an independent 54-line passage to create the present poem. It is uncertain whether Emerson intended to include lines 61−79 of the earlier draft in the final version (they are printed in "Fragments on the Poet and the Poetic Gift" in RE and CE). In Emerson's journal the full earlier draft reads:

> Poet of poets
> Is Time the distiller;
> Time the refiner,
> He hath a vitriol
> Which can dissolve
> Towns into melody.
>   Burn up the libraries,
>   Down with the colleges,
>   Raze the foundations,
>   Drive out the doctors,
>   Rout the philosophers,
>   Harry the critics,—

Men of particulars,
Narrowing niggardly,
Something to nothing;
All their ten thousand ways
End in the néant.

All thro' the countryside
Rush locomotives;
Prospering grocers
Poring on newspapers
Over their shop-fires
Settle the State.
But for the poet,—
Seldom in Centuries
Comes the well-tempered
Musical man.
He is the waited-for
He is the complement
Of one man & all men
The random wayfarer.
Thinks the poet of his kin
This is he that should come
Tongue of the secret
Key of the caskets
Of past & of future.
Sudden the lustre
That hovered round cities,
Round closets of power,
Or Chambers of Commerce,
Round banks, or round beauties,
Or State-rending factions,
Has quit them, & perches
Well pleased on his form.

The bard never cared
To pave his welcome to the great
Costs him time to live with them
Which the genius ill supplies
Preengaged to woods & skies
The poet received
Foremost of all
Badge of nobility,
Charter of earth,
Free of the city,
Free of the field
Knight of each order
Mate of each class

Fellow of monarchs,
And, what is better,
Fellow of all men.

But over all his crowning grace
Wherefor thanks God his daily praise
Is the purging of his eye
To see the people of the sky
From blue mount & headland dim
Friendly hands stretch forth to him
Him they beckon, him advise
Of heavenlier prosperities,
And a more excelling grace
And a truer bosom-glow
Than the wine-fed feasters know.
They turn his heart from lovely maids
And make the darlings of the earth
Swainish, coarse, & nothing worth
Teach him gladly to postpone
Pleasures to another stage
Beyond the scope of human age
Freely as task at eve undone
Waits unblamed tomorrow's sun

412.30   meadows] Alternative reading: "forest".

413.8   When . . . first incloses] In the manuscript, this line appears twice, the second time in a corrected clear copy.

413.22   Emblem] Alternative reading: "Science".

414.13−30   The patient . . . ode.] In RE and CE, these lines are included in "Fragments on Nature and Life."

416.19   Pale Genius . . . alone,] In RE and CE, included in "Fragments on the Poet and the Poetic Gift."

416.27−30   Go, speed . . . souls.] Emerson used these lines as the motto to "Intellect" in *Essays: First Series* (1847).

417.6−7   Intellect . . . broods] The editor of CE titled the poem "Intellect" in his edition, where the first line begins "Gravely it broods".

418.3   *Vae solis!*] "Go alone!"

418.4−11   I found . . . own] These lines are the first part of a poem that Emerson experimentally combined with another poem (slightly revising both), to create the text reproduced here. He continued to revise "I found this" as a separate work, and in later versions it opened with Saadi as speaker (the editors of RE and CE combined "The civil world" with both parts of "I found this" in their editions). The second part reads:

> And thus the high muse treated me
> Directly never greeted me
> But when she spread her dearest subtle spells
> Feigned to speak to some one else
> I was free to overhear
> Or was welcome to forbear
> But that idle word
> Thus at random overheard
> Was the song of all the spheres
> And proverb of the following years
> All the planets with it shone
> A livery all events put on
> It fell in rain it grew in grain
> It wore flesh in friendly forms
> It frowned in enemies
> It spoke in Tullius Cicero
> In Milton & in Angelo
> I travelled & found it at Rome
> Eastward it filled all Heathendom
> And lay on my hearth when I came home

419.1   Dark . . . Cheshire]   Mt. Monadnoc, in Cheshire County, southern New Hampshire. The poem is titled "Monadnoc from Afar" in RE and CE.

420.3   Wisp . . . falling]   Titled "The Heavens" in CE.

421.14   A patch . . . upland]   Titled "The Waterfall," stanzas 1, 4, and 5 are printed in RE, and 1, 4–7 in CE.

424.2–3   Why did . . . Sale.]   In CE these lines, printed under the date "1854", appear in a group titled "Webster" (see also pages 332.9–12 and 355.1–22 and notes). However, the couplet appears to have been written in 1852.

424.4   The atom . . . beside]   Emerson's heading for these lines reads "Third Person. *Poet*". In RE and CE, published among the "Fragments on the Poet and the Poetic Gift."

424.12   All day . . . rock,]   Titled "Nahant" in CE.

426.16   Papas Blondine]   Emerson wrote the poem to his daughter Ellen in her early teens, according to his son Edward.

427.29   Flatter . . . ease]   In the manuscript, "Stoop to" is written below this line.

428.25   Asmodaean]   Asmodeus is an evil spirit, sometimes king of demons, in Hebrew tradition.

429.17   And fled . . . darkness]   Alternative reading for "darkness" is "frowns".

430.14   Teach me . . . stars!]   In CE, these lines are joined to the quatrain "When all their blooms the meadows flaunt" (page 451.18–21 in this volume).

430.18   O sun! . . . clouds,]   These lines were originally intended to be part of "Ode. Sung in the Town Hall, Concord, July 4, 1857" (page 161.18 in this volume).

432.21   *Maia*]   In Hindu philosophy, "cosmic illusion," the sensory world of manifold phenomena that conceals the unity of absolute being.

437.10   October . . . wherein]   Titled "October" in CE.

438.1   How drearily . . . hall]   See note 461.1.

439.1   The land . . . electric]   The poem, written in 1859, was occasioned by John Brown's raid on the federal arsenal at Harpers Ferry, Virginia.

440.16   The heavy . . . chain]   Emerson's source was a prose translation of Taliesin's "Preiddeu Annwn" ("Spoils of the Day") in Edward Davies, *The Mythology and Rites of the British Druids* (London, 1809). An early three-line version is titled "The Exile. / (After Taliessin)" in RE and CE.

442.20   Paques]   Easter.

442.23   Hoel]   Hywel ab Owain Gwynedd (d. 1170), Welsh prince and poet.

445.1   A queen . . . peers,]   Printed under the title "The Walk" in RE and CE.

445.9   By kinds . . . check,]   Emerson's heading reads "Nature."

446.10   At Plymouth . . . crowd]   Emerson presented this poem to his wife Lidian as an 1868 New Year's gift.

447.1   *To the Clock*]   A versification by Emerson of passages in his aunt Mary Moody Emerson's journals.

447.13   Enceladus]   In Greek mythology, a rebellious giant struck down by the gods.

448.16   Too late . . . came]   Emerson wrote the poem for his son, Edward, to accompany a lithograph of William Morris Hunt's painting *The Bugle Call*.

448.18   Ediths]   Emerson's daughter's.

449.5   Try . . . affords,]   Emerson's heading reads "*Poet*".

449.16   In Music]   Alternative reading for "In" is "To".

449.22   Beauty to fire]   Alternative reading for "fire" is "burn".

450.1 *Song of Taliesin*] An adaptation by Emerson of an English translation of a Welsh poem of Taliesin in David William Nash, *Taliesin; or, The Bards and Druids of Britain* (London, 1858), p. 164.

450.20 Nature saith,] Emerson's versification of a passage in his aunt Mary Moody Emerson's journal.

451.8 *a Well*] Built 1866 near the Milton, Massachusetts, home of Sarah Swain and John Murray Forbes; Sarah Forbes, who commissioned the inscription, donated the "memorial fountain" to the town.

451.12 *Letters*] The title is taken from an earlier version.

451.18–21 When all . . . fear?] These lines originally appeared within drafts of "May-Day" (page 131.1 in this volume) and were later combined with other verses to produce the present text.

454.7 The best . . . muse] A versification by Emerson of a passage in his aunt Mary Moody Emerson's journal. Not in CE; in RE, a version beginning "Best boon of life" is printed among the "Fragments on the Poet and the Poetic Gift".

454.17–455.16 Behold . . . yore.] These stanzas were originally written for "Boston Hymn" (page 163.1 in this volume).

456.1 Eve roved . . . heard] Emerson presented this poem with a gift of luggage to his daughter Ellen around 1864.

456.13–14 *Trimountain . . . nobis*] See notes 232.1, 2, 5.

458.21 Abdiel] Angel who opposes Satan's revolt in Milton's *Paradise Lost*.

459.2 By patriots] Alternative reading: "Which".

460.12 have heard] Alternative reading: "preferred".

460.18 phrase] Alternative reading: "dress".

461.1 In my garden . . . meet] Titled "Walden" in RE; under the same title in CE, only the first eight stanzas are printed, with "How drearily in College hall" (page 438.1 in this volume) added as a new ending.

465.1 TRANSLATIONS] Emerson's main sources for Persian poetry were the German translations of Joseph von Hammer-Purgstall (see note 104.16); the majority of his translations of Hafiz are from *Diwan*, and of other Persian poets, from *Geschichte*. His source for the poetry of Michelangelo was *Rime di Michelangelo Buonarroti il vecchio . . .* (Paris, 1821).

465.22 Hafiz] See note 104.14.

466.8–9 so firm . . . gray] Alternative reading for "so firm" is "a mass", and for "gray", "rock".

466.11 Has already . . . broke] Alternative reading: "The pile in shivers broke".

466.28–29   Asaph . . . language,]   In Muslim tradition, Solomon had Asaph for his vizier, the east wind for his courser, and could understand the language of birds.

471.11   [   ]out]   Partly illegible in this draft; in an earlier draft: "soon as without".

471.24   destroyed]   After this, in an earlier draft, the translation concludes with four lines: "Hast thou Hafiz in thy heart / Hope of safety thee before / Then wilt thou sit henceforth / In the dust of the votary's door".

473.20–21   Jamschid . . . Kai]   Iranian kings of history and legend.

473.23   Ferhad, . . . Schirin]   In Persian legend, the sculptor Farhad loved Shirin, who was also desired by Prince Khosru. Fearing that Farhad might be favored, the prince offered to defer to him if he could cut a path through a great mountain. Farhad committed suicide when the prince, seeing that he was succeeding, sent false word of Shirin's death.

473.26   desolate]   Alternative readings are "wasted" and "decayed".

474.9   Jethro]   Priest or prince in Midian and father-in-law of Moses, who kept his flocks.

476.28   Again arable]   In the manuscript: "Again *urbar* arable fruitful". Below this line, Emerson noted: "Ur = ox."

477.1   Blame me . . . preacher]   Emerson wrote his own mark of authorship at the end of this poem, but in other manuscripts attributed it to Hāfiz. Another version reads: "Not mine, sour priest, not mine the blame, / Did not wise god approve / Who lit in me this quenchless flame / What maiden should I love?"

477.14   Our Shah's . . . efflux]   Emerson's heading reads "Compliments".

478.1   If thy darling . . . thee]   Emerson's heading reads "Friendship".

478.20   seal of Solomons]   Alternative reading for "seal" is "ring". In Islamic tradition, King Solomon's signet ring signified his sovereignty and his dominion over the spirit world.

479.12   Who dedicates . . . glass]   Emerson's heading reads "Wine".

479.22   *Hafiz?*]   Attribution uncertain.

480.26   laid as in]   In the manuscript, "laid (as) in"; parentheses usually signify Emerson's uncertainty as to whether he should keep a word.

481.8   The love-bias given.]   Emerson ended the line "&c" and did not complete the translation.

481.14   *Hafiz?*]   Attribution uncertain.

481.18   Are . . . morsel]   Emerson appended following this: "[and the whole of that ode. p 443]," a reference to *Diwan*, vol. I.

481.21   Into the Sinderud,]   At the end of this line, Emerson wrote "(river)".

482.4   Should . . . playground]   Emerson ended the line "&c &c" and did not complete the translation.

483.15   world]   In the manuscript: "(world or fortune)".

483.17   Jam & Keikobad]   See note 473.20–21.

486.9–12   Ferhad . . . Schirin]   See note 473.23.

486.24   Gives . . . May]   Emerson ended the line "&c&c" and did not complete the translation.

489.1   "Drink wine, . . . heaven]   An earlier, longer translation reads:

> If thou drink wine the heaven
> Free on earth itself diffuses
> Fear not sinning, which
> Also has its uses
>
> Without scruple gather all
> All which is thine own
> Since the murdersword of Fate
> Without scruple hews thee down
>
> I adjure thee o my love
> At thy graceful feet I crave
> That thou come to my deathbed
> Come thou to my grave
>
> Ah what is heaven or hell
> Angel or man
> This Temperance is ever
> A heresy
>
> The Builder of heaven
> Has shut in the earth
> So that no street
> Leads out of it forth
>
> On wonderful roads
> Wine leads the mind forth
> The vault stands unmoved
> Until the Last Day
>
> Yet *via* the Cup
> Goest thou clean over all away
> May the wish of pious hearts
> Ever attend thee Hafiz

490.7–8   pictures . . . Mani]   "Mani grounded the divinity of his mission on the masterpieces of painting, as Mahomet on the Masterpiece of Arabian Poetry, the Koran."—Emerson's note, translating a footnote to the poem in *Diwan*.

491.7   Saadi]   See note 15.22.

491.19   *Salve senescentem*]   Latin: "Hail, Old Age."

492.6   Jussuf]   Yūsuf in the Koran (the Biblical Joseph of Genesis); he became the emblem of masculine beauty.

493.5   *Ibn Jemin*]   See note 215.7.

493.6–494.21   Shah Sandschar . . . *Enweri*]   See note 216.6.

494.26   *Feisi*]   See note 268.12.

495.1   *The Soul*]   From *Geschichte*, p. 197; one of the surviving fragments of verses sung by "whirling dervishes" sometime after the death of Jalāl ad-Dīn ar-Rūmī (see note 215.15).

495.11   Teach . . . meal]   This and the following two translations are of Persian aphorisms in Chardin's *Voyages du Chevalier Chardin, en Perse, et Autres Lieux de l'Orient* . . . , vol. 5, ed. L. Langlès (Paris, 1811). Emerson's heading reads "Persian".

496.1   *Arabian Ballad*]   Emerson translated the untitled ballad from *Noten und Abhandlungen zu besserem Verstndnis des West-östlichen Divans*, vol. 6, pp. 12–17, in Goethe's *Werke* (1828–33).

496.18   message]   Alternative readings are "word" and "tidings".

496.24   Whose dearest friend]   Alternative reading: "Him whose guest".

496.25   Was left unhurt.]   Alternative reading: "Was never harmed."

499.11   working]   Alternative reading: "operation".

499.22   Fortune . . . port,]   From the Latin of Christian poet Prudentius (b. A.D. 348), quoted in Robert Burton's *The Anatomy of Melancholy*, part 2, section 3, member 6. Another version by Emerson reads: "Fortune & Hope no more beguile, / Farewell, ye gay deceivers; / You've led me many a weary mile, / Go flatter young believers."

500.1   Alas, . . . betrayed]   Madrigal 51.

500.13   Wo is me . . . think]   Madrigal 52.

500.18   For not . . . new to me]   Emerson marked the end of the line with an asterisk and enclosed this and the following line in parentheses; his footnote to the line reads: "Grimm's translation runs 'New to me is nothing which /blinds/dazzles/beguiles/ men' ", referring to a German translation in Herman Friedrich Grimm's *Essays* (Hanover, 1859), p. 250.

500.26 Sweet, . . . stone,] A translation of "Riposta, In Persona della Notte".

501.1 The power . . . heaven] Emerson's headnote cites "Michel Angelo's Third Sonnet."

502.2 *The New Life*] This 1843 translation predates the first complete English translation, published by Charles Lyell in 1846. Emerson's principal source was an Italian text of 1576, *Vita nuova di Dante Alighieri*, edited by Bartolomeo Sermartelli, which did not include section breaks or section numbers, and in which Dante's words were frequently altered or misspelled (Emerson may have used a different edition for a few revisions that he made).

502.3 1] Emerson did not divide his translation into sections; this volume includes those section breaks and section numbers in J. Chesley Matthews' edition of Emerson's translation that follow the standard critical edition, *Le opere di Dante Alighieri* (Florence, 1921), edited by Michele Barbi.

504.19 Vide cor tuum.] Behold your heart.

512.1 Fili . . . nostra.] My son, it is time that we put an end to our disimulations.

532.12 Æole . . . tibi] Aeolus, for to you.

532.14–15 Tuus . . . fas est] It is yours, O queen, to ponder carefully what you wish concerning this task; I will earnestly strive to carry out your command.

532.18 Dardanidae duri] O bold Trojans.

532.20 Multum . . . armis.] Rome, you owe much to civil arms.

532.24 Dic . . . virum.] Tell me, Muse, of the man.

532.27 Bella . . . ait.] Wars I see, wars are in store for me, he said.

534.5–23 I say that . . . of Love.] Mathews gave these lines the section numbers "(xxvii)" and gave the remaining sections two sets of numbers, e.g., "XXVII (xxviii)", "XLII (xliii)", to reflect the numbering in some translations of *Vita Nuova* in which the "XXVI" section was divided into two parts.

543.16 lady] After this, Emerson left space in the manuscript to complete his translation of the sonnet but did not return to it.

Index of Titles and First Lines

CATALOGING INFORMATION

Emerson, Ralph Waldo, 1803–1882.
  [Poems. Selections]
  Collected Poems and Translations / Ralph Waldo Emerson.
  Edited by Harold Bloom and Paul Kane.
  (The Library of America ; 70)
  Contains Emerson's published poetry, plus selections of his unpublished
poetry from journals and notebooks, and some of his translations of poetry
from other languages, notably Dante's Vita Nuova.
  Includes bibliographical references and index.
  1. Poetry—Translations into English. I. Title. Collected peoms and
translations. II. Title. Poems, Emerson 1847. III. Title. May-Day and other
pieces, Emerson 1867. IV. Series.
PS1624.AI   1994   93–40245
811′.3—dc20
ISBN 0–940450–28–3 (alk. paper)

THE LIBRARY OF AMERICA SERIES

*This book is set in 10 point Linotron Galliard,
a face designed for photocomposition by Matthew Carter
and based on the sixteenth-century face Granjon. The paper
is acid-free Ecusta Nyalite and meets the requirements for perma-
nence of the American National Standards Institute. The binding
material is Brillianta, a 100% woven rayon cloth made by
Van Heek-Scholco Textielfabrieken, Holland. The com-
position is by Haddon Craftsmen, Inc., and The
Clarinda Company. Printing and binding
by R. R. Donnelley & Sons Company.
Designed by Bruce Campbell.*